National Geographic
Picture Atlas of
OUR
WORLD

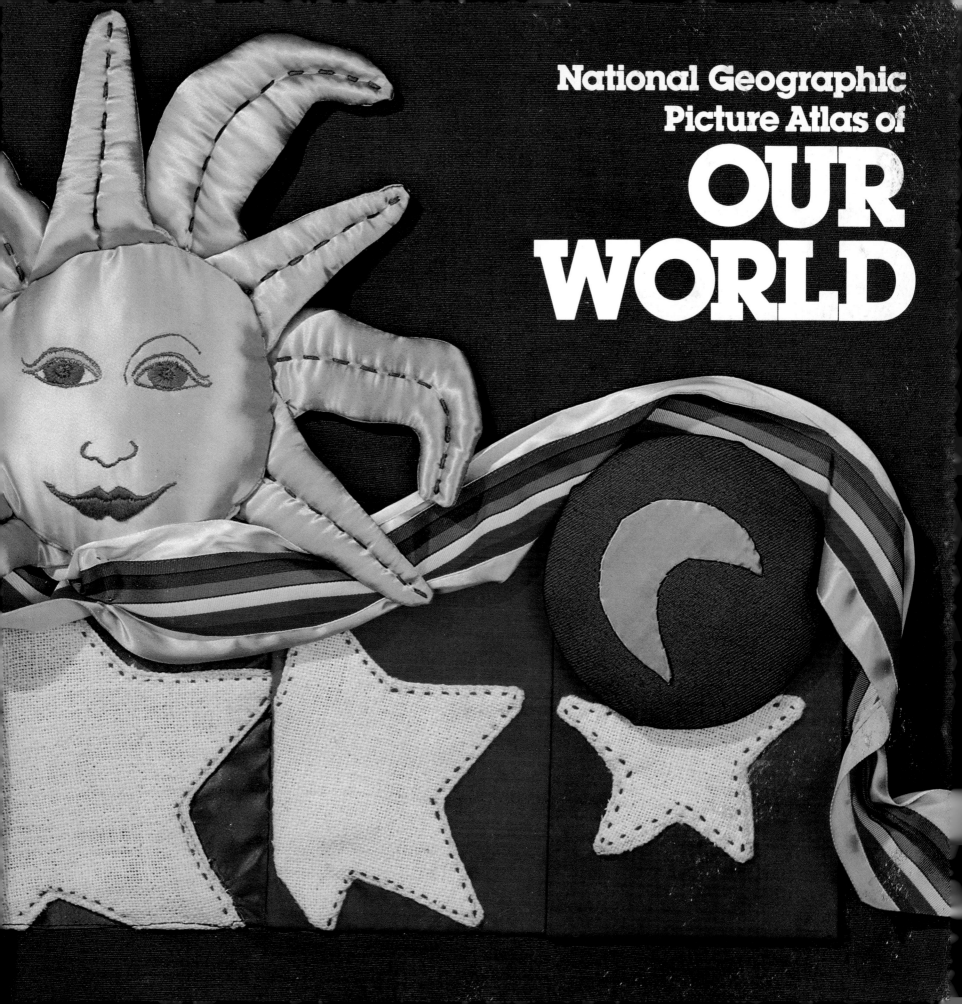

National Geographic
Picture Atlas of

OUR WORLD

NATIONAL GEOGRAPHIC
PICTURE ATLAS OF
OUR WORLD

PUBLISHED
BY THE
NATIONAL
GEOGRAPHIC
SOCIETY

PREPARED BY
NATIONAL GEOGRAPHIC BOOK SERVICE
CHARLES O. HYMAN, *Director*

Staff for this book
ROSS S. BENNETT
Editor

ANNE DIRKES KOBOR
Illustrations Editor

CAROL BITTIG LUTYK
Chief Researcher

CONSTANCE BROWN BOLTZ
DAVID M. SEAGER
Associate Art Directors

THOMAS B. ALLEN
JULES B. BILLARD
MELANIE ANN CORNER
MARY DICKINSON
SEYMOUR L. FISHBEIN
MARY SWAIN HOOVER
SUZANNE P. KANE
EDWARD LANOUETTE
ELIZABETH L. NEWHOUSE
DAVID F. ROBINSON
MARGARET SEDEEN
VERLA LEE SMITH
SUSAN ECKERT SIDMAN
JONATHAN B. TOURTELLOT
KAREN HOFFMAN VOLLMER
ANNE ELIZABETH WITHERS
Editorial Staff

ROBERT C. FIRESTONE
Production Manager

KAREN F. EDWARDS
Assistant Production Manager

RICHARD S. WAIN
Production Assistant

MOLLY KOHLER
Illustrations Research

LISE M. SWINSON
Editorial Assistant

JOHN T. DUNN
Engraving and Printing

JOHN D. GARST, JR.
PETER J. BALCH
VIRGINIA L. BAZA
CHARLES W. BERRY
SUSANAH B. BROWN
GEORGE COSTANTINO
MARGARET DEANE GRAY
DEWEY G. HICKS, JR.
DEBORAH HORNE
VICTOR J. KELLEY
MARK SEIDLER
KATHERINE TUERR
CATHY WELLS
ALFRED ZEBARTH
Map Design, Research, and Production

JOLENE M. BLOZIS
MARTHA K. HIGHTOWER
Index

Contributions by
JOHN HANLY ADAMS
WAYNE BARRETT
CHARLES F. CASE
JAN COOK
JANICE F. DELANEY
BETTIE DONLEY
EDWARD J. HOLLAND
DAN HUTNER
ELLIOTT JONES
KARIN KINNEY
PENELOPE A. LOEFFLER
DIANE S. MARTON
SANDY McGREW
LINDA BRUMBACH MEYERRIECKS
ANNE OMAN
SUKEY RYAN
SHIRLEY L. SCOTT
TED SHEPHERD
CAROL SIMONS
CHARLES L. STERN

*547 Illustrations
in full color, including
108 maps*

Contents

The Globe Beneath Our Feet

BANG! That's how the universe began, some scientists say—in a huge explosion of tightly packed matter. According to this "big bang" theory, the fragments have been spraying outward ever since, and at unimaginable speeds. You and our whole galaxy are zipping through space at more than a million miles an hour!

You can see a few of the largest fragments on any starry night. Most of those pinpoints of light are suns like the one that lights up our world. Several others are planets that circle our sun, companions in space to the planet Earth. Together, the sun and its planets—plus the various moons and other bodies—make up our solar system. It's a smoothly running clockwork that took shape, scientists say, as bits of dust and gas

from the big bang swirled in a giant cloud of matter. Like droplets in a rain cloud, the particles bumped into each other and clung together. As small clusters grew bigger, they attracted more and more particles to them with a pull we call gravity.

Imagine the Earth forming in this way, sweeping around the sun like a vacuum cleaner, gobbling up the drifting matter in its path and getting heavier as it goes. Gradually it condenses into a solid ball.

Solid? Actually the outer part of its core is believed to be mostly molten iron. This hot core is encased in a great ball of rock called the mantle, and the outer portion of that—a layer about 150 miles thick—is also partly molten. From this hot layer come most of the gases and lava, together called magma, that

fire up our awesome volcanoes. Some magma is pretty close to the surface—so close, in fact, that if the Earth were the size of a chicken egg, the crust that separates us from the magma would be thinner than the eggshell. Are your feet feeling hot? Relax; most of the crust is many miles thick.

Not even the land we're standing on is stable. If we could speed up time and make a thousand years pass in a second, we would see great slabs of land actually moving this way and that across the face of the globe. Hundreds of millions of years ago, the place that is now New York City lay on the Equator, the Earth's imaginary waistline. And millions of years from now, if present movement continues, Los Angeles will be swept past San Francisco on its way to Alaska.

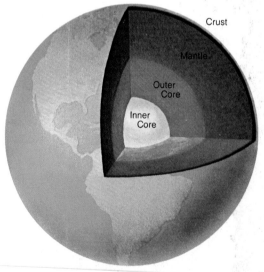

Born of dust *ringing a glowing sun, young planets take shape in this artist's-eye view (opposite). Falls and fountains of molten rock light up the Hawaiian sky (left) and tell of intense heat in parts of Earth's layered interior (above). Our weathered planet shows its age: an estimated 4.6 billion years.*

The Wandering Continents

| 200 million years ago | 135 million years ago | 65 million years ago | Today |

When Columbus set sail in 1492, he knew the world was round. But he thought that all the dry land was gathered together in one big continent. He expected to cross the world's one-and-only ocean and drop anchor on the continent's far side, the Indies. That's why the natives he met in the New World came to be called Indians, and the islands he reached became known as the West Indies.

If Columbus had sailed 200 million years ago, he probably would have found that most of the land was locked in a super-continent we now call Pangaea, which means "all lands." It was surrounded by a super-ocean called Panthalassa, which means "all seas."

If Columbus sailed today, he would find the journey from Europe to North America slightly longer than it was in 1492. That's because the seven continents are part of slow-moving pieces of ancient Pangaea, creeping across Earth's surface. Scientists have a name for this process of continental movement; they call it plate tectonics.

Roughly, here's how they believe it works. The Earth's crust is cracked into about a dozen huge slabs called plates (below). Like giant rafts up to 80 miles (129 km) thick, they float on the partially molten upper mantle, carrying landmasses like passengers. In some places the plates rub edges as they slip past each other, wrenching the countryside with earthquakes.

In other places the plates ram head-on; mountains rise as one plate's edge crumples like a bashed fender. The edge of one plate may slip underneath the other, forming a deep trench as the plate slowly slides down into the upper mantle.

Where two plates are pulled apart, magma oozes up through the rift to build new crust as the old is recycled. That's how the Atlantic Ocean grows wider—by an inch or so a year—as the Pacific Ocean shrinks. That's how the volcanic island of Surtsey was born in 1963 off the coast of Iceland.

Pieces of Pangaea *form the continents of today. Pushed and pulled about by slow churnings in the upper mantle—where tremendous heat and pressure make "solid" rock actually flow—great slabs of crust jostle each other about. An artist's imaginary cross-section (opposite) shows some of the forces at work.* Subduction *pulls one plate edge-first under another.* Sea floor spreading *tears open an ocean bed as two plates are moved apart; flows of lava patch the seam with new crust. Such forces ripped Pangaea and scattered its pieces to the seven seas (above).*

Where plates meet, volcanoes and quakes mark the restless boundaries. Nine-tenths of Earth's quakes and eruptions occur at the edges of the Pacific plates (right). No wonder the seams are called the Ring of Fire.

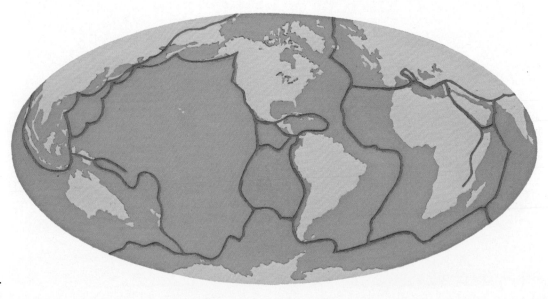

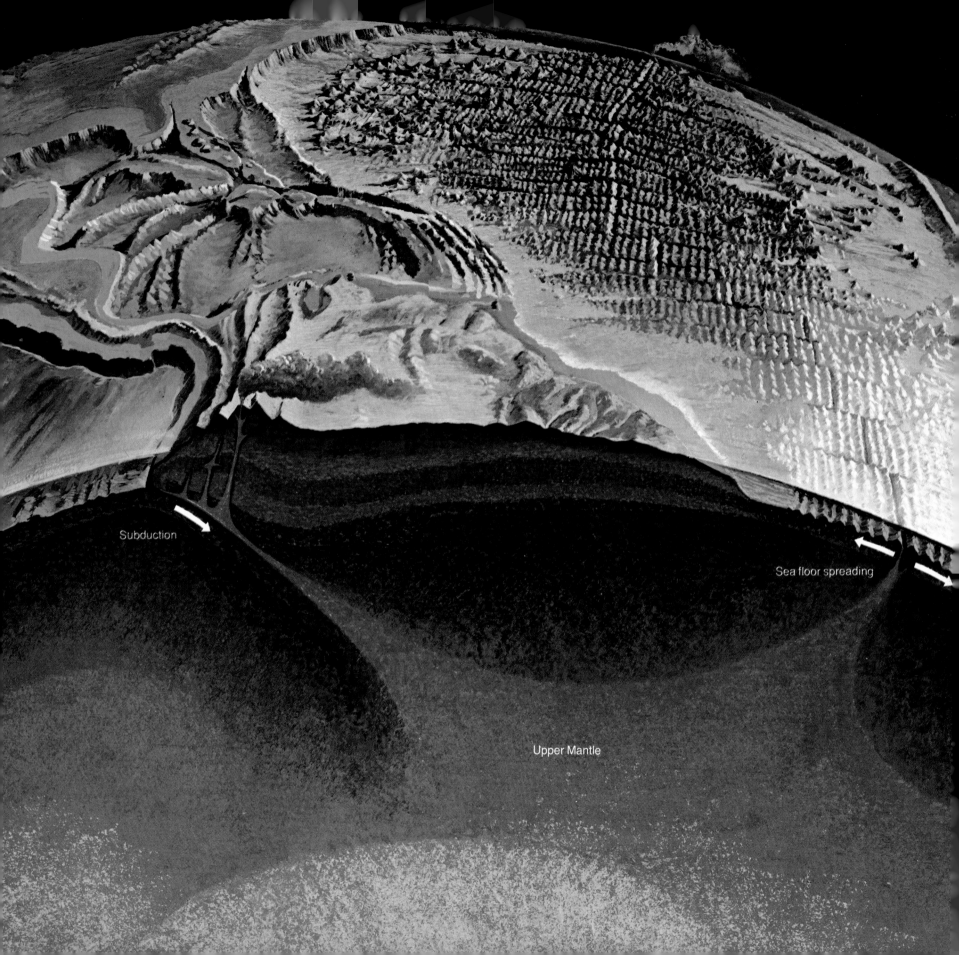

Crustal Crunch: an Earthquake

Want to see how an earthquake happens? Put your hands flat together, as if you were saying a prayer. Push them hard against each other. Now try to slide them on each other, one up and the other down. If your hands are clean and dry, they won't slip smoothly. They will move in "jumps."

If your palms were the edges of two of Earth's crustal plates, each jump would be an earthquake. Where two plates try to slip past each other, neither colliding nor pulling apart, their edges can jam together and appear firmly locked for many years. But as the plates keep moving, the tension builds along the seam until—jump!—it breaks loose, actually splitting rocks and grinding the plate edges against each other as they jolt to a new position. On Earth's great ball it is only a twitch. But to humans a quake can spell disaster. An earthquake in China in 1556 killed 830,000 people.

Quakes from a variety of causes rattle Earth's surface every day. But most are too small to be noticed, except by scientists called seismologists. They use a seismograph, a sensitive instrument that indicates the distance and strength of a quake.

Seismologists hope someday to predict and control major earth tremors. Until then, earthquakes will continue to kill an average of 14,000 people a year.

Earth has its faults; *they mark places where one portion of the crust has moved relative to another. Along California's San Andreas Fault (right, upper), two crustal plates have been grinding against each other for many millions of years. A great shudder along this fault system demolished much of San Francisco in the tragic earthquake of 1906 (opposite). Smaller shocks frequently rattle dishes and crack windowpanes.*

This kind of movement occurs on what is called a strike-slip fault. Roads zigzag and mountains split apart along the fault as the passing plates carry one part one way and the rest another (right).

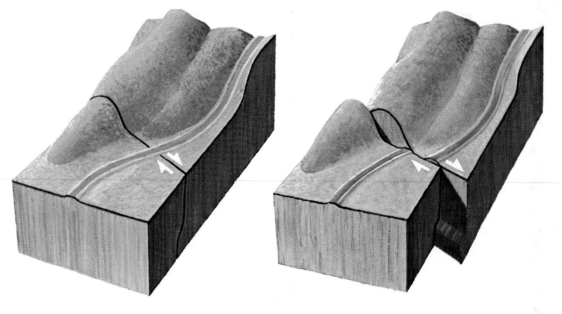

The Making of Mountains

When cars or continents collide, the result is wrinkles. And when India rammed Asia, the wrinkles made the highest mountains on Earth—the mighty Himalayas.

The landmass that is now India once was carried toward Asia on a crustal plate that was being subducted—that is, it was slipping under the edge of the Asian landmass and melting again into the mantle beneath. Why didn't India sink with it? Scientists have found that most landmasses are lighter in weight than the plates on which they ride. Thus, India "floated" while its plate sank, much the way packages on an escalator would pile up at the top while the stair treads "subducted" into the floor.

The restless Earth builds mountains in several ways. The Himalayas and Appalachians are typical of folded mountains, formed as one landmass plows into another. Block mountains form when vast chunks of crust break loose and tilt, like ice cracking into slabs at the center of a pond. That's how some of the Rocky Mountains rose.

Now and then molten rock or magma, squeezed by tremendous pressures, wells up beneath the crust but doesn't quite break through to the surface. Instead the pressure may push up a huge bulge in the crust, and the result is a dome mountain. The magma cools and hardens into rock, and the crustal material above it begins to wear away by erosion. Sometimes magma does burst through and a fiery volcano is born.

Folded, block, dome, or volcano, each of Earth's mountains rises above the land only to be worn down again, inch by inch, in a losing battle with erosion. Many even hasten their own end by forcing moist winds to ride up and over their summits. The rising air cools, the moisture condenses—and down comes rain or snow to pry boulders loose and wash soil away.

Like a cookie *on a conveyor belt, the land we know as India seems to have been moved northeastward away from Africa millions of years ago. Ahead, its plate slid under the Eurasian Plate, probably forming a deep trench offshore (below, left). When land met land, India's edge rumpled, pushing up peaks called folded mountains (below). The trench is gone; in its place stand the Himalayas (right).*

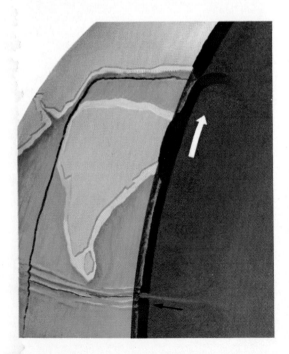

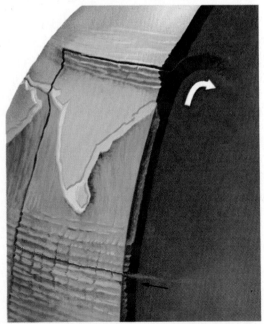

Shaping the Face of the Land

Water, water everywhere — well, almost everywhere. Seventy percent of Earth's surface is covered by it. And on the 30 percent that is land, the ceaseless work of water leaves its mark, slowly changing the look of the lands we inhabit.

Evaporating mainly from the seas, water is drawn up into the atmosphere in the form of a gas. There, changing temperatures and pressures turn the water vapor into liquid drops that eventually fall as rain. When rain falls on land, it drains back into the seas in a complex round trip called the hydrologic cycle. Falling as snow, then packing into ice, water builds glaciers that gouge valleys and grind down mountains. Our human ancestors survived the Ice Age, when great glaciers advanced and melted back. Some covered millions of square miles and lay nearly two miles thick in places.

Falling as rain or running off as snowmelt, water gathers in rivulets and builds into cascading streams and mighty rivers that cut ever deeper into the land. Muddy water tells you that a stream is still at work, carrying away the soil a speck at a time. Enough specks, enough time, and it will carve you a canyon.

Columbia Glacier *sticks out its frozen tongue at the Gulf of Alaska (opposite). On its sprawling tip, a fair-size city would sit like a lemon drop. Nature's mighty bulldozer, a glacier can tear away many tons of rock and soil and deposit them miles away. But don't wait for delivery; glaciers usually move only inches a year.*

Water is a patient worker. For millions of years the Colorado River has been carving out Marble Canyon (right) in the Arizona desertland. Downstream it has worked an even greater wonder: the Grand Canyon. There in a side canyon, Havasu Falls spills over a 100-foot (30 m) stairstep (upper). Rain upstream has turned the water brown with sediment that once was solid rock. Someday it may become rock again as it settles to the bottom, becomes packed down under new sediment, and forms sandstone.

Spinning Out the Seasons

Our Earth is a seasoned traveler. Autumn cools into winter and spring warms up to summer as we journey with the globe on its year-long circuit of the sun. And it all happens because the whirling Earth doesn't stand up straight.

Imagine its orbit as the edge of an oval table, with the sun as a centerpiece. Like a cockeyed top, the Earth spins around the table edge, leaning at an angle of 23½°. Without that tilt, we would have no seasons. Every day and every night would be 12 hours long, no matter where you lived or what month it was.

When a person in Kansas squints up at the sun in June, he sees it passing nearly overhead, since the North Pole is then tilted toward the sun. No wonder he mops his brow; the sun's rays are hitting Kansas almost straight-on. It makes little difference that the Earth is beginning to swing farther away from the sun in its oblong orbit. The sun radiates energy, but not in the form of heat; sunlight only produces heat when it strikes something it can't go through, like a road or a roof or a sunbather's skin.

To see how this happens, go to a window and hold your hand in the sunlight coming through the glass. Feel the warmth? Now feel the glass. It's cold because the sunlight passes right through it.

Another reason summer is warmer is that the days are longer than the nights. The dark then covers more of the Southern Hemisphere than of the Northern. Direct sunlight, long days—that's summer!

Now it's December, and the North Pole is tilted away from the sun. And so is Kansas. The sun's rays now strike at an angle and much of the heat is lost. And night's black skullcap has shifted northward, giving the sun less time to warm things up. Long nights, a cool sun low in the southern sky—that's winter!

In Australia the seasons are just the opposite; folks there sweat while people in the Northern Hemisphere shiver. In the tropics, a wide belt that straddles the Equator, the weather stays warm all year—and often gets very hot. But at the poles, the sun's angle is always low—thus the ice caps.

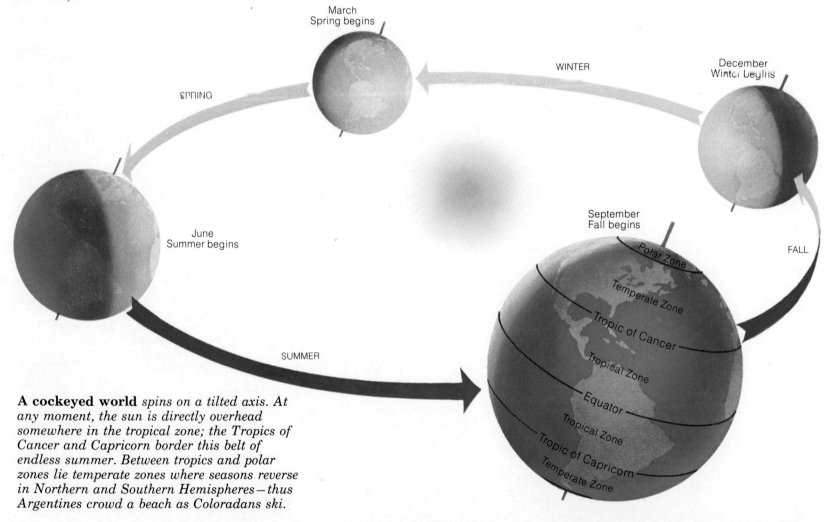

A cockeyed world *spins on a tilted axis. At any moment, the sun is directly overhead somewhere in the tropical zone; the Tropics of Cancer and Capricorn border this belt of endless summer. Between tropics and polar zones lie temperate zones where seasons reverse in Northern and Southern Hemispheres—thus Argentines crowd a beach as Coloradans ski.*

Home Is Where the Niche Is

Shaped by many forces, Earth offers a variety of niches, or habitats—and life in endless variety takes up the offer. Science has studied 1.5 million kinds of plants and animals; millions more wait to be discovered. At Yellowstone National Park in Wyoming, bacteria thrive in pools so hot the water almost boils. In Antarctica tiny plants grow in a sub-zero pond. Fish in ocean depths withstand pressures that would squash us. Some birds fly at altitudes where we humans would die from lack of oxygen. No matter what we find in outer space, there are plenty of wonders here on Planet Earth.

Snow and Ice
Tundra
Evergreen Forest
Deciduous Forest
Tropical Forest

A hike up *a mountain can be like a walk from Equator to North Pole. You start in warm, wet forests and end in frozen wastes. Plants and animals change as you pass from zone to zone. Here an artist brings together creatures from various continents, each in its typical place on a "magic mountain" of life.*

Snow and ice. *Not much grows here to feed (from left) the pseudoscorpion, mayfly, jumping spider, and tiny springtail. Life at the top of the world depends partly on insects and pollen carried upslope by winds from below.*

Tundra. *Ground-hugging plants support a limited family of creatures. A golden eagle needs eagle eyes to spot pikas. Blood pheasant, bighorn sheep, marmots, and the sure-footed chamois also inhabit this zone of cold winds and little shelter.*

Evergreen forest. *Trees that keep their leaves all year do best in these cool heights. Many other plants share the zone, creating varied environments for moose, lynx, water ouzel—or "dipper" bird— beaver, snowshoe hare, and grizzly bear.*

Deciduous forest. *Deciduous trees are those that lose their leaves in autumn. Here they spread their shade over sparrow hawk, gray squirrel, flying squirrel (which doesn't fly but glides), white-tailed deer, little brown bat, and burrowing owl.*

Tropical forest. *Steamy jungles hide the bird of paradise, chimpanzee, toucan, boa, spider monkey, alligator, and a big fruit-eating bat—the flying fox. Sometimes we call them exotic, but that means out-of-place. Here a pika would be exotic.*

Continental shelf. *In the shallows near the land, the ocean's abundance fills the waters with the Portuguese man-of-war jellyfish, seal, snail, scallop, lobster, crab, sea horse, fiddler crab, haddock, shark, and sea otter. Most of our seafood grows here.*

Open ocean. *The albatross may wander around the world on slender wings. In the deep seas below swim the huge right whale, the nightmarish giant squid— and, to the fisherman's delight, the herring, the big bluefin tuna, and the cod.*

At Home on Planet Earth

Suppose we had a big picnic and invited everybody. Not just everybody we know, but every person in the world. And suppose each of our guests sat on a blanket one yard square (0.8 sq m). Now that *would* be a big picnic; it would sprawl across more than 1,300 square miles. But this is a big planet — about 93 million square miles. Our picnic would easily fit on New York's Long Island. And that would leave 99.997 percent of the world's land unoccupied.

"Everybody." Taken literally, the word meant over four billion men, women, and children at home on Planet Earth in 1979. In about 40 years it will mean eight billion. If that growth rate could continue (it can't, for reasons we will explore later), those picnickers on their blankets would completely cover every square yard of the world's dry land by A.D. 2600. And in another thousand years or so, the people then alive would weigh as much as the earth itself — a whopping 6.6 thousand billion billion tons.

Scientists who study the tools and fossilized remains left behind by the earliest humans have found that mankind appears to be several million years old. If so, it took nearly all of those millions of years to build up a worldwide population of one billion people. But then it took only the next 120 years to add a second billion, another 32 years to build up a third, and only 15 years more to add a fourth. If this "population explosion" continues at its present rate, the next billion should take only a little more than a decade. "Everybody" is a pretty big word, and it gets bigger by about 200,000 persons every day.

A lot has happened to the human family in our long and shadowy saga. Experts tell us that our prehistoric ancestors roamed in small bands. Their numbers were kept low by the fact that they were hunters and gatherers — a life-style that takes a lot of work and risk to get only a small amount of food. And a lot of territory, too; it must have taken at least 500 square miles (805 sq km) for a band of about 25 of these primitive humans to feed themselves.

Then, perhaps about 300,000 years ago, *Homo sapiens* or "wise man" appeared. This is the current model; it includes you and the Pygmy and the Eskimo and the Australian Aborigine. Everybody. But just how wise is this maker of tools, this master of fire and language, this believer in gods, this grower of crops and herder of animals, this shaper of the ancient face of earth? "Not very," some say. Draw your own conclusions as we take a closer look at our species and how we have managed the resources of our world.

You can start by taking a look at yourself. Except for your clothes and your hairstyle, you probably don't look much different from a Neolithic or "New Stone Age" youngster of 8,000 years ago. Are you black? White? Oriental? Sometime after *Homo sapiens* appeared on the scene, the species began to develop into distinct races — chiefly these three, known to science as Negroid, Caucasoid, and Mongoloid.

Today over half the world's people are white, a third are yellow, and the rest are black. But over the centuries the "colors" have blended as peoples intermixed. Today the small, dark-skinned Pygmies of Africa's Ituri Forest probably are the only pure racial group in the human family.

No one knows exactly how or why the different racial traits developed, but there are some good guesses. The "black" in blacks comes from melanin, a pigment in the skin that protects its owners from overdoses of the sun's ultraviolet rays — a great asset to peoples rooted in sunny lands such as Africa. In hot climates it also helps to be tall, since you then have more skin area from which to give off body heat. Thus, desert dwellers tend to tower over Arctic peoples whose smaller surface area helps them to conserve warmth. Eye folds and cheeks padded with fat help to make Eskimo eyes appear "slanted" to others; actually such traits may have developed over the ages as ways of protecting the sinuses from the icy blasts of winter.

Whatever your racial traits, wear them proudly, like badges earned in the long struggle of our ancestors to populate every cranny of this varied planet. From the cradle of our species — now thought to be Africa — these ancient pioneers gradually spread throughout the continents and along the island chains, making homes for themselves in steamy jungle and shimmering desert, on mountain slope and valley floor, in green forest and on rocky plain, in tents of animal hide called yurts and houses of snow called igloos. This we humans do better than any other creature: We adapt to almost any environment.

We're number one at other things, too. We learn. We invent. And we change our environment to suit us. As hunter-gatherers learned the ways of fish in the streams, they invented snares to catch them. They saw herds of deer thriving in meadows and

How's that again? *Voices of the world greet you in tongues as varied as human homes. From a Swiss chalet comes German. A curving Sumatran roof echoes speech of the Batak tribe. English rings from a split-level, Eskimo from an igloo, Swahili from a cone-topped African home, Aymara from a reed house on South America's Lake Titicaca. From everyone: "Good morning!"*

brushy clearings; and, like American Indians in historic times, they probably made new clearings with stone axes or with a tool that humans alone have mastered: fire. In new environments or old, early people fought off their enemies—both animal and human—with a slowly improving arsenal of weapons. And in all these tasks, they learned to cooperate, to work together in doing things they could not do by themselves.

Suppose you and some friends decide to build a tree house. Can you do it without talking? Sure you can. Just point to a board, and your friend knows you want him to pick it up. Frown, and he knows there's something wrong. A smile says all's okay. Scientists have listed *seven hundred thousand* different combinations of face and body movements humans can use to convey meaning to others. But what a way to build a tree house! You'd all be so busy nodding and pointing and gesturing that you'd never seem to do much work. Waves and winks are fine, but words get things done.

Long ago, people learned to make sounds that expressed their thoughts. How did the sounds become language? No one knows. One guess was that humans began to talk by imitating the sounds of animals—but scoffers labeled this idea the "bowwow theory." Did language begin with grunts of pleasure while eating—the "yum-yum theory"? Or with shouts of alarm—the "oh-oh theory"? Experts think language sprang from more complex roots than these. What's *your* theory? It could be as good a guess as any.

Today humankind speaks 3,000 different languages—plus dialects, or variations, be-

yond counting. How, then, does one nation manage to communicate with another? Fortunately, at most stages of history, one particular language has become a kind of "universal language," understood by various peoples in addition to their own.

In days of the Roman empire it was Latin. Today it is probably English, used and taught over more of the world's area than any other tongue. Chinese actually has more users—at least twice as many—but when nation talks with nation, or scientist to scientist, or businessman to businessman, they turn most often to English as a way around the language barrier.

Whatever the differences may have been in language, race, or life-style, peoples in every chapter of the human story have faced the same challenge: the need for food. How would your family be meeting this challenge today if no one had ever noticed that a seed dropped on the ground will sprout a whole new plant? You'd probably be hunter-gatherers, like the Semang in the jungles of present-day Malaysia. With no crops to harvest, you'd eat whatever you could find or catch. Your lunch might be a lizard, your dinner a soup of leaves and plant pulp boiled in a section of bamboo. Anyone for a snack of snails?

Very few still follow this oldest way of getting food. Those who do must make a living on land no one else wants. Theirs is a difficult life-style: The men hunt, the women forage and raise the children, and no one has time for much else.

Farming began perhaps 10,000 years ago. With agriculture came civilization. As people learned to plant the foods they wanted,

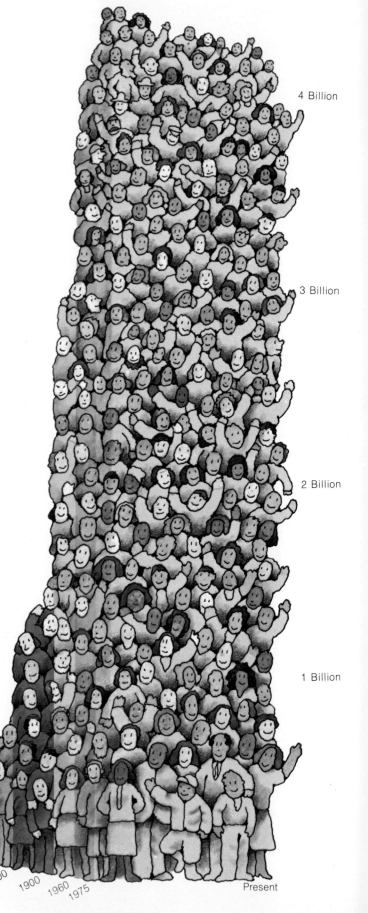

4 Billion

3 Billion

2 Billion

1 Billion

1000 1100 1200 1300 1400 1500 1600 1650 1750 1800 1900 1960 1975

Present

they too began to take root in the land. Larger and larger groups could be fed on the acres that once supported only a few. Villages sprouted, grew to towns, blossomed into cities. The slow rate of population growth began to speed up. Forested lands were cleared, plowed, planted; some became pastures. Ditches were dug to lead water to the crops. Gradually the hand of mankind began to change the face of the earth.

People changed, too. Farming allowed some to specialize, to work as makers of tools, judges of disputes, keepers of records, teachers of the young. Less time was used in getting food, so more could be devoted to inventing ways of growing, storing, and defending it. With each new invention, humankind took another step toward the computers and satellites and lasers that serve us today.

More leisure time freed the mind to think of other things...of art and music and dance and story...of how fish breathe and where the wind comes from...of trade and politics. And, yes, of war. A grim habit, and a heavy price to pay for the progress it sometimes achieved in cementing peoples together into societies.

Yet much of the human story has been another kind of war, a life-or-death battle with the whims of nature. From our beginnings, we have tried to influence nature's workings by rituals and sacrifices and by building temples to the gods we saw behind these awesome forces.

Many faiths guide the human family today. About a billion of us are Christian, nearly 600 million are Muslim, and more than 500 million are Hindu. Some 260 million follow the teachings of Buddha, 174 million the lessons of Confucius. There are 55 million Shintoists, 31 million Taoists, and 15 million Jews. Countless other beliefs enrich our religious heritage, from ancient Druidism to modern "cargo cults." These cults arose when South Pacific islanders watched in awe as the white man's ships and planes poured out wondrous objects: tools of metal and plastic, shirts and pants, talking boxes called radios. Now they imitate the intruders, hoping to tap the magic that brings such gifts to other people.

We have a name for that magic; it is called technology. Science and invention, feeding on a storehouse of raw materials and cheap energy that once seemed endless, have filled our daily lives with miracles. Dial a few numbers, and in seconds your telephone will ring the one you want out of dozens of millions. Tap a pocket calculator, and it does your arithmetic in an instant and gets an A+ for accuracy. In 1969 you could turn a knob and watch live as a man stepped onto the moon a quarter-million miles away.

But the real miracle is the sun. From that burning ball comes nearly all the energy of Earth. Energy to warm the crust. Energy to heat the air and set it in motion. Energy to turn the water in lakes and oceans into vapor that sprinkles the land with rain. Energy to create those marvels of technology. Energy to power the engines of life itself.

Green plants are the vital link. They catch the sun's outpouring energy and turn it into food for other life forms here on Spacecraft Earth. Coal and oil that began to form millions of years ago, lumber and firewood grown in our lifetimes, an orange picked yesterday — these and countless other plant products are "batteries" of energy that once fell to earth as sunlight.

When ancient farmers began to plant seeds, they tapped yet another storehouse of the sun's energy: the rich topsoil built up

It's a small world, *and a crowded one. Wild animals, diseases, and a limited food supply once kept human numbers low. Largely free of these brakes, population zoomed. At this rate, we would outweigh our own planet in 16 more centuries. Or, long before then, we might breathe away our oxygen, devour all our food, or bake in the heat given off by our own bodies. But experts say we won't. We might reach a crowded 20 billion — but a top figure of about 8 billion is more likely.*

over the centuries as plants wilted, rotted, and enriched the dirt with humus. Seeds grew well in the Middle East, North Africa, Greece—so people clustered there and built great civilizations.

But in some places their axes toppled the trees whose roots helped hold that fertile topsoil in place, and their irrigation projects upset the natural water levels in the ground. Farming faltered as erosion swept more and more topsoil away. Livestock could live where crops couldn't—but the animals nibbled away young plants that would have halted the loss. Now vast stretches of these once-rich farmlands lie thin and rocky and almost useless.

Today, with fertilizers and better farming methods, the people of Israel work hard to make their nation fruitful—far beyond the "land of milk and honey" it was in Bible times. Other Mediterranean countries also have labored to turn weary lands green again. But in areas with less money and know-how, hunger runs wild.

Too many people, not enough food: could it happen in America? Since colonial times, this nation has lost about a third of its topsoil—some 50 billion tons—to erosion. And as the population rises, houses and factories and highways and shopping centers gobble up farmland—about 15 million acres in the 1970's alone. Will enough be left to feed America's growing millions and those who need its food exports?

Technology to the rescue! Modernized American farms coax more food from less land at lower cost, with plenty left to export. In Ghana, two-thirds of a family's budget goes for food; in the United States, food eats up only 16 percent, the lowest in the world. A scientist has even calculated that if we moved underground—everybody—and farmed the entire surface of the earth with plants that made the best use of sunlight, our planet could feed *three trillion people!* But would you want to be one of these human earthworms, forever banned from building a tree house or organizing a picnic because you might keep the sunlight

Look for life *where the crops grow best. Food and fiber to feed our millions have kept the human family largely at home in the warm, fertile regions of Earth. Fewer folk live where forests and desert offer only a limited supply of food. Fewer still can survive where ice, snow, and tundra hold sway. Half the world's people farm a third of its land; there they tend livestock and about 100 major crops.*

Arctic Tundra	Wheat, Barley, Rye, and Oats	Potatoes
Forest	Corn	Root Crops
Farmland and Prairie	Sorghum and Millet	Soybeans
Desert and Wasteland	Rice	

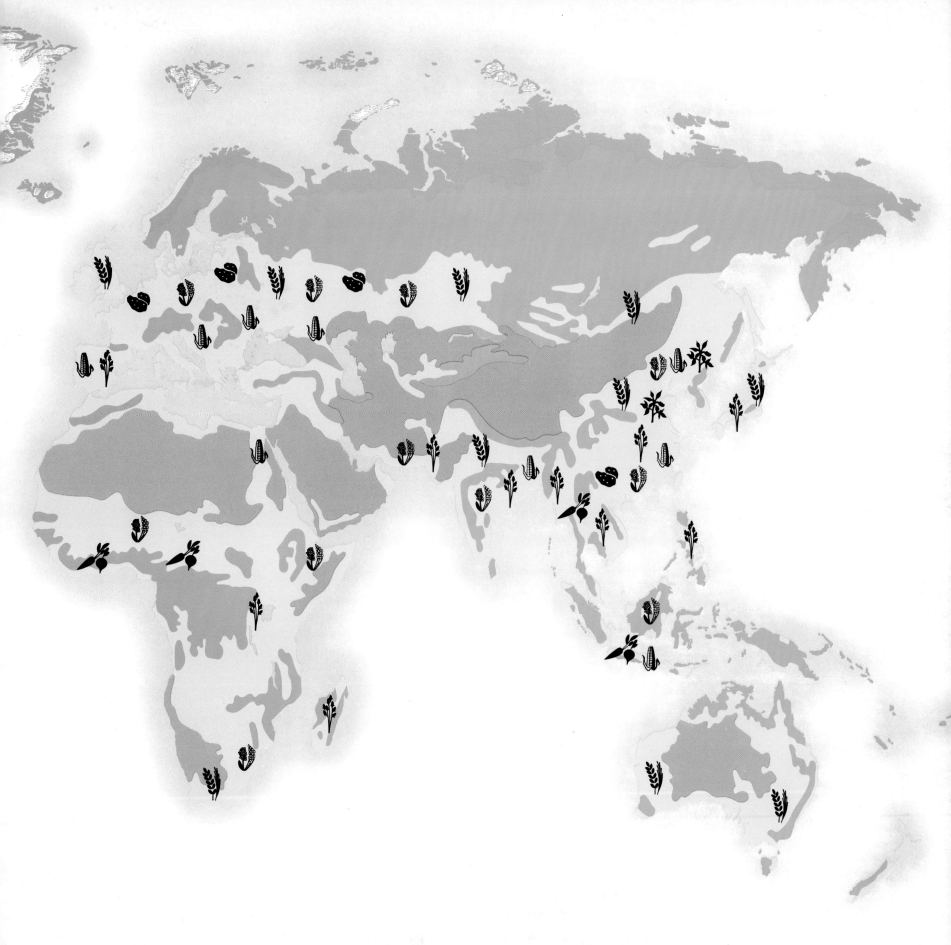

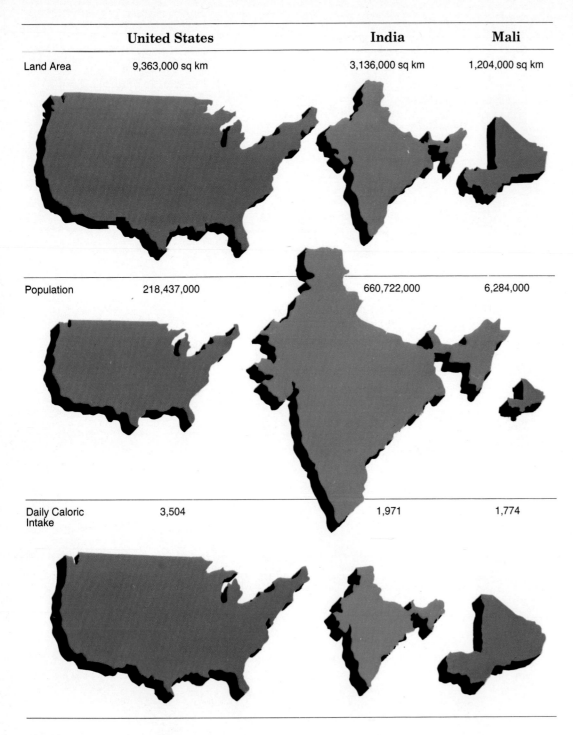

	United States	India	Mali
Land Area	9,363,000 sq km	3,136,000 sq km	1,204,000 sq km
Population	218,437,000	660,722,000	6,284,000
Daily Caloric Intake	3,504	1,971	1,774

Who's got what *on this unevenly divided planet? Compared to Mali, the United States has 35 times as many people, India 105 times. If land were in the same ratio, the three lands would look as they do at center (above). But they don't; as shown at top, it takes three Malis to cover India, eight to equal America. The United States looms even larger at mealtime. Then an average American eats twice the calories of an Indian or Malian. Trade helps to even the balance. Americans export corn, wheat— and the jumbo jet, one of the fruits of industrial know-how. Africa sells peanuts and diamonds, South America coffee and bananas. Europe's factories export watches; from rural areas come cheeses and wines. Rice pours from Asia, and so do cameras and TV sets. Why is the Arab boy smiling? Because the world runs on oil.*

off a patch of those all-important plants?

Technology to the rescue again! As a nation builds up its industries, it tends to become better educated, more aware of the links between population and the quality of life. Its growth rate tends to level off. Some experts think human numbers will peak in the next century and go no higher: five billion Asians and roughly another billion each in Africa, Europe, and the Americas. Two to a blanket, and your picnic for eight billion "everybodies" would take up no more room than it would today.

Technology to the rescue? Let's take a closer look. Making a calculator, airing a TV program, and counting down a moon shot all eat up those raw materials that once were so plentiful. The United States has one-twentieth of the world's people, yet uses a third of its energy output. And a fourth of its non-energy-producing minerals—copper, lead, iron, zinc, aluminum, and so on.

Fuels burned are gone forever, leaving smoke and ash that clog the air. But Earth's thin blanket of air acts like a greenhouse; sunlight pours through but only some of its heat can escape back out into space. The more fuels we burn, the more carbon dioxide we dump into the air—and the less heat can escape through it. It would take only a few degrees' rise in Earth's average air temperature to throw climates off kilter. A rise of only a few degrees could melt the ice caps and drown harbors all over the globe.

Metals, too, are often gone forever. The chromium in American bike handlebars comes from abroad; none has been found in the United States. Yet when the bike wears out, it's thrown away. Three-fourths of the metals used in the United States are used once and then junked—even though it takes *20 times* more energy to get new metal than it does to recycle the old.

Farming was mankind's first great leap forward; the Industrial Revolution was the second. What we do now with the benefits and problems each has brought us will show just how wise *Homo sapiens* really is.

Mapping Our Round World

The wind howls. Terrified sailors pray for their lives. A savage storm tosses the tiny ship carrying Christopher Columbus and his men homeward from the New World in 1493. Lost at sea? Yes—and they had been lost many times since leaving Spain nine months before. Through that triumphant voyage of discovery there had been weeks of danger and doubt. Often Columbus had not known where he was. Often, when he felt most sure, he was wrong.

How much *did* Columbus know about the Earth? Like the ancient Greeks, he knew it was round. He was a mapmaker and had studied the charts of great geographers. From them he got two wrong ideas. First, he believed the world to be much smaller than it is. Second, he thought that only an ocean and small islands lay between western Europe and Asia. In the 15th century, no one in Europe suspected that the continents of North and South America even existed.

However, as explorers like Columbus reached out, maps reflected their discoveries. The map below was drawn by Juan de la Cosa, a shipmate of Columbus. It is the first to show the American continents. English flags represent the voyages to Canada made by the Cabots in 1497 and 1498. Tiny ships show Vasco da Gama's 1498 trip to India, and the 1500 voyage to Brazil by Cabral.

Then came the boldest gamble of those times. In three miserable and dangerous years, Ferdinand Magellan's crew sailed completely around the world, returning to Spain in 1522. Soon globes and maps began to picture a world that looks much more like the one we know today.

The word "map" comes from "mappa," the Latin name for the linen material that Roman cartographers used for their drawings—so you don't need paper to make maps. The oldest maps known were drawn on clay tablets, about 2300 B.C. in Babylon. Early Eskimos and Indians made sketches on skin, bone, and wood. Juan de la Cosa drew his map on parchment—sheepskin.

You don't need writing to make maps. Just imagine how often your earliest ancestors might have taken a stick and scratched a picture in sand to show where the good hunting was, or where the fearful enemy lurked. In the past, maps of new regions could be made only if someone went to see what lay beyond the horizon. But today, as you will see on the following pages, science helps us map places we've never been.

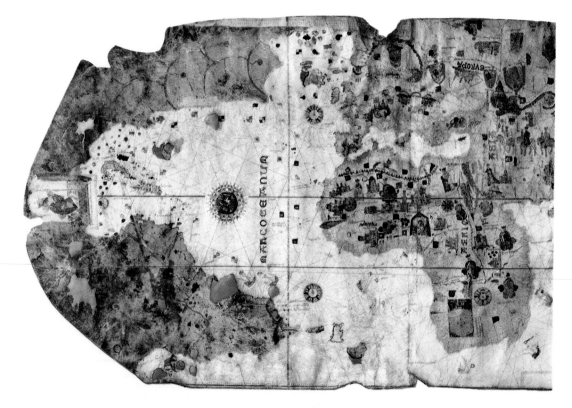

The New World, *green as a plant, springs to life on this map drawn about the year 1500. The crisscross lines give compass headings. In the Pacific Ocean, islanders navigated by bamboo charts (above). Tiny shells represented islands, and bent twigs showed the direction of waves and winds.*

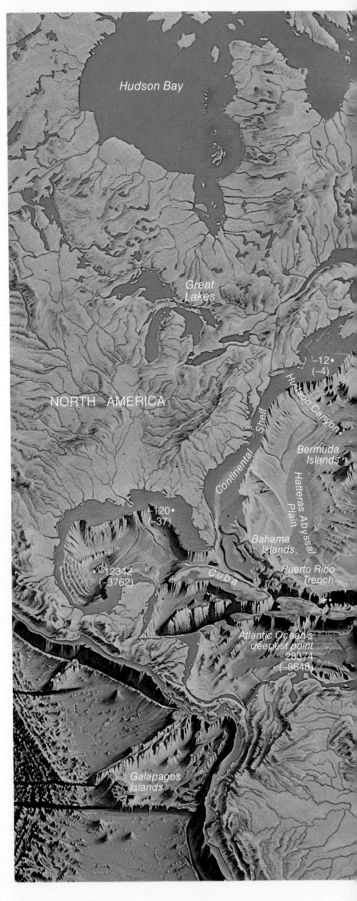

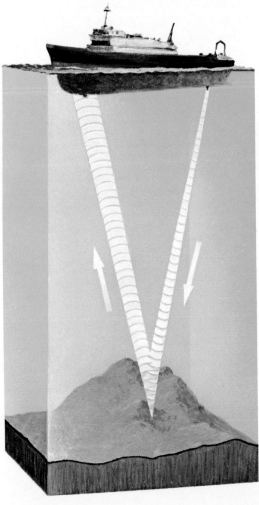

Delicate instruments *become eyes and ears for today's explorers. Arctic ice gives way to the U.S. nuclear submarine* Skate *(top). Underwater,* Skate *sensed the speed and direction of the Earth's rotation as the sub neared, then found, the North Pole.*

Blue-winged satellite Mariner 9 *(above) orbits Mars alongside the Martian moon Phobos. Mariner's cameras photomapped the red planet, showing us volcanoes, mountains—a land no human has traveled.*

We can't drain the ocean, but sound waves "see" its floor. To make this map, ships' instruments bounced echoes off the bottom (right) and measured its ups and downs. They saw a great mountain range, twisting through the Atlantic Basin like a 10,000-mile-long (16,093 km) crocodile.

Hudson Bay

Great Lakes

NORTH AMERICA

Continental Shelf

Hudson Canyon

−12•
(−4)

Bermuda Islands

Hatteras Abyssal Plain

−120•
(−37)

Bahama Islands

Puerto Rico Trench−

•12342
(−3762)

Cuba

Atlantic Ocean's deepest point 28374 (−8648)

Galapagos Islands

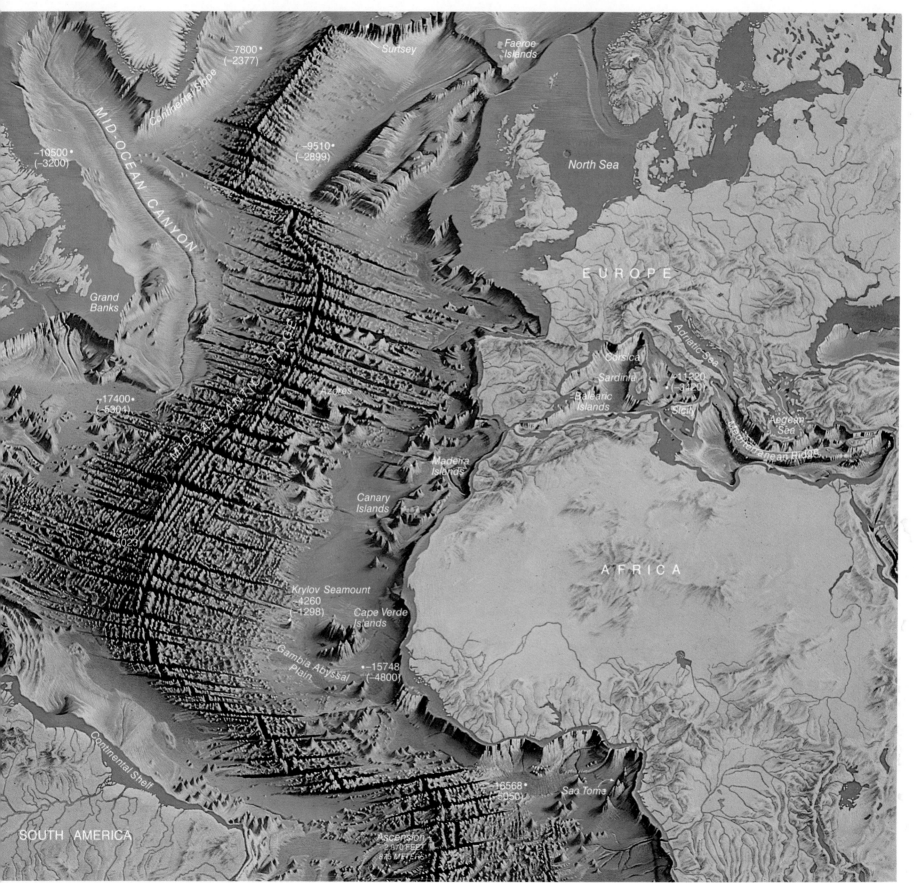

Faeroe
Islands

Surtsey

−7800•
(−2377)

Continental Slope

MID-OCEAN CANYON

−9510•
(−2899)

North Sea

EUROPE

−10500•
(−3200)

Grand
Banks

MID-ATLANTIC RIDGE

Azores

Corsica

Sardinia

Adriatic Sea

Balearic
Islands

−11220•
(−3420)

Sicily

Aegean
Sea

−17400•
(−5304)

Madeira
Islands

Mediterranean Ridge

Canary
Islands

−19200•
(−4023)

AFRICA

Krylov Seamount
−4260•
(−1298)

Cape Verde
Islands

Gambia Abyssal
Plain

•−15748
(−4800)

Continental Shelf

•−16568
(−5050)

Sao Tome

SOUTH AMERICA

Ascension
2870 FEET
875 METERS

• −12000 (−3658) Depth in feet (meters) below sea level. Average depth of abyssal plains is 16000 feet (4877 meters)

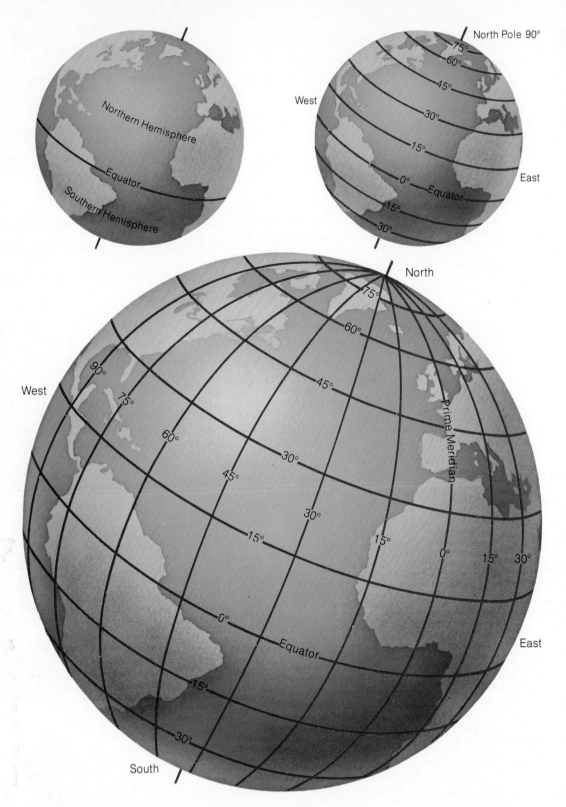

Street Corners of the Globe

Suppose you want to meet a friend on the corner of Third Avenue and Main Street. To find the intersection, you follow one street until it meets the other. The grid of latitude and longitude is like a city's grid of streets, but it can locate any place on Earth.

Look at a globe or at the map in the pocket of this book. Where 80° west longitude crosses 40° north latitude, you'll find Cleveland, Ohio. Durban, South Africa, is at 30° East, 30° South. If your friend said, "Come to my home at 70° North, 160° West," would you pack a swimming suit? Or boots and a parka? It shouldn't be hard to decide; your friend is an Eskimo. Take a parka.

The Time of Your Life

Meridians separate worldwide Standard Time zones (opposite). In some places, borders bend so neighbors can have the same time. These 24 zones exist so that, wherever you live, watches will be close to sun time and agree with the clocks of everyone else in the same zone. Travelers going west set their watches back an hour each time they cross into a new time zone. Eastbound, they set their watches ahead.

The Date Line, an imaginary line on the 180th meridian (broken line opposite), divides the old day from the new. The date on the calendar changes here. If you cross the Date Line westbound, on a Thursday, you pass into Friday. Eastbound, you'll go back to Wednesday.

Each time zone equals about 15° of longitude. The sun takes one hour to cross the zone. Once every 24 hours the Earth makes a complete rotation on its axis. As morning arrives, you are turning toward the sun. At noon you are passing directly in front of it. At dusk you are turning away from it. When your part of the globe is dark, the opposite part is lighted by the sun.

Imaginary lines *grid the Earth. At top left, the Equator divides the globe equally into Northern and Southern hemispheres. At right, parallels of latitude run east and west, and measure distance in degrees (°) north and south—from 0° at the Equator* *to 90° at the North or South Pole. Above, longitude lines called meridians run north and south to complete the grid. They measure distance for 180° east and 180° west of 0°, or the Prime Meridian, which passes near Greenwich, England.*

The Round Earth on Flat Paper

The only true map of our round Earth is a globe. A flat map can never tell the whole truth because there is no way to flatten the "skin" of a globe without tearing or stretching it. But we cannot carry globes in our pockets when we travel. Mapmakers, using geometry, have developed ways to make flat maps called *projections*.

When we show pictures on a screen, we say that we "project" them. Imagine a transparent globe, and a light shining through it from opposite the point where you will touch the globe with a flat surface or "plane." You can see how a shadow of the Northern Hemisphere is projected onto the flat screen. Where it touches, at the North Pole, shapes are accurate. At the outer edges of the map, areas are distorted.

Cartographers draw maps for special purposes by using various ways to draw the grid of parallels and meridians. A plane projection is good for showing large areas such as continents or hemispheres. But with any projection, mapmakers make the point of contact where they want most accuracy. Here are a few kinds of projections:

Plane projection

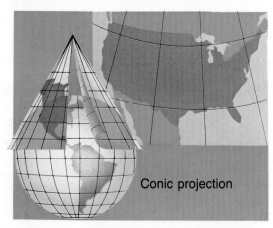

Conic projection

A conic projection is made as though a cone-shaped screen were placed on a globe. Here, to map the United States, the point of the cone is directly above the North Pole. The area where the cone touches the globe—the middle of the United States—will appear without distortion. Away from the line of contact, distortion grows.

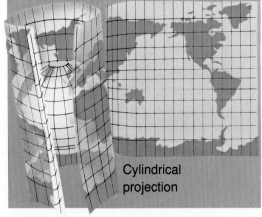

Cylindrical projection

A cylinder is a curved surface which can be flattened. About 1569, Gerhardus Mercator, a Flemish cartographer, made a cylindrical projection. It is still used today for navigation because all points lie in their correct compass directions from each other. Shapes are accurate at the Equator, badly distorted near the Poles.

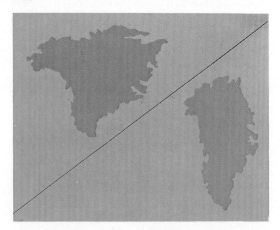

Greenland *reaches from about 20° to about 74° west longitude. When the meridians—as on a globe—lie in their true positions, Greenland can be shown in its true shape (lower). On a Mercator projection, to be in the correct place, Greenland must stretch far out of shape (upper). In scale, it would look nine times bigger than it really is.*

Map Legend

🐂	Cattle and Hides
🐑	Sheep
🌾	Grains
🥔	Potatoes
🍇	Grapes
🌰	Oilseeds
🐟	Fishing
⛏	Mining
🛢	Oil
🏭	Manufacturing

Map Labels

A
Arica

B
Iquique

C
Chuquicamata

D
Antofagasta
Salta
CHACO
Paraguay River
Iguazu Falls

E
Pan American Highway
San Miguel de Tucuman
Resistencia
Paraguay River

F
Mount Ojos del Salado
22,572 FEET
6,880 METERS
Corrientes
Parana River
Uruguay River

PACIFIC OCEAN

G
Mount Aconcagua
22,834 FEET
6,960 METERS
Highest point in South America
Cordoba
Santa Fe
Rivera

H
Vina del Mar
Valparaiso
Mendoza
Rosario
Salto
Paysandu
URUGUAY

J
SANTIAGO
Rancagua
BUENOS AIRES
La Plata
MONTEVIDEO
Rio de la Plata

CHILE

K
Talca
La Plata

Concepcion
Chillan
PAMPAS

L
Temuco
Valdivia
Mar del Plata
Bahia Blanca

M
Negro River
ATLANTIC OCEAN

ARGENTINA

N
Lake Nahuel Huapi
San Carlos de Bariloche
Valdes Peninsula
Puerto Montt
Chiloe Island
Rawson
-131 FEET
-40 METERS
Lowest point in South America

O

P
Comodoro Rivadavia

ANDES

Q
PATAGONIA

R

Strait of Magellan

S

T
Punta Arenas
Tierra del Fuego

U
Ushuaia
Puerto Williams
Cape Horn

N

0 — 800
KILOMETERS
0 — 600
STATUTE MILES

How to Find a Place

Look up *Punta Arenas, Chile,* in the Index. You'll find **98** T4. Turn to page **98.** Place a finger on the number 4 on the grid at the bottom of the map, and another on the letter T along the side. Then follow the imaginary lines across the page until the fingers meet. There you'll find Punta Arenas.

Stories Maps Tell

Each map is a story. Words tell part of the story. With the language of symbols, you can read the rest. See what you can discover about the countries on this page. Where is the capital of Argentina? The star tells you: Buenos Aires. The agriculture symbols show the main crops farmers grow. Other symbols tell you where people work in mines, factories, oil fields. How far is it from one end of Chile to the other? With the scale, you can measure.

In your *Picture Atlas,* each country has a biography, plus a summary that lists major economic activities alphabetically and gives the most numerous religions, languages, and ethnic groups. (Turn to page 298 for explanations of some unfamiliar terms.) Facts and figures are the most up-to-date available, *but nothing stands still.* Nations change their flags, their capitals, their borders, and even their names.

The figures in the fact boxes have been rounded off. Foreign words and place names often have markings for use in pronunciation. These marks appear on the map in the back pocket, but in the book the words have been Anglicized—changed into English.

A list of general map symbols follows:

★ **OTTAWA** *Capital*

● **Birmingham** *over 1 million people*

● **San Juan** *over 100,000 people*

● Colima *over 50,000 people*

• Galway *under 50,000 people*

Lake, Reservoir	*Swamp*
Intermittent Lake	.... *Political Boundary*
Dry Salt Lake	*Disputed Area*
River	——— *Road*
Intermittent River	—+— *Railroad*
Disappearing River	)(*Pass, Tunnel*
Canal	• *Low Place*
Reef	ı *Dam*
Mountains	+ *Mountain Peak*
Glaciers	▫ *Site*

GREENLAND
(DENMARK)

SOVIET UNION

ALASKA
(U.S.)

CANADA

JAPAN

NORTH PACIFIC OCEAN

UNITED STATES

NORTH ATLANTIC OCEAN

BAHAMAS

MEXICO

HAWAII
(U.S.)

CUBA

DOMINICAN REPUBLIC

HAITI

PUERTO RICO (U.S.)

BELIZE
JAMAICA

DOMINICA

GUATEMALA
HONDURAS

ST. VINCENT ST. LUCIA

EL SALVADOR
NICARAGUA

GRENADA
BARBADOS

COSTA RICA

TRINIDAD AND TOBAGO

PANAMA

VENEZUELA
GUYANA

SURINAME

COLOMBIA

FRENCH GUIANA

KIRIBATI

ECUADOR

NAURU

SOLOMON
ISLANDS

TUVALU

PERU

BRAZIL

WESTERN SAMOA

FIJI

BOLIVIA

SOUTH PACIFIC OCEAN

TONGA

PARAGUAY

CHILE

This world map *gives an accurate picture*
of the shapes of the continents at the center,
but distorts them as we move toward the
left and right edges of the map. On the
left, the continents "lean" toward the
right, especially near the top of the page.
On the right, they "lean" toward the
left. This is the reason why the portion
of the Soviet Union which appears at
both edges of the map—and is really the
same piece of land—has a different shape.

URUGUAY

ARGENTINA

AUSTRALIA

NEW ZEALAND

ICELAND

SWEDEN

NORWAY

FINLAND

SOVIET UNION

UNITED
KINGDOM

DENMARK

IRELAND

NETHERLANDS

EAST
GERMANY

POLAND

BELGIUM
LUXEMBOURG

WEST
GERMANY

CZECHOSLOVAKIA

MONGOLIA

SWITZERLAND
LIECHTENSTEIN

AUSTRIA

HUNGARY

FRANCE

SAN
MARINO

ROMANIA

ANDORRA

MONACO

YUGOSLAVIA

BULGARIA

NORTH KOREA

PORTUGAL

ITALY

ALBANIA

CHINA

SPAIN

VATICAN
CITY

GREECE

TURKEY

SOUTH KOREA

JAPAN

MALTA

CYPRUS

SYRIA

AFGHANISTAN

TUNISIA

LEBANON

MOROCCO

ISRAEL

IRAQ

IRAN

JORDAN

KUWAIT

PAKISTAN

NEPAL

BHUTAN

ALGERIA

LIBYA

EGYPT

BAHRAIN

TAIWAN

QATAR

UNITED ARAB
EMIRATES

BANGLADESH

CAPE
VERDE
ISLANDS

MAURITANIA

SAUDI ARABIA

OMAN

INDIA

BURMA

MALI

NIGER

LAOS

SENEGAL

CHAD

SUDAN

NORTH
YEMEN

SOUTH
YEMEN

THAILAND

VIETNAM

PHILIPPINES

GAMBIA

GUINEA-
BISSAU

GUINEA

UPPER
VOLTA

DJIBOUTI

KAMPUCHEA
(CAMBODIA)

SIERRA LEONE

BENIN

NIGERIA

BRUNEI
(U.K.)

LIBERIA

IVORY
COAST

GHANA

ETHIOPIA

SRI LANKA

CENTRAL AFRICAN
EMPIRE

SOMALIA

MALDIVES

MALAYSIA

TOGO

CAMEROON

NAURU

EQUATORIAL GUINEA

SAO TOME AND PRINCIPE

GABON

CONGO

UGANDA

KENYA

SINGAPORE

ANGOLA

RWANDA
BURUNDI

SEYCHELLES

INDONESIA

PAPUA
NEW GUINEA

SOLOMON
ISLANDS

ZAIRE

TANZANIA

SOUTH ATLANTIC OCEAN

COMORO ISLANDS

INDIAN OCEAN

ANGOLA

ZAMBIA

MALAWI

MOZAMBIQUE

MADAGASCAR

MAURITIUS

NAMIBIA
(SOUTH-WEST AFRICA)

ZIMBABWE
RHODESIA

BOTSWANA

AUSTRALIA

BOPHUTHATSWANA

SWAZILAND

SOUTH AFRICA

LESOTHO

TRANSKEI

NEW ZEALAND

0   4000

KILOMETERS

0   3000

STATUTE MILES

North America

How wide is North America? Close to 4,000 miles if you measure from Newfoundland across Alaska. Yet it's less than 30 miles wide where the Panama Canal links the Atlantic and Pacific oceans. They and the Arctic Ocean wash the longest coastline of any continent— more than 96,000 miles.

Islands fringe both the northern and southern shores. Most of Greenland, the largest island in the world, wears a thick blanket of ice. A thousand years ago Vikings gave this frozen place its misleading name to lure settlers. No fib is needed to bring winter tourists to the West Indies, where palm trees wave in tropical breezes the year round.

Forests cover much of the mainland. A wide band of evergreens stretches across North America from Labrador to Alaska and down through California's mountains. Forest green also colors the southeastern United States and the tropics of Middle America.

Fired by earth's inner furnace, Old Faithful blows its top in a whoosh of vapor. Some 12,000 gallons roar up in a few minutes of fury. Then calm returns to this famous geyser in Yellowstone National Park while water refills its underground "plumbing." Unfaithful to any schedule, Old Faithful waits from 33 to 120 minutes between blasts.

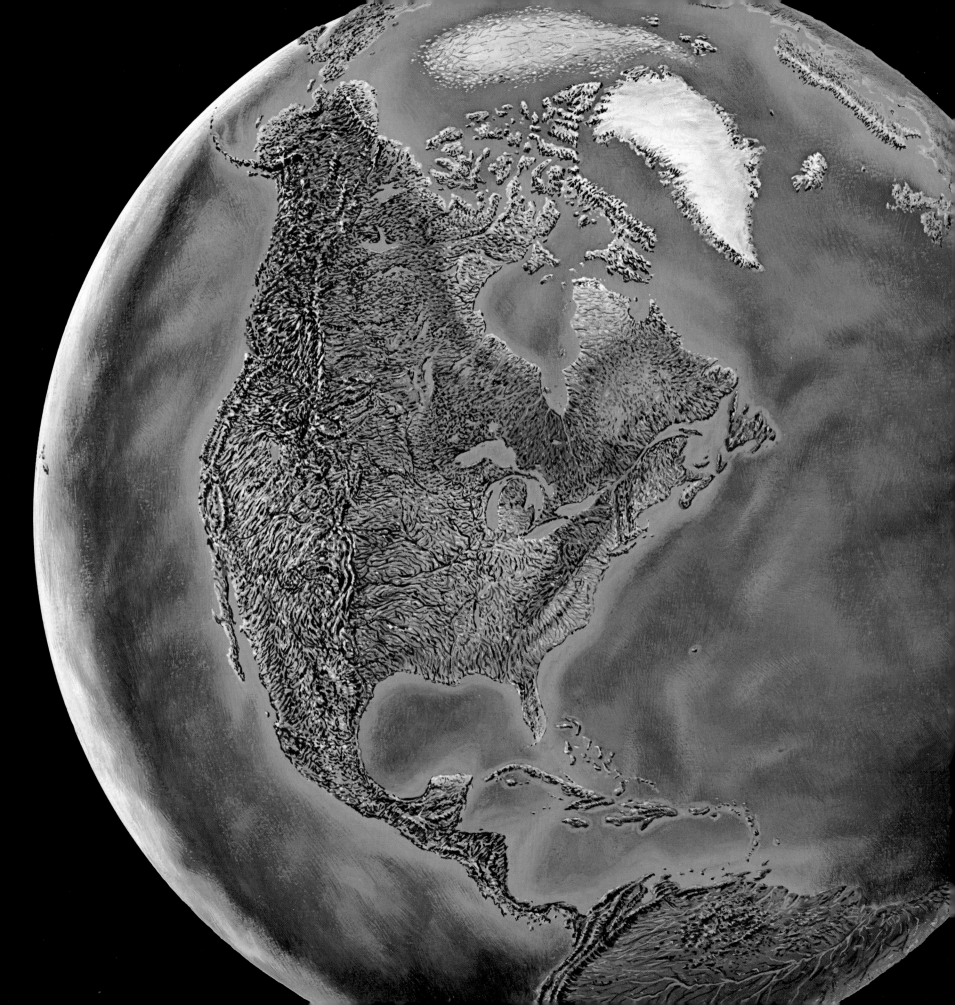

Gold is another important color. At harvest time, ripe grain glistens across the breadbasket of North America. The deep, rich soils of the United States' Midwest and Canada's prairie provinces produce bumper crops of wheat to help feed the world.

But few plows had yet turned this soil when covered wagons were crossing the grasslands, bound for California's goldfields. Some prospectors struck it rich. Half a century later, the gold-rushers streamed into Alaska. In Juneau, later the capital of the state, they worked the largest gold mine in the world. Today engineers drill for black gold—oil—in both Alaska and Mexico.

Seeking cities of gold, Spanish explorers had ranged over Mexico and the southern United States in the early 1500's. Hernando Cortes, conqueror of the Aztec Indians, once crumpled a sheet of parchment and called it "a map of Mexico." The crinkles represented mountains. If he had known what we know, he would have crumpled many sheets to show all the mountains in North America. They range from the smoking volcanoes of Mexico and Costa Rica to the ice-capped peaks of Ellesmere Island, Canada's northernmost point on the Arctic Ocean.

The Rocky Mountains and nearby chains provide superb scenery. Places such as Yosemite National Park in California's Sierra Nevada awe millions of visitors a year. But few of the continent's wonders surpass Grand Canyon, the world's largest gorge. It could hold more water than 20 Lake Eries.

The five Great Lakes form earth's largest group of freshwater "seas." Up the St. Lawrence Seaway, freighters sail to ports more than 2,000 miles from the Atlantic. Much of North America's wealth travels such great waterways. The mainstream for commerce is the Mississippi River, where tugs push barges loaded with machinery, grain, coal, and ores. Fast rivers like the Columbia and Colorado produce energy at hydroelectric dams. Logs are rafted down swift Canadian streams.

North America was Vinland the Good to Leif Ericson, the Viking who probably landed in northern Newfoundland around A.D. 1000. Almost 500 years later, Columbus stepped ashore on San Salvador in the West Indies. On many of the islands lived Carib Indians, for whom the Caribbean was named.

The very first Americans arrived thousands of years ago, out of Asia and across a now-flooded land bridge linking Siberia to Alaska. They fanned out across the continent and became the ancestors of the American Indians. Some eventually founded civilizations in Mexico and Central America.

Today mestizos—people with a mixture of European and Indian blood— populate much of this southern region. Caribbean Negroes, like blacks in the United States, trace their ancestors back to African slaves.

For 400 years European settlers of every nationality brought a variety of cultures to the continent. With them came ideas of self-reliance and a spirit of adventure that helped build new societies in which all could share.

Facts About North America

SIZE: 9,368,000 sq mi (24,265,000 sq km)

POPULATION: 359,000,000

DENSITY: 38 persons for every sq mi (15 per sq km)

HIGHEST POINT: Mount McKinley, Alaska, 20,320 ft (6,194 m) above sea level

LOWEST POINT: Death Valley, California, 282 ft (86 m) below sea level

LARGEST COUNTRY: (by area) Canada 3,850,000 sq mi (9,971,500 sq km)

LARGEST COUNTRY: (by population) United States 218,437,000

LARGEST METROPOLITAN AREAS: (by population)

Mexico City	11,300,000
New York	9,600,000
Chicago	7,100,000
Los Angeles	7,100,000
Philadelphia	4,900,000

LONGEST RIVERS: (mi and km)

Mackenzie	2,600	4,100
Missouri	2,500	4,000
Mississippi	2,300	3,700
Yukon	1,900	3,000
Rio Grande	1,800	2,900

LARGEST LAKES: (sq mi and sq km)

*Superior	31,700	82,100
Huron	23,000	59,500
Michigan	22,300	57,700
Great Bear	12,000	31,000
Great Slave	11,000	28,400

*World Record

UNITED STATES

Map Labels:

Seattle, WASH., Columbia River, Portland, OREGON, CASCADE RANGE, IDAHO, Boise, Snake River, MONTANA, NORTH DAKOTA, SOUTH DAKOTA, MINNESOTA, Lake Superior

San Francisco, San Jose, Monterey Peninsula, NEVADA, Salt Lake City, Great Salt Lake, UTAH, ROCKY MOUNTAINS, WYOMING, GREAT PLAINS, NEBRASKA, Mississippi River, Missouri River, St. Paul, WIS., Lake Michigan, Lake Huron, MICH., Milwaukee, Chicago, Detroit, Cleveland, Lake Erie, Lake Ontario, N.Y., Hudson River, VT., N.H., Boston, MASS., CONN., R.I., New York, N.J., Philadelphia, Baltimore, DEL., MD.

Pasadena, Los Angeles, San Diego, SIERRA NEVADA, CALIF., Las Vegas, Death Valley -282 FEET -86 METERS Lowest point in North America, Colorado River, ARIZONA, COLO., Denver, Pikes Peak 14,110 FEET 4,301 METERS, KANSAS, Platte River, Omaha, IOWA, ILLINOIS, INDIANA, St. Louis, MISSOURI, OHIO, Columbus, INDIANA, Indianapolis, Ohio River, KY., W. VA., VA., WASHINGTON, D.C., Outer Banks

PACIFIC OCEAN, Phoenix, NEW MEXICO, Rio Grande, OKLAHOMA, Red River, ARKANSAS, Nashville, TENN., Memphis, Mississippi River, Arkansas River, APPALACHIAN MOUNTAINS, N.C., S.C., ATLANTIC OCEAN

Dallas, TEXAS, LA., MISS., ALA., GEORGIA, Atlanta, Jacksonville

San Antonio, Houston, New Orleans, GULF OF MEXICO, FLORIDA, Cape Canaveral, Miami

ME.

Alaska inset:
BROOKS RANGE, ARCTIC CIRCLE, Nome, Yukon River, Fairbanks, ALASKA, Mount McKinley 20,320 FEET 6,194 METERS Highest point in North America, Anchorage, Juneau, Sitka, BERING SEA, ALEUTIAN ISLANDS, GULF OF ALASKA

N

Legend:

★	Capital City
✈	International Airport
—	Roads
+	Railroads
🐄	Livestock
🐄	Dairy Products
🐔	Eggs and Poultry
🌾	Grains
🥔	Potatoes
🌱	Soybeans
🍇	Fruit
🍊	Citrus Fruit
🥬	Sugar Beets
🎋	Sugarcane
🍃	Tobacco
☁	Cotton
🌳	Wood
🐟	Fishing
⛏	Mining
🛢	Oil or Natural Gas
🏭	Manufacturing

KILOMETERS 0 — 750

STATUTE MILES 0 — 500

United States

In the family of nations the United States comes in fourth—two times. In area, the Soviet Union, Canada, and China are larger; in population, China, India, and the Soviet Union take first, second, and third places.

Yet America is a giant. Although only 6 percent of the world's people live in the United States, they own close to half the world's wealth. Americans can claim the largest government budget of any nation, the busiest airways, and the biggest postal service. Americans produce the most meat and mine the most coal. But there are penalties, too: America uses up the most energy; it has the most cars—and some of the worst air pollution; the most candy and soda pop—and the most dentists to fill the cavities.

Imagine you are out in space with a powerful telescope. From here you can see how Americans have used—and changed—their land, turning wilderness into farm and factory. In New England the rooftops of old red-brick mills show where rivers powered the country's first industries. Around the harbors that welcomed early English colonists lie gray patches—grids of streets dotted with buildings, the great port cities from Boston south to Baltimore.

The largest patch is New York City. America's nickname, the Melting Pot, comes from the country's great variety of peoples, and nowhere does the pot bubble as excitingly as here. New Yorkers can boast that their city has more Puerto Ricans than San Juan, more Jews than Tel Aviv, more Italians than Venice—plus blacks, Irish, Arabs, Chinese, and many others. Elsewhere other groups have made their own contributions to the pot: Cubans in Miami, Scandinavians in the northern Midwest, Scotch-Irish—and African slaves—in the South, and the biggest wave of newcomers, the Mexican-Americans of the Southwest.

Now turn westward from New York. Beyond the Appalachians, where the long, low ridges look like wrinkles on an old man's forehead, lie the flat cornfields, pastures, and cities of the Midwest. When settlers first cleared this region, they divided the land into squares, a mile on a side. The farm roads of today still follow that pattern.

Past the Mississippi, the Great Plains rise like a slightly tilted tabletop. West of Denver the checkered tablecloth of wheat fields suddenly changes to a rumpled picnic blanket—the Rocky Mountains. Beyond spread deserts, canyons, more mountains, and the grazing land of Indian sheepherders.

Irrigation canals bring Colorado River water to vegetable farms in Southern California. Only 10 of the country's 30 largest metropolitan areas lie west of the Mississippi—Los Angeles, the biggest, sprawls across a mountain-rimmed basin.

North along the rocky Pacific coast, your telescope shows one way America pays for its riches: Scars left by loggers speckle the Cascade Range. But where Alaska's glaciers sparkle in the sun little has changed—so far—despite the big oil pipeline, more people, and Anchorage's multilane highways. In a wilderness two times the size of Texas, Eskimos still trail the caribou.

Hawaii, too, shows contrast to our eye in the sky—big-city Honolulu, the drowsy villages of Kauai, lush blankets of sugarcane, fiery lava spilling from Kilauea Crater.

OFFICIAL NAME: United States of America
AREA: 3,615,200 sq mi (9,363,400 sq km)
POPULATION: 218,437,000
CAPITAL: Washington, D. C. (pop. 674,000)
ETHNIC GROUPS: Europeans, also Latin Americans, blacks. **LANGUAGE:** English. **RELIGION:** Protestant, Roman Catholic, also Jewish. **ECONOMY:** chemicals, coal, cotton, dairy products, fish, fruit, grain, iron, livestock, machinery, meat, natural gas, oil, paper, potatoes, publishing, soybeans, steel, sugar, tobacco, transportation equipment, wood. **CURRENCY:** dollar.

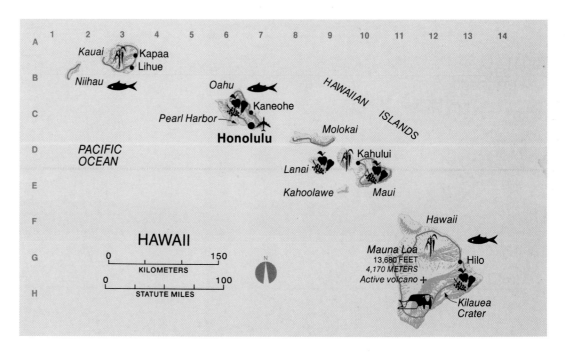

United States

1 America's symbol, a bald eagle spreads its wings—up to eight feet (2.4 m) wide!

2 Golden Oklahoma wheat pours from a chute, headed perhaps for the bakeries of New York—or Nigeria. The United States usually exports more grain than all other nations combined.

3 World's tallest identical twins, the 110-story towers of New York's World Trade Center soar above the Hudson River. More people ride the buildings' 208 elevators on a busy day than live in the entire city of Boise, Idaho.

4 Farm machines creep across a giant land—the Montana plains. They harvest wheat, grown in mile-long ribbons to trap water and prevent wind erosion.

5 Fun afloat fills a summer afternoon on a tributary of the Suwannee River in northern Florida. The river, made famous as Swanee in Stephen Foster's song "Old Folks at Home," helps drain the Okefenokee Swamp in Georgia.

United States

1 *Denali, "the Great One"—Alaskans often call Mount McKinley by its Indian name. The peak, North America's tallest, rises almost four miles. Nearby, Dall sheep keep to the high slopes, where they feel safest. With cupped hoofs they can cling to hillsides and escape their enemies.*

2 *San Francisco skyscrapers—the thin pyramid of the Transamerica Building among them—catch the rays of sunset. Wharves reach into San Francisco Bay, world's largest natural harbor. If you sailed out of the picture to the left, you would soon reach the Pacific Ocean.*

3 *At the Jet Propulsion Laboratory in Pasadena, California, aliens from the planet Earth ready a Mariner space probe to invade the skies of Mars.*

4 *A booming sea crashes against rocky headlands along California's Monterey Peninsula. Most of the U. S. Pacific coast is steeper and rockier than the sloping, sandy Atlantic shoreline.*

1

2

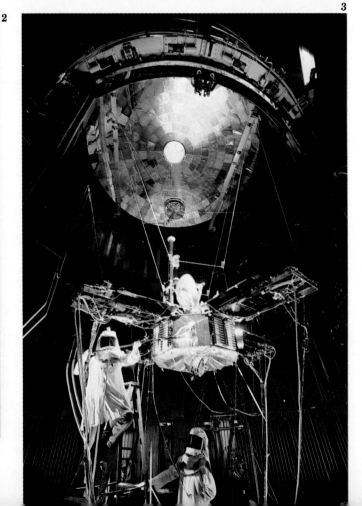

3

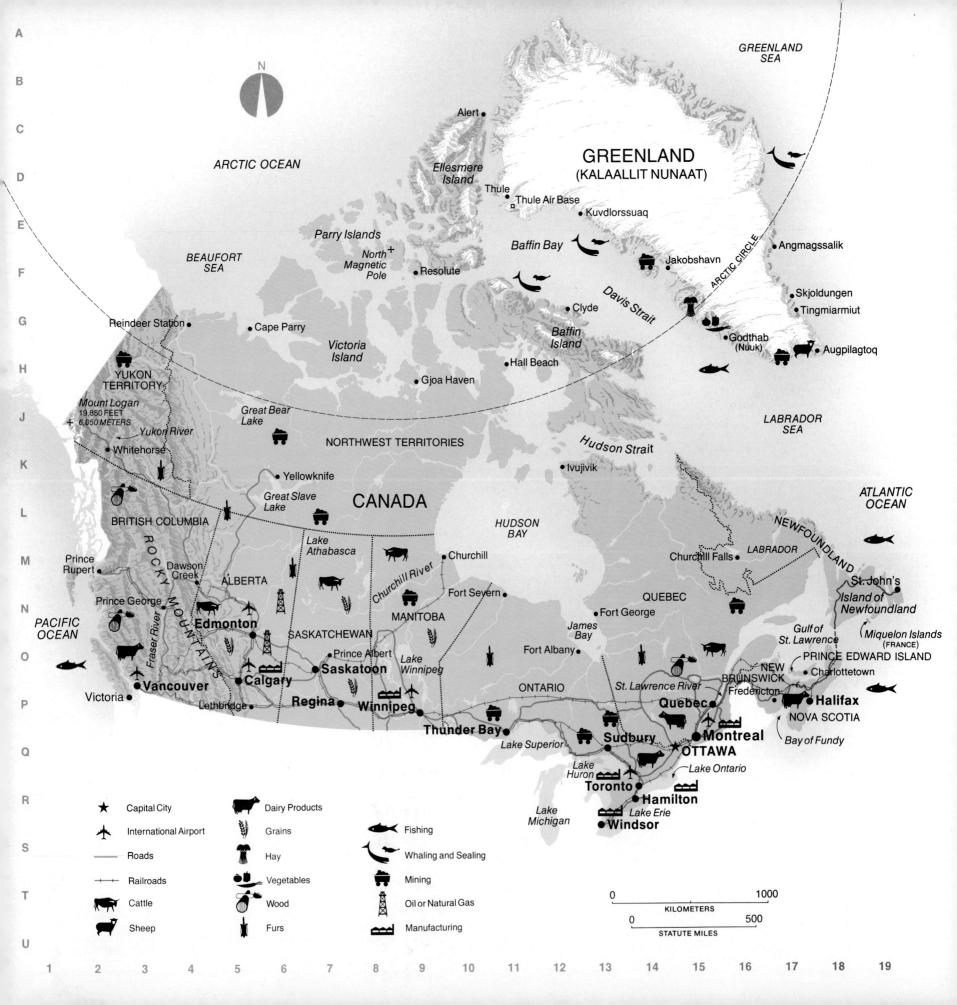

A B C D E F G H J K L M N O P Q R S T U

1 2 3 4 5 6 7 8 9 10 11 12 13 14 15 16 17 18 19

N

ARCTIC OCEAN

GREENLAND
(KALAALLIT NUNAAT)

GREENLAND
SEA

Alert

Ellesmere
Island

Thule
Thule Air Base
Kuvdlorssuaq

Parry Islands

BEAUFORT
SEA

North
Magnetic
Pole

Resolute

Baffin Bay

Jakobshavn

ARCTIC CIRCLE

Angmagssalik

Skjoldungen

Tingmiarmiut

Reindeer Station

Cape Parry

Clyde

Davis Strait

Victoria
Island

Baffin
Island

Godthab
(Nuuk)

Augpilagtoq

Hall Beach

YUKON
TERRITORY

Gjoa Haven

Mount Logan
19,850 FEET
+ 6,050 METERS

Great Bear
Lake

Yukon River

LABRADOR
SEA

Whitehorse

NORTHWEST TERRITORIES

Hudson Strait

Yellowknife

CANADA

Ivujivik

ATLANTIC
OCEAN

Great Slave
Lake

HUDSON
BAY

NEWFOUNDLAND

BRITISH COLUMBIA

ROCKY MOUNTAINS

Prince
Rupert

Dawson
Creek

ALBERTA

Lake
Athabasca

Churchill

LABRADOR

Churchill Falls

Churchill River

Fort Severn

St. John's

Prince George

Fraser River

Edmonton

SASKATCHEWAN

MANITOBA

Fort George

QUEBEC

Island of
Newfoundland

PACIFIC
OCEAN

James
Bay

Gulf of
St. Lawrence

Miquelon Islands
(FRANCE)

Prince Albert

Lake
Winnipeg

Fort Albany

Saskatoon

ONTARIO

St. Lawrence River

PRINCE EDWARD ISLAND

Vancouver

Calgary

Regina

Winnipeg

NEW
BRUNSWICK

Charlottetown

Victoria

Lethbridge

Thunder Bay

Lake Superior

Sudbury

Quebec

Fredericton

Halifax

NOVA SCOTIA

OTTAWA

Montreal

Bay of Fundy

Lake
Huron

Lake Ontario

Toronto

Hamilton

Lake Erie

Lake
Michigan

Windsor

★ Capital City
✈ International Airport
━ Roads
┼┼ Railroads
Cattle
Sheep

Dairy Products
Grains
Hay
Vegetables
Wood
Furs

Fishing
Whaling and Sealing
Mining
Oil or Natural Gas
Manufacturing

0   1000
KILOMETERS
0   500
STATUTE MILES

Canada

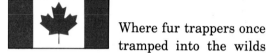

Where fur trappers once tramped into the wilds after beavers and foxes, Canada's frontiersmen now arrive by plane. They harness rivers with dams to make electricity. They mine ore from open pits in the frozen wilderness. Bush pilots ferry in supplies to villages in snowcapped polar regions and to logging camps tucked away in deep forests far from civilization.

Canada's people lead lives as varied as the land itself. A young Eskimo on Baffin Island hunts whales with his harpoon. Cowboys on horseback drive cattle in Alberta. A farmer of French-speaking Quebec Province cuts hay with a scythe. A Nova Scotian, dressed in the plaid kilt of his Scottish forebears, sounds his bagpipe. Two Indians on a lake in Manitoba harvest wild rice with sticks; one knocks the grain from the stalks into the canoe while the other paddles.

Such scenes from the past enrich Canada's lively present. Some Eskimos use snowmobiles rather than dogsleds. Indians with no fear of heights help raise glittering skyscrapers. Midwestern farmers reap grain with the latest tractors and combines.

Most Canadians live near the southern border. Here a highway and railroad link the oceans and connect exciting cities: Vancouver, the nation's leading seaport, with spectacular views of mountains and sea . . . Toronto, home of skyscrapers, museums, and peoples from around the world . . . Montreal, the biggest French-speaking city in the world—outside of Paris. To Montreal's docks come ships from the Atlantic. By canals and the St. Lawrence River some reach the Great Lakes.

Three wilderness barriers slow down settlement of Canada's interior. They are the frozen Arctic region of the north; the band of Rocky Mountains; and the vast Canadian Shield, which cups Hudson Bay.

The crustal slab that is the Shield (some of its rock is 3.6 billion years old) reaches from Newfoundland to the eastern part of Saskatchewan and north to the Arctic islands. Its thin soil produces thick forests, but limits farming. North of the tree line the land turns into forbidding tundra—mucky soil over frozen subsoil. But the Shield contains riches: metals, asbestos, natural gas, oil, and coal. Forests yield half the world's newsprint. Only about a third of the Shield's resources have been explored.

Thousands of rivers and lakes cross the Shield, providing waterpower for big hydroelectric plants. The project at Churchill Falls in Labrador is one of the largest power plants in the world. In western Canada, mountains of the Yukon Territory, once rich with gold, now attract another "rush" of explorers seeking copper, lead, and silver.

Much different are the populated areas of southeast Canada. Here people work on timberlands and ocean fishing grounds of the Atlantic provinces. Productive farms stretch from southern Quebec and Ontario westward to the broad prairies.

OFFICIAL NAME: Canada
AREA: 3,850,000 sq mi (9,971,500 sq km)
POPULATION: 23,632,000
CAPITAL: Ottawa (pop. 303,000)
ETHNIC GROUPS: European. **LANGUAGE:** English, French. **RELIGION:** Protestant, Roman Catholic. **ECONOMY:** chemicals, copper, dairy products, fish, furs, grains, iron, livestock, natural gas, nickel, oil, paper, transportation equipment, wood, zinc. **CURRENCY:** dollar.

Greenland

Picture a soft mud pie. Press the palm of your hand down on it. See the way the mud squishes up around your hand? That's how Greenland is shaped.

On the world's largest island, the Ice Age has never ended. Greenland lies under the weight of an ice cap that is two miles (3.2 km) thick in places and rimmed by mountains. These rugged coastal areas offer the only footholds for human life. Most of the people live in scattered villages on the south and west coasts. They hunt seals, walrus, and foxes, and fish for halibut and salmon. In winter, villagers haul chunks of ice from nearby icebergs back to the "water house." There the ice is melted down for the daily supply of fresh water.

Most islanders claim both Eskimo and Scandinavian ancestors. A Viking, Eric the Red, founded a colony here in the year 982. Hoping to attract more colonists, he called the place "Greenland" after the grassy valleys of the southwest coast. Long before, Eskimos trickled in across the ice bridge from Ellesmere Island.

In today's Greenland, old Eskimo ways mix with modern. If Henrik's father goes on a seal hunt, he uses his dogsled. But when Henrik is old enough for boarding school in town, he will leave their isolated village by helicopter. That's the only way out when ice keeps ships from entering the fjords. Many young people are giving up village life for the towns, where they can live in apartments and work in offices and stores or in fish and shrimp processing plants.

Greenland won home rule from Denmark in 1979. Place names in Greenlandic then became official: Kalaallit Nunaat for the island, Nuuk for its capital.

OFFICIAL NAME: Kalaallit Nunaat
AREA: 840,000 sq mi (2,175,600 sq km)
POPULATION: 50,000
CAPITAL: Nuuk (Godthab) (pop. 7,000)
ETHNIC GROUPS: Eskimo, also Danish. **LANGUAGE:** Danish, Greenlandic. **RELIGION:** Lutheran. **ECONOMY:** fish, hay, sealing, sheep, skins, vegetables, zinc. **CURRENCY:** krone.

1

Canada

1 *Fertile fields, rimmed by huge grain elevators, display the bounty of northern Alberta. In this most northerly of Canada's major farming regions, the first frost may come in August.*

2 *London? No, Ottawa. The changing of the guard on Parliament Hill looks like the same pageant at Buckingham Palace for good reason: A free Canada still has close ties to the Crown of England.*

3 *A Cree Indian in Quebec's north woods airs out a string of felt moccasin liners called "duffels." She may wear three pairs at one time when winter chills the air to -40° F (-40° C) at her tribal home near James Bay.*

4 *Fairytale spires of a grand hotel, the Chateau Frontenac, tower over the St. Lawrence River at Quebec City. Stone houses 300 years old dot parts of the town. It is the capital of Quebec, Canada's French-speaking province.*

5 *TILT! A British Columbia timber barge empties itself by tipping until its load of logs slides into the water. The crew controls the slant by pumping water in and out of tanks. Lumbering earns half the money this province makes.*

2

3   5

4

1

3

2

Canada

1 *Mother's just a furry milk bottle to this harp seal pup. It grows up on ice floes in the Gulf of St. Lawrence with thousands of other seals. Its mother can tell it apart from the look-alike mob by its own special whimper and smell. A month after birth it will be on its own, wearing a coarse gray coat instead of this soft white one.*

2 *Several tons of droopy-horned musk oxen thud across the Arctic tundra on Ellesmere Island. In their shaggy coats the 800-pound (363 kg) animals carry a feather-light treasure: a silky undercoat of wool called qiviut, which the oxen shed every spring. A four-foot (1.2 m) scarf made of qiviut weighs less than an ounce and feels like fine cashmere. Now protected, musk oxen once faced extinction from overhunting.*

4

5

Greenland

3 When your harbor looks like this, it's hard to believe it's summer. Residents of Augpilagtoq, a fishing village at Greenland's southern tip, see plenty of ice, even in August. One village chops icebergs into ice cubes and ships them abroad to chill drinks. If all Greenland's ice melted, seas would rise some 20 feet.

4 Awash in shrimp, the fishing boat Karl Birgithe earns its skipper a good income. In a land too cold to grow many crops, Greenlanders turn to the sea for much of their food—or to supermarkets stocked with groceries from Denmark.

5 "I can survive!" his look seems to say. This Polar Eskimo boy will need such spunk to live like his father, the seal hunter, who uses dogsleds and kayaks for treks amid mountains and ice floes.

Mexico

5 ▶

1 *Cupped hands hold promise: newfound oil to fuel Mexico's needy economy.*

2 *Mexico City balloon man has enough even for this carload. The fast-growing capital may one day rank as the world's largest metropolitan area.*

3 *Parading cowgirls make a carousel of color at a charreada, a Mexican rodeo.*

4 *A smiling guitarist wears the traditional sombrero. The word comes from the Spanish* sombra, *shade.*

5 *Land meets sky on the sleeping volcano Popocatepetl. In its shadow a church built by Spanish conquerors perches on an overgrown Indian pyramid.*

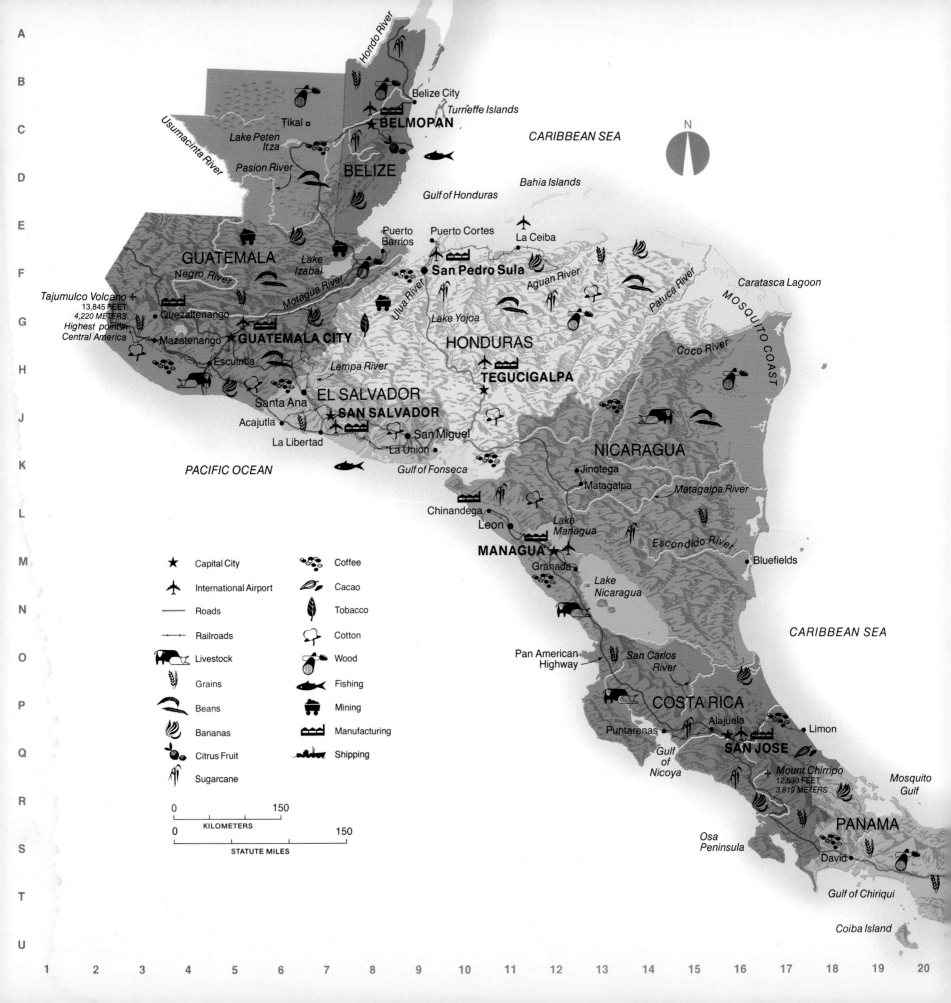

A B C D E F G H J K L M N O P Q R S T U

1 2 3 4 5 6 7 8 9 10 11 12 13 14 15 16 17 18 19 20

Hondo River

Belize City
Turneffe Islands
★ **BELMOPAN**

CARIBBEAN SEA

N

Usumacinta River
Tikal □
*Lake Peten
Itza*
Pasion River
BELIZE

Gulf of Honduras
Bahia Islands

Puerto
Barrios
Puerto Cortes
La Ceiba

GUATEMALA
Negro River
*Lake
Izabal*
San Pedro Sula
Aguan River

Caratasca Lagoon

+ Tajumulco Volcano
13,845 FEET
4,220 METERS
Highest point in
Central America

• Quezaltenango
Motagua River
Ulua River
Lake Yojoa
HONDURAS

M O S Q U I T O   C O A S T

Coco River

• Mazatenango
★ **GUATEMALA CITY**
✈ **TEGUCIGALPA**
★

• Escuintla
Lempa River

Santa Ana
EL SALVADOR
★ **SAN SALVADOR**

Acajutla
• San Miguel
La Libertad
La Union
Gulf of Fonseca

NICARAGUA

Jinotega
•
• Matagalpa
Matagalpa River

PACIFIC OCEAN

Chinandega •
Leon •
*Lake
Managua*
Escondido River

• Bluefields

★ **MANAGUA** ✈
Granada •

*Lake
Nicaragua*

CARIBBEAN SEA

Pan American
Highway
*San Carlos
River*

Mount Chirripo
+ 12,530 FEET
3,819 METERS

COSTA RICA

Puntarenas •
Alajuela •
• Limon
★ ✈
*Gulf
of
Nicoya*
SAN JOSE

*Mosquito
Gulf*

*Osa
Peninsula*
PANAMA

David •

Gulf of Chiriqui

Coiba Island

Legend

★ Capital City	Coffee
✈ International Airport	Cacao
— Roads	Tobacco
┼ Railroads	Cotton
Livestock	Wood
Grains	Fishing
Beans	Mining
Bananas	Manufacturing
Citrus Fruit	Shipping
Sugarcane	

0   150
KILOMETERS

0   150
STATUTE MILES

Belize

Belize is odd man out in Spanish-speaking Central America. Most Belizeans speak English, and the mixed population of blacks, Indians, and Europeans gives this small country a British flavor unlike that of its Latin neighbors.

Most Belizeans live along the steamy, swampy coast. The world's second longest coral reef, after Australia's, lies offshore—175 miles (282 km) of brightly colored coral and tropical fish. Wood houses near the sea stand on stilts to capture cooling breezes and withstand floods. In 1961 Hurricane Hattie's monstrous 10-foot (3 m) tides destroyed much of Belize City, which sits only 18 inches (46 cm) above sea level.

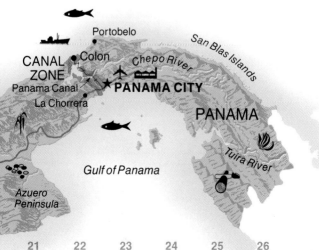

Now Belizeans have moved their capital to a safer place: Belmopan, a new city bulldozed out of the inland jungle. The forests—which provide a major export, wood—hold other cities too. But these towns are silent and empty, ruins left by the Maya Indians who lived here centuries ago.

Belize, once called British Honduras and still a colony, awaits independence.

OFFICIAL NAME: Belize
AREA: 8,900 sq mi (23,000 sq km)
POPULATION: 152,000
CAPITAL: Belmopan (pop. 5,000)
ETHNIC GROUPS: blacks, also mestizos, Indian.
LANGUAGE: English, Spanish, Maya, Carib. RELIGION: Roman Catholic, Protestant. ECONOMY: bananas, beans, citrus fruit, fish, grains, livestock, molasses, rum, soap, sugar, wood. CURRENCY: dollar.

Costa Rica

 When Christopher Columbus saw the glittering gold jewelry worn by Indians here, he named the area Costa Rica, or "rich coast." He was wrong about the gold; it came from elsewhere. Costa Rica has few known mineral riches. But the people—they call themselves Ticos—have found another kind of wealth: peace and prosperity. Ticos boast they have less poverty and better schools than most other Central American countries. And, in 1949, they abolished their armed forces.

Small fields cover a rolling landscape in the country's fertile upland basins. Some farmers still carry coffee and other crops to market in hand-painted carts drawn by oxen. Families paint their own colorful designs on the carts, and pass the intricate patterns from generation to generation.

OFFICIAL NAME: Republic of Costa Rica
AREA: 19,700 sq mi (51,000 sq km)
POPULATION: 2,119,000
CAPITAL: San Jose (pop. 229,000)
ETHNIC GROUPS: Spanish, also mestizos. LANGUAGE: Spanish. RELIGION: Roman Catholic. ECONOMY: bananas, cacao, coffee, grains, livestock, meat, sugar, textiles. CURRENCY: colon.

El Salvador

 Women balance baskets filled with fruit, vegetables—even live chickens—on their heads. Tables stacked with food items line narrow streets. Meat hangs from big hooks. A street market in El Salvador bustles with activity. The children of women who work at the market play in a nearby day-care center. The youngsters are bathed, fed, and checked by a nurse each day. Some children have little schooling, because there are not enough schools.

Mountains cover most of El Salvador, smallest of the Central American republics. Only the coast and central plateau offer flat land. Farmers plant all available acres, even the slopes of volcanoes. Some of their plots are so steep the farmers joke that they risk falling out of their cornfields.

Volcanoes can be seen from almost any place in El Salvador. Eruptions leave fields of hardened lava. Even the Pacific beaches are black volcanic sand. Fearing earthquakes, people often build low houses with massive stucco walls. Pink or red tile roofs add touches of color.

OFFICIAL NAME: Republic of El Salvador
AREA: 8,300 sq mi (21,400 sq km)
POPULATION: 4,515,000
CAPITAL: San Salvador (pop. 387,000)
ETHNIC GROUPS: mestizos, also Indian, Spanish.
LANGUAGE: Spanish. RELIGION: Roman Catholic. ECONOMY: beans, coffee, cotton, grains, oil refining, sugar, textiles. CURRENCY: colon.

Guatemala

 In the lowland jungles of Guatemala, archeologists have uncovered entire cities built long ago by Maya Indians. The ruins of Tikal are perhaps the most famous. Here scientists found temples and pyramids, paved causeways, and palaces of kings and nobles. Today descendants of the Maya live in the same region. Some tap

chicozapote trees for chicle, which puts the "chew" into chewing gum. Many Indians also live in the highlands, where they use simple farming methods to grow corn on steep hillsides. They go to town on market days or for fiestas (celebrations). You can tell which village a farmer comes from by the pattern of his colorful clothes.

Guatemala City sits in the highlands too. There, volcanoes cradle dazzling-blue lakes, and the weather is cooler than in the less populated tropical coastlands.

OFFICIAL NAME: Republic of Guatemala **AREA:** 42,000 sq mi (108,900 sq km) **POPULATION:** 6,621,000 **CAPITAL:** Guatemala City (pop. 718,000) **ETHNIC GROUPS:** Indian, mestizos. **LANGUAGE:** Spanish, Maya-Quiche dialects. **RELIGION:** Roman Catholic. **ECONOMY:** bananas, beans, coffee, cotton, grains, lead, livestock, meat, sugar, textiles, wood, zinc. **CURRENCY:** quetzal.

Honduras

 Most of Honduras's people live on the mountain-rimmed central highlands. The country has less than a thousand miles of paved roads, and many people never travel more than a few miles from home.

Tegucigalpa, the capital, has no railroad. Even the Pan American Highway through Central America bypasses the city. It spreads out on hillsides so steep that some streets are built like stairs. But frequent air service connects the capital with the rest of Honduras and the outside world.

In northern Honduras, on the coastal plain sweeping inland from the Caribbean Sea, banana plantations cover thousands of acres. Until a few years ago, big American companies ran them like separate little countries. Each had its own schools, hospitals, even railroads. These plantations once grew about a third of the world's bananas— mostly shipped to the United States.

Honduras turns out many valuable products besides bananas. Forests supply fine woods such as mahogany. Mountain mines yield silver and small amounts of gold, lead, and zinc. Farms grow sugarcane, coffee, and tobacco.

Because it is not so heavily populated, Honduras attracts settlers from crowded El Salvador, its neighbor on the Pacific Ocean coastline.

OFFICIAL NAME: Republic of Honduras **AREA:** 43,300 sq mi (112,100 sq km) **POPULATION:** 3,517,000 **CAPITAL:** Tegucigalpa (pop. 274,000) **ETHNIC GROUPS:** mestizos, also Indian. **LANGUAGE:** Spanish. **RELIGION:** Roman Catholic. **ECONOMY:** bananas, beans, coffee, cotton, grains, meat, metals, oil refining, sugar, textiles, tobacco, wood. **CURRENCY:** lempira.

Nicaragua

 Volcanoes in Nicaragua gave the world its only freshwater sharks. Many years ago, lava flows walled off Lake Nicaragua from the Pacific Ocean, trapping sharks and other saltwater fish. Rains slowly turned the water fresh, but some sea fish adapted to the new conditions and survived.

Engineers eye Nicaragua's lakes as a second route across Central America. If linked to both the Atlantic and Pacific by modern waterways, the lakes would be an alternative to the Panama Canal. Nicaraguan cities cluster along the lakes. But residents live with a violent earth. Earthquakes destroyed Managua in 1931 and again flattened it in 1972.

Most Nicaraguans live in low valleys near the Pacific. The vast eastern area has few people, especially in the insect-ridden swamp called Mosquito Coast, where most of Nicaragua's few Indian tribes live.

OFFICIAL NAME: Republic of Nicaragua **AREA:** 57,100 sq mi (147,900 sq km) **POPULATION:** 2,409,000 **CAPITAL:** Managua (pop. 376,000) **ETHNIC GROUPS:** mestizos, also European, blacks, Indian. **LANGUAGE:** Spanish. **RELIGION:** Roman Catholic. **ECONOMY:** beans, cattle, chemicals, coffee, cotton, grains, meat, metals, sugar, textiles. **CURRENCY:** cordoba.

Panama

 Panama, a country with an unusual twist, is shaped like the letter S. This strip of hilly jungle doubles back on itself. Look at the map. You will see that a ship going through the Panama Canal doesn't head west to reach the Pacific Ocean. It goes east!

People have been crossing Panama for centuries. About 30 miles wide (48 km) at its narrowest point, it offers a shortcut between the Atlantic and Pacific. Spanish explorers shipped gold across the narrow part of the isthmus by mule. When the United States wanted to build a waterway for ocean-going ships in 1903, it chose much the same route.

Today, ships from around the world line up for the 15-hour journey through the Panama Canal, often saving themselves a 9,000-mile (14,400 km) voyage around South America. Locks lift the ships over an 85-foot (26 m) rise, and let them down at the other end. Control of the canal will pass to Panama under a treaty signed in 1978.

Panama City and Colon thrive on trade from the busy Canal. The rest of Panama is a quiet land of tropical forests, villages, and farms. Men often wear white "Panama" hats—made in Ecuador.

OFFICIAL NAME: Republic of Panama **AREA:** 29,200 sq mi (75,600 sq km) **POPULATION:** 1,812,000 **CAPITAL:** Panama City (pop. 416,000) **ETHNIC GROUPS:** mestizos, also blacks, Indian, Spanish. **LANGUAGE:** Spanish, also English. **RELIGION:** Roman Catholic, also Protestant. **ECONOMY:** bananas, coffee, meat, metals, oil refining, shrimp, sugar, wood. **CURRENCY:** balboa.

Guatemala

▶ *The Maya city of Tikal slept 1,000 years under a jungle blanket. Now such ruins offer clues to Maya life in A.D. 800. The Maya developed writing and kept precise calendars; their mathematical system, like ours, made use of the zero.*

Panama

1 *Unable to walk on his hooklike claws, a sloth clings to life in the trees.*

2 *Bananas by the bag—Panama's biggest export—come to your breakfast table.*

3 *Chopper pilot gets a whirlybird's-eye view of shipping in the Panama Canal.*

Costa Rica

4 *Mountains of fruit brighten market stalls in Costa Rica's cool central highlands.*

Belize

5 *A fisherman spears a fish amid coastal coral. He dives to work six hours a day.*

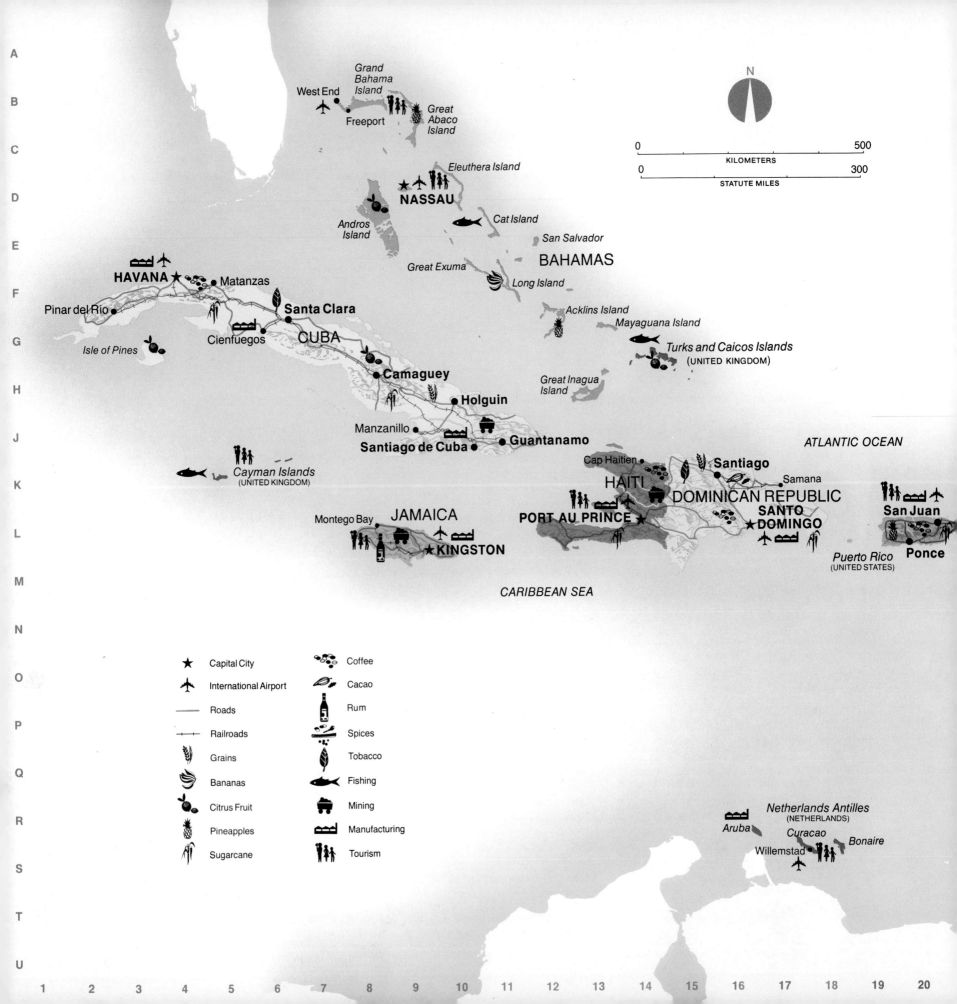

West End

Grand Bahama Island

Freeport

Great Abaco Island

Eleuthera Island

★ **NASSAU**

Cat Island

Andros Island

San Salvador

BAHAMAS

Great Exuma

Long Island

HAVANA ★ Matanzas

Pinar del Rio

Santa Clara

Cienfuegos

CUBA

Isle of Pines

Acklins Island

Mayaguana Island

Turks and Caicos Islands
(UNITED KINGDOM)

Camaguey

Holguin

Great Inagua Island

Manzanillo

Santiago de Cuba

Guantanamo

ATLANTIC OCEAN

Cayman Islands
(UNITED KINGDOM)

Cap Haitien

Santiago

Samana

HAITI

DOMINICAN REPUBLIC

★ **SANTO DOMINGO**

★ **San Juan**

Montego Bay

JAMAICA

PORT AU PRINCE

Puerto Rico
(UNITED STATES)

Ponce

★ **KINGSTON**

CARIBBEAN SEA

★ Capital City

✈ International Airport

— Roads

Railroads

🌾 Grains

Bananas

Citrus Fruit

Pineapples

Sugarcane

Coffee

Cacao

Rum

Spices

Tobacco

Fishing

Mining

Manufacturing

Tourism

Netherlands Antilles
(NETHERLANDS)

Aruba

Curacao

Bonaire

Willemstad

N

0 — 500
KILOMETERS
0 — 300
STATUTE MILES

Antigua

Christopher Columbus named this island after a church in Spain. Antiguans boast that they have a different beach for every day of the year. The stretches of powdery white sand lure vacationers to luxurious and fashionable resorts in this Caribbean island state under British control.

In one of the many harbors sits Nelson's Dockyard, an important base for Britain's fleet in colonial days. Inland, life moves at a donkey's pace. Frequent droughts parch the island — instead of flowers, shells of sea conchs decorate yards. A favorite meal: *fungi* and *coo-coo* — cornmeal and okra.

OFFICIAL NAME: State of Antigua
AREA: 108 sq mi (280 sq km)
POPULATION: 73,000
CAPITAL: St. John's (pop. 22,000)
ETHNIC GROUPS: blacks. **LANGUAGE:** English.
RELIGION: Protestant. **ECONOMY:** cotton, oil refining, sugar, tourism. **CURRENCY:** dollar.

Bahamas

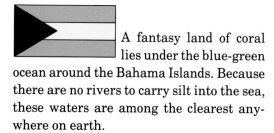 A fantasy land of coral lies under the blue-green ocean around the Bahama Islands. Because there are no rivers to carry silt into the sea, these waters are among the clearest anywhere on earth.

The Spanish word *bajamar,* for "shallow waters," gave the Bahamas their name. Yet there are deep channels, too — where fishermen catch record-size tuna and marlin, and where Spanish galleons once sailed. On one of the 700 islands, San Salvador, Columbus first landed in the New World.

OFFICIAL NAME: The Commonwealth of The Bahamas
AREA: 4,400 sq mi (11,400 sq km)
POPULATION: 226,000
CAPITAL: Nassau (pop. 3,300)
ETHNIC GROUPS: blacks, also British, Canadian, mulattos. **LANGUAGE:** English. **RELIGION:** Protestant, also Roman Catholic. **ECONOMY:** cement, fish, fruit, medicines, oil refining, rum, salt, tourism, vegetables, wood. **CURRENCY:** dollar.

Barbados

 Sam Lord, a buccaneer, hung lights from palm and tamarind trees in Barbados to imitate a harbor. This trick lured treasure-laden ships into reefs off the Barbados coast. Now the islanders make most of their money from molasses and the tourist trade. Though overpopulated and poor, Barbados keeps a feel of England (it once was a British colony) with tennis and cricket courts, and smoked fish for breakfast. Names like Yorkshire, Hastings, and Windsor can be found on the island, and the north coast is called the Scotland District.

OFFICIAL NAME: Barbados
AREA: 166 sq mi (430 sq km)
POPULATION: 258,000
CAPITAL: Bridgetown (pop. 9,000)
ETHNIC GROUPS: blacks, also mulattos. **LANGUAGE:** English. **RELIGION:** Protestant, also Roman Catholic. **ECONOMY:** clothing, molasses, rum, sugar, tourism. **CURRENCY:** dollar.

Cuba

 People in Key West, Florida, can easily tune in radio stations in Havana, only 100 miles (161 km) away. For years radio was almost the only contact Americans had with Cuba, because of quarrels between the United States and the Communist government of Fidel Castro. But in the 1970's the two nations began allowing tourists to trickle back.

Visitors find a long, mostly flat island with mountains at the eastern end. The white buildings of Havana, largest city in the Caribbean, have a worn look, because the government has spent its money in the countryside building new apartments. These slowly replace the old *bohios,* huts where rural folk have lived for centuries between thatched roofs and mud floors.

At the age of 12, many children go off to boarding school, where they study half the day and tend crops the other half. When it's

---

Map labels

✈ 👥👨👩
U.S. Virgin Islands
— *British Virgin Islands*

👥👨👩 *Anguilla* (UNITED KINGDOM)
St. Martin (St. Maarten) (FRANCE & NETHERLANDS)
St. Barthelemy (FRANCE)

Saba (NETH.)
St. Croix *St. Eustatius* (NETH.)
(U.S.) *Barbuda* (UNITED KINGDOM)

St. Christopher-Nevis *Antigua* (UNITED KINGDOM)
(UNITED KINGDOM) *Montserrat* (UNITED KINGDOM)

Guadeloupe
(FRANCE) Pointe-a-Pitre
Basse Terre

DOMINICA
ROSEAU ★

Le Carbet *Martinique*
Fort de France (FRANCE)

CASTRIES ★ ST. LUCIA

St. Vincent BARBADOS
Kingstown
The **BRIDGETOWN**
Grenadines

ST. GEORGE'S ★ GRENADA

Tobago
TRINIDAD AND TOBAGO
PORT OF SPAIN ★
Trinidad

time to harvest sugarcane, even adult city dwellers travel to the lush plains to help. "Sugar is our life," one worker explains. Cuba exports more sugar than any other country, mostly to Russia.

But Cuba's second crop may be the more famous: tobacco, hand-rolled into prized "Havana" cigars. When Christopher Columbus landed in Cuba his sailors saw Indians smoking cigars — *tobacos* in the Indian tongue — and took the idea back to Europe.

OFFICIAL NAME: Republic of Cuba
AREA: 44,200 sq mi (114,500 sq km)
POPULATION: 9,797,000
CAPITAL: Havana (pop. 1,755,400)
ETHNIC GROUPS: mulattos, Spanish, also blacks. **LANGUAGE:** Spanish. **RELIGION:** Roman Catholic. **ECONOMY:** chemicals, citrus fruit, coffee, grains, nickel, oil refining, paper, potatoes, sugar, textiles, tobacco, wood. **CURRENCY:** peso.

Dominica

Until 1978 Dominica belonged to Great Britain. Now independent, it remains the same wildly beautiful island Columbus discovered. Lush foliage drapes cloud-shrouded volcanic peaks. Drenched by rain, Dominica measures amounts that fall during the year in feet, not inches.

Sparkling streams splash into glistening pools. The forests are alive with rare animals. They include the world's largest parrot, a beaver without a tail, and a giant frog prized as a delicacy by Dominicans. They call it "mountain chicken." Most of the people farm small plots near the coast.

Dominica has the area's only Carib Indian reservation. Legend says fierce Caribs would eat dirt and die to avoid capture.

OFFICIAL NAME: Dominica
AREA: 305 sq mi (790 sq km)
POPULATION: 81,000
CAPITAL: Roseau (pop. 10,200)
ETHNIC GROUPS: blacks. **LANGUAGE:** English, French patois. **RELIGION:** Roman Catholic, Protestant. **ECONOMY:** cacao, coconut, fruit, tourism. **CURRENCY:** dollar.

Dominican Republic

Sharing the island of Hispaniola with Haiti, the Dominican Republic saw the beginning of European settlements in the New World. From Santo Domingo, oldest European city in the Americas, Spanish explorers set forth in their quest for gold.

Today the country's wealth springs from oil refineries, bauxite and other minerals, the growing of coffee, and the processing of foods such as tomato paste.

Most Dominicans still work on farms, but new hotels bring increasing business from tourists. Visitors eat goat meat along Santo Domingo's Avenida George Washington, go sportfishing off the peninsula of Samana, or shop for jewelry made from amber. This hard, clear, yellow-brown substance is fossilized sap from pine trees that grew here 20 million years ago. Some specimens have prehistoric insects embedded inside them.

OFFICIAL NAME: Dominican Republic
AREA: 18,800 sq mi (48,700 sq km)
POPULATION: 5,393,000
CAPITAL: Santo Domingo (pop. 674,000)
ETHNIC GROUPS: mulattos, also Spanish, blacks. **LANGUAGE:** Spanish. **RELIGION:** Roman Catholic. **ECONOMY:** bauxite, cement, coffee, gold, grains, molasses, nickel, oil refining, silver, sugar, textiles, tobacco, tourism. **CURRENCY:** peso.

Grenada

The crater of an ancient volcano provides the harbor for St. George's, the capital of Grenada. This small city has red-roofed houses painted in soft colors. They nestle in the hills above the harbor. North of St. George's, Grenada rises sharply to a mountain range. Here you can see another volcano crater — far above sea level.

Volcanoes gave Grenada its black sand beaches. In the island's rich soil, banana and nutmeg trees thrive. From the inner seeds of the nutmeg comes the spice used to flavor cookies and eggnog. The cover of the nutmeg is not thrown away but ground into mace, another spice widely used in cooking. Now you know why 17th-century sailors called this the "Isle of Spice."

OFFICIAL NAME: Grenada
AREA: 133 sq mi (344 sq km)
POPULATION: 108,000
CAPITAL: St. George's (pop. 7,303)
ETHNIC GROUPS: blacks, also mulattos. **LANGUAGE:** English, also French patois. **RELIGION:** Protestant, also Roman Catholic. **ECONOMY:** bananas, cacao, mace, nutmeg. **CURRENCY:** dollar.

Haiti

Late in the night, when all is quiet, you can sometimes hear them, far back in the mountains: voodoo drums. Voodoo, a religion of spirit worship and magic spells, grew from beliefs brought to Haiti by West African slaves. In 1804 the slaves overthrew their French masters and made Haiti the first black republic in the world.

Most farmers in this crowded land till plots of ground about two acres in size. Families often make less than $100 a year, so children tag after tourists in downtown Port au Prince, hoping to earn a few cents as tour guides. In city markets women sell fruits, vegetables, and handicrafts.

Markets appear in many of Haiti's famous paintings, done by self-taught artists. Their brightly-colored brushstrokes often show people washing clothes in streams that flow past mud-walled, thatch-roofed houses surrounded by flowers.

OFFICIAL NAME: Republic of Haiti
AREA: 10,700 sq mi (27,700 sq km)
POPULATION: 5,534,000
CAPITAL: Port au Prince (pop. 459,000)
ETHNIC GROUPS: blacks, also mulattos. **LANGUAGE:** French, Creole. **RELIGION:** Roman Catholic, also Protestant; voodoo widely practiced. **ECONOMY:** bauxite, beans, cement, coffee, grains, handicrafts, peas, sisal, sugar, textiles, tourism. **CURRENCY:** gourde.

Jamaica

 The motto of Jamaica, "Out of many, one people," describes these islanders well. Their forebears include the original Arawak Indians, who died out under Spanish rule; African slaves imported to work sugarcane plantations; East Indians brought in after slavery was abolished; Spanish and English colonists; and Chinese merchants.

Jamaica's calypso songs show this heritage, blending African rhythms with words that are both funny and a little sad.

About half of all Jamaicans work on the land, growing sugarcane, coffee, and other crops. Jamaica produces more bauxite (aluminum ore) than any other country. Thousands of tourists create jobs for artists, entertainers, and scuba-diving instructors. Visitors play in waterfalls cascading down a rock stairway to the sea, and take raft trips past jungles along the Rio Grande River.

OFFICIAL NAME: Jamaica
AREA: 4,400 sq mi (11,400 sq km)
POPULATION: 2,201,000
CAPITAL: Kingston (pop. 604,000)
ETHNIC GROUPS: blacks, also mulattos. **LANGUAGE:** English. **RELIGION:** Protestant, also Roman Catholic. **ECONOMY:** alumina, bauxite, cacao, coconut, coffee, fruit, pimiento, rum, sugar, textiles, tourism. **CURRENCY:** dollar.

Puerto Rico

Raoul drives on a freeway to his job in a San Juan chemical plant. He passes high-rise buildings and luxury hotels, and he may even stop for a snack at a fast-food restaurant. Except for the signs in Spanish, San Juan looks like a United States city. Originally San Juan was the name of the island, and the capital was called Puerto Rico.

Thirty years ago the island had only a few factories and industries. Now there are more than 2,000 manufacturing plants. They bring in six times more income than the sugar, coffee, and pineapples that had been the main source of earnings for the island for hundreds of years.

Puerto Ricans are United States citizens. They enjoy a higher income than most other people in Latin America. Yet the hardships of poverty still burden many families in this overcrowded land. Because so many things have to be imported, prices are high. Hurricanes and droughts damage the island from time to time.

Yet families like Raoul's, and thousands of tourists each year, enjoy Puerto Rico's year-round warm climate. Visitors like to go sailing on Phosphorescent Bay. It's named for tiny sea animals that send out showers of emerald-green sparks, lighting up the waters. And people picnic at El Yunque, the rain forest near San Juan. There the rainfall reaches more than 200 inches each year, and ferns grow as tall as trees.

OFFICIAL NAME: Commonwealth of Puerto Rico
AREA: 3,400 sq mi (8,900 sq km)
POPULATION: 3,337,000
CAPITAL: San Juan (pop. 453,000)
ETHNIC GROUPS: Spanish. **LANGUAGE:** Spanish, English. **RELIGION:** Roman Catholic. **ECONOMY:** chemicals, coffee, machinery, molasses, oil refining, pineapples, rum, sugar, tobacco, tourism. **CURRENCY:** dollar.

St. Christopher-Nevis

Two major islands make up the West Indies country called St. Christopher-Nevis, usually shortened to St. Kitts. Most of the people live on St. Christopher, which Columbus named after his patron saint. It is a mountainous island covered with plantations. Mt. Misery has a lake in its volcanic crater. Sugarcane is the big money crop there, but nearby Nevis grows cotton.

The first European settlers found life hard. Of 500 who sailed from France in 1627, almost half died aboard ship. Another 100 died shortly after arrival. The survivors lived in huts and dined on turtles and iguanas. With the introduction of slavery, tobacco plantations prospered. By 1800, some 4,000 whites and 26,000 slaves populated St. Kitts. Slavery ended in 1833.

In 1979, St. Kitts was expecting to receive its independence from Great Britain.

OFFICIAL NAME: State of St. Christopher-Nevis
AREA: 120 sq mi (310 sq km)
POPULATION: 48,000
CAPITAL: Basseterre (pop. 13,000)
ETHNIC GROUPS: blacks. **LANGUAGE:** English. **RELIGION:** Protestant, Roman Catholic. **ECONOMY:** coconut, cotton, molasses, salt, sugar. **CURRENCY:** dollar.

St. Lucia

 *Obeah.* It's one form of black magic, and its practice survives on St. Lucia. Believers seek out an obeah man to provide love potions or a murderous spell. His tools may be cats' skulls, dead frogs, dogs' teeth, parrots' beaks, dirt from a grave.

Many of St. Lucia's people are farmers. They live on an island of towering volcanoes, wild orchids, giant ferns, and bubbling sulfur springs so hot you can hard-boil an egg in seconds. Twin peaks, the Pitons, jut sharply from the sea in the southwest.

In British-French wars, St. Lucia changed hands nine times. Britain, the final owner, granted independence in 1978.

OFFICIAL NAME: St. Lucia
AREA: 238 sq mi (616 sq km)
POPULATION: 119,000
CAPITAL: Castries (pop. 39,000)
ETHNIC GROUPS: blacks. **LANGUAGE:** English, French patois. **RELIGION:** Roman Catholic. **ECONOMY:** cacao, coconut, fruit, spices, sugar, tourism. **CURRENCY:** dollar.

St. Vincent

In 1979 part of St. Vincent blew up. The Soufriere volcano shot ash and grit so high into the air that high-altitude winds carried the dust around the globe. A sixth of the island's people fled from the area near Soufriere. (Both Guadeloupe and Montserrat also have volcanoes called "Soufriere"; the name means "place of sulfur" in French.)

Most people here live on the island's calmer southern end, where they farm or fish. Every Saturday, schooners from the nearby Grenadines bring goats, vegetables, and fruit to Kingstown's dockside market.

Long linked to Great Britain, the island expects to gain its independence soon.

OFFICIAL NAME: State of St. Vincent
AREA: 150 sq mi (389 sq km)
POPULATION: 105,000
CAPITAL: Kingstown (pop. 17,000)
ETHNIC GROUPS: blacks, mixed, also European, East Indian, Carib Indian. **LANGUAGE:** English, also French patois. **RELIGION:** Protestant, Roman Catholic. **ECONOMY:** arrowroot, bananas, coconut, fish. **CURRENCY:** dollar.

Trinidad and Tobago

 Trinidad leaps into frenzied fun-making each year at Carnival time. For two days before Ash Wednesday—the first day of the 40-day Lenten fasting period—parades fill the streets. Costumed merrymakers dance all through the night to the throbbing beat of steel bands. In earlier days, wealthy plantation owners attended elegant balls during Carnival. Later, freed slaves added the folk traditions of Africa to the island's celebrations.

From Trinidad sprang calypso—rhythmic tunes spiced with witty sayings. Another invention: musical drums made from empty oil drums. Coves ring Tobago, said to be the setting for *Robinson Crusoe*.

OFFICIAL NAME: Republic of Trinidad and Tobago
AREA: 2,000 sq mi (5,100 sq km)
POPULATION: 1,045,000
CAPITAL: Port of Spain (pop. 61,000)
ETHNIC GROUPS: blacks, East Indian, also mixed. **LANGUAGE:** English. **RELIGION:** Roman Catholic, Protestant, Hindu, Muslim. **ECONOMY:** bananas, cacao, citrus fruit, coffee, grains, oil, sugar, tourism. **CURRENCY:** dollar.

British Territories

Britain's remaining possessions in the West Indies—in recent years many have been granted independence—include islands with colorful, violent histories. The British Virgin Islands sheltered such notorious buccaneers as Blackbeard and Captain Kidd. The pirates, awaiting Spain's gold-laden galleons, hid in the hundreds of coves that dent the islands. Islets were given swashbuckling names such as Gallows Cay, Rum Island, and Dead Chest.

Because of its flat, curved shape, tiny Anguilla was named by explorers after the French word for eel. Many men of the Cayman Islands take up a livelihood of fishing for sharks and turtles. On Montserrat, steep cliffs rise straight from the sea at some places. The first Irish settlers called this the Emerald Isle after their homeland. There is little green about Turks and Caicos Islands, since they get little rainfall.

Anguilla, British Virgin Islands, Cayman Islands, Montserrat, Turks and Caicos Islands
OFFICIAL NAME: British West Indies
AREA: 400 sq mi (1,050 sq km)
POPULATION: 49,000
ETHNIC GROUPS: blacks, European, Indian, mixed. **LANGUAGE:** English, also French patois. **RELIGION:** Protestant, Roman Catholic. **ECONOMY:** arrowroot, cacao, coconut, cotton, fish, fruit, livestock, sugar, tourism, turtle meat and shells, vegetables. **CURRENCY:** dollar.

French Antilles

May 8, 1902. Breakfast time in the city of St. Pierre on Martinique, one of France's two major islands in the Caribbean. Suddenly nearby Mount Pelee erupts, sending an avalanche of flame into the town. In less than three minutes the city is destroyed and more than 30,000 people die.

Luckily, no such disaster came to Guadeloupe, the other main island, when its Soufriere volcano rumbled in 1976. Mountains and volcanoes can even be helpful. The mountains trap moist air, bringing rain.

Fertile volcanic soil helps produce good sugarcane, banana, and pineapple crops.

St. Barthelemy (St. Barts) and part of St. Martin, dependencies of Guadeloupe, have valuable salt deposits.

OFFICIAL NAME: Department of Martinique; Department of Guadeloupe
AREA: 1,100 sq mi (2,900 sq km)
POPULATION: 659,000
CAPITAL: Martinique—Fort de France (pop. 99,000); Guadeloupe—Basse Terre (pop. 16,000)
ETHNIC GROUPS: blacks, mulattos, also European, Indian. **LANGUAGE:** French, Creole. **RELIGION:** Roman Catholic. **ECONOMY:** bananas, cement, oil refining, pineapples, rum, sugar, tourism. **CURRENCY:** franc.

Netherlands Antilles

The Netherlands Antilles—Dutch possessions that govern themselves—consist of two widely separated groups of islands. The coral-fringed ABC's (Aruba, Bonaire, and Curacao) lie off the coast of Venezuela. More northerly are the Dutch Windward Islands of St. Maarten (which is part French), St. Eustatius, and a volcanic peak called Saba.

Except for Saba, these islands share a common problem—a shortage of drinking water. Homes and hotels have cisterns to catch any rain that falls, usually in the July-to-October period. On Curacao and desertlike Aruba, islanders distill salty seawater to get fresh water for cooking.

At St. Maarten ships bring water tanks to Philipsburg, one of several "free ports"—where taxes are low or may not be collected at all. Visitors find bargains in cameras, watches, and china from all over the world.

OFFICIAL NAME: Netherlands Antilles
AREA: 386 sq mi (1,000 sq km)
POPULATION: 247,000
CAPITAL: Willemstad (pop. 46,000)
ETHNIC GROUPS: blacks, European, Indian, mixed. **LANGUAGE:** Dutch, English, also Papiamento. **RELIGION:** Roman Catholic, also Protestant. **ECONOMY:** oil refining, phosphate, tourism. **CURRENCY:** florin.

United States Virgin Islands

Columbus named the islands The Virgins in 1493 because of their serene, unspoiled beauty. By the 1700's vigorous pirates had disturbed the serenity, and sugarcane plantations had spoiled the scenery. But the beauty of the islands could not be hidden. They now lure throngs of tourists. Sugar and livestock produce other income.

The islands—there are about 50, counting those that are only outcroppings of rock—have an average yearly temperature of 78° F (26° C), considered to be the best climate in the Caribbean.

On St. Thomas, tropical flowers splash color along the sidewalks in the capital of Charlotte Amalie—also noted for its tax-free shops. More than half of St. John, smallest of the three main islands, is a national park where the natural environment is to remain unspoiled. On St. Croix, largest of the islands, you can see oil refineries, explore colonial Christiansted, and swim underwater trails in Buck Island National Monument. The United States bought the Virgin Islands from Denmark in 1917.

OFFICIAL NAME: United States Virgin Islands
AREA: 132 sq mi (340 sq km)
POPULATION: 110,000
CAPITAL: Charlotte Amalie (pop. 12,000)
ETHNIC GROUPS: blacks, also European. **LANGUAGE:** English. **RELIGION:** Protestant, Roman Catholic. **ECONOMY:** cattle, gin, jewelry, metals, oil refining, perfumes, rum, sugar, textiles, tourism, watches. **CURRENCY:** dollar.

Jamaica

1 *Breadfruit by the head-load—you can eat this starchy food baked, roasted, or fried.*

Martinique

2 Thwap! *By beating the water, a boatman keeps fish from leaping out of his net, which hangs from the floats below him.*

3 *Kaleidoscope of Carnival helps draw 300,000 tourists to Martinique yearly.*

Netherlands Antilles

1 *Could you sing to the noise of a drum, a file, a banging hoe, and a cowbell? That's* tambu, *the throbbing music of Curacao. These singers make up words as they go, in the Papiamento tongue.*

2 *Far from the cool North Sea, Dutch-style houses bake in tropical Willemstad. Buildings have worn soft colors ever since a Dutch governor complained that the glare of white walls hurt his eyes.*

Cuba

3 *A mechanical claw loads sugarcane into an ox-drawn cart. Sugar accounts for more than four-fifths of Cuba's exports.*

6

Dominican Republic

4 *The taste of tobacco brings a smile and a paycheck to a Santiago cigar worker. His nation is richer than neighboring Haiti—and has close to twice as much land area for the same number of people.*

Haiti

5 *Muscles, not motors, pull much of Haiti's load. Only one person in 400 owns a car.*

6 *The fort that killed thousands without firing a shot: The Citadel. Stories say 20,000 men died of overwork building it. A mad Haitian king, Henry Christophe, designed it to stop an invasion by Napoleon—an invasion that never came.*

South America

Two words dominate South America's geography: Amazon and Andes.

Beginning as a trickle on a mountain in Peru, headwaters of the Amazon River gain force as they crash through rocky gorges on the eastern slopes of the Andes Mountains. The flow levels out in the flat rain forests. Other streams swell the flood until it is miles wide.

Though not quite as long as the Nile, the Amazon is bigger in every other way. More water flows from the Amazon than from all eight of the world's next biggest rivers put together! Its channel is so deep that ocean ships can sail all the way upstream to Iquitos, Peru's "port on the Atlantic." The river drains the Amazon Basin, an area two-thirds the size of the United States. Large areas remain unexplored. In 1975, Brazilian mapmakers detected a 400-mile river never charted before.

In the basin live more than 100,000 kinds of plants and animals. Water lilies grow leaves so wide a child can lie down on one. Piranha, ferocious fish with teeth like daggers, can strip the meat from a drowning calf in a minute.

The jungles shelter people too, many of them Stone Age Indian tribes. An entire tribe may live in a single village and speak a language heard nowhere else.

Indians along Brazil's Xingu River capture an anaconda, or water boa, South America's largest snake. Some grow 30 feet (9 m) long. This one could have crushed a swimming child in its coils. Indians of the jungle hunt forest animals for food and hides, and clear small plots to raise corn and root crops. Sometimes they raid neighboring villages.

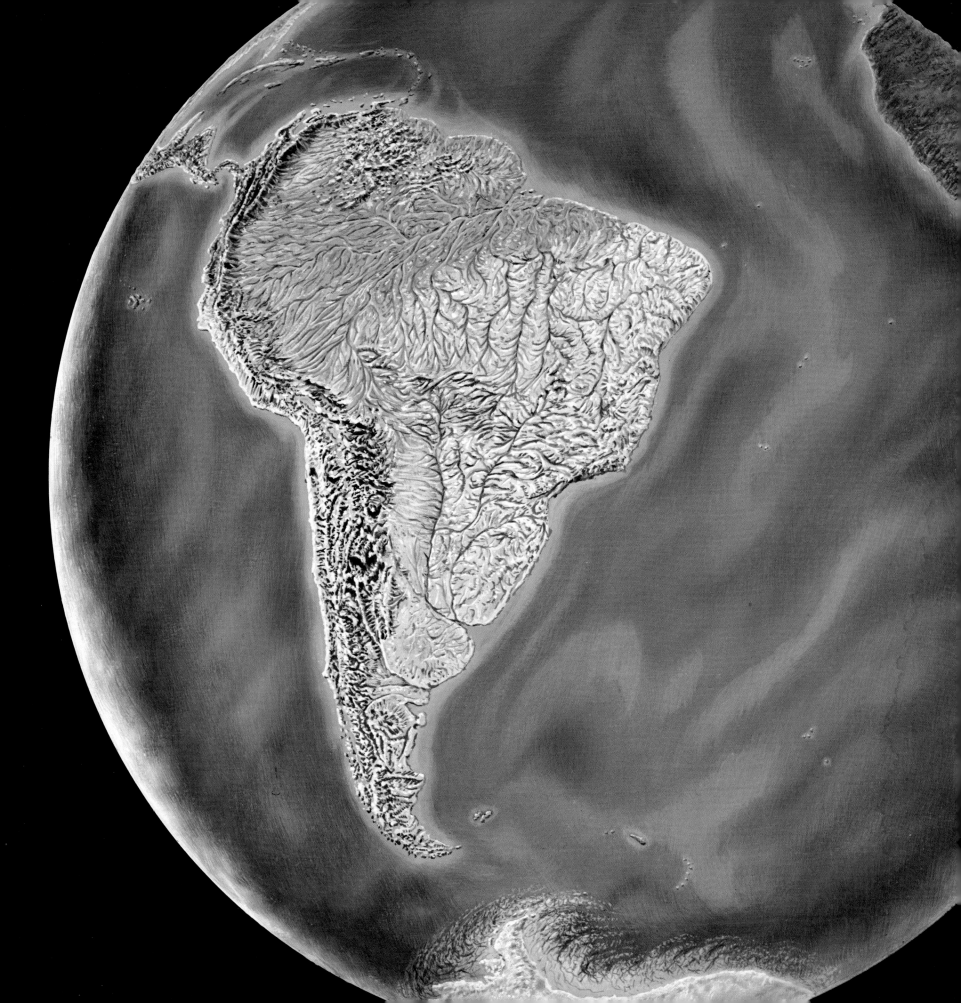

If you think of South America as a triangle-shaped flag, then the Andes form the pole from which it flies. For 4,500 miles (7,200 km), peak after snow-capped peak stands in a line, from cold and windy Cape Horn north to the sunny beaches of the Caribbean Sea. The Andes are both the world's longest mountain chain and its second highest, next to the Himalayas of Asia. On the Chile-Argentina border, mighty Aconcagua crowns the Western Hemisphere.

Earthquakes and erupting volcanoes often shake these mountains. Just offshore, deep in an ocean trench, a section of the Pacific Ocean floor called the Nazca Plate is creeping downward to its destruction under the South American Plate. The slow-motion collision keeps pushing the Andes higher.

In spite of the quakes, many people live in the Andes. Most are Indians descended from civilizations that flourished before the Spanish arrived. They wear brightly colored wool clothes made from the hair of alpacas, vicunas, and sheep. The people have extra-large hearts and lungs that help them breathe the thin air at high altitudes.

South America has other highland regions, much lower than the Andes. The Guiana Highlands meet the Amazon Basin in the north. To the south rise the Brazilian Highlands, forming a plateau that slopes away into the pampas, the fertile plains of Argentina.

Half of South America—the Brazil half—speaks Portuguese. Most of the other half speaks Spanish. The reason is nearly 500 years old. To settle an argument, a line was drawn in 1494 that gave Portugal the eastern bulge of the continent. Spain got all the rest.

So the Portuguese settled the coast of Brazil, and a small band of gold-hungry Spaniards headed for the Andes. These bold conquistadores (conquerors) had heard tales of a fabulous Indian empire there. In the land of the Incas, stretching from Ecuador to Chile, gold was so common it was called "sweat of the sun," and silver "tears of the moon." The Spaniards destroyed the Inca empire. They killed the emperor, stripped the gold and silver from the temples, and set the Indians to work in mines, seeking still more treasure. Gold and silver became the sweat and tears of the Indian.

Today, most South Americans still live near the edges of their continent. They crowd into huge cities—Rio de Janeiro, Buenos Aires, Santiago, Lima, Caracas. Gleaming skyscrapers seem to be in a race against muddy slums, to see which can grow faster. In the west, from Bolivia north to Colombia, the Andes have fenced people into cramped valleys. Towering ridges and deep gorges have kept the people cut off from each other, and isolated them from the hundreds of miles of empty lowlands in the Amazon and Orinoco basins.

Now things are changing. To solve the problem of too many people in some places and too few in others, South Americans have set out to conquer their own backyards. The Andean countries are building roads down into the jungle. And Brazilians are clearing forests and planning brand new cities, like Brasilia, in the wilderness.

Facts About South America

SIZE: 6,866,000 sq mi (17,783,000 sq km)

POPULATION: 229,000,000

DENSITY: 33 persons for every sq mi (13 per sq km)

HIGHEST POINT: Mount Aconcagua, Argentina, 22,834 ft (6,959 m) above sea level

LOWEST POINT: Valdes Peninsula, Argentina, 131 ft (40 m) below sea level

LARGEST COUNTRY: (by area) Brazil 3,290,000 sq mi (8,521,100 sq km)

LARGEST COUNTRY: (by population) Brazil 115,415,000

LARGEST METROPOLITAN AREAS: (by population)

Sao Paulo	9,900,000
Buenos Aires	8,700,000
Rio de Janeiro	8,300,000
Lima	3,400,000
Bogota	3,000,000
Santiago	3,000,000

LONGEST RIVERS: (mi and km)

Amazon	4,000	6,400
Parana	2,500	4,000
Purus	2,100	3,300
Madeira	2,000	3,200
Sao Francisco	1,900	3,000

LARGEST LAKES: (sq mi and sq km)

Maracaibo	5,200	13,400
Titicaca	3,200	8,200

CARIBBEAN SEA

Guajira Peninsula
Paraguana Peninsula
Margarita Island

Santa Marta
Barranquilla
Cartagena
Cristobal Colon Peak
+ 18,947 FEET
5,775 METERS
Maracaibo
Cabimas
Barquisimeto
CARACAS
Petare
San Francisco de Yare
Maracay
Cumana

Monteria
Magdalena River
Lake Maracaibo
Valera
Valencia
Maturin

Merida
+ Bolivar Peak
16,427 FEET
5,007 METERS
LLANOS
Apure River
Orinoco River
Ciudad Guayana

Cucuta
San Cristobal
VENEZUELA
Ciudad Bolivar

Bucaramanga
Atrato River
Arauca
ANDES
Puerto Paez
Puerto Carreno
GUIANA HIGHLANDS
Angel Falls
LA GRAN SABANA

Medellin
Muzo
LLANOS
Meta River

PACIFIC OCEAN
Manizales
Pereira
Ibague
BOGOTA
Villavicencio

Buenaventura
Cali
Neiva
Siberia
Guaviare River
Obando
Orinoco River

Tumaco
COLOMBIA
San Jose del Guaviare
San Felipe

Pasto
Whiskey
Vaupes River
ANDES

N
Puerto Leguizamo
Caqueta River

Putumayo River
La Pedrera

0   400
KILOMETERS
0   300
STATUTE MILES
Arica

Amazon River
Leticia

	Legend		
★	Capital City		Sugarcane
✈	International Airport		Coffee
	Roads		Cotton
	Railroads		Fishing
	Cattle		Mining
	Dairy Products		Oil and Natural Gas
	Grains		Manufacturing
	Bananas and Plantains		

ATLANTIC OCEAN

Colombia

During the 16th century, Spanish conquistadores marched up the valley of the Magdalena River into the Andes Mountains. They hoped to find gold. Legend told of El Dorado, an Indian king who took part in a dramatic ceremony. His attendants powdered him with gold dust, then rowed him into a lake. He submerged himself, and his subjects tossed in emerald and gold ornaments as offerings to the gods.

Today Colombia, with more than 600 mines, is a leading producer of gold in South America. Most mines lie near the country's second largest city, Medellin. Colombia also produces 90 percent of the world's emeralds. The green crystals come from mines near Bogota. And what delicate mining it is. No dynamite blasts and mountain-eating machinery. Workers chip away at the thin veins with hand tools, just as Indians did centuries ago. In the capital and largest city, the Gold Museum displays a 1,796-carat emerald the size of a woman's fist.

For all its gold and emeralds, however, Colombia's real treasure is coffee. Some 300,000 farms, of about eight acres each, cling to the slopes of the Andes. In the shade of banana trees, the berries of the coffee trees slowly ripen, turning from dark green to yellow to bright red. The whole family helps pick the berries by hand and spread them to dry in the sun. After three weeks they remove the skins and pack the coffee beans into large sacks. Trucks carry the sacks down the "coffee road" to town for sale.

Other major crops grow here, where the Andes Mountains split into three razorback ranges. If you stood at the foot of an imaginary mountain with a telescope, you could see sugarcane and cotton fields in the lowlands, coffee trees in the cool slopes above 3,000 feet (914 m), and potatoes in the colder regions above 6,500 feet (1,981 m).

Even though western Colombia contains steep terrain, the majority of Colombians live there. Farm villages cling to alpine ridges, and modern cities seem to crawl up the sides of valleys.

In Colombia's wild, wild east a few cowboys tend herds of cattle on the plains north of the Guaviare River. Indians live in jungle villages to the south, a region soggy with rivers that flow into the Amazon.

To help themselves travel around their rugged land, Colombians pioneered South America's first airline in 1919.

OFFICIAL NAME: Republic of Colombia
AREA: 440,000 sq mi (1,139,600 sq km)
POPULATION: 25,559,000
CAPITAL: Bogota (pop. 2,855,000)
ETHNIC GROUPS: mestizos, also European, mulattos, blacks. **LANGUAGE:** Spanish. **RELIGION:** Roman Catholic. **ECONOMY:** bananas, cattle, chemicals, coffee, cotton, grains, metals, oil, plantains, sugar, textiles. **CURRENCY:** peso.

Venezuela

After jumping into his jeans, Jose grabs his mitt. The *beisbol* game has already started in the sandlot across the street from the high-rise apartment building where he lives. If he's lucky, traffic will have jammed to a stop in the street. It often does in the crowded city of Caracas.

About 500 miles to the south, the Indian boy Moawa has risen with the sun. Taking his bow and arrow, he leaves the dwelling in which his entire tribe sleeps and pads barefoot into the jungle to hunt.

Jose and Moawa are both citizens of Venezuela. Jose lives in the cool highlands of the northern coast. Moawa lives in the tropical forest of the southeast. In between are the *llanos*, or plains, which flood half the year and dry up hard as rock the other half.

Like birds on a branch, most of the people, factories, and farms of Venezuela perch on a range of the Andes Mountains—although the government tries to attract workers into less crowded areas like Ciudad Bolivar on the Orinoco River. The city is named for Simon Bolivar, who freed Venezuela and neighboring countries from Spanish rule in the early 19th century.

It is lonely in the vast plains north of the Orinoco River. But the land is alive with natural wonders—red howler monkeys, crocodile-like caimans, and the world's largest rodent, the blunt-nosed capybara that can weigh as much as 100 pounds (45 kg). From one of the Guiana Highland's flat-topped mountains plunges the world's highest waterfall, Angel Falls, 3,212 feet (979 m). Jimmy Angel, an American aviator, discovered it in 1935 while searching for the gold that brought conquistadores to South America in the 1500's.

Spanish explorers saw the Indian huts built on stilts in shallow Lake Maracaibo, and the dugout canoes, like Italian gondolas, that ferried to and fro. So they called the country "little Venice"—Venezuela. Today oil wells punched in Lake Maracaibo and elsewhere in the country pump the "black gold" that makes Venezuela one of the world's leading oil producers.

OFFICIAL NAME: Republic of Venezuela
AREA: 352,000 sq mi (911,600 sq km)
POPULATION: 14,058,000
CAPITAL: Caracas (pop. 1,659,000)
ETHNIC GROUPS: mestizos, also European, blacks. **LANGUAGE:** Spanish. **RELIGION:** Roman Catholic. **ECONOMY:** cattle, cement, chemicals, coffee, fish, grains, iron, natural gas, oil, sugar, textiles. **CURRENCY:** bolivar.

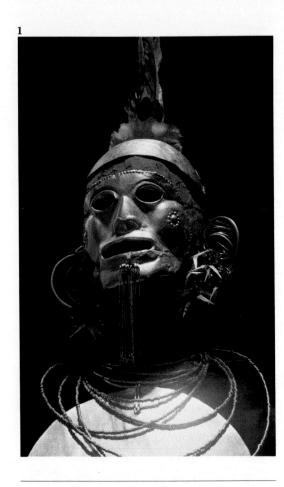

Colombia

1 *Gold mask and ornaments, on display in a Bogota museum, belonged to Indian warriors. Colombia's Chibcha Indians, like the Incas to the south, worshiped the sun. The Spanish conquered them in the 1530's.*

2 *For centuries, traders used rivers, like the Atrato, as watery highways to travel through the swampy jungles.*

3 *Tucano Indians haul their canoe around a waterfall on the Vaupes River in the southeast. Trackless jungle has long discouraged settlement here.*

4 *Coffee trees, here shaded by banana trees, grow best on hillsides. Healthy coffee trees may live fifty years.*

5 *Most of the world's emeralds, like these cut and uncut specimens, come from Colombia. The country also produces South America's only platinum.*

Venezuela

1 *Colorful macaw, a kind of parrot found in the tropics, can be taught to "talk"— but it really only mimics words.*

2 *Angel Falls, world champion with the greatest uninterrupted drop, is 16 times higher than Niagara Falls.*

3 *Men dressed as devils dance in the streets of San Francisco de Yare on Corpus Christi Day. The ritual symbolizes chasing away the devil.*

4 *Derricks pump oil from Lake Maracaibo. More than 80 percent of Venezuela's wealth comes from the production of oil.*

5 *Yanomamo Indian boys play at being warriors, sneaking up on a target. Charcoal on the face is the raiding color. Constant practice with bow and arrow develops enough skill to hit a small bird 60 feet (18 m) up in a tree.*

3

4

5

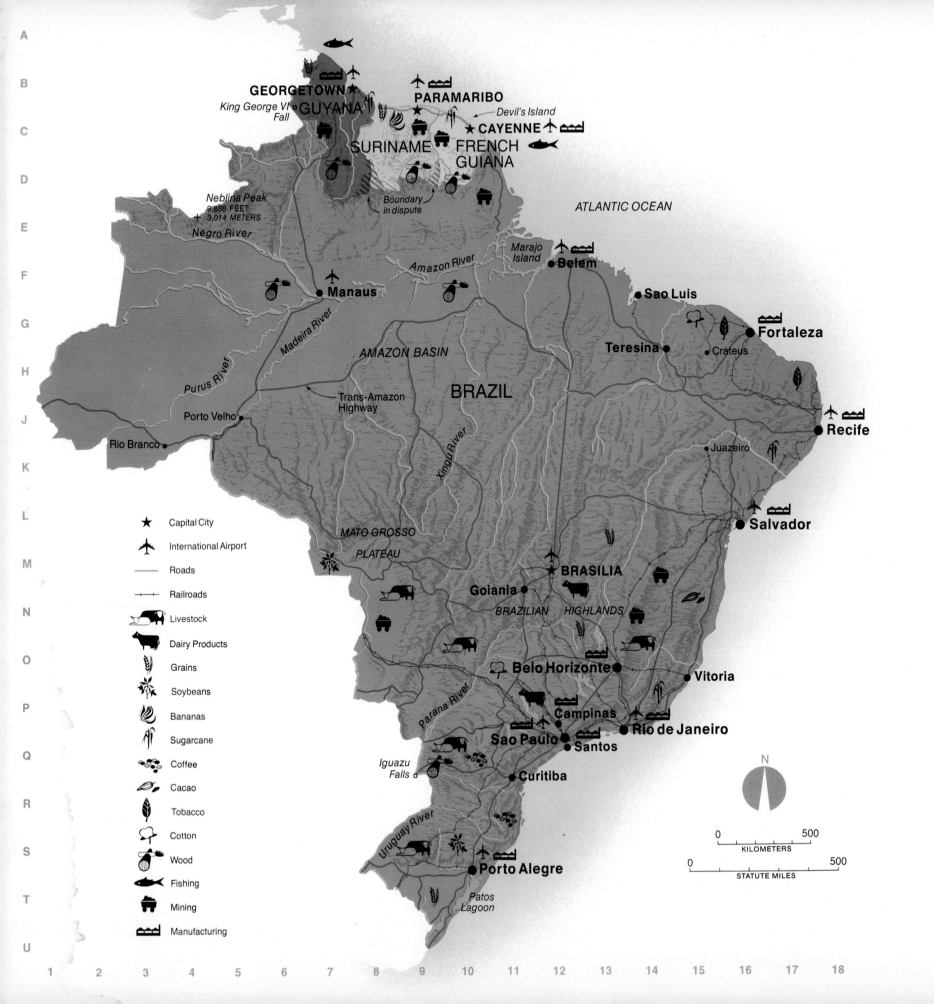

A B C D E F G H J K L M N O P Q R S T U

1 2 3 4 5 6 7 8 9 10 11 12 13 14 15 16 17 18

GEORGETOWN ★
King George VI
Fall
GUYANA

PARAMARIBO
★
← Devil's Island
CAYENNE ★
SURINAME
FRENCH
GUIANA

Boundary
in dispute

ATLANTIC OCEAN

Neblina Peak
9,888 FEET
3,014 METERS
Negro River

Amazon River

Marajo
Island
Belem

Sao Luis

Fortaleza
Teresina
Crateus

AMAZON BASIN

BRAZIL

Madeira River

Manaus

Purus River

Trans-Amazon
Highway
Porto Velho

Rio Branco

Xingu River

Recife
Juazeiro

MATO GROSSO
PLATEAU

Salvador

BRASILIA ★

Goiania

BRAZILIAN   HIGHLANDS

Belo Horizonte

Vitoria

Parana River

Campinas

Rio de Janeiro
Sao Paulo
Santos

Iguazu
Falls

Curitiba

Uruguay River

Porto Alegre

Patos
Lagoon

N

0   500
KILOMETERS

0   500
STATUTE MILES

★ Capital City
✈ International Airport
── Roads
┼┼ Railroads
Livestock
Dairy Products
Grains
Soybeans
Bananas
Sugarcane
Coffee
Cacao
Tobacco
Cotton
Wood
Fishing
Mining
Manufacturing

Brazil

Cowboys who are called *vaqueiros*.... Prospectors panning for gold along jungle streams.... Indians roaming trackless forests. Much like the United States many years ago, Brazil is vast and mostly unsettled, with a wild frontier in the western region. It even has cattlemen pitted against farmers, and settlers crushed by hardships, as in the old American West. But Brazil is changing.

Long known as "the land of the future," Brazil has an economy that grows like Jack's beanstalk. With more farmland than all of Europe, the country raises about one-third of the world's coffee and much of its beef, cotton, and sugarcane.

Forests yield lumber, nuts, wax from the carnauba palm tree, and latex from rubber trees. A papermill built in Japan was shipped across the ocean and erected in northeast Brazil to use pulpwood from the immense Amazon forests.

Brazil has rich deposits of iron ore, bauxite for the manufacture of aluminum, and manganese used in making steel, as well as gold, diamonds, and semiprecious gemstones such as amethysts. Its factories turn out cars, textiles, steel, and cement.

Covering nearly half of South America, Brazil has plenty of room to grow for its many kinds of people. They are a mixture of races and nationalities: Indians, Europeans, Africans, and Asians. Most live along the 4,250 miles (6,840 km) of the nation's Atlantic Ocean coastline.

To attract people into the interior, the government built a new capital, Brasilia, far inland from the coast. A network of highways now includes the Trans-Amazon Highway across the Amazon jungle.

Through the heart of this green tangle flows the Amazon River, 4,000 miles (6,400 km) long. With its tributaries it drains more land than any other river system on earth. In the Amazon Basin you can see monkeys, giant snakes, more than 3,000 kinds of butterflies, and Indians who still paddle canoes and hunt with bows and arrows.

Far from that wilderness are the great coastal cities. Sao Paulo, an industrial giant that is South America's largest city, has more skyscrapers than Chicago. Rio de Janeiro earns fame for beautiful beaches, a yearly carnival, and a 180,000-seat soccer stadium. A deep moat circles the playing field to protect players and referees from overexcited fans in the stands.

OFFICIAL NAME: Federative Republic of Brazil
AREA: 3,290,000 sq mi (8,521,100 sq km)
POPULATION: 115,415,000
CAPITAL: Brasilia (pop. 350,000)
ETHNIC GROUPS: European, also mixed, blacks, Indian. **LANGUAGE:** Portuguese. **RELIGION:** Roman Catholic. **ECONOMY:** cacao, cement, chemicals, coffee, cotton, grains, iron, meat, milk, motor vehicles, shoes, soybeans, sugar, steel, textiles, wood. **CURRENCY:** cruzeiro.

French Guiana

For nearly 100 years, France sent many of its convicts to Devil's Island, just off the coast of French Guiana. The mainland held other prison camps. Some 70,000 criminals spent years in these guarded settlements, which gained a reputation for cruelty. Unused to working in tropical heat, some prisoners died. The French government closed the dreaded prison colonies in 1945.

Now, French Guiana hopes to become known more for its new space research center near Cayenne than for prisons. The space center is helping, but many problems remain. Lying some 200 miles north of the Equator, French Guiana is hot and rainy, with few roads and no real industry or good farmland.

Most people are of mixed black and white ancestry, and live in or near the capital. The Guianese are French citizens, since the country is an overseas *departement,* or administrative district, of France and is represented in the Parliament.

OFFICIAL NAME: Department of French Guiana
AREA: 35,100 sq mi (90,900 sq km)
POPULATION: 60,000
CAPITAL: Cayenne (pop. 25,000)
ETHNIC GROUPS: blacks, mulattos. **LANGUAGE:** French. **RELIGION:** Roman Catholic. **ECONOMY:** bananas, cassava, gold, grains, rum, shrimp, sugar, wood. **CURRENCY:** franc.

Guyana

Native Indians called the area between the Orinoco and Amazon rivers *guiana,* "land of waters." From low mountains in the west and south, four big rivers flow north across this former British colony to the Atlantic Ocean. Other streams drop from highlands in waterfalls that include 1,600-foot (488 m) King George VI Fall.

The low and fertile coastal plain is protected from river floods by dikes, which also keep out the ocean. Dikes and a seawall guard Georgetown, the capital city, because it lies six feet (1.8 m) below sea level.

Nearly all Guyanese live along the coast. They dig canals to drain off water from heavy rains, and grow sugarcane on large plantations and rice on smaller farms. Strange as it may sound, many farmers speak Hindi. That's because the British, after they abolished slavery in Guyana and other nearby areas in 1834, brought in farm workers from India. Today, descendants of those Asian workers make up half of the people in Guyana.

Inland from Guyana's coast lie rich deposits of bauxite—the raw material for making aluminum—and immense forests of hardwood trees, which cover 85 percent of the land. Diamond miners find gems by dredging the bottoms of inland rivers.

OFFICIAL NAME: Cooperative Republic of Guyana
AREA: 83,000 sq mi (215,000 sq km)
POPULATION: 813,000
CAPITAL: Georgetown (pop. 64,000)
ETHNIC GROUPS: East Indian, blacks. **LANGUAGE:** English. **RELIGION:** Christian, also Hindu, Muslim. **ECONOMY:** alumina, bauxite, diamonds, grains, molasses, rum, shrimp, sugar, wood. **CURRENCY:** dollar.

Suriname

Rain forests, highland timber, wooded swamps —forests cover most of Suriname, with at least 2,000 kinds of trees. Hardwoods like the greenheart tree yield lumber that resists termites and decay.

Many Surinamese live and work on small rice farms near the ocean. But a small part of the population lives in the forest. They are native Indians and blacks called Bush Negroes, descendants of African slaves who ran away from coastal plantations.

Residents of Paramaribo speak "Taki Taki"—a mixture of French, English, Dutch, and other tongues. This former Dutch colony was originally owned by the British. In 1667 the British gave it to the Dutch in exchange for the colony of New Netherland, which became New York.

OFFICIAL NAME: Republic of Suriname
AREA: 55,100 sq mi (142,700 sq km)
POPULATION: 385,000
CAPITAL: Paramaribo (pop. 103,000)
ETHNIC GROUPS: East Indian, also mulattos, Javanese, blacks. **LANGUAGE:** Dutch. **RELIGION:** Christian, also Hindu, Muslim. **ECONOMY:** aluminum, bananas, bauxite, cacao, coffee, grains, sugar, wood. **CURRENCY:** guilder.

Brazil

1 *Sprawling across a high tableland, Sao Paulo leads Brazilian cities in traffic, industry, population, and pollution.*

2 *Sparkling lights of Rio de Janeiro dance beneath Sugar Loaf Mountain, granite guardian of the city's harbor entrance.*

3 *Carnival fever infects fun-loving Brazilians during four days before Lent.*

4 *A taste-tester sniffs and sips coffee bound for the United States. He grades about 24 samples in less than a minute.*

Brazil

1 *Pet birds spend their days on their master's shoulders in Xingu National Park. This Indian and wildlife reserve is at the headwaters of the Xingu River.*

2 *Time out! pants a jaguar resting in a Brazilian zoo. This animal symbolizes the rich wildlife of the Amazon Basin that may be threatened by highways, cities, and farms carved into the jungle.*

3 *After frost ruined the 1975 coffee crop, many Brazilians planted soybeans in alternating strips with rice plots. Now Brazil is a leading soybean exporter.*

Suriname

4 *People known as Bush Negroes ride the rapids in a dugout canoe. Nearly 30 ethnic groups, races, and nationalities mingle in this steamy, Iowa-size land.*

Guyana

5 *A field worker carries a heavy bundle of sugarcane on his head. Huge plantations lie along Guyana's hot and humid coast.*

French Guiana

6 *Be prepared for rain from December to July in Cayenne, capital and chief port of French Guiana. About 150 inches (381 cm) fall on the small city yearly.*

4   5

6

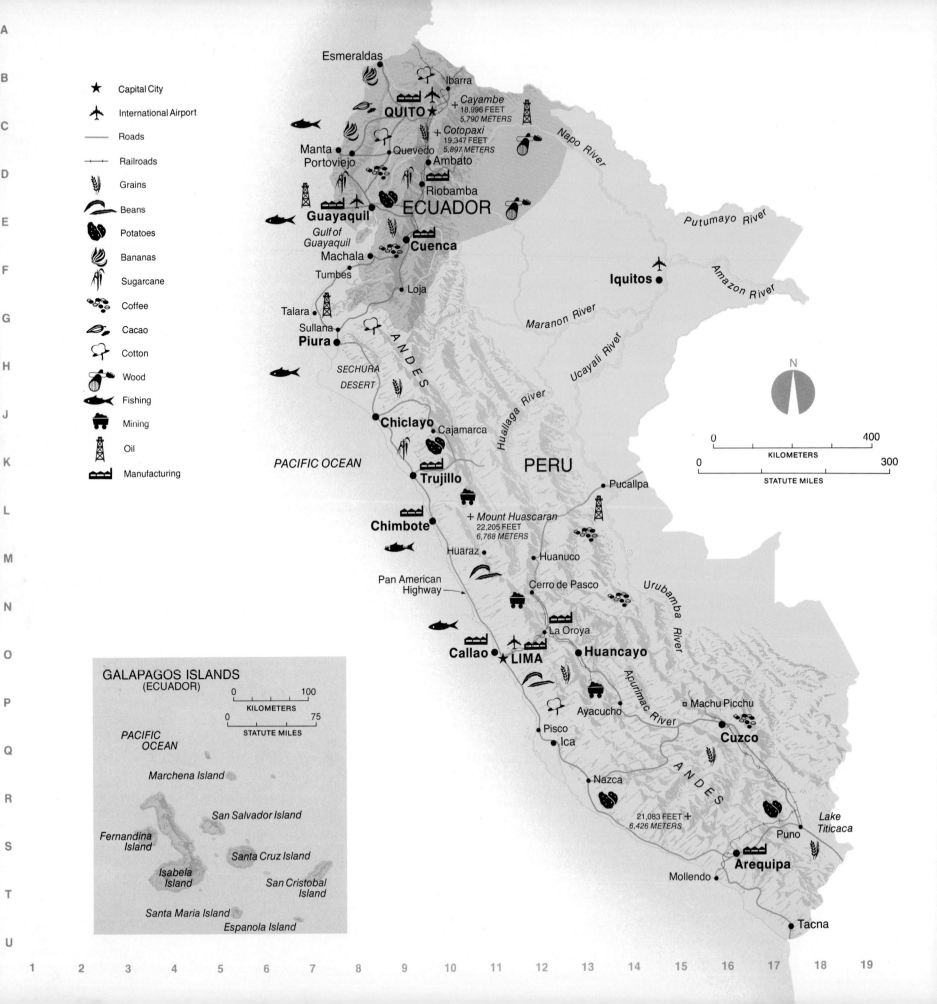

Esmeraldas
Ibarra
QUITO ★
Cayambe
18,996 FEET
5,790 METERS
Cotopaxi
19,347 FEET
5,897 METERS
Manta
Quevedo
Portoviejo
Ambato
Riobamba
ECUADOR
Guayaquil
Gulf of Guayaquil
Cuenca
Machala
Tumbes
Loja
Talara
Sullana
Piura

SECHURA DESERT

A N D E S

Chiclayo
Cajamarca

PACIFIC OCEAN

Trujillo

Napo River

Putumayo River

Amazon River

Iquitos ✈

Maranon River

Ucayali River

Huallaga River

PERU

Pucallpa

Chimbote
+ *Mount Huascaran*
22,205 FEET
6,768 METERS
Huaraz
Huanuco
Cerro de Pasco

Urubamba River

Pan American
Highway →

La Oroya

Callao ★ **LIMA**
Huancayo

Apurimac River

Ayacucho

☐ Machu Picchu

Pisco
Ica

Cuzco

Nazca
21,083 FEET +
6,426 METERS

A N D E S

Puno
Lake Titicaca

Arequipa
Mollendo

Tacna

Legend

★ Capital City
✈ International Airport
━ Roads
┼┼┼ Railroads
🌾 Grains
🫘 Beans
🥔 Potatoes
🍌 Bananas
🌱 Sugarcane
☕ Coffee
🫘 Cacao
☁ Cotton
🪵 Wood
🐟 Fishing
⛏ Mining
🛢 Oil
🏭 Manufacturing

Compass
N

Scale
0   400
KILOMETERS
0   300
STATUTE MILES

GALAPAGOS ISLANDS
(ECUADOR)

0   100
KILOMETERS
0   75
STATUTE MILES

PACIFIC OCEAN

Marchena Island
San Salvador Island
Fernandina Island
Isabela Island
Santa Cruz Island
San Cristobal Island
Santa Maria Island
Espanola Island

Ecuador

How would you like to throw snowballs from one hemisphere to another? Go to Ecuador, a nation named after the Equator and the only place on earth where latitude and temperature both reach zero. Cayambe, an inactive volcano, holds the only glacier on earth's "hot" line.

The eastern region of this Colorado-size country slopes through forests and valleys to end in Amazon jungles. Indians with spears and blowguns hunt colorful birds — and one tribe, the Jivaro, until recently practiced the art of headshrinking. The ocelot, jaguar, and vampire bat also make their home in the forests.

Highlands bordered by giant volcanoes, some of them still active, make up central Ecuador. Poncho-clad Indians on large estates harvest barley with sickles under the eyes of overseers. And here stands Quito, Ecuador's capital. Once part of the Inca empire, Quito survived the Spanish conquest. The conquistadores rushed north to Colombia and south to Peru in search of Inca gold.

West of the Andes lie the coastal lowlands. A rich agricultural belt yields coffee, cacao, and rice. Balsa trees tower to 100 feet (30 m). On the docks of Guayaquil, Ecuador's largest city with nearly a million people, you may see a stevedore carry a log of balsa wood the size of a telephone pole on his shoulder. The port also handles such major products as oil and the world's largest export of bananas.

Westward, 600 miles out in the Pacific, lie the Galapagos Islands. Tortoises with shells as big as bathtubs wander over the archipelago that was named for them. Lizards a yard long feed on prickly pear. The islands' strange forms of wildlife inspired naturalist Charles Darwin to develop his theory of evolution.

Today Ecuador mixes the new with the old. Hi-fi sets blare — and in rural houses pet guinea pigs run free, as they fatten for the cook pot. Modern rigs pump oil — and scrubland laborers collect kapok from ceibo tree pods. Kapok is the fluffy stuffing of life preservers and cushions.

OFFICIAL NAME: Republic of Ecuador
AREA: 106,000 sq mi (274,500 sq km)
POPULATION: 7,549,000
CAPITAL: Quito (pop. 598,000)
ETHNIC GROUPS: Indian, mestizos, also European. **LANGUAGE:** Spanish, Quechua. **RELIGION:** Roman Catholic. **ECONOMY:** bananas, cacao, chemicals, coffee, cotton, fish, grains, oil, potatoes, sugar, textiles, wood. **CURRENCY:** sucre.

Peru

Peru offers a wide variety of different worlds. It is a golden desert world, so dry in places even cactus won't grow. Skiers glide down slopes of sand. From this coastal desert comes much of Peru's wealth, including oil. Crops grow in the irrigated valleys and oases. Just beneath the bone-dry sand, archeologists have found thousands of mummies and colorful textiles buried thousands of years ago.

Peru's palm-fringed coast faces the cold blue Pacific, filled with tiny fish. They are ground into fishmeal to feed pigs and poultry all over the world. Seabirds also eat these fish, and the bird droppings coat the rocky offshore islands with guano. Peruvian farmers use this rich fertilizer to help make the desert bloom.

Breezes blow the smell of fish from Callao, Peru's chief port, to Lima, her capital. Lima, once the center of Spanish power in South America, is an industrial city. Skyscrapers look down on colonial palaces with graceful patios and shuttered balconies. Guitar and flute melodies drift through the noise of traffic-choked streets. During Holy Week, worshipers carry candles in outdoor processions. By Easter the melted candle wax makes some streets slippery.

Peru is a world of snowcapped mountains. Indians in woolen caps and ponchos graze sheep in the shadows of peaks that soar to 22,000 feet (6,700 m). They farm rocky plateaus, homeland of the "Irish" potato. They work in mines that produce almost all the major metals. Indians on Lake Titicaca live on floating islands woven from reeds. They also use reeds to build boats, houses, even a soccer field.

Highland Indians still speak the Quechua language of their Inca ancestors, rulers of a mighty empire that covered much of western South America. In 1533 a handful of Spaniards overthrew the Incas. Some Incas may have hidden at Machu Picchu, a mountain stronghold so high above the Urubamba River that modern explorers did not find the "lost city" until 1911.

Peru's eastern frontier is a world of steamy green jungle, where painted Indians hunt with blowguns and poison darts. In the wooded foothills, plantations grow coffee, tea, cacao, cotton, and sugar. This frontier has hardly been touched, but Peru's future may lie in these rich farmlands, dense forests, and oil reserves.

OFFICIAL NAME: Republic of Peru
AREA: 496,000 sq mi (1,284,600 sq km)
POPULATION: 16,818,000
CAPITAL: Lima (pop. 341,000)
ETHNIC GROUPS: Indian, mestizos, also European. **LANGUAGE:** Spanish, Quechua. **RELIGION:** Roman Catholic. **ECONOMY:** beans, cement, coffee, copper, cotton, fish, grains, iron, lead, oil, potatoes, steel, sugar, zinc. **CURRENCY:** sol.

4

Ecuador

1 *Plantains aplenty! These starchy cousins of Ecuador's chief export, the banana, bend the back of a Cofan Indian.*

2 *Chains of sausage sell briskly at a market in the busy seaport of Guayaquil.*

3 *A colorful marine iguana keeps an eye out for enemies on the rocky beaches of the Galapagos. After chilling dips in the sea, the cold-blooded reptile sunbathes on rocks as hot as 120° F (49° C).*

4 *Snowcapped Cotopaxi, an active volcano, soars almost two miles above Quito, the capital and oldest city of Ecuador.*

5 *Fishing boats made of balsa logs skim homeward over calm Pacific waters. Balsa wood is even lighter than cork.*

5

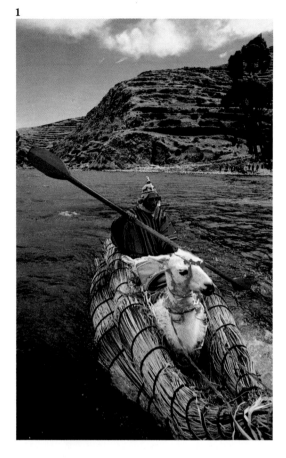

Peru

1 *An Indian paddles his reed boat to an island in Lake Titicaca. His passenger, a white llama decorated with ribbons, will be sacrificed to bring good crops.*

2 *Narrow streets twist through Cuzco, oldest continuously inhabited city in the New World. Indians lived here as long as 900 years ago. Walls of many Inca buildings still stand. Some of the stones weigh more than 100 tons.*

3 *A packtrain of llamas carrying brush marches past an inactive volcano. If overloaded or annoyed, llamas will bite, spit, and refuse to move.*

4 *Only one gateway led to Machu Picchu, mountain fortress of the ancient Incas. Long stairways join the aqueducts, garden terraces, and roofless houses.*

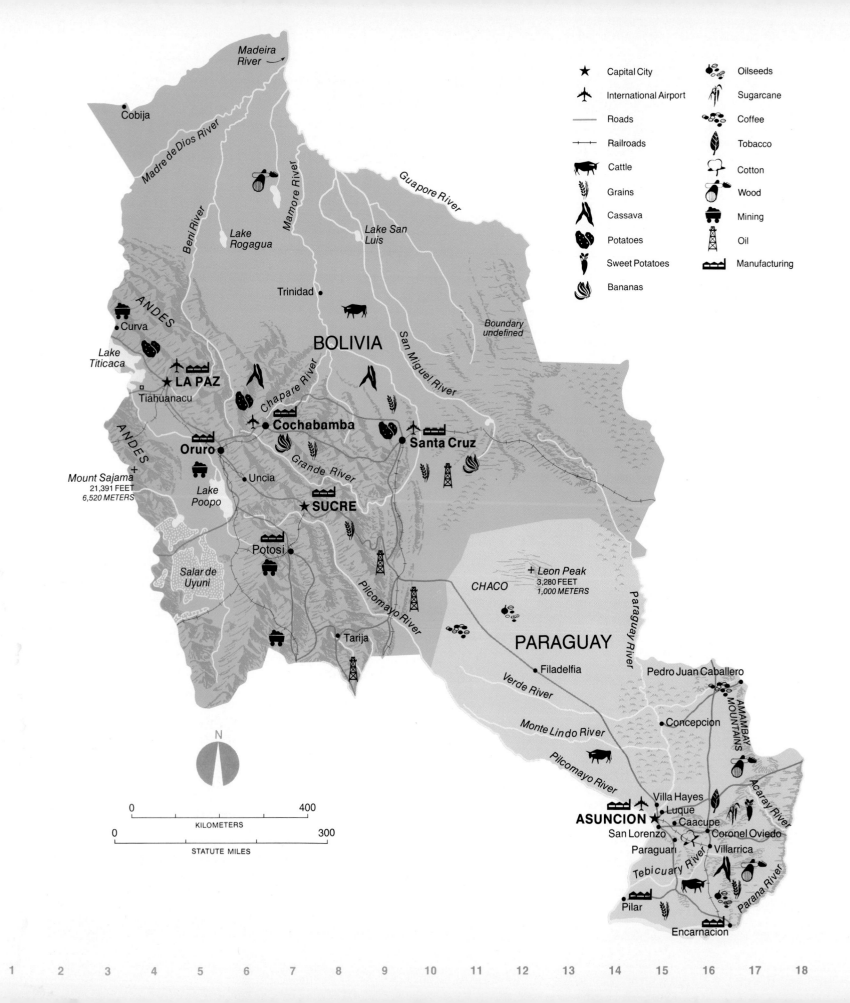

A	
B	Madeira River
C	Cobija
D	Madre de Dios River
E	Lake Rogagua · Mamore River · Lake San Luis
F	Beni River · Trinidad · Guapore River
G	ANDES · Curva · BOLIVIA · San Miguel River · Boundary undefined
H	Lake Titicaca · LA PAZ · Chapare River
J	ANDES · Tiahuanacu · Cochabamba · Santa Cruz
K	Oruro · Grande River
L	Mount Sajama 21,391 FEET 6,520 METERS · Uncia · Lake Poopo · SUCRE · Leon Peak 3,280 FEET 1,000 METERS
M	Salar de Uyuni · Potosi · CHACO · PARAGUAY · Paraguay River
N	Pilcomayo River
O	Tarija · Filadelfia · Pedro Juan Caballero
P	Verde River · Concepcion · AMAMBAY MOUNTAINS
Q	Monte Lindo River · Pilcomayo River · Acaray River
R	Villa Hayes · Luque · ASUNCION · Caacupe · Coronel Oviedo · Parana River
S	San Lorenzo · Paraguari · Villarrica · Tebicuary River
T	Pilar · Parana River
U	Encarnacion

Legend

- ★ Capital City
- ✈ International Airport
- — Roads
- ┼ Railroads
- Cattle
- Grains
- Cassava
- Potatoes
- Sweet Potatoes
- Bananas
- Oilseeds
- Sugarcane
- Coffee
- Tobacco
- Cotton
- Wood
- Mining
- Oil
- Manufacturing

N

0	400
KILOMETERS	
0	300
STATUTE MILES	

1 2 3 4 5 6 7 8 9 10 11 12 13 14 15 16 17 18

Bolivia

It's hard to start a fire in La Paz, the world's highest capital. At 11,900 feet (3,627 m), the thin air provides less oxygen than at sea level, and fires need oxygen.

The altitude has other odd effects. Planes at La Paz's airport need more time to get airborne, so the runways are extra long. Motorboats on nearby Titicaca, the world's highest navigable lake, can operate at only 70 percent of their engines' full power. And the people who live on the altiplano, the windswept plateau around La Paz, have developed larger-than-normal hearts and lungs to help them breathe. They also have more red corpuscles in their blood.

Bolivia's constitution names Sucre as the country's legal capital, site of the Supreme Court. But Congress and all other government bodies sit at La Paz. The city governs a land that ranges from rain forests and grasslands to towering mountains. The lowlands produce oil, cattle, and lumber. The peaks harbor the Andean condor, the world's largest bird of prey with a wingspan that can reach ten feet (3 m). From deep, green valleys, called *yungas,* on the east slopes of the Andes come coffee, grains, and fruits.

The altiplano is home to 70 percent of the population, mostly Quechua and Aymara Indians and mestizos, descendants of Indians who married Europeans after the Spaniards came in 1538. The people speak 32 different tongues. Many Indians work in the tin mines at Potosi, helping to keep Bolivia one of the largest producers of this metal in the world. Others use terraces on the hills around Titicaca to grow potatoes. Andean Indians may have been the first people in history to cultivate the white or "Irish" potato, a tuber native to the Americas. Some Indians raise vicunas and alpacas for their fine wool. Products of the area are loaded on the llama, the "camel of the Andes," which can live on moss and lichens.

Indians also cultivate the coca plant, source of cocaine. For centuries they have chewed the narcotic leaves to dull the pain of cold and hunger. A different form of relief comes at weekend festivals when Indians dance in village streets to the tune of flutes and other pipes. They carry tin fishes, an age-old symbol of religion. Traditional derby hats worn by women indicate the region where they live—brown for La Paz, white for Cochabamba, black for Santa Cruz.

OFFICIAL NAME: Republic of Bolivia
AREA: 424,000 sq mi (1,098,100 sq km)
POPULATION: 5,081,000
CAPITAL: La Paz, administrative (pop. 655,000)
  Sucre, legal and judicial (pop. 64,000)
ETHNIC GROUPS: Indian, also mestizos, European. **LANGUAGE:** Spanish, Aymara, Quechua.
RELIGION: Roman Catholic. **ECONOMY:** bananas, cassava, grains, lead, oil, potatoes, silver, sugar, textiles, tin, zinc. **CURRENCY:** peso.

Paraguay

This is the only country in the Americas where the people speak an Indian language as often as they do the official language, Spanish. Nearly everyone can communicate in the old Indian tongue, Guarani. The country's name may have come from a Guarani word meaning "a place with a great river."

Because roads in this California-size country are few and rough, rivers provide most of the transportation for cargo and people. A major river, the Paraguay, divides the country into two regions: the Region Oriental, a fertile plateau in the east, and the Chaco, a flat region of grassy plains and scattered woodlands in the west.

Though the Region Oriental contains less than half the country's land, most of the people live there. They farm small plots with simple tools. Often, the children must help with the work.

Few people live in the harsh Chaco. In the dry season the plains become parched. The rainy season turns them into a swamp whose underground water is too salty for irrigation or drinking. Yet ranchers are able to raise cattle here because they catch rainwater in storage tanks for their stock.

A variety of wild animals—crocodiles, wild hogs, jaguars, deer—manage to survive in the Chaco. Even the vegetation is tough. A famous hardwood of the region, called *quebracho,* "ax-breaker," is used to make railroad ties and even to pave streets. From quebracho also comes tannin, used for curing leather.

Paraguay boasts other unusual products. One is petitgrain oil, an extract of the orange tree used to make perfumes and marmalade. Another is the finely woven lace called *nanduti,* "spiderweb."

Most Paraguayan peasants smoke black cigars. Just about everybody drinks *yerba mate,* a tea made from the leaves of holly trees. From time to time, rural folk catch wild monkeys by getting them drunk on a liquid made from molasses and sugarcane. Those monkeys not sold are dressed in red suits. Like scarecrows, they frighten raiding monkeys away from garden plots.

OFFICIAL NAME: Republic of Paraguay
AREA: 157,000 sq mi (406,600 sq km)
POPULATION: 3,095,000
CAPITAL: Asuncion (pop. 393,000)
ETHNIC GROUPS: mestizos. **LANGUAGE:** Spanish, Guarani. **RELIGION:** Roman Catholic. **ECONOMY:** beer, cassava, cement, coffee, cotton, grains, meat, oilseeds, sugar, sweet potatoes, textiles, tobacco, wood. **CURRENCY:** guarani.

Bolivia

1 *Garden terraces share a hilltop with the thatch-roofed houses of Curva, hometown of ancient and modern medicine men.*

2 *Dressed for warmth, a miner drills into a vein of tin ore beneath a glacier.*

3 *An Indian baby spends most of its time strapped to its mother's back. Her stovepipe hat shows that she is Quechua. Aymara women wear derby hats.*

Paraguay

4 *Beware! Man-eating fish! Maka Indians wade bravely through a piranha-filled lagoon near the Paraguay River. The men trap piranhas and other fish in nets strung between long poles.*

5 *Fish from the day's catch sizzle over an open fire. Maka weavers use piranha jaws instead of scissors to cut thread.*

1

2

3

4

5

A
Arica

B
Iquique

C
Chuquicamata

D
Antofagasta
Salta
CHACO
Paraguay River
Iguazu Falls

E
Pan American Highway
San Miguel de Tucuman
Resistencia

F
Mount Ojos del Salado
22,572 FEET
6,880 METERS
PACIFIC OCEAN
Corrientes
Parana River
Uruguay River

G
Mount Aconcagua
22,834 FEET
6,960 METERS
Highest point in South America
Cordoba
Santa Fe
Salto
Rivera

H
Vina del Mar
Valparaiso
Mendoza
Rosario
Paysandu
URUGUAY

J
SANTIAGO
Rancagua
CHILE
BUENOS AIRES
MONTEVIDEO
Rio de la Plata
La Plata

K
Talca
Chillan
Concepcion
PAMPAS

L
Mar del Plata
Bahia Blanca

M
Temuco
Valdivia
Negro River
ARGENTINA
ATLANTIC OCEAN

N
Puerto Montt
Lake Nahuel Huapi
San Carlos de Bariloche
Valdes Peninsula

O
Chiloe Island
Rawson
-131 FEET
-40 METERS
Lowest point in South America
ANDES

P
Comodoro Rivadavia
PATAGONIA

Q

R

S
Strait of Magellan

T
Punta Arenas
Tierra del Fuego

U
Ushuaia
Puerto Williams
Cape Horn

Legend:
★ Capital City
✈ International Airport
— Roads
+—+ Railroads
🐂 Cattle and Hides
🐑 Sheep
🌾 Grains
🥔 Potatoes
🍇 Grapes
Oilseeds
🐟 Fishing
Mining
Oil
Manufacturing

0 — 800
KILOMETERS

0 — 600
STATUTE MILES

0° 20° 40°
100° 80° 60° 40° 20°

Argentina

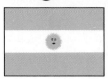

How would you like to take your summer vacation in January and February and go skiing in the mountains in August? That's what many children in Argentina do each year. Because they live below the Equator, their seasons are the opposite of the Northern Hemisphere. From Buenos Aires, people go north to warm up in winter and south to cool off in summer.

Sprawled on the bank of the Rio de la Plata, Buenos Aires is one of the world's great ports. A third of Argentina's people live in or around their capital. That wasn't always so. For 300 years after its founding by the Spanish in the 1500's, Buenos Aires was an outpost on the edge of a vast region of fertile plains that the Indians called *pampa*, meaning "space."

Life on the pampas in the last century sounds like something out of the Old West in the United States. On *estancias*, or ranches, cattle and horses roamed the open range. Gauchos, the Argentine cowboys, rounded up the herds. Forts guarded the frontier against Indian raids.

By the 1880's the Indians had been subdued. Then immigrants from Europe came to settle, fencing off much of the land for farms. Cultivation of the rich pampas rapidly increased. Argentina became a great agricultural country, and the little port of Buenos Aires grew into one of the world's largest and busiest metropolitan areas.

Today nearly half of the pampas remain grazing land. With some 60 million head of cattle, Argentina ranks as the world's second largest exporter of beef. Argentines themselves love beef. They eat about 200 pounds (91 kg) a year per person, twice the United States average.

You have to get away from the pampas to appreciate Argentina's great geographical variety. Go west and you'll see the towering Andes. They stretch the length of the country's border with Chile. Go north to the Chaco and you'll feel some of the continent's hottest temperatures. Go northeast to the subtropical forest and you'll find chattering monkeys, jungle plants, and colorful parrots. Go south to Patagonia, a scrubby, arid plateau, and you'll hear the cutting wind blowing across huge sheep ranches.

Farthest south lies Tierra del Fuego, Land of Fire. Explorer Ferdinand Magellan, sailing around the tip of South America, named it that in 1520 when he saw huge fires blazing along the shore. Primitive natives, who wore no clothes even in snowstorms, built the fires to keep warm.

OFFICIAL NAME: Argentine Republic
AREA: 1,070,000 sq mi (2,771,300 sq km)
POPULATION: 26,487,000
CAPITAL: Buenos Aires (pop. 2,973,000)
ETHNIC GROUPS: European, also Indian. LANGUAGE: Spanish. RELIGION: Roman Catholic. ECONOMY: chemicals, grains, hides, livestock, machinery, meat, metals, motor vehicles, oil, oilseeds, printing, textiles, wool. CURRENCY: peso.

Chile

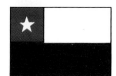

You must think in superlatives when you consider Chile. It's the longest skinny country in the world. Stretched across the United States it would reach from New York to San Francisco. It has one of the driest deserts, some of the heaviest rainfall, and the second highest mountain range in the world.

The desert and the Andes made Chile difficult to explore. Imagine the disappointment of Spanish adventurers. Led by Pedro de Valdivia, they came south from Peru in the 16th century looking for gold. Instead, they found hundreds of miles of desert to cross. The Atacama Desert has since produced a treasure in other minerals, especially copper. But the desert is so dry that U. S. astronauts trained there for the moon landing. Some places haven't seen a *drop* of rain in 400 years!

Spanish colonists found other unpleasant surprises in Chile. Earthquakes wiped out their settlements again and again. Pirates infested the coast. And in the south lived the tough Araucanian Indians, a tribe never conquered by force.

Araucanians killed Pedro de Valdivia. Legend says they poured molten gold down his throat since it was gold he was after. They killed hundreds of other Spaniards. They also married many. Today most Chileans have both Indian and Spanish blood.

Valdivia founded Santiago, now Chile's capital. In the heart of Chile's central valley, Santiago has palm trees downtown and snow-covered mountains less than an hour away by car. But it's surrounded by slums called *callampas,* or "mushroom towns," because they sprout up so quickly.

Most of the population is packed onto 18 percent of the land in the central valley, about the only part of the country where crops will grow. Here are vast vineyards and fields of alfalfa, wheat, and barley. Even so, Chile has to import two-thirds of its food. Most of it comes through Valparaiso, Chile's chief port.

South of the heartland lies a forested region that attracts tourists, even though nearly 100 inches (254 cm) of rain falls every year. Volcanic peaks rise above shimmering lakes and waterfalls. Chile's few remaining Indians live here.

Main roads south end at Puerto Montt, but there's still more to Chile, the Chilean archipelago. Storms and earthquakes regularly hit this wilderness of forest-covered islands. Around the Strait of Magellan, sheep outnumber people fifty to one. Hardy shepherds mix with oil drillers in Punta Arenas, the world's southernmost major town.

OFFICIAL NAME: Republic of Chile
AREA: 286,000 sq mi (740,700 sq km)
POPULATION: 10,689,000
CAPITAL: Santiago (pop. 3,263,000)
ETHNIC GROUPS: mestizos, European. LANGUAGE: Spanish. RELIGION: Roman Catholic, also Protestant. ECONOMY: copper, fish, fruit, grains, iodine, iron, nitrates, paper, potatoes, steel, textiles. CURRENCY: peso.

Uruguay

"Monte vide eu!" ("I see a mountain!") So cried a Portuguese sailor on explorer Ferdinand Magellan's ship as it swung up the Rio de la Plata in 1520. That's how Uruguay's capital is supposed to have gotten its name.

Uruguay hasn't any real mountains. Neither has it many forests. Rolling pastureland covers most of the country and feeds more than 30 million sheep and cattle, Uruguay's greatest source of wealth. Wild flowers called verbena color the pastures in spring. They give Uruguay its nickname, "the purple land."

For more than a century, Uruguay was a battleground between the Portuguese in Brazil and the Spanish in what is now Argentina. Until it won its independence in 1828, Uruguay was known as the *Banda Oriental,* or "East Bank," because of its location on the Uruguay River. Even today Uruguayans are often called "Orientals."

OFFICIAL NAME: Oriental Republic of Uruguay
AREA: 72,200 sq mi (187,000 sq km)
POPULATION: 2,893,000
CAPITAL: Montevideo (pop. 1,230,000)
ETHNIC GROUPS: European, also mestizos. LANGUAGE: Spanish. RELIGION: Roman Catholic. ECONOMY: cement, grains, hides and skins, livestock, meat, oil refining, plastics, shoes, textiles, wool. CURRENCY: peso.

Argentina

1 *Winds gusting at more than 100 miles an hour blow a plume of snow from the top of Mount Aconcagua, tallest peak in the Western Hemisphere. High winds and below-zero temperatures have killed dozens of mountain climbers here.*

2 *Chilled sides of beef swing from truck to ship in the port of Buenos Aires. People around the world eat beef, lamb, and mutton from Argentina, where both cattle and sheep outnumber residents.*

3 *Gauchos tend flocks prized for meat and fine wool in Patagonia. Blue-ribbon sheep often wear canvas robes and hoods to protect their wool. Welsh shepherds gave their names to many towns, like Rawson, in Argentina's southern region.*

4 *Breadbasket of South America, Argentina exports much of her bounty of corn and other grains. Pampa soil is so rich that most farmers do not use fertilizer.*

Uruguay

1 *Home on the range, a gaucho charges after stray cattle. Long ago a gaucho custom-fitted his own boots by pulling a horse skin over his leg and foot. Today ranch hands buy ready-made boots. Many still wear the traditional poncho.*

2 *Cattle fatten on lush grass that grows three feet (.9 m) high in some places.*

Chile

3 *Wines made from Chilean grapes grace dinner tables in North America.*

4 *Giant-size steps dwarf trains and a huge shovel at Chuquicamata, one of the world's largest open-pit copper mines.*

5 *From June to September, skiers from around the world glide down the slopes at a winter resort near Santiago.*

6 *A girl cuddles a pet lamb on Tierra del Fuego, an island the size of Belgium.*

6

Europe

Europe could be called "The Continent that Conquered the World." At one time or another Europeans have ruled, with very few exceptions, every piece of land on earth. In North America, for instance, the British, French, Spanish, Dutch—even the Russians—have left their marks. Most former European colonies now govern themselves, but Europe's touch is lasting. European languages—English, Spanish, French, and others—are heard around the globe.

Much of the world's best-known art, science, literature, and music could be stamped "Made in Europe."

Yet Europe is not even a real continent. It's more like a peninsula of Asia, beginning where the Ural Mountains cross Russia. Together the two "continents" are called "Eurasia." Only tradition keeps them separate in name.

So how did Europe become such a master of history? Experts argue about that, but surely geography helped.

Eisriesenwelt: In German the name means "giant ice world." It's a good word-picture of the world's largest ice cave, which reaches 25 miles (40 km) into the Austrian

Alps south of Salzburg. Snowmelt and wintry winds carry moisture into the limestone caverns. There it freezes into a fairyland of columns and draperies.

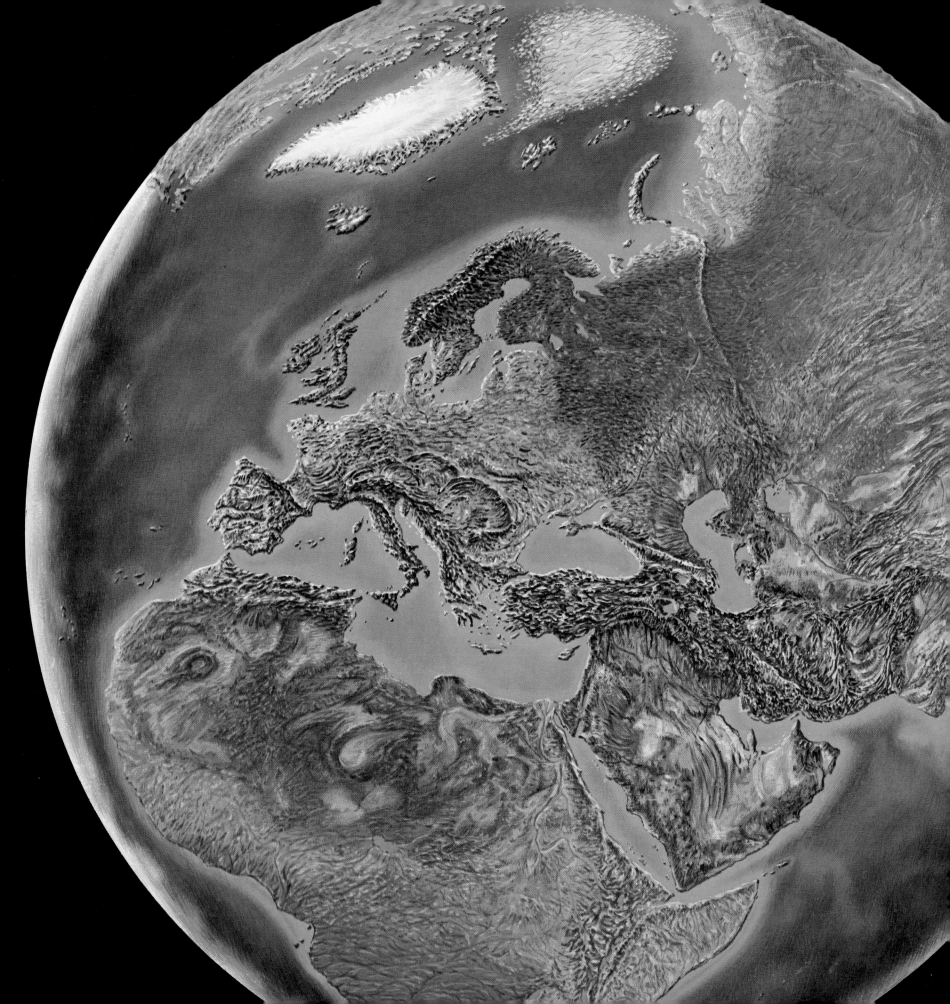

For one thing, Europe is situated in a good place for world exploration. Europeans could practice sailing long distances on their own sheltered mini-ocean, the Mediterranean Sea. "Mediterranean" means "in the midst of lands," and that's a good name for Europe too. You need to travel no more than 4,000 miles from Spain to reach any of the four biggest continents.

Europe also profits from warm summers, cool winters, and plenty of rain—just right for farming. Because Europe's climate is like theirs, some Americans think England, for instance, is straight across the Atlantic from New York. It's actually opposite icy Labrador! But warm water from the ocean's Gulf Stream keeps the European climate mild, in spite of the northern latitude.

I t takes a lot of people to run an empire or an industry, and—sure enough—Europe has what it takes. Though about the size of Canada, Europe embraces a bigger population than North and South America together!

Europeans live in a jumble of mountains, gulfs, plains, bays, and islands. The gulfs and seas become shipping highways for trade and exploration, as do the many short rivers. But water and mountain also split Europe into many countries. Languages, customs, even ways of cooking may differ from one nation to another nation.

Sunny southern Europe is unusually patchy, because it's made of peninsulas: the Iberian Peninsula, shared by Spain and Portugal; boot-shaped Italy; and the fat Balkan Peninsula between the Adriatic and Black seas. A mountain range caps each—the Pyrenees, the Alps, and the Carpathians.

Farther north beats the industrial heart of Europe. If you made a wide, curving brushstroke on the map, from England, down over Belgium and northern France, and across Germany to southern Poland, you would have covered the larger part of Europe's busy cities and roaring factories.

Squeezed among them, and spread over vast rural areas, are some of the world's richest croplands. A fourth of Europe's people farm half its land. Some has been plowed for thousands of years.

To Americans accustomed to a vast land, Europe seems crowded, yet cozy—full of old villages with steep roofs, narrow streets, and neat gardens. It's a picture from a fairy tale—not surprising, since that's where many fairy tales came from. Europe, however, has also been a leader in superhighways, television, and whip-fast trains.

Amid Europe's tangle of borders, war often comes easy. For centuries Europeans have invaded each other. Even now, nations of non-Communist Western Europe stand opposed to those of Communist Eastern Europe.

Hopes are high that Europeans are at last smoothing over divisions that their patchwork geography created. Nine of the western countries have formed an economic European Community, and three more nations wait to join. A European Parliament is even taking shape. Soon the people may be calling themselves, not Belgians, Germans, or Italians but "Europeans."

Facts About Europe

SIZE: 4,024,000 sq mi (10,422,000 sq km)

POPULATION: 671,000,000

DENSITY: 167 persons for every sq mi (64 per sq km)

HIGHEST POINT: Mount Elbrus, U.S.S.R., 18,510 ft (5,642 m) above sea level

LOWEST POINT: Caspian Sea, 92 ft (28 m) below sea level

LARGEST COUNTRIES: (by area) European Russia 2,123,300 sq mi (5,499,500 sq km); France 213,000 sq mi (551,600 sq km)

LARGEST COUNTRIES: (by population) European Russia 192,036,000 West Germany 61,474,000

LARGEST METROPOLITAN AREAS: (by population)

London	11,200,000
Moscow	11,000,000
Paris	9,200,000
Leningrad	5,200,000
Madrid	3,900,000
Berlin (West)	3,900,000
(East)	1,100,000

LONGEST RIVERS: (mi and km)

Volga	2,200	3,500
Danube	1,700	2,700
Ural	1,500	2,400
Dnieper	1,400	2,200
Don	1,200	1,900
Dniester	800	1,200
North Dvina	800	1,200
Rhine	800	1,200

LARGEST LAKES: (sq mi and sq km)

Ladoga	6,800	17,600
Onega	3,700	9,500
Vanern	2,100	5,400

A

B

C

D

E

F

G

H

J

K

L

M

N

O

P

Q

R

S

T

1 2 3 4 5 6 7 8 9 10 11 12 13 14 15 16 17 18

North Cape

• Hammerfest

N

• Tromso

LAPLAND

ICELAND

• Akureyri

Jokulsa River

Thjorsa River

Vatnajokull

★REYKJAVIK

Selfoss •

Heimaey • Vik

Surtsey

ATLANTIC OCEAN

FAEROE ISLANDS
(DENMARK)

Streymoy

Torshavn •
Sandoy

Suduroy

0 ——————— 500
KILOMETERS
0 ——————— 300
STATUTE MILES

NORWEGIAN
SEA

Lofoten Islands

Narvik •

Bodo •

• Kiruna

Tornio River

Kemi River

ARCTIC CIRCLE

• Rovaniemi

• Kemi

• Lulea

Oulu •

Lule River

Oulu River

FINLAND

Namsen River

Angerman River

Ume River

• Umea

Kuopio •

• Joensuu

Trondheim •

NORRLAND

• Ostersund

Vaasa •

Jyvaskyla •

Great Saimaa Lake System

NORWAY

Geirangerfjorden

SWEDEN

• Sundsvall

GULF OF BOTHNIA

Pori •

Tampere

Lappeenranta •

Glittertind +
8,110 FEET
2,472 METERS

Lagen River

Glama River

Klar River

Dal River

Aland Islands

Lahti •

Bergen •

OSLO ★

Stavanger •

Karlstad •

Vasteras

SVEALAND

Uppsala

Lake Malaren

★**STOCKHOLM**

GULF OF FINLAND

Turku

★**HELSINKI**

Skien •

Lake Vanern

Orebro

Norrkoping

Kristiansand •

Lake Vattern

Linkoping

NORTH SEA

Frederikshavn •

Goteborg

Jonkoping •

Visby •

Gotland

Boras

GOTALAND

Oland

Alborg

DENMARK

Arhus

JUTLAND

COPENHAGEN

Halsingborg

Karlskrona •

BALTIC SEA

Esbjerg •

Odense

ZEALAND

Malmo

Bornholm

★ Capital City
✈ International Airport
— Roads
+ Railroads
🐄 Livestock
🐄 Dairy Products
🦌 Reindeer
🌾 Grains
🍄 Hay

🥕 Vegetables
🥔 Potatoes
🍓 Fruit
🥕 Sugar Beets
🪵 Wood
🐟 Fishing
⛏ Mining
🛢 Oil or Natural Gas
🏭 Manufacturing

Denmark

In Denmark even the trains ride on the ferry. They must, because this small nation is made up of a peninsula in the North Sea—Jutland—and more than 400 islands. When a train arrives at the water's edge, workers divide it into lengths of a few cars each. Then they load the cars, with the passengers still aboard, side by side on a ferry. After the boat reaches the opposite shore, workers put the train back together and it heads on down the track.

Zealand is Denmark's largest island and site of busy Copenhagen with its famous Tivoli amusement park, a fairyland of rides, cafes, open-air theaters for acrobats and musicians, and thousands of colored lights. Danes are Scandinavians, related to Norwegians and Swedes by language and history. Unlike their northern cousins, however, the Danes are flatlanders. The tallest hill in Jutland would stand only waist-high to New York's Empire State Building.

Small, tidy farms and woodlots dot the green countryside. From here come those prized Danish hams and cheeses that you can buy in American supermarkets.

The Danes like to run their country as carefully as they prepare their food. Taxes are high, but it's hard to find a slum. Modern, glass-walled apartments rise near neat village houses unchanged since the 1830's, a period that saw the publication of the first fairy tales by Denmark's famed storyteller, Hans Christian Andersen.

OFFICIAL NAME: Kingdom of Denmark
AREA: 17,100 sq mi (44,300 sq km)
POPULATION: 5,148,000
CAPITAL: Copenhagen (pop. 546,000)
ETHNIC GROUPS: Scandinavian. **LANGUAGE:** Danish. **RELIGION:** Lutheran. **ECONOMY:** chemicals, dairy products, electronics, fish, furs, grains, livestock, machinery, meat, metals, root crops, shipbuilding, textiles, transportation equipment. **CURRENCY:** krone.

Finland

A boy and girl stand on shore waiting for a tugboat to chug down the waterway between two of Finland's 55,000 lakes. The tug pulls a string of log rafts—bundles of long, white birch trunks headed for sawmills to be cut into lumber.

As the last raft floats by, half a mile behind the tug, the boy and girl splash out and hop on for a ride.

In this southern part of Finland, the country seems more lake than land, as if scraps of forest had been scattered over a mirror of blue water. But north of here the woods thicken, covering the rolling land all the way to Lapland at the Arctic Circle. Finns use their timber well, making paper and furniture to sell to the rest of the countries of Europe.

The Finns are believed to have come originally from central Asia. Their language is related to Hungarian. Racially, they have mixed most often with Swedes and Germans, though history binds them closest to Sweden. In Helsinki both Finnish and Swedish appear on the street signs.

Finland's best-known gift to the world is the refreshing sauna bath. First heat a small, wood-lined room with hot rocks. Then pour water on them, and bake yourself in the steam. When you've had enough, step outside—and dive into an icy lake!

OFFICIAL NAME: Republic of Finland
AREA: 130,000 sq mi (336,700 sq km)
POPULATION: 4,748,000
CAPITAL: Helsinki (pop. 503,000)
ETHNIC GROUPS: Finnish, also Swedish, Lappish. **LANGUAGE:** Finnish, also Swedish. **RELIGION:** Lutheran. **ECONOMY:** copper, dairy products, grains, livestock, machinery, paper, potatoes, ships, shoes, wood. **CURRENCY:** markka.

Iceland

Winter in Iceland, and time for a swim—outdoors. Although Icelanders live only a few splashes from the Arctic Circle, they can soak with steamy comfort in water from natural hot springs. The springs warm swimming pools and heat homes and offices in the capital of Reykjavik, where the world's oldest parliament meets.

The springs are warmed by fires from volcanoes, part of an underwater mountain chain. Drifting continents help form such volcanoes; on page 8 you can read how.

In 1963 molten lava from one of the volcanoes erupted from the ocean floor south of Iceland and made a new island, Surtsey. In 1973, on the nearby island of Heimaey, a volcano buried part of the island's port city in lava and ash.

Older lava, now cooled into hard, broken rock, covers much of mainland Iceland. Some fields are clothed by soft moss or grass, where sheep graze.

Most Icelanders live in coastal valleys and fishing villages, away from the moonlike interior. Some work in greenhouses heated by hot springs. Here grapes, melons, even bananas grow under the subarctic sun.

OFFICIAL NAME: Republic of Iceland
AREA: 39,700 sq mi (103,000 sq km)
POPULATION: 223,000
CAPITAL: Reykjavik (pop. 85,000)
ETHNIC GROUPS: Celtic, Norwegian. **LANGUAGE:** Icelandic. **RELIGION:** Lutheran. **ECONOMY:** aluminum, dairy products, diatomite, fish, hay, potatoes, sheep, turnips. **CURRENCY:** krona.

Norway

The people huddle on a snowy hillside above the city of Tromso. They look south, waiting in the January cold. It is almost noon, but the sun has not risen. In fact, it has not risen for two months. Tromso lies 210 miles (338 km) north of the Arctic Circle—so far north that early winter days are dark from beginning to end.

The sky brightens. Suddenly a fiery glow appears on the horizon. Everyone cheers. "See the sun!" *Morketiden,* the "dark time," is over. From now on, each day will get longer. By the middle of May, Tromso will belong to "The Land of the Midnight Sun," its days without end.

Most Norwegians live farther south, where their narrow, rugged country is warmer. Though near the Arctic, southern Norway can depend on ocean currents to keep its winters no colder than January in the state of Maine.

Norwegians have lived closely with the ocean—"the blue meadow" some call it—since the time of the Vikings a thousand years ago. Shipping, fishing, and shipbuilding help keep Norway prosperous. The ocean's latest gift is oil, pumped from beneath the North Sea.

All along Norway's 1,110-mile (1,786 km) length, fingers of ocean called fjords wind inland between steep mountains. Small farms squeeze into the valleys. Sometimes Norwegian children vacation high in the mountains in old wooden houses once used as "summer farms" for cheesemaking. Here they can explore the steep meadows until the smell of woodsmoke drifts through the evening air, calling them in to the fire.

OFFICIAL NAME: Kingdom of Norway
AREA: 149,000 sq mi (386,200 sq km)
POPULATION: 4,061,000
CAPITAL: Oslo (pop. 462,000)
ETHNIC GROUPS: Scandinavian, also Lappish.
LANGUAGE: Norwegian. RELIGION: Lutheran.
ECONOMY: chemicals, fish, fruit, grains, livestock, metals, natural gas, oil, paper, ships, vegetables, wood. CURRENCY: krone.

Sweden

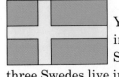

You'd better like living in an apartment if you're Swedish. Two of every three Swedes live in apartments, mostly in cities and towns of southern Sweden.

This is the fourth largest country in Europe after Russia, France, and Spain. In the late 1800's Sweden was a poor land. A fifth of the people moved away to seek their fortunes in the United States. Many went to Illinois, Minnesota, and Wisconsin. But new industries—steel, lumber, hydroelectric power—have now changed Sweden into one of the richest countries in Europe.

Sweden has three regions. Swedes call the northern half of their country Norrland. Here Lapp nomads wander with reindeer herds through a snowbound wilderness. Lapps also live in Norway and Finland.

In the wooded hills of central Sweden, called Svealand, Viking kings lie buried under huge mounds of earth. In summer, swarms of vacationers make a beeline for the shores of Sweden's many lakes, which cover as much space as all the nation's farms. East of Stockholm, sailboats race among thousands of islands that speckle the Baltic Sea. Even when winter flattens the waves into ice, young Swedes go right on sailing—in boats fitted with steel runners.

On the western coast of Gotaland, the name for southern Sweden, herring fishermen begin their workdays at 2 a.m. Skilled workers build large ships at the port of Goteborg. A few workers go to jobs far underground. Although free of war for 150 years, cautious Sweden has buried some of her factories and power plants in bombproof shelters as far down as 85 feet (26 m).

OFFICIAL NAME: Kingdom of Sweden
AREA: 173,000 sq mi (448,100 sq km)
POPULATION: 8,273,000
CAPITAL: Stockholm (pop. 666,000)
ETHNIC GROUPS: Scandinavian, also Lappish.
LANGUAGE: Swedish. RELIGION: Lutheran.
ECONOMY: dairy products, grains, iron, machinery, motor vehicles, paper, precision equipment, ships, steel, wood. CURRENCY: krona.

1

2

Sweden

1 Surrounded by waters of Lake Malaren, Sweden's capital of Stockholm sprawls across 14 islands linked by 50 bridges. The city has grown from a small trading port 700 years ago into a major hub of European commerce. About 12 miles (19 km) of docks handle seagoing ships. One of every six Swedes calls Stockholm home, as do thousands of immigrants from Finland and southern Europe.

Norway

2 A breathtaking flight awaits this youngster in an Oslo ski-jumping contest. Sports-loving Norwegians learn to ski almost as soon as they can walk. They excel in ski jumping, a sport Norway introduced to the world a century ago.

3 Narrow arm of the sea, Geirangerfjorden slices between steep, rocky mountains. Warm ocean currents keep Norway's watery highways ice-free all year long. Peasants of long ago thought they saw gigantic, scary trolls lurking in the shadows of these misty hills.

3

1

3   2

Iceland

1 *On Iceland's restless crust, rivers of ice creep to the edge of hot springs, steaming geysers, pools of bubbling mud.*

2 *Silver treasure from the Atlantic, herring spurt from a huge net aboard an Icelandic trawler. The island's chief exports are fish and fish products.*

Denmark

3 *The Little Mermaid, heroine of a Hans Christian Andersen fairy tale, gazes across Copenhagen's crowded harbor.*

Finland

4 *On the eve of May Day, Helsinki's Market Square displays balloons and toys instead of carrots and cabbages.*

5 *During summer vacation a teenager sorts potatoes on a farm near Tampere, second largest city in Finland.*

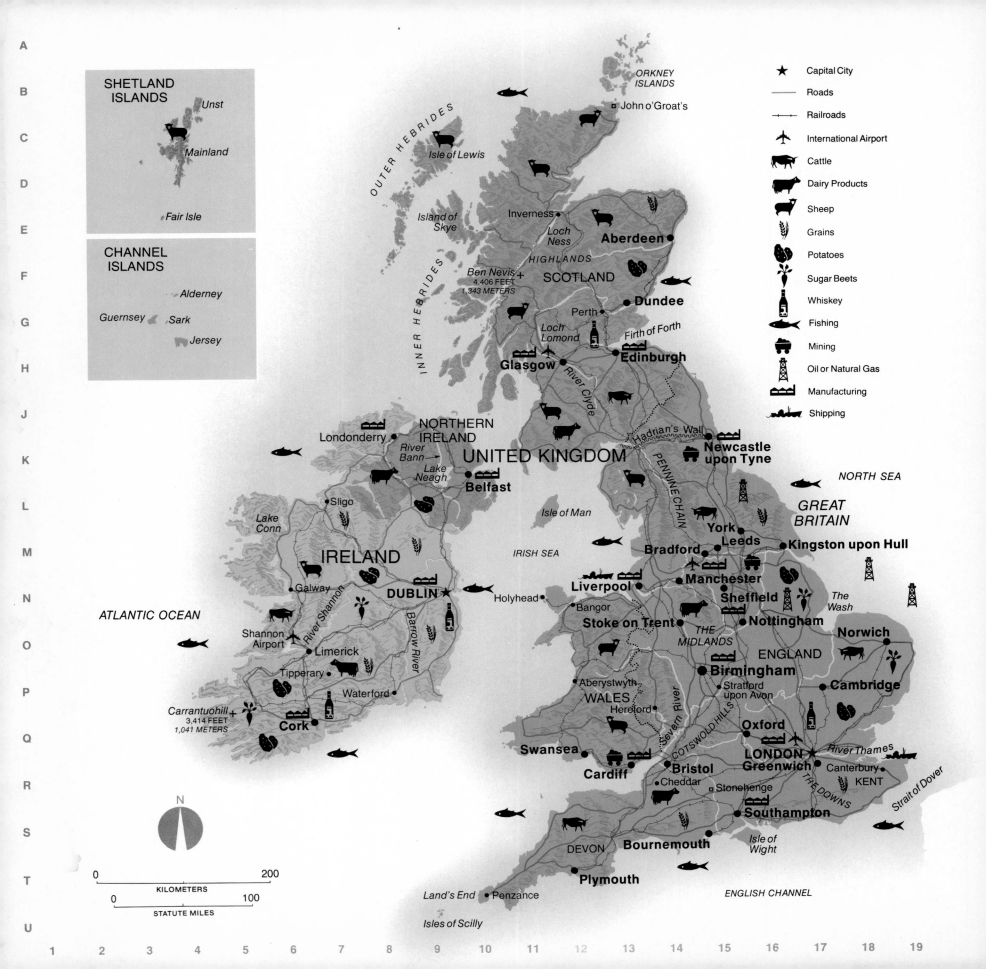

A B C D E F G H J K L M N O P Q R S T U

SHETLAND ISLANDS

Unst

Mainland

Fair Isle

CHANNEL ISLANDS

Alderney

Guernsey   Sark

Jersey

ORKNEY ISLANDS

John o'Groat's

OUTER HEBRIDES

Isle of Lewis

Island of Skye

INNER HEBRIDES

Inverness

Loch Ness

HIGHLANDS

Aberdeen

Ben Nevis
4,406 FEET
1,343 METERS

SCOTLAND

Dundee

Perth

Loch Lomond

Firth of Forth

Glasgow   **Edinburgh**

River Clyde

Hadrian's Wall

PENNINE CHAIN

Newcastle upon Tyne

NORTH SEA

Londonderry

NORTHERN IRELAND

River Bann

Lake Neagh

Belfast

UNITED KINGDOM

Isle of Man

IRISH SEA

GREAT BRITAIN

York

Leeds

Bradford

Kingston upon Hull

Sligo

Lake Conn

IRELAND

Liverpool

Manchester

Sheffield

The Wash

Galway

DUBLIN ★

Holyhead

Bangor

Stoke on Trent

THE MIDLANDS

Nottingham

Norwich

ATLANTIC OCEAN

River Shannon

Barrow River

Shannon Airport

Limerick

Tipperary

Waterford

ENGLAND

Birmingham

Aberystwyth

Stratford upon Avon

WALES

Hereford

Cambridge

Carrantuohill
3,414 FEET
1,041 METERS

Cork

Oxford

Severn River

COTSWOLD HILLS

LONDON ★

Greenwich

River Thames

Canterbury

KENT

Strait of Dover

Swansea

Cardiff

Bristol

Cheddar

Stonehenge

THE DOWNS

N

Southampton

DEVON

Bournemouth

Isle of Wight

0   200
KILOMETERS

0   100
STATUTE MILES

Plymouth

Land's End   Penzance

ENGLISH CHANNEL

Isles of Scilly

★ Capital City

Roads

Railroads

✈ International Airport

🐄 Cattle

🐄 Dairy Products

🐑 Sheep

🌾 Grains

Potatoes

🫛 Sugar Beets

🍾 Whiskey

🐟 Fishing

Mining

Oil or Natural Gas

Manufacturing

Shipping

1 2 3 4 5 6 7 8 9 10 11 12 13 14 15 16 17 18 19

Ireland

Some people like to call Ireland the Emerald Isle because of the brilliant green of its rolling hills and valleys. Limestone does it. The mineral-rich underlying rock nourishes the thick sod from below while abundant rains and mists water it from above.

Low, gentle mountains—hardly more than hills—sprawl across the northern and southern ends of this fabled island. The highest peak, Carrantuohill, rises a mere 3,414 feet (1,041 m) among the Mountains of Kerry in the southwest.

Between the mountains, in a wide belt across the middle of the country, stretch the fertile lowlands. Small farms grow hay, barley, and wheat. Cattle graze in fields. Here, too, lie vast, treeless peat bogs, made up of thick, spongy layers of partly rotted moss. Over thousands of cool, damp years, the moss has decayed slowly to form a substance midway between soil and coal. The bogs cover about a sixth of the land. It's lucky they do, for Ireland has little coal of its own and no oil at all. Irishmen slice the peat into loaf-size chunks and burn it as fuel in their cookstoves and fireplaces.

Western Ireland, with a coastline as ragged as broken glass, is often swept by North Atlantic gales. Fingers of the sea poke inland here, creating harbors where fishermen live and take shelter from the storms.

To outsiders, Ireland may seem an isle of enchantment—a land of song and drink and tales of elves and leprechauns. Here are winding lanes and thatch-roofed cottages, haunted ruins and the cheery glow of a tavern where patrons play darts and drink a rich, dark beer called stout.

But Ireland is a poor country. It has a little manufacturing—machinery, whiskey, fine woolen clothes, and linens. It ships out some livestock and meat, too, mostly to England. But its greatest exports have been its people—the thousands of men and women who fled the great potato famines of the 1840's. Since those days many of the Irish have continued to seek jobs and opportunities in other lands.

Ireland is a land divided. In 1920, six northern, largely Protestant counties split off from the rest of the country to stay under British rule—Northern Ireland. The rest of Ireland, mostly Catholic, won complete independence from England in 1949.

OFFICIAL NAME: Ireland
AREA: 27,000 sq mi (69,900 sq km)
POPULATION: 3,228,000
CAPITAL: Dublin (pop. 568,000)
ETHNIC GROUPS: Celtic. **LANGUAGE:** English, Gaelic. **RELIGION:** Roman Catholic. **ECONOMY:** beer, chemicals, dairy products, grains, livestock, machinery, meat, potatoes, sugar, textiles, transportation equipment. **CURRENCY:** pound.

United Kingdom

Four storied provinces form the United Kingdom. The largest, England, covers an area the size of New York State and shares the island of Great Britain with Scotland and Wales. The smallest member, Northern Ireland, occupies a corner of Ireland. All four provinces fly the same flag, the Union Jack. It waves also over such widely separated possessions as Gibraltar, the rocky fortress at the Atlantic entrance to the Mediterranean Sea, and the colony of Hong Kong on the South China coast. Once the Union Jack flew over a worldwide empire that included countries such as Canada and India. Now independent, they still belong to the British Commonwealth of Nations.

The heart of the kingdom is its largest city, London. Bobbies (policemen) direct traffic in streets brightened by red double-decker buses. Red-coated guardsmen sometimes ride by on horseback. Rush-hour crowds favor London's Underground. The world's first subway, it opened in 1863.

London straddles the Thames, Britain's longest river. The Thames rises in the Cotswold Hills, a gently rolling land of pastures and tile-roofed cottages.

Highways, some planned by Roman colonists almost 2,000 years ago, crisscross the land. Motorists stay to the left. The custom started in the age of knighthood, when a rider kept an approaching horseman on his sword-arm side. Country lanes lead past castle ruins, which recall settings for plays by England's most famous writer, William Shakespeare. His house at Stratford-upon-Avon attracts a million tourists a year.

Southward to the English Channel roll the Downs, grassy hills that break off in chalk cliffs or end in sandy beaches. In the southeast, mild climate and rich soil favor Kent, the "Garden of England." Vine-grown hops, used by breweries to put flavor in beer, dry out in cone-shaped "oasthouses."

Fruitful too is the West Country, with its Cheddar cheese, Devon cream, and Hereford cider. Golden barley ripens on the Salisbury Plain. Here stands Stonehenge, a ring of giant stones set in place as a calendar by a mysterious people 4,500 years ago. Beyond Land's End lie the Scilly Isles. Each spring their daffodils are rushed to London markets. On the Channel Islands, near the coast of France, Jersey and Guernsey cattle fatten in lush pastures. More French than English in custom, the islanders call Britain's Queen the Duchess of Normandy.

Countryside gives way to industrial areas in England's Midlands. Birmingham, the second largest city in Britain, turns out automobiles, machine tools, and plastics. Nottingham produces lace fit for Maid Marian. Her Robin Hood roamed Sherwood Forest, parts of which remain in nearby parks.

Fisheries on the east coast and potato fields in drained marshes called the fens supply the ingredients for a favorite English snack—fish and chips (chunks of potatoes). On the west coast of England, ships laden with ores and grains tie up at Liverpool docks. A 35-mile (56 km) canal links the port to Manchester, which manufactures everything from computers to cotton fabric.

Wales is known for poets, singers—and coal. Tons of it pour through Cardiff on the Severn River. Limestone is quarried from low mountains in northern Wales.

Rounded hills, the Pennines, reach northward to Scotland. Hadrian's Wall, a stone barrier built by the Romans to keep out hostile tribes of Picts and Scots, still stands near the Scottish border. Sheep graze on Scottish lowlands. In green valleys glisten lakes, called lochs by Scots. The most famous is Loch Ness, where some people believe a monster dwells. Far to the north tiny Shetland ponies roam the sparsely populated Shetland Islands. Off the islands' rugged coasts, drilling platforms tap oil deposits under the North Sea.

Some of the Scots' ancestors originally came from northern Ireland. Many Scottish people migrated back to the region, called Ulster, in the 18th century. Two-thirds of Ulster's residents are Protestants of Scottish and English descent. The rest are Irish Catholics. Some people can still speak Gaelic, the ancient Celtic language once used all over the island.

OFFICIAL NAME: United Kingdom of Great Britain and Northern Ireland
AREA: 94,200 sq mi (244,000 sq km)
POPULATION: 55,894,000
CAPITAL: London (pop. 7,029,000)
ETHNIC GROUPS: Anglo-Saxon, Celtic, Norman, Scandinavian. **LANGUAGE:** English, also Gaelic, Welsh. **RELIGION:** Protestant, also Roman Catholic. **ECONOMY:** chemicals, clothing, dairy products, grains, livestock, machinery, metals, motor vehicles, paper, potatoes, sugar, textiles, whiskey. **CURRENCY:** pound.

United Kingdom

1 *A whirling grindstone shapes a kitchen knife in Sheffield, long known for its fine blades and silverware. This Midlands town forged some of the Bowie knives used on the American frontier.*

2 *Splendid in their plumed helmets, the Queen's Life Guards clip-clop through a London park. The click-click of tourists' cameras often goes with them.*

3 *Not London Bridge, as some visitors think, but Tower Bridge. Its upper span is a walkway, now closed. A drawbridge below carries traffic over the Thames.*

4 *In a 220-year-old coach the red-robed Lord Mayor of London takes an official ride. The area he rules, the "City" of London, actually covers only one of Greater London's 610 square miles. Each year the City pays a traditional rent to the Crown: six horseshoes, 61 horseshoe nails, one hatchet, and one billhook (a kind of pruning tool).*

2

4

6

5 **4**

United Kingdom

1 *Sunglasses, rarely needed in misty Scotland, lend a 20th-century look to this piper's traditional dress. The bagpipe's reedy sound, called a skirl, once led Scottish clans into battle.*

2 *This Highland shepherd will soon clip his rams and take the fleece to market. The Scots use wool to make everything from blankets to kilts and tweed suits.*

3 *Honest dirt—lots of it! A blackened miner in Wales uses an air-powered pick to break off slabs from a wall of coal.*

4 *Fishermen haul a cocoon-shaped net of silver eels from a river in Northern Ireland. Much of this catch will end up on London's dinner plates. Europeans consider the oily flesh a tasty treat.*

Ireland

5 *Ireland's woodpiles are made of peat. This stack will warm the cottage in winter. The stringy lumps of sod, which the Irish call turf, burn slowly, like charcoal in a barbecue grill.*

6 *How many kinds of green can you see among these Irish farms? Some people say a true Irishman can tell apart 40 shades of the color. To that, others might reply "blarney!—nonsense!"*

A B C D E F G H J K L M N O P Q R S T U

1 2 3 4 5 6 7 8 9 10 11 12 13 14 15 16 17 18

BALTIC SEA

North Frisian Islands

Kiel Bay

Kiel Canal

• Kiel

Stralsund

• Rostock

• Wismar

Lübeck

NORTH SEA

East Frisian Islands

West Frisian Islands

Bremerhaven

Schwerin

Lake Müritz

Oder River

Wilhelmshaven

Emden

Hamburg

Elbe River

Groningen

Oldenburg

Bremen

NORTHERN LOWLANDS

West Berlin

EAST BERLIN

Frankfurt an der Oder

IJsselmeer

NETHERLANDS

Ems River

Weser River

Wolfsburg

Potsdam

Alkmaar

Edam

Hannover

Magdeburg

Haarlem

AMSTERDAM

Osnabrück

Braunschweig

EAST GERMANY

Dessau

Cottbus

The Hague

Delft

Utrecht

Rhine River

Münster

Bielefeld

HARZ MOUNTAINS

Rotterdam

Gouda

Maas River

Halle

Neisse River

Baarle Hertog (BELGIUM)

Essen

Hamm

Göttingen

Leipzig

Duisburg

Dortmund

Ruhr River

Stolberg

Ostend

Bruges

Düsseldorf

Wuppertal

Kassel

Dresden

Ghent

Antwerp

WEST GERMANY

Erfurt

Gera

Karl Marx Stadt

BRUSSELS

Cologne

Jena

Aachen

BONN

Zwickau

BELGIUM

Liège

Plauen

Namur

Koblenz

ARDENNES

Wiesbaden

Frankfurt

LUXEMBOURG

Mainz

Darmstadt

Würzburg

N

Mosel River

LUXEMBOURG CITY

Mannheim

Nuremberg

Saarbrücken

Heidelberg

BAVARIA

Heilbronn

Regensburg

Karlsruhe

Rhine River

Stuttgart

Danube River

Neckar River

Augsburg

Munich

BLACK FOREST

Freiburg

Neuschwanstein

BAVARIAN ALPS

Lake Constance

Garmisch-Partenkirchen

★ Capital City

Sugar Beets

✈ International Airport

Wine

Roads

Flax

Railroads

Plants and Flowers

Cattle

Fishing

Hogs

Mining

Dairy Products

Natural Gas

Grains

Manufacturing

Potatoes

Shipping

0   250
KILOMETERS

0   150
STATUTE MILES

Belgium

Belgique? Or is it Belgie? They both mean "Belgium," but in different languages — French and Flemish, a Dutch dialect. It's an important fact of Belgian life: Walloons in the French-speaking south have many differences with their Flemish neighbors in the north.

Belgians in the capital, Brussels, use both languages. Many speak German, too. Their city serves as headquarters for Western military forces in Europe, and for the European Community, a nine-nation trading group. Some people think Brussels may someday be the capital of a united Europe.

If Belgium were an old-fashioned craft shop, it could hang out this sign: "Guns and Glass, Leather and Lace." The hard-working Belgians make all these things and more. The eastern two-thirds of the small country bulges with people and factories. Here, too, Europe's armies have clashed, from Roman times to World War II. They found Belgium, with its mostly flat landscape, an easy pathway for invasions.

Today the invaders are weekend bicycle riders. They whiz along tree-lined canals and pedal past fields of flax, the plant used to make linen. And in the south they wheel through the low, twisty Ardennes, forested mountains where wild pigs roam.

OFFICIAL NAME: Kingdom of Belgium
AREA: 11,800 sq mi (30,500 sq km)
POPULATION: 9,835,000
CAPITAL: Brussels (pop. 153,000)
ETHNIC GROUPS: Fleming, Walloon. **LANGUAGE:** Flemish, French. **RELIGION:** Roman Catholic.
ECONOMY: chemicals, engineering, gemstone cutting, grains, livestock, metals, oil refining, potatoes, steel, sugar, textiles. **CURRENCY:** franc.

East Germany

Taking a shortcut down cobblestone streets, Ilse, 13, pedals her bicycle home. She's happy because her farm youth group won a prize. Their chickens produced more eggs than required.

Like most youngsters in Communist East Germany, Ilse takes part in youth group projects, and works four hours a week in a factory. She also is on her school's gymnastic team, and she plans to become an engineer. East German women are active in all career fields. Eight out of ten women work or take training outside their homes.

East Germany is an industrial leader among Communist states. Petrochemical refineries use oil from a Russian pipeline. Strip mines for lignite (soft, brown coal) sometimes border fields of grain and sugar beets, food factories, and steel plants.

The western border of East Germany was drawn in 1949, when Germany was divided into two countries. Berlin was also split into two parts. A wall of concrete and barbed wire put up by East Germans separates East Berlin from West Berlin.

OFFICIAL NAME: German Democratic Republic
AREA: 41,800 sq mi (108,200 sq km)
POPULATION: 16,775,000
CAPITAL: East Berlin (pop. 1,119,000)
ETHNIC GROUPS: Germanic. **LANGUAGE:** German. **RELIGION:** Protestant, also Roman Catholic. (Government discourages religion.) **ECONOMY:** chemicals, coal, electronic equipment, grains, livestock, machinery, metals, potash, ships, sugar, textiles. **CURRENCY:** mark.

West Germany

Children in West Germany sometimes look like Hansel and Gretel. The girls wear bright print jumpers and lacy blouses — dirndl dresses. Boys sport lederhosen — leather shorts with suspenders. Older youths wear jeans and T-shirts. They play soccer, the national sport, and attend *Gymnasium* (high school) or work as apprentices with master craftsmen. About one in five goes to college.

In West Germany's crowded cities, town walls and cathedrals dating back to the Middle Ages stand side by side with modern glass-and-steel high-rise buildings. But within a short drive by the *Autobahn* — the freeway — lies the quiet countryside.

Hiking trails, where you may not meet another person for hours, wind through wheat fields and oak forests. Wanderers can set out on a cross-country hike from the Bavarian Alps. Here snowcapped mountains tower over villages. Dairy cows graze on hillside meadows. Craftsmen turn out wood carvings and toys.

Traveling westward, the hikers reach fir-studded hills in the Black Forest. This is the land of cuckoo clocks, thatched roofs, and Mercedes-Benz car factories.

The Rhine River forms the Black Forest's western boundary. Tourist steamers and tugboats crowd freighters carrying coal, machinery, and timber on Europe's busiest waterway. Between Mainz and Dusseldorf the Rhine threads through a deep gorge. Castles hundreds of years old perch on hilltops. Vineyards line the river banks.

As the land levels off, the hikers detour around the smoky, industry-crammed Ruhr Valley. Crossing a vast pastureland they come to moors and sand dunes, windmills and dairy farms along the North Sea. In the Frisian Islands, fishermen whose ancestors were pirates bring in boatloads of herring. The trail next passes Hamburg, West Germany's greatest port, and then ends at the border of Denmark. Only Berlin cannot be reached on foot. You must go in by car, train, or plane. The city was separated from West Germany by the division of Germany which took place after World War II.

OFFICIAL NAME: Federal Republic of Germany
AREA: 96,000 sq mi (248,600 sq km)
POPULATION: 61,474,000
CAPITAL: Bonn (pop. 285,000)
ETHNIC GROUPS: Germanic. **LANGUAGE:** German. **RELIGION:** Protestant, Roman Catholic. **ECONOMY:** cement, chemicals, coal, grains, iron, livestock, machinery, motor vehicles, potatoes, ships, steel, sugar, textiles. **CURRENCY:** mark.

Luxembourg

Most all Luxembourgers speak Letzeburgesch, a form of the German language. But newspapers, books, and school texts in this tiny nation usually are written in French or standard German. Since Luxembourg has no university, its young people often go to neighboring France or Germany to get a higher education for a profession.

Luxembourg City, built on rocky heights, was one of the mightiest fortresses in medieval Europe. Four of its rulers reigned as Holy Roman emperors, and Luxembourg governed an area nearly 400 times its present size. Now the country is 51 miles (82 km) by 35 miles (56 km) at its longest and widest points. You can drive across modern Luxembourg in less than half an hour.

Rugged mountains and dense forests spread over northern Luxembourg. Streams often form natural moats around castles. Farms prosper in the central valley, vineyards in the east. Iron ore deposits in the south supply a vital steel industry.

OFFICIAL NAME: Grand Duchy of Luxembourg
AREA: 990 sq mi (2,580 sq km)
POPULATION: 358,000
CAPITAL: Luxembourg (pop. 79,000)
ETHNIC GROUPS: Germanic, also French, Italian. **LANGUAGE:** French, German, and Letzeburgesch, English. **RELIGION:** Roman Catholic. **ECONOMY:** beets, chemicals, engineering, grains, iron, metals, potatoes, steel, textiles, tires. **CURRENCY:** franc.

Netherlands

Netherlands means "the low lands." About one-third of the country lies below sea level. Huge dikes block off the North Sea. From the top of such a dike, you can sometimes see waves cresting higher than the pastureland behind you.

For about a thousand years the Dutch have fought back the sea. They drain the land with ditches, then plant reeds to dry out the ground. Pumps, formerly driven by windmills but now electric powered, hum steadily to keep seawater off sections of reclaimed land called *polders*. A crack in a dike could spell disaster. Yet the Dutch keep pushing back the sea, creating about 12 square miles of new land a year.

Farmers, fishermen, and children usually wear wooden shoes because the soil is often wet. The land is so level that boats cruising on the waterways look as if they are sailing through the farm fields.

A maze of canals links the major cities. In Amsterdam, houses must be built on pilings because the ground is waterlogged. With little land to waste, houses only one room wide often rise four stories high.

Holland's seat of government is at The Hague, where the queen opens Parliament each year. The World Court hears cases involving treaties and international laws.

Rotterdam, busiest seaport in the world, handles fleets of cargo ships, and supertankers bringing oil to Western Europe.

In spring, tourists flock to Holland to see the tulips. They eat cheeses from the towns of Edam and Gouda, admire Delft blue china, and watch diamond cutters work.

OFFICIAL NAME: Kingdom of the Netherlands
AREA: 13,100 sq mi (33,900 sq km)
POPULATION: 13,929,000
CAPITAL: Amsterdam (pop. 741,000)
The Hague, seat of government (pop. 472,000)
ETHNIC GROUPS: Germanic. **LANGUAGE:** Dutch. **RELIGION:** Protestant, Roman Catholic. **ECONOMY:** chemicals, engineering, grains, livestock, machinery, metals, natural gas, oil, plants and flowers. **CURRENCY:** guilder.

1

Netherlands

1 *A helicopter sprays rows of tulips to kill insects and fungi. Growers cut the flowers so the bulbs will grow larger. Excess blossoms are fed to cows or dumped at sea. Tulips first came to Holland from Turkey in the 16th century.*

2 *Porters hustle a heavy load of golden Edam cheeses for weighing at the market in Alkmaar. Suspended from shoulder harnesses, the cheese-piled barrows often weigh more than 300 pounds.*

3 *Hugging an armful of tulips, a Dutch boy hitches a ride on his mother's bicycle. The whole family pitches in to plant in the fall, care for the spring blooms, and harvest new bulbs in the summer.*

Belgium

4 *The waterfront of Ghent, mirrored in the River Lys, reflects architectural styles that date back to the plain, gray grain warehouses of the 13th century. Nourished by two rivers, Ghent grew to greatness during the Middle Ages as an important seaport and weaving center.*

East Germany

1 *A four-woman team harvests sugar beets near Wismar. Here at the northern edge of East Germany, harvesters must hurry when frost threatens to kill their crop.*

2 *Stolberg, a Harz Mountains resort, boasts many half-timbered houses. This style of building—a wood frame filled in with plaster—was started in the Middle Ages.*

West Germany

3 *Volkswagens take shape at Wolfsburg. Popular VW's help make West Germany a world leader in the value of its exports.*

4 *The Rhine curves past a watchtower, a cliff-top castle, grape-clad hills. At harvest time, school's out for children who help workers bring in the grapes.*

5 *Bavaria, in southern Germany, is famed worldwide for its pretzels, beer, sausages, and castles such as Neuschwanstein.*

3

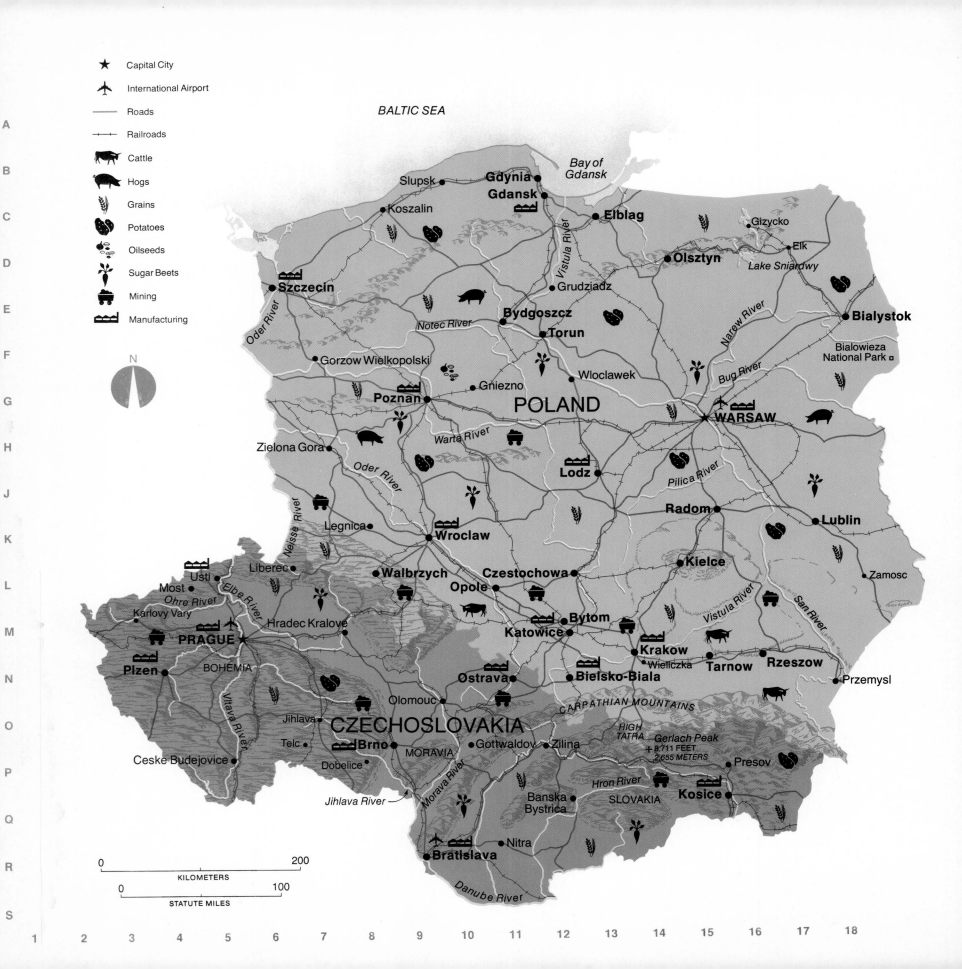

Legend

★ Capital City
✈ International Airport
— Roads
╬ Railroads
🐂 Cattle
🐖 Hogs
🌾 Grains
Potatoes
Oilseeds
Sugar Beets
Mining
Manufacturing

N

BALTIC SEA

Bay of Gdansk

Slupsk
Gdynia
Gdansk
Koszalin
Elblag
Gizycko
Elk
Olsztyn
Lake Sniardwy

Szczecin
Grudziadz
Bialystok

Notec River
Bydgoszcz
Torun
Narew River
Bialowieza
National Park

Oder River
Gorzow Wielkopolski
Bug River

Gniezno
POLAND
Poznan
Wloclawek

Warta River
WARSAW

Zielona Gora
Lodz
Pilica River

Oder River
Radom
Lublin

Legnica
Wroclaw
Kielce
Zamosc

Neisse River
Walbrzych
Czestochowa
Opole
Vistula River
San River

Liberec
Bytom
Katowice
Usti
Krakow
PRAGUE
Wieliczka
Tarnow
Rzeszow
Karlovy Vary
Ohre River
Elbe River
Hradec Kralove
Ostrava
Bielsko-Biala
Przemysl

Plzen
BOHEMIA
Olomouc
CARPATHIAN MOUNTAINS
HIGH TATRA
Presov

Jihlava
CZECHOSLOVAKIA
Gerlach Peak
+8,711 FEET,
2,655 METERS

Vltava River
Telc
Brno
MORAVIA
Gottwaldov
Zilina
Kosice

Ceske Budejovice
Dobelice
Hron River
Banska
Bystrica
SLOVAKIA

Jihlava River
Morava River
Nitra

Bratislava

Danube River

0 _____ 200
KILOMETERS

0 _____ 100
STATUTE MILES

Czechoslovakia

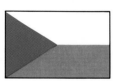

The music of carols fills a small apartment. Gifts lie under the Christmas tree. From the stove come mouth-watering smells of steaming carp—the fish that is as traditional to Czechoslovakians on Christmas Eve as turkey is to Americans on Thanksgiving. Children save carp scales, which they believe bring good luck.

In Prague a statue of St. Wenceslas, the "Good King" of the well-known Christmas carol, stands on a broad avenue. Cars and streetcars jam the streets. Shops and movie houses line arcades. In these covered walkways, shoppers munch sausages while students in blue jeans strum guitars and browse in bookstores. Spires of St. Vitus's Cathedral soar above Prague Castle, whose beginnings go back one thousand years. Throughout the nation, some 2,500 castles still stand. Several are on the Vltava River.

That gentle stream flows through hills and forests of Bohemia, largest of the nation's three regions. Where the Ohre meets the Tepla (Warm) River—heated by hot springs—sits Karlovy Vary (Karlsbad). Here workers enjoy mineral-water baths once frequented by nobility. Craftsmen fashion fine crystal and porcelain. At Plzen (Pilsen), famed for weapons of war and Pilsner beer, smokestacks crowd the sky.

Moravia, the central region, has rich coal fields and modern steel mills as well as fertile plains. On collective farms, peasants harvest sugar beets, wheat, and barley. Women in babushkas (head scarves) and aprons bicycle to jobs in Brno, the second largest city in Czechoslovakia. Visitors can go boating on underground rivers in grottoes—caves enlarged to make passages.

In summer, singers and dancers dress up in bright costumes for folk festivals. On Christmas Eve, country girls still follow the old custom of tossing a shoe over a shoulder to find out how soon they will marry. A shoe pointing away from the house means that a wedding is likely within the year.

Slovakia, in the east, joined Bohemia and Moravia in 1918 to form Czechoslovakia. Mountains shield Bratislava, a major port on the Danube, from cold winds.

OFFICIAL NAME: Czechoslovak Socialist Republic
AREA: 49,400 sq mi (127,900 sq km)
POPULATION: 15,136,000
CAPITAL: Prague (pop. 1,176,000)
ETHNIC GROUPS: Slavic. **LANGUAGE:** Czech, Slovak. **RELIGION:** Roman Catholic, also Protestant. **ECONOMY:** chemicals, coal, grains, machinery, metals, potatoes, sugar, textiles, transportation equipment. **CURRENCY:** koruna.

Poland

School is out. Teenagers carrying knapsacks and hitchhiking booklets set out on Poland's highways. Anyone over 17 can buy a booklet. Each provides accident insurance and contains sheets of coupons. After a hitchhiker is picked up, he gives the driver coupons for the number of kilometers traveled. Coupons entered in a lottery may win the driver a new car.

Automobiles share narrow roads with horse-drawn carts, still a major form of transportation. But most people travel by rail across Poland's rolling plains and flat lakelands. Coal and grain barges move along the navigable Oder and Vistula rivers, which drain the New Mexico-size nation. Oceangoing freighters call at the Baltic seaports of Gdansk and Szczecin.

Poland saw great destruction in World War II. Monuments mark grim sites where people suffered mass murder in Nazi concentration camps. Now cities have been rebuilt. In Warsaw, historic Old Town with its royal palace and ancient marketplace has been restored. On the capital's outskirts sprawl small factories and huge industrial plants. Women hold jobs operating cranes, sweeping streets, and directing traffic.

Near Warsaw is the birthplace of composer Frederic Chopin. His lively music reflects the Polish spirit. Villagers in embroidered vests celebrate festive occasions with folk dances. In the High Tatra of southern Poland, mountain men, *gorals,* quiet their flocks of bleating sheep by playing the *kobza,* a bagpipe-like instrument fitted with a goat's head carved from wood.

In Masuria, the northeast region bordering the Soviet Union, red-brick castles rise from green meadows. Sailboats skim over blue lakes. Giant oaks and pines shade Bialowieza National Park. Farther south descendants of Slavic tribesmen called Polanians—"dwellers of the fields"—cut wheat and rye, and dig potatoes by hand.

University students crowd cafes in the ancient city of Krakow. Its castles and churches recall seven centuries of history. Old St. Mary's Church is a reminder that Catholics hail the Mother of Jesus as "Queen of Poland." In 1978 they rejoiced as one of their countrymen became Pope John Paul II. He was the first non-Italian cardinal elected Pope in 456 years.

OFFICIAL NAME: Polish People's Republic
AREA: 120,600 sq mi (312,400 sq km)
POPULATION: 35,030,000
CAPITAL: Warsaw (pop. 1,463,000)
ETHNIC GROUPS: Slavic. **LANGUAGE:** Polish. **RELIGION:** Roman Catholic. **ECONOMY:** chemicals, coal, grains, machinery, meat, metals, oilseeds, potatoes, ships, sugar, sulfur. **CURRENCY:** zloty.

Czechoslovakia

1 *Elegant town houses built centuries ago gaze down on the cobblestone streets of Telc. Once protected by a moat, the town is now preserved as a historic monument. Its houses are still occupied, and its shops continue to attract customers.*

2 *As a gigantic "bicycle chain" turns 70 tons (63.5 t) of glowing steel ingot, a worker in Ostrava flakes off crusty scales. In the heart of the rich coalfields near the Polish border, Ostrava's huge factories turn out three-fourths of Czechoslovakia's iron and steel.*

3 *Musicians march from village to village calling everyone to a harvest festival at Dobelice. An evergreen sprig on the trombonist's cap also announces the celebration. In this swiftly modernizing country, people practice old customs and wear old costumes only for special events.*

Poland

4 Black smoke from a factory drifts above a farmer and son plowing fields at Katowice, center of Poland's coal and steel region. Forests and strips of open land, scattered throughout the industrial area, help purify the air. A nation of small farmers, Poland ranks as a world leader in agriculture. But industry dominates her economy, with coal miners the highest paid workers.

5 Reliving the past, students perform the graceful dances of their ancestors at the harvest festival in Opole. Dance halls hundreds of feet below ground were hand-carved out of salt in the centuries-old mine at Wieliczka. The chambers sparkle with light from huge chandeliers coated with glittering salt crystals. Horses hauling salt to the surface worked in the dark for so many years that they became blind.

N

Salzach
River

*Lake
Constance*
Bregenz

Inn River

Innsbruck

A L P S

+ Gross Glockner
12,457 FEET
3,797 METERS

*Krimml
Waterfall*

Oberndorf
Wels
Steyr

Linz

Danube River

Krems

St. Polten

★ **VIENNA**

Salzburg

Erzberg
+

Enns River

AUSTRIA

*Neusiedler
Lake*

Sopron

Gyor

Tatabanya

Szombathely

Graz

Raba River

Veszprem

Dunaujvaros

Miskolc

Eger

Nyiregyhaza

★ **BUDAPEST**

Debrecen

Szekesfehervar

Szolnok

HUNGARY

Kecskemet

Bekescsaba

Villach

Klagenfurt

Maribor

*Lake
Balaton*

SLOVENIA

Kaposvar

Pecs

Szeged

Subotica

Ljubljana

Drava River

Zagreb

CROATIA

Karlovac

Danube River

Osijek

Zrenjanin

Novi Sad

Rijeka

Istria

Pula

Cres

Pag

Banja Luka

Tuzla

Sava River

YUGOSLAVIA

SERBIA

BELGRADE ★

*Danube
River*

Zadar

D A L M A T I A N

BOSNIA-
HERCEGOVINA

Zenica

Kragujevac

Morava River

Sibenik

Split

Brac

Vis

Hvar

Korcula

C O A S T

Sarajevo

Drina River

MONTENEGRO

Pec

Pristina

Nis

*ADRIATIC
SEA*

Dubrovnik

Titograd

Bar

*Lake
Scutari*

Skopje

MACEDONIA

Vardar River

Ohrid

Bitola

*Lake
Ohrid*

*Lake
Prespa*

Legend

★ Capital City
✈ International Airport
— Roads
‡ Railroads
🐂 Cattle
🐑 Sheep
🐖 Hogs
🌾 Grains

🥔 Potatoes
🌱 Oilseeds
🌿 Sugar Beets
🍾 Wine
🍃 Tobacco
🪵 Wood
⛏ Mining
🏭 Manufacturing

0 ——————————— 300
KILOMETERS

0 ——————————— 200
STATUTE MILES

(3,797 m) the highest point in the Austrian Alps. Houses with sloped roofs cluster around castles here and in Lower Austria, the largest province in the country.

Second in size is Styria, green with vineyards and dense forests except where open-pit mines scar the face of Erzberg, a mountain of iron ore.

The heart of the nation beats in Vienna, a city of palaces, gardens, and gaiety. Close by flows the Danube, once blue but now a brown and busy highway for barges and excursion boats. Near the sprawling Hofburg, the long-ago palace of emperors, coffeehouse customers sip *Melange mit Schlag* — milk, coffee, and whipped cream — and eat delicious Vienna pastries.

Austria

From spruce-clad Alps to winding Danube River the air is often filled with sounds of music — Strauss waltzes, thrumming guitars, mountaineers' yodels. On Christmas Eve, "Silent Night" echoes from St. Nikolas Church in Oberndorf, where Franz Gruber composed the hymn in 1818. In summer, crowds pour into Salzburg for the Mozart festival, honoring the great composer of classical music.

Land Salzburg, one of the country's nine provinces, boasts Europe's highest waterfall — the Krimml, which plunges 1,250 feet (381 m). The province also has salt (*Salz*) mines that give the region its name, and hot springs. Snowy slopes here and in Tyrol attract skiers. Innsbruck, once a vacation spot for royalty, welcomed the 1976 Olympic Games. To reach some mountain resorts, you ride up the slopes in small railway-like cars hanging from cables.

Spring thaws bring the opening of Gross Glockner Highway, a twisting toll road that in some places is roofed for protection against avalanches. Motorists drive up to see glaciers and peaks bathed in reddish alpenglow. The tollway ends in Carinthia Province at Gross Glockner, at 12,457 feet

OFFICIAL NAME: Republic of Austria
AREA: 32,400 sq mi (83,900 sq km)
POPULATION: 7,517,000
CAPITAL: Vienna (pop. 1,593,000)
ETHNIC GROUPS: Germanic. LANGUAGE: German. RELIGION: Roman Catholic, also Protestant. ECONOMY: chemicals, coal, grains, livestock, machinery, metals, paper, potatoes, sugar, textiles, wood. CURRENCY: shilling.

Hungary

Hungary has a double city for a capital. Hilly Buda on the west side of the Danube and flat Pest on the east joined to form Budapest in 1873. Seagoing ships can steam up the Danube to dock right in the heart of this landlocked nation.

Magyars — fierce mounted nomads from the east — settled on the Great Hungarian Plain in the ninth century. Their language, now called Hungarian, remained distinct from that of neighboring Slavs.

Today the plains, under Communist collective farming, produce corn and wheat. Paprika, ground from scarlet peppers, flavors national dishes. Fields of lavender, a flower that yields a sweet-smelling oil, grow near Lake Balaton, a resort area in the hilly west. On lowland ranges, cowboys called *csikos* crack whips and drive cattle. Prairie

shepherds, in shaggy sheepskin cloaks, look like overgrown sheep themselves.

About 300,000 Gypsies live in Hungary. Gypsy violinists once led the country's armies into battle. Medieval castles recall other wars, fought by knights in armor. Now many castles serve as tourist hotels.

OFFICIAL NAME: Hungarian People's Republic
AREA: 35,900 sq mi (93,000 sq km)
POPULATION: 10,693,000
CAPITAL: Budapest (pop. 2,090,000)
ETHNIC GROUPS: Magyar. LANGUAGE: Hungarian. RELIGION: Roman Catholic, also Protestant. ECONOMY: bauxite, chemicals, coal, engineering, grains, machinery, metals, potatoes, sugar, textiles, wine. CURRENCY: forint.

Yugoslavia

In Croatia, one of Yugoslavia's six states, children learn the Roman alphabet with its ABC's. But in the state next door, Serbia's pupils study the Cyrillic alphabet with letters like Б(B), Ф(F), and Э(E).

A melting pot of different cultures, the "Land of the South Slavs" has numerous languages and three religions. The land is as varied as the people, with plains, mountains, and an island-studded coast on the Adriatic Sea.

Half of all Yugoslavs still work the land, many behind ox-drawn plows. Others mine coal in Slovenia in the north, tend flocks of sheep in Macedonia in the south, or cut trees in central Bosnia's beech forests. Seeking a better life, young people stream into Belgrade, a modern city with traffic jams, sleek buildings, and colorful *diskotekas*.

OFFICIAL NAME: Socialist Federal Republic of Yugoslavia
AREA: 98,800 sq mi (255,900 sq km)
POPULATION: 21,973,000
CAPITAL: Belgrade (pop. 771,000)
ETHNIC GROUPS: Slavic. LANGUAGE: Macedonian, Serbo-Croatian, Slovene. RELIGION: Eastern Orthodox, Roman Catholic, also Muslim. ECONOMY: chemicals, coal, grains, livestock, machinery, metals, oilseeds, sugar, textiles, tobacco, wine, wood. CURRENCY: dinar.

Austria

1 *Patient hands of a wood-carver put the finishing touches on a sculpture. Austrian craftsmen also work in leather, porcelain, silver, enamel, glass, and lace. Embroidery adorns purses. Some designs have 1,600 stitches a square inch.*

2 *Men in masks and costumes that make them look like women celebrate Fasching, Austria's long carnival season of festive dances, parties, and parades. Revived in recent times, the festival dates back to the Middle Ages. So does the custom of wearing disguises at such celebrations; then it allowed nobles and commoners to mix and poke fun at each other without being recognized.*

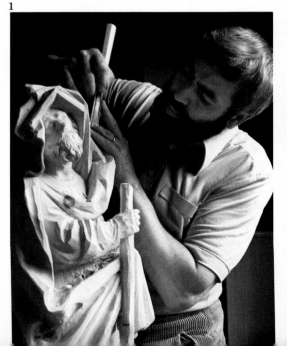

4

3

3 *Quiet valleys in the Yugoslav republic of Bosnia-Hercegovina have endured centuries of bloody wars and conquest. From cliffs such as these, Yugoslav guerrillas attacked enemy troops during World War II. In Sarajevo, capital of the region, the murder of Austrian Archduke Franz Ferdinand in 1914 led to the outbreak of World War I.*

Hungary

4 *Aglow in the setting sun, Hungary's Parliament Building looks out over the Danube River at Budapest. More than 400 pounds of gold decorate the ornate halls and staircases of the legislature.*

A B C D E F G H J K L M N O P Q R S T

1 2 3 4 5 6 7 8 9 10 11 12

Satu Mare
Baia Mare
Suceava
Iasi
Oradea
Cluj-Napoca
Tirgu Mures
Bacau
Arad
Sighisoara
ROMANIA
Timisoara
Resita
Sibiu
Olt River
Brasov
Galati
Mures River
TRANSYLVANIAN ALPS
Braila
Tulcea
Danube River Delta
Iron Gate Dam
Pitesti
Ploiesti
BUCHAREST
Craiova
Constanta
Vidin
Danube River
Ruse
Belogradchik
Iskur River
Pleven
Varna
BLACK SEA
BULGARIA
SOFIA
Gabrovo
Pernik
Stara Zagora
Burgas
Plovdiv
Maritsa River
← Tundzha River
Lake Scutari
Shkoder
Struma River
RHODOPE MOUNTAINS
Evros River
Drin River
Durres
TIRANA
Drama
Komotini
Elbasan
Lake Ohrid
Lake Prespa
Serrar
Kavala
ALBANIA
Korce
Veroia
Thasos
Vlore
Mount Olympus + 9,570 FEET 2,917 METERS
Salonica
Corfu
Ioannina
Trikala
Larisa
Lemnos
Volos
AEGEAN SEA
Lesbos
Mitilini
GREECE
IONIAN SEA
Agrinion
Euboea
Chios
Patrae
Andros
Cephalonia
Corinth
ATHENS
Samos
Zante
Piraeus
Siros
Mikonos
PELOPONNESUS
Melos
Naxos
Kalamai
Sparta
Kos
Thera
Rhodes
Cerigo
Rhodes
SEA OF CRETE
Carpathos
MEDITERRANEAN SEA
Khania
Iraklion
CRETE

Prut River
CARPATHIAN MOUNTAINS
Siret River

★ Capital City
✈ International Airport
— Roads
+−+ Railroads
🐄 Livestock
🌾 Grains
🥬 Vegetables
🍎 Fruit

🫒 Olives
Oilseeds
Tobacco
Cotton
Wood
Mining
Oil or Natural Gas
Manufacturing

0   KILOMETERS   300
0   STATUTE MILES   200

N

Albania

A young shepherd plays his flute-like panpipe as his flock grazes in a mountain meadow. Ask where he lives, and he will reply *Shqiperia*—Land of Eagles.

Albania is a land of craggy mountains and rushing streams, of forest and dense scrub. Huts of stone and mud cling to hillsides. The people follow many old ways in spite of changes urged by the Communist government. In some villages *kulle*—towering fortress-like houses—still stand, reminders that tribal differences often started blood feuds in the past.

Customs, language, dress (baggy clothes with raised designs on the cloth) have survived through centuries of invasions. Roman legions marched through the lowlands along the coast. Crusaders landed at Durres, now a major seaport and rail center.

OFFICIAL NAME: People's Socialist Republic of Albania
AREA: 11,100 sq mi (28,700 sq km)
POPULATION: 2,569,000
CAPITAL: Tirana (pop. 175,000)
ETHNIC GROUPS: Gheg, Tosk. LANGUAGE: Albanian, Greek. RELIGION: Muslim, also Eastern Orthodox, Roman Catholic. (Government prohibits public observances.) ECONOMY: asphalt, cement, chromium, coal, cotton, fruit, grains, metals, oil, sugar, textiles, tobacco, vegetables, wine, wood. CURRENCY: lek.

Bulgaria

A basketball player hits a jump shot. Pleased teammates shake their heads from side to side. That means "good" in Bulgaria. Up and down nods mean "no."

Traditions live on in this Balkan land of sunshine and flowers. You see reminders of the past in every town and city, in spite of rebuilding programs by the Communist government. In villages, thatch-roofed cottages stand in the shade of modern apartment buildings of concrete and stone. In Sofia, whose coat of arms proclaims "Grows, but grows not old," the ancient Church of St. George shares a courtyard with a hotel. Nearby you see the nine domes of the Bouyouk Mosque, built by Ottoman Turks in the 15th century. The mosque now houses an archeological museum.

Bulgaria lies on the main trade route between Europe and Asia Minor. The countryside dazzles your eye with grainfields in the lowlands, gardens that checkerboard the high plains, and snow-topped mountains. Lush vineyards and fields of brilliant sunflowers stretch along the Danube. Most spectacular: the Valley of Roses, where tons of petals are crushed to make perfume.

At Varna on the Black Sea, Bulgaria's vacation playground begins. Resorts with sand beaches mix with Roman ruins and richly decorated monasteries. Vacationers enjoy mud baths, music festivals, and hearty meals. Creamy yogurt, a Bulgarian favorite, wins approving shakes of the head from diners in restaurants.

OFFICIAL NAME: People's Republic of Bulgaria
AREA: 43,200 sq mi (111,900 sq km)
POPULATION: 8,848,000
CAPITAL: Sofia (pop. 1,021,000)
ETHNIC GROUPS: Slavic, also Turkish. LANGUAGE: Bulgarian, also Turkish. RELIGION: Eastern Orthodox, also Muslim. ECONOMY: chemicals, cigarettes, coal, fruit, grains, machinery, metals, textiles, transportation equipment, vegetables, wood. CURRENCY: leva.

Greece

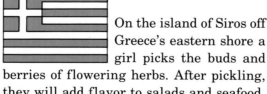

On the island of Siros off Greece's eastern shore a girl picks the buds and berries of flowering herbs. After pickling, they will add flavor to salads and seafood. Herbs grow wild on the sunny islands of Greece. More than 400 in number, they make up about one-fifth of the country.

Plato and other thinkers of early Greece gave the Western world many of its most important ideas. From Greek for "power of the people" came our word "democracy." The poet Homer wrote great stories of ancient gods, and of heroes such as Odysseus.

If you sail the Aegean Sea where Odysseus wandered, you can visit Kos, birthplace of Hippocrates, the father of medicine. At Rhodes you see the site where a bronze statue called the Colossus once towered a hundred feet or more. On Crete, largest of the islands, you discover ruins and artifacts of vanished peoples and ways of life.

In the Ionian Sea rises the island of Corfu. Women there spin wool into cloth and fishermen mend their nets in age-old fashion. Whitewashed huts against blue sea and sky remind you of Greece's white and blue flag. Other colors glow in flower blossoms bearing names from mythology: Iris, goddess of the rainbow; Narcissus, the youth who died from love for his own reflection; Hyacinthus, a young man accidentally killed by the god Apollo.

Mount Olympus, tallest peak in mountainous Greece, was said to be the home of Zeus, the most powerful god. About 150 miles south of Olympus the capital city of Athens spreads across a plain. Athenians jam trolley buses, shop in boutiques, relax in *tavernas*. Smog from industry and traffic stings eyes and eats away at marble ruins.

The crowning glory of Athens is the Acropolis, a hilltop gleaming with remains of classic temples. Below the limestone heights lie ruins of the Agora, the marketplace of ancient Athens and birthplace of democracy. Here the philosopher Socrates walked and St. Paul preached. From the battlefield of Marathon, 26 miles (42 km) northeast of Athens, a runner raced with news of a Persian defeat in 490 B.C. His feat, and games held at Olympia on the Peloponnesus, inspired today's Olympics.

OFFICIAL NAME: Hellenic Republic
AREA: 51,200 sq mi (132,600 sq km)
POPULATION: 9,309,000
CAPITAL: Athens (pop. 867,000)
ETHNIC GROUPS: Greek. LANGUAGE: Greek. RELIGION: Eastern Orthodox. ECONOMY: aluminum, chemicals, cotton, fruit, grains, oil refining, olives, textiles, tobacco. CURRENCY: drachma.

Romania

"Buna ziua—Good day," says a Romanian peasant in colorful folk dress. The words sound Latin, and for good reason. Emperor Trajan's Roman legions left their language behind after conquering this land, then known as Dacia.

Tatars and Turks have also invaded, but the seeds of today's Romanian language and way of life survived, far back in the mountains and remote castles of Transylvania. The fortress where Prince Dracula was born in the 15th century still stands in the hilltop town of Sighisoara. Surrounding houses almost miraculously survive from the 17th century, when a destructive earthquake hit the area.

Another quake in 1977 leveled much of Bucharest, city of monuments. With its parks and its streets lined with horse chestnut and lime trees, the capital is called by some "Paris of the Balkans."

Romania under Communism has seen industry grow, from reborn Ploiesti oil fields, target of Allied bombers in World War II, to a giant hydroelectric plant at Iron Gate Dam on the Danube. At the Black Sea this river comes apart like a rope's end and fans out through a marshy delta, home of herons, flamingos, and pelicans.

Technology has brought change to Romania, but old skills are kept alive. Woodcarvers, potters, and carpet weavers pursue their crafts. Villagers in the north wear fur caps and sheepskin vests like those worn 500 years ago. Mothers rock their babies in hand-carved wooden cradles.

OFFICIAL NAME: Socialist Republic of Romania
AREA: 91,700 sq mi (237,500 sq km)
POPULATION: 21,868,000
CAPITAL: Bucharest (pop. 1,807,000)
ETHNIC GROUPS: Romanian, also Magyar. **LANGUAGE:** Romanian, also Hungarian, German.
RELIGION: Eastern Orthodox, also Protestant, Roman Catholic. **ECONOMY:** chemicals, coal, fruit, grains, livestock, machinery, metals, natural gas, oilseeds, potatoes, textiles, transportation equipment, wood. **CURRENCY:** lei.

1

2

Romania

1 *Refineries at Ploiesti help make Romania a leading producer of oil in Europe.*

Bulgaria

2 *Once a Turkish stronghold, the fortress of Belogradchik guards a mountain pass.*
3 *The valley home of this foal and boy produces cheese made from sheep's milk.*

Greece

4 *A young girl and her grandmother share the pleasure and profit of making sweaters of wool from the family sheep.*
5 *As many as 14 cruise ships a day call at Mikonos, once a hideout for pirates.*

3

4

5

A B C D E F G H J K L M N O P Q R S T U

1 2 3 4 5 6 7 8 9 10 11 12 13 14 15 16 17 18 19

Brenner Pass

ALPS
ALPS

+ Mont Blanc
15,771 FEET
4,807 METERS

Lake Como

Bolzano

Plave River

Udine

Bergamo

Lake Garda

Trieste

Milan

Brescia

Verona

Venice

Turin

Padova

Po River

Parma

Ferrara

Genoa

Bologna

La Spezia

LIGURIAN
SEA

Collodi

Rimini

★ SAN MARINO

Pisa

Florence

Livorno

Arno River

Tiber River

Ancona

Elba

Lake
Trasimeno

Perugia

A
P
E
N
N
I
N
E
S

ADRIATIC

SEA

Lake
Bolsena

Terni

ITALY

Pescara

Civitavecchia

VATICAN CITY

★ **ROME**

Volturno
River

Foggia

Bari

SASSARI

Olbia

TYRRHENIAN

SEA

Mount Vesuvius
4,190 FEET
1,277 METERS

Naples

Brindisi

Pompeii

Isle of Capri

Taranto

SARDINIA

Tirso River

GULF OF
TARANTO

Cosenza

IONIAN
SEA

Cagliari

Palermo

Messina

Reggio Calabria

Victoria

Gozo

Mount Etna
10,902 FEET
3,323 METERS

Comino

SICILY

Catania

MALTA

Sliema

Gela

Syracuse

Rabat

★ **VALLETTA**

Malta

MEDITERRANEAN SEA

MEDITERRANEAN SEA

Legend

★ Capital City
✈ International Airport
— Roads
+ Railroads
🐄 Livestock
🌾 Grains

🫑 Vegetables
🍇 Fruit
🫒 Olives
🍾 Wine
🏭 Manufacturing
👪 Tourism

0 _____ 300
KILOMETERS

0 _____ 200
STATUTE MILES

N

0 _____ 15
KILOMETERS

0 _____ 10
STATUTE MILES

Italy

It's evening in Italy, and the brightly lit *piazza,* or square, still bustles with activity. Groups of all ages fill the sidewalk cafes, eating ice cream and drinking coffee from tiny cups. Children—they're allowed to stay up late in Italy—dance to the tunes of a strolling accordion player. Because Italians love crowds and the open air, the piazza is where their life centers.

Northern Italians complain their country is like a crippled giant, with a powerful head and strong shoulders but small feet and wobbly ankles that slow him down. You can see what they mean, because southern Italy, with its stony land, dry climate, and poor farms, lags behind the modern north in producing wealth. The Po Valley, near the Alps, has two-thirds of Italy's fertile soil and most of its industry as well. The factories of Milan, Turin, and Genoa help make Italy an industrial power.

Some 2,000 years ago the Roman empire included all the lands surrounding the Mediterranean Sea. The ancient Romans were great builders. The Appian Way, one of the major roads into Rome, was first paved in 312 B.C. It is still in use today. Before Italy was unified almost 120 years ago, the country was divided into small, often warring, city-states. One of these, Florence, dazzled 14th- and 15th-century Europe with its works of art. In 1966 a flood on the Arno River buried many art treasures in mud. Students who helped restore them were called *Angeli del Fango*—Angels of the Mud.

Venice, another great city-state, was established on a group of islands by Italians fleeing barbarians 15 centuries ago. Venice has canals instead of streets. Canoe-like boats called gondolas serve as taxis. In Sicily, an island off southern Italy, you see Mount Etna, Europe's highest volcanic peak. It often coughs up smoke and ashes.

OFFICIAL NAME: Italian Republic
AREA: 116,300 sq mi (301,200 sq km)
POPULATION: 56,711,000
CAPITAL: Rome (pop. 2,884,000)
ETHNIC GROUPS: Italian. LANGUAGE: Italian.
RELIGION: Roman Catholic. ECONOMY: chemicals, fruit, grains, machinery, motor vehicles, olives, steel, textiles, wine. CURRENCY: lira.

Malta

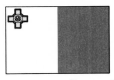

Picture a group of five islands smack at the crossroads of the Mediterranean Sea and you'll see why Malta has been invaded so often. Today yachts replace warships in the Grand Harbor, and thousands of tourists are the invaders.

Malta needs tourists because the former British colony (it became independent in 1964) has few natural resources. Fresh water is scarce and the thin soil is not productive. Under the soil lies limestone, which people use to build honey-colored houses. Many Maltese earn a living by tending vineyards or weaving lace garments.

OFFICIAL NAME: Republic of Malta
AREA: 121 sq mi (313 sq km)
POPULATION: 334,000
CAPITAL: Valletta (pop. 15,200)
ETHNIC GROUPS: Arab, British, Italian, Norman, Spanish. LANGUAGE: English, Maltese. RELIGION: Roman Catholic. ECONOMY: citrus fruit, eggs, flowers, grains, grapes, livestock, textiles, tourism, vegetables. CURRENCY: pound.

San Marino

The world's oldest republic is so small you could drive by it on a foggy day and not see it. Named after the stonecutter Marinus, its founder in A.D. 301, San Marino winds around a mountain in northeastern Italy. Its tiny capital, on the mountaintop, has medieval walls and towers.

Most San Marinese farm or sell souvenirs and postage stamps to more than two million tourists each year. Until recently the government sold titles to anyone who wanted to be called duke or count and was willing to pay $25,000 for the privilege.

OFFICIAL NAME: Republic of San Marino
AREA: 23 sq mi (62 sq km)
POPULATION: 20,000
CAPITAL: San Marino (pop. 4,400)
ETHNIC GROUPS: Italian. LANGUAGE: Italian.
RELIGION: Roman Catholic. ECONOMY: cement, ceramics, grains, grapes, livestock, postage stamps, textiles, tourism. CURRENCY: lira.

Vatican City

"Viva il Papa! Long live the Pope!" Throngs in St. Peter's Square greet the white-clad figure as he appears each Sunday in his palace window. Not only is he the head of the Roman Catholic Church and its 700 million members, he's also ruler of Vatican City, the world's smallest nation, inside Rome.

Only as big as a golf course, Vatican City has its own jail, newspaper, and army. People who live there try to get home early. Gates are locked promptly at 11:30 p.m.

OFFICIAL NAME: State of the Vatican City
AREA: .2 sq mi (.5 sq km)
POPULATION: 1,000
ETHNIC GROUPS: Italian. LANGUAGE: Italian, Latin. RELIGION: Roman Catholic. ECONOMY: contributions, museum fees, postage stamps, publications, tourist mementos. CURRENCY: lira.

Italy

1 *Main street of Venice, the Grand Canal welcomes a floating carnival of oared boats to recall medieval days when the city celebrated its "wedding" to the sea. The annual ceremony, in which the chief magistrate tossed a ring into the Adriatic, symbolized a partnership with the sea that made Venice a great maritime power.*

2 *Pinocchio was a character thought up by Italian author Carlo Collodi. The needle-nosed puppet wanted to be a real boy, perhaps like this youngster from the Italian village of Collodi.*

Vatican City

3 *Like giant cupped hands, curving columns reach around St. Peter's Square. On holy days worshipers fill it to receive the Pope's blessing. Designs like the obelisk in the center and the dome atop St. Peter's Basilica have become popular for monuments and important buildings.*

2

Switzerland

Glaciers and palm trees, yodeling shepherds and solemn bankers—that is the kind of contrast you find in surprising Switzerland, a small nation dominated by giant mountains. Nearly one-fourth of this country is barren rock and ice. The Jura Mountains in the northwest and the Swiss Alps in the south frame a central plateau. Rivers in the Alps flow away in so many directions that the rainfall from a single Swiss storm can end up in four different seas—Adriatic, Black, North, or western Mediterranean.

Skiers and climbers love Switzerland. A famed slope at Davos provides a thrilling run of more than seven miles. Swiss mountaineers developed many of the best climbing techniques and equipment. The Swiss also use their slopes as grazing land. Goats browse in alpine pastures and give milk for cheesemaking; cow's milk makes both cheese and famous Swiss milk chocolate.

Skilled workers turn out watches, instruments, and textiles famed for quality.

The Swiss federal union of 23 states, called cantons, unites four regions with different languages—but with a strong nationalism. German is spoken over a large central and northern area, French in the west. A small group in the southeast speak Romansh, a Latin dialect. In the south, people of the Ticino area speak Italian and live in a Mediterranean climate. Palm trees and camellias flourish among terraced houses; visitors bask in the warm climate of the lake country along the Italian border.

OFFICIAL NAME: Swiss Confederation
AREA: 16,000 sq mi (41,400 sq km)
POPULATION: 6,293,000
CAPITAL: Bern (pop. 147,000)
ETHNIC GROUPS: Germanic, also French, Italian. **LANGUAGE:** German, also French, Italian.
RELIGION: Protestant, Roman Catholic. **ECONOMY:** banking, chemicals, dairy products, machinery, metals, precision instruments, textiles, watches. **CURRENCY:** franc.

Switzerland

1 Bathed in sunset's warm glow, the Jungfrau (right) and neighboring peaks tower above fields in Bern canton, a Swiss state. Europe's highest railroad stops at 11,333 feet (3,454 m), nearly at the top of the Jungfrau. Little electric trains carry as many as 12,000 passengers an hour to resort villages nestled in these forbidding giants.

2 Climbers work their way up the rugged Rimpfischhorn. Behind them rises the Matterhorn, 14,690 feet (4,477 m) high. First climbed in 1865, that famous mountain is now scaled by thousands of guide-led tourists each year.

France

1 Cowboys drive half-wild horses across a flooded plain on the Camargue, a marshy region in the Rhone River delta. Horses have run free here since Roman times.

2 Sickle in hand, a harvester gathers lavender. An acre of flowers yields up to 30 pounds (13.6 kg) of sweet-smelling oil for perfume. Southern France reigns as the floral-oil capital of the world.

3 Sunbathed vineyards and hardworking Burgundians in eastern France produce some of the world's best wines.

4 A villager on Corsica gently strips the outer bark from a live cork oak tree. The tender inner layer will form the next cork harvest six to nine years later. Factories on the mainland turn raw cork into wine-bottle stoppers.

5 Fine wines and unusual dishes attract visitors to the Burgundy region. Snails are raised on farms to meet the demand.

6 Symbol of Paris, the Eiffel Tower soars above the French capital. Framed by the tower's legs, the military academy where Napoleon studied glows in the distance.

6

4

5

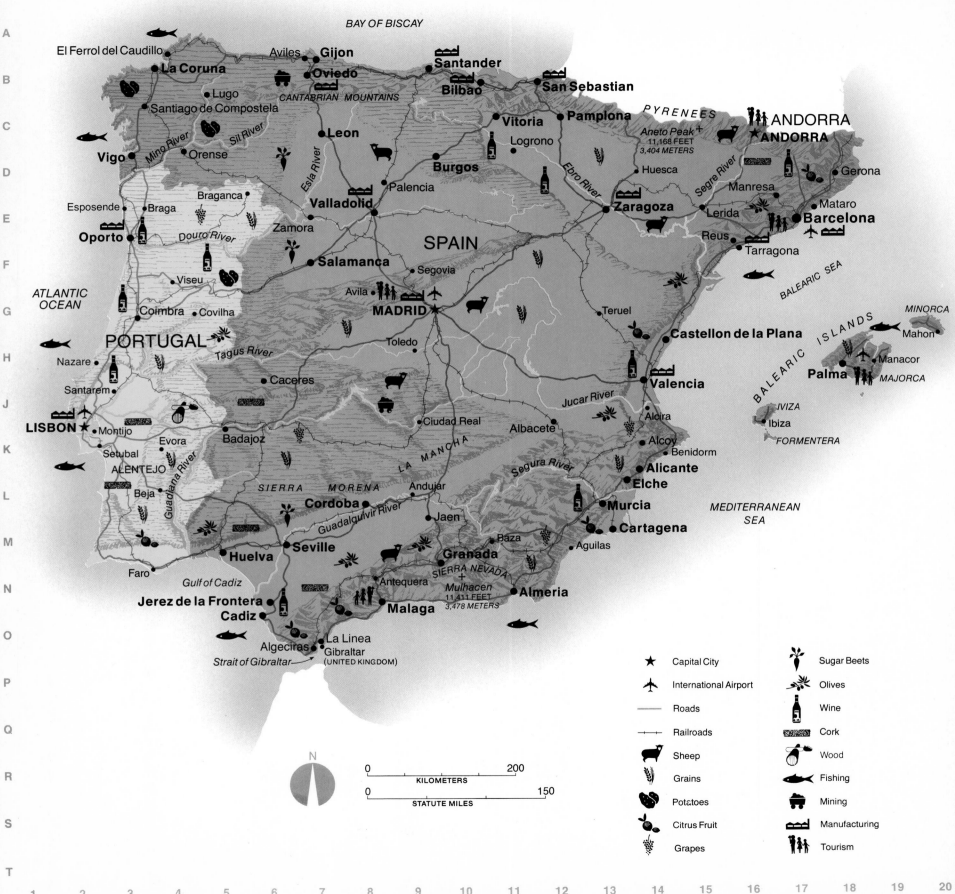

BAY OF BISCAY

A
El Ferrol del Caudillo
Aviles **Gijon**
La Coruna **Oviedo** **Santander**
B Lugo **Bilbao** San Sebastian
Santiago de Compostela CANTABRIAN MOUNTAINS PYRENEES
Vitoria **Pamplona** ANDORRA
C **Vigo** Orense **Leon** Logrono Aneto Peak **ANDORRA**
Mino River Sil River 11,168 FEET
3,404 METERS
Esposende Braga Esla River **Burgos** Huesca Gerona
D Braga Bragança Palencia Manresa Mataro
Oporto Zamora **Valladolid** **Zaragoza** Lerida **Barcelona**
E Douro River Reus
ATLANTIC Viseu SPAIN Tarragona
OCEAN Coimbra Covilha **Salamanca** Segovia
F Avila BALEARIC SEA
Nazare Tagus River **MADRID** Teruel BALEARIC ISLANDS MINORCA
G Santarem Caceres **Castellon de la Plana** Mahon
PORTUGAL Toledo
H LISBON Montijo **Valencia** Manacor
Evora Ciudad Real Albacete Alcira **Palma** MAJORCA
J Setubal Badajoz Jucar River Alcoy IVIZA
ALENTEJO Segura River Benidorm Ibiza
Beja LA MANCHA **Alicante** FORMENTERA
K Andujar **Elche**
SIERRA MORENA **Murcia**
L **Cordoba** Jaen **Cartagena** MEDITERRANEAN
Guadalquivir River Baza SEA
M **Huelva** **Seville** Aguilas
Faro **Granada**
N Gulf of Cadiz Antequera SIERRA NEVADA **Almeria**
Jerez de la Frontera Mulhacen
O **Cadiz** La Linea 11,411 FEET
Algeciras Gibraltar 3,478 METERS
Strait of Gibraltar (UNITED KINGDOM)
P

N
0   200
KILOMETERS
0   150
STATUTE MILES

★ Capital City   🌱 Sugar Beets
✈ International Airport 🫒 Olives
── Roads   🍾 Wine
┼ Railroads   ▦ Cork
🐑 Sheep   Wood
🌾 Grains   🐟 Fishing
🥔 Potatoes   Mining
🍊 Citrus Fruit   Manufacturing
🍇 Grapes   Tourism

Andorra

For centuries, Andorran farmers in the rugged Pyrenees have made extra money by creeping through pine valleys and mountain passes. Leading loaded donkeys, they smuggle goods — from clothing to car parts — into France and Spain.

Tourists give Andorra its biggest business now. Hotels and shops crowd the capital. Low taxes and prices draw three million bargain hunters a year. In alpine meadows, hikers camp near grazing sheep. In snowy peaks that once isolated Andorra, skiers enjoy a six-month season.

Semi-independent under both French and Spanish co-princes, Andorra is known as a co-principality. It has no army, airport, or railroad. But the governments provide two of everything else: courts, post offices, currencies. Kids can even choose to attend a French or a Spanish school.

OFFICIAL NAME: The Valleys of Andorra
AREA: 180 sq mi (466 sq km)
POPULATION: 29,000
CAPITAL: Andorra (pop. 2,000)
ETHNIC GROUPS: Spanish, also Catalan, French.
LANGUAGE: Catalan, Spanish, French. **RELIGION:** Roman Catholic. **ECONOMY:** sheep, tobacco, tourism, wood. **CURRENCY:** franc, peseta.

Portugal

Along the Douro River Valley in northern Portugal, vineyards on terraces cling to hillsides. In autumn, pickers fill baskets with purple grapes. Then workers press out the juice in huge vats by treading on the grapes with bare feet.

Another important product is cork. It comes from the rolling hills of the Alentejo area. Here workers strip bark off cork-oak trees. It is used in bottle stoppers, insulation, and life jackets. The Alentejo's farms and ranches also produce wheat, beef, pork, and bulls specially bred for bullfighting.

The eventual result: port wine. It is shipped all over the world from Oporto, where the Douro empties into the sea. Both the famed wine, and Portugal itself, were named after "the port of Oporto."

The Portuguese have always looked toward the sea. Portugal's explorers created a worldwide empire. Most overseas possessions are gone, but the nation remains a leader in shipping and fishing. Dried codfish is a national dish, and Portuguese housewives say they know 365 ways to cook it — one for every day in the year.

OFFICIAL NAME: Portuguese Republic
AREA: 36,400 sq mi (94,300 sq km)
POPULATION: 9,830,000
CAPITAL: Lisbon (pop. 830,000)
ETHNIC GROUPS: Arab, Berber, Celtic, Iberian.
LANGUAGE: Portuguese. **RELIGION:** Roman Catholic. **ECONOMY:** chemicals, cork, fish, grains, metals, oil refining, olives, paper, resin, shoes, textiles, wine, wood. **CURRENCY:** escudo.

Spain

In a tiled kitchen in Valencia, a Spanish girl helps prepare supper for her family. While she lightly fries bits of pork, sausage, and chicken in olive oil, her mother readies clams and mussels. All are combined with shrimp, lobster, peas, and saffron rice. The result is *paella,* a classic dish flavored with the history and geography of Spain.

Cut off from Europe by the Pyrenees Mountains, ancient Spain was wide open to the sea. A succession of visitors came to call: Phoenicians, Greeks, Carthaginians. The Romans conquered and departed. In 711 the Moors — Muslim Arabs from Africa — came and stayed nearly 800 years. Besides art and learning they brought *za faran* — saffron — the spice that colors rice in paella yellow. Spanish courtyards filled with greenery and splashing fountains are another legacy of the desert people.

Central Spain is mostly a dry, barren plateau crisscrossed by mountain ranges. Romans, and later the Moors, brought irrigation plans but little else to the farm villages huddled around turreted castles. Life was better in coastal towns, where fishing added to the food supply.

In 1492 the Moors were driven out. The separate regions of Spain united under Catholicism, and Columbus's daring voyage launched the Spanish empire. The colonies are gone, but the church, supported by the state, still is central to Spanish life. Hundreds of fiestas, or festivals, honor saints each year — and delight tourists.

Farming remains important, for Spain is a leading supplier of olives, wine, cork, and citrus fruit. But more than half the people live and work in cities. The busy factories of Madrid, Barcelona, and Bilbao no longer shut down so workers can take an afternoon siesta, or nap. Even the bullfight, the traditional pageant of danger and courage, is losing ground. The country's most popular sport today is soccer.

OFFICIAL NAME: Spanish State
AREA: 195,000 sq mi (505,100 sq km)
POPULATION: 36,734,000
CAPITAL: Madrid (pop. 3,500,000)
ETHNIC GROUPS: Andalusian, Castilian, Catalan, Galician, Valencian. **LANGUAGE:** Spanish, also Catalan, Galician. **RELIGION:** Roman Catholic. **ECONOMY:** chemicals, cork, fish, fruit, grains, iron, mercury, motor vehicles, olives, potatoes, sheep, shoes, steel, sugar, textiles, tourism, wine. **CURRENCY:** peseta.

1

2

Spain

1 *Pageants all over Spain mark Easter's Holy Week, a time to remember Christ's last days and a time to repent one's sins. Hoods date from days when sorrowful sinners sought to keep faces hidden.*

2 *With red* muleta *the matador guides the charging bull, risking death gracefully before he makes the kill. Banderillas stuck in the bull's neck keep the head low. Bullfighting, not for all tastes, is the traditional sport of Spain.*

3 *International sport of beach bathing fills the lovely Mediterranean shore of Benidorm—and the high-rises on its rim. Some years the number of tourists in Spain may equal the nation's population.*

Portugal

4 *Portugal lives on fish. From every port boats set out each day to try their luck. Sometimes, like the* Marbel *here at Nazare, they return to a nasty surf.*

5 *What the boats bring in, fishwives put up for sale. So do canneries; Portugal is a world leader in producing sardines.*

3

5

4

Asia

Lashed by icy blizzards, snow-covered Mount Everest towers into the clouds, five and a half miles above sea level. Few climbers have conquered its windswept summit. But they continue to try, as one of them said, "Because it is there." The highest point on earth, Everest crowns the Himalayas.

Larger than North and South America combined, Asia makes up almost a third of the earth's land surface. From the eastern Mediterranean to the shores of the Pacific, it stretches some 6,000 miles. It reaches from the Arctic to the Equator, from frozen Siberian coasts to Indonesia's steaming jungles.

Where Asia touches Europe, mapmakers have drawn the boundary. It runs along the Ural Mountains, down through the Caspian and Black seas into the Mediterranean, and on through the Suez Canal and the Red Sea. The Indian Ocean laps against southern Asia. Its jagged shoreline ranges from the dry sands of the Arabian Peninsula in the west to the green rain forests of the Malay Peninsula in the east.

From Himalayan heights mighty rivers flow. Southward into the Indian Ocean drain the Indus, the Brahmaputra, and the sacred Ganges, where Hindu pilgrims come to wash away their

Mount Everest wears a feather of cloud in its snowy cap as it beckons expert climbers to high adventure. The topmost of our planet's peaks, this Himalayan giant reaches up 29,028 feet (8,848 m) between the lofty lands of Nepal and Tibet. The summit was first photographed by air in 1933 and first climbed in 1953.

sins. Through Southeast Asia snakes
the Mekong River, lifeline for millions.
The Yangtze and Yellow plunge from
Tibetan highlands and twist across China's plains. Most of northern Asia's river systems empty into the Arctic Ocean.

Flat, frozen tundra covers northernmost Asia. South of it stretches the
taiga, a belt of dense evergreen forest
larger in area than the United States.
Vast treeless plains sweep across central Asia. In these sparsely populated
regions, herdsmen drive cattle and live
in tents. Nomads roam huge deserts
that cut across the continent, from the
Gobi in Mongolia to the Empty Quarter
on the Arabian Peninsula.

Monsoon rains drench Southeast
Asia. In terraced paddies and flooded
fields, peasants bend their backs to harvest rice, the basic food of Asia's millions. When the seasonal rains fail to
come, famines kill thousands.

More than half the world's people
live in Asia, most of them in the
lowlands of India and China. Despite
birth control measures, population expands at the rate of 100,000 a day. People live longer because of better medical
care. In Calcutta an average of 80,000
persons jam every square mile.

Population pressures put impossible
demands on Asia's food resources. Crop
failures, crude agricultural methods,
and the destruction of war have forced
many countries to import food from the
Western world. Western farming practices are also being adopted. In some
areas the introduction of new strains of
rice and other grains have produced

more food. But the spreading of desert
areas, particularly in India and Pakistan, limits production.

Asia gave birth to the world's great
religions. Hinduism has the most followers. Buddhism flowed from India to
Sri Lanka, Southeast Asia, China, and
Japan. Almost 20 percent of Asians are
Muslims. Christianity has more believers throughout the world than any other
faith. But, outside Lebanon, Cyprus,
Russia, and the Philippines, relatively
few Christians live in Asia.

Great civilizations took hold in Asia
some 50 centuries ago. Between the Tigris and Euphrates rivers flourished the
Sumerians, who invented a way of writing on clay tablets. Then came the Babylonians, who developed a system of
writing down a code of laws and built
walled cities. New ideas spread through
the Indus Valley in what is now Pakistan and along the Yellow River in China. From Asia came the wheel, mechanical printing, silk, and gunpowder.

For centuries nomadic tribes surged
out of central Asia to loot and conquer.
Aryans, Huns, Tatars, and Mongols all
left their marks. During the 13th century Kublai Khan ruled most of Asia.

Mongoloid peoples (Mongolians, Chinese, Japanese, Koreans) make up one
of Asia's principal racial groups. Many
people of Caucasian stock live in India
and western Asia. Some black groups
are native to the Malay Peninsula, the
Philippines and other island clusters.

Many languages echo throughout the
continent, and dialects number in the
thousands. The people of one Indian
state alone speak nearly 400 tongues.

Facts About Asia

SIZE: 17,300,000 sq mi
(44,808,000 sq km)

POPULATION: 2,602,000,000

DENSITY: 150 persons for every sq mi
(58 per sq km)

HIGHEST POINT: *Mount Everest,
Nepal/Tibet, 29,028 ft (8,848 m)
above sea level

LOWEST POINT: shore of *Dead Sea,
Israel/Jordan, 1,302 ft (397 m) below
sea level

LARGEST COUNTRY: (by area)
*U.S.S.R., excluding European
Russia, 6,471,000 sq mi (16,760,000
sq km)

LARGEST COUNTRY: (by population)
*China 1,003,855,000

LARGEST METROPOLITAN AREAS:
(by population)
*Tokyo   24,900,000
Shanghai   10,900,000
Calcutta   9,100,000
Seoul   8,700,000
Peking   7,600,000
Bombay   6,800,000

LONGEST RIVERS: (mi and km)

Yangtze	3,400	5,400
Yellow	2,900	4,600
Amur	2,700	4,300
Lena	2,600	4,100
Mekong	2,600	4,100

LARGEST LAKES: (sq mi and sq km)

*Caspian Sea	143,500	371,600
Record saltwater lake		
Aral Sea	25,300	65,500
Lake Baykal	11,700	30,300
Lake Balkhash	7,100	18,300

*World Record

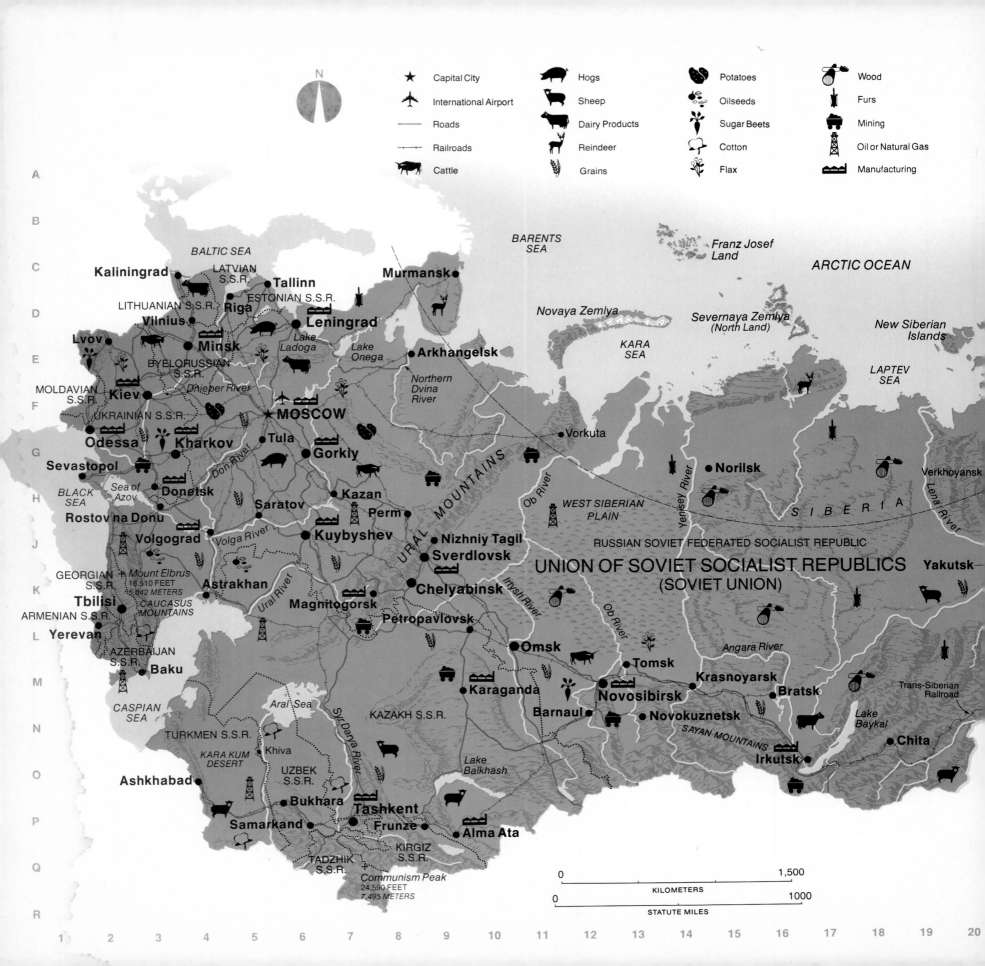

Legend

★ Capital City
✈ International Airport
— Roads
╫ Railroads
🐂 Cattle

🐖 Hogs
🐑 Sheep
🐄 Dairy Products
🦌 Reindeer
🌾 Grains

🥔 Potatoes
Oilseeds
🌱 Sugar Beets
Cotton
Flax

Wood
Furs
Mining
Oil or Natural Gas
Manufacturing

UNION OF SOVIET SOCIALIST REPUBLICS (SOVIET UNION)

RUSSIAN SOVIET FEDERATED SOCIALIST REPUBLIC

ARCTIC OCEAN

BARENTS SEA
KARA SEA
LAPTEV SEA

Franz Josef Land
Novaya Zemlya
Severnaya Zemlya (North Land)
New Siberian Islands

BALTIC SEA

Kaliningrad
LATVIAN S.S.R.
Tallinn
ESTONIAN S.S.R.
Murmansk
LITHUANIAN S.S.R.
Riga
Vilnius
Leningrad
Lvov
Minsk
BYELORUSSIAN S.S.R.
Lake Ladoga
Lake Onega
Arkhangelsk
Northern Dvina River
MOLDAVIAN S.S.R.
Kiev
Dnieper River
UKRAINIAN S.S.R.
MOSCOW
Odessa
Kharkov
Tula
Gorkiy
Vorkuta
Norilsk
Verkhoyansk
Sevastopol
Don River
SIBERIA
Lena River
BLACK SEA
Sea of Azov
Donetsk
Saratov
Kazan
Perm
URAL MOUNTAINS
Ob River
WEST SIBERIAN PLAIN
Yenisey River
Rostov na Donu
Nizhniy Tagil
Volgograd
Volga River
Kuybyshev
Sverdlovsk
Yakutsk
GEORGIAN S.S.R.
Mount Elbrus 18,510 FEET 5,642 METERS
Astrakhan
Ural River
Chelyabinsk
Irtysh River
Ob River
Tbilisi
CAUCASUS MOUNTAINS
Magnitogorsk
Angara River
ARMENIAN S.S.R.
Yerevan
Petropavlovsk
Omsk
Tomsk
Krasnoyarsk
Bratsk
AZERBAIJAN S.S.R.
Baku
CASPIAN SEA
Aral Sea
Karaganda
Barnaul
Novosibirsk
Novokuznetsk
Trans-Siberian Railroad
KAZAKH S.S.R.
Lake Baykal
TURKMEN S.S.R.
KARA KUM DESERT
Khiva
Syr Darya River
Lake Balkhash
SAYAN MOUNTAINS
Chita
Irkutsk
Ashkhabad
UZBEK S.S.R.
Bukhara
Samarkand
Tashkent
Frunze
Alma Ata
KIRGIZ S.S.R.
TADZHIK S.S.R.
Communism Peak 24,590 FEET 7,495 METERS

0		1,500

KILOMETERS

| 0 | | 1000 |

STATUTE MILES

CHUKCHI SEA

Bering Strait

Wrangel Island

EAST SIBERIAN SEA

Kolyma River

ARCTIC CIRCLE

SIBERIA

BERING SEA

Kamchatka Peninsula

Oymyakon

Magadan

Petropavlovsk Kamchatskiy

SEA OF OKHOTSK

Sakhalin Island

Kuril Islands

Komsomolsk

Amur River

Khabarovsk

Vladivostok

SEA OF JAPAN

U.S.S.R.

This is the biggest country on earth, so vast that a popular saying goes, "The Soviet Union is not a country but a world." It stretches some 3,000 miles north and south, and about 6,800 miles east and west, spanning 11 time zones. It is more than twice the size of the United States, including Alaska.

The varied landscape, spilling into both Europe and Asia, is a lesson in geography. In the icy north the ground remains permanently frozen. Winter temperatures in Siberia average 50° below zero F (–46° C); some people even sleep on top of their ovens. Wolves and reindeer roam the snow-shrouded pine forests. Siberia's Lake Baykal is 25 million years old and a mile deep — oldest and deepest lake on earth. It holds a fifth of the world's fresh water.

Far to the southwest, camels plod the sand dunes of central Asia. The world's longest irrigation canal, planned to stretch more than 800 miles, is bringing new life — cotton, melons, grapes — to the Kara Kum Desert. The minarets and mosques of Bukhara and fabled Samarkand reveal Muslim, Turkish, and Persian influences.

West of the Ural Mountains, European Russia begins, dominated by the great cities of Moscow and Leningrad. Boats and barges ply the 2,290-mile (3,685 km) Volga River, the longest in Europe. Wheat and corn grow in the Ukraine's black soil — the fertile sediment of Ice Age glaciers.

The people are as varied as the land. Many of us think of the Soviet Union as Russia and everyone as Russians. But Russia is just one of 15 republics in a country that embraces more than 100 cultures.

The Russians, just over half the population, are Slavic in origin. An Estonian farmer is blond and speaks a Finnic tongue as well as Russian. Georgians, famed for living long lives, write their language in an ancient alphabet used nowhere else. The Kazakh cowboy has Oriental features and speaks a Turkic language. The Tuvans, who live in the snowy Sayan Mountains, travel on fur-covered skis. (The hairs keep skis from slipping backward.)

The heart of the country is Moscow. And the heart of Moscow is the Kremlin. This city-within-a-city is the seat of government and headquarters of the Communist Party. Forbidding brick walls surround palaces, churches, museums, and offices.

It was back in the 15th century that Moscow expanded from a small village into the center of a large and powerful state. Under such rulers as Catherine the Great, Peter the Great, and Ivan the Terrible, rich and poor alike lived under the shadow of the tsars, or kings. Under the system of serfdom peasants were bound to a master as if they were slaves. Tsar Alexander II freed the serfs in 1861. Then, in 1917, Tsarist Russia came tumbling down, and the October Revolution of that year brought the Communist Bolsheviks to power. Revolutionaries later killed Tsar Nicholas II and his family. Today statues of the Communist leader V. I. Lenin stand in town squares; his portraits look down on Soviet classrooms.

In 1922 the country was proclaimed the Union of Soviet Socialist Republics. "Soviet" refers to citizens' councils that meet to discuss government affairs. The government decides everything: how many apartments will be built, how much wheat the farmers will plant, who will mine coal, and who will dance ballet. Careers outside the home are open to women. Seventy percent of the doctors, half the factory workers, and a third of all graduate engineers are women.

In the cities families live in small apartments, but rents are cheap. At the end of the day, workers go grocery shopping. They buy what's available, usually milk, potatoes, bread, cheese, and cabbage.

The farms are not privately owned. Some farmers work together on collectives and share earnings. Others work for wages on huge state farms run by the government. Skillful workers earn rewards. A silkworm breeder near Samarkand, who often brought in bumper crops of cocoons, won the Order of Lenin, the Order of the October Revolution, a car, and free vacations to resorts in the Caucasus Mountains.

Some families till small plots of state-owned land on their own, selling their fruits and vegetables in local markets. It's one way that farmers earn extra money.

Nowadays many Soviet citizens from both cities and farms are beginning new lives in Siberia. For centuries Siberia was feared as a frozen wasteland, a place for prisoners and runaway serfs. Verkhoyansk and Oymyakon, where temperatures drop to 96° below zero F (–71° C), are the coldest towns in the world. Yet today Siberia is called the "land of the long ruble" because workers receive extra pay to help develop the land. Under all that snow and ice is a vast fortune in oil, gas, coal, gold, and other resources. A legend says that when God created Earth, he dropped a sack of riches on Siberia. Why? Because his hands were frozen.

OFFICIAL NAME: Union of Soviet Socialist Republics
AREA: 8,594,500 sq mi (22,259,800 sq km)
POPULATION: 259,234,000
CAPITAL: Moscow (pop. 7,644,000)
ETHNIC GROUPS: Russian, Ukranian, other Slavic groups, also Turkic. **LANGUAGE:** Russian, other Slavic tongues, also Turkic languages. **RELIGION:** Russian Orthodox, Muslim. (Government discourages religion.) **ECONOMY:** coal, cotton, flax, furs, grains, iron, livestock, machinery, natural gas, oil, oilseeds, potatoes, steel, sugar, wood. **CURRENCY:** ruble.

1

3

4

U.S.S.R.

1 *Some two million reindeer, 80 percent of the world's total, roam Siberia. They provide transportation, clothing, and food for many northern nomads.*

2 *Milksicles? You can buy your milk solid during winter in Irkutsk. Use the stick frozen in the center for carrying your chunk of milk home to thaw and drink.*

3 *A farmer wearing the bushy sheepskin hat of the Turkmen steers his cart down a street in Khiva, Uzbekistan.*

4 *Wheat thrives in the rich black soil of the Ukraine, among the most fertile of Soviet republics. Small compared to Russia, the Ukraine is still larger than the largest nation in non-Soviet Europe.*

U.S.S.R.

1 *Moscow's Red Square looks its color on May Day, when troops carrying crimson flags honor this national holiday. Atop the Kremlin's walls a clock tower faces onion-domed St. Basil's Cathedral. Red Square's name actually has nothing to do with politics; it comes from an old Russian word for "beautiful."*

2 *In costumes white as the snow outside, ballet dancers perform in an opera hall at Novosibirsk, largest city in Siberia. This land doesn't always shiver; summer temperatures may soar into the nineties.*

3 *A tractor army marches off the assembly line in Volgograd—"City of the Volga." Russians sometimes call their great river Mother Volga, because their nation grew to importance along its banks.*

N

0 ——————————— 500
KILOMETERS

0 ——————————— 300
STATUTE MILES

★ Capital City
✈ International Airport
— Roads
┼┼ Railroads
🌾 Grains
🥬 Vegetables
🍒 Fruit
🌿 Sugar Beets
🎋 Sugarcane
🪣 Wood
🐟 Fishing
🛒 Mining
🏭 Manufacturing

NORTH KOREA

Paektu
9,003 FEET
2,744 METERS ✚

Tu man River

Najin
Chongjin

Manpo

Yalu River

Kimchaek

Sinuiju

Taedong River

Hungnam

PYONGYANG ★ ✈

Korea Bay

Nampo

Wonsan

Kosong

Kaesong

Sokcho

Inchon

Chunchon

SEOUL ★

Suwon

SOUTH KOREA

YELLOW SEA

Han River

Chongju

Taejon

Naktong River

Chonju

Taegu

Pohang

Kwangju

Masan

Ulsan

Mokpo

Yosu

Pusan

Cheju Island Cheju

KOREA STRAIT

Kitakyushu

Fukuoka

Suo Sea

Sasebo

Beppu

Goto Retto

✚ *Mount Aso*

SHIKOKU

Matsuyama

Nagasaki

Kumamoto

EAST CHINA SEA

Kagoshima

KYUSHU

Osumi Islands

Teshio River

Asahigawa

Ishikari River

Sapporo

Kushiro

HOKKAIDO

Uchiura Bay

Hakodate

Tsugaru Strait

Aomori

Hachinohe

Akita

Morioka

HONSHU

Kitakami River

Sendai

Sado

Niigata

Shinano River

JAPAN

SEA OF JAPAN

Oki Islands

Toyama

Kanazawa

Nagano

Utsunomiya

Maebashi

Wakasa Bay

Gifu

Lake Biwa

TOKYO ★

Yokohama

Himeji

Kyoto

Nagoya

Okayama

Kobe

Osaka

Mount Fuji
12,388 FEET
3,776 METERS

Sakai

Shizuoka

Hiroshima

Wakamaya

Hamamatsu

Inland Sea

PACIFIC OCEAN

Amami Islands

Okinawa

Naha

Sakishima Islands

RYUKYU ISLANDS

Japan

Hikers carrying sleeping bags and canteens challenge the highest mountain in Japan—Mount Fuji. The 12,388-foot (3,776 m) peak is held sacred by followers of the Buddhist and Shinto religions. About halfway to the top, Fuji climbers stop at a way station to spend the night. Before dawn they awake and hurry in the morning chill to reach the summit, where they can see the sun rising over the Pacific. More than 100,000 people make the climb every year.

At night the distant lights of Tokyo can be seen from Fuji. Tokyo is the heart of the world's largest metropolitan area. Including Yokohama, it totals more than 24 million people. Their Westernized life-styles and hard-driving work habits show the spirit of the new Japan—rebuilt from World War II ruins to top-rank industrial power.

Along neon-lit streets of Tokyo's Ginza district, shoppers crowd restaurants and stores. Tables are set up in some streets on weekends, when cars are banned. Diners may feast on *sushi* (raw fish and rice), noodles, or broiled sparrow. On weekdays commuters jam the subways, where uniformed "people pushers" shove them into the cars. "Bullet trains" to Osaka reach speeds of more than 150 miles an hour.

Most Japanese live in teeming cities on Honshu, largest of the nation's four major islands. Apartments and cottages reflect modern influences as well as old ways. Refrigerators and televisions share space with charcoal stoves and mats that serve as beds. Children bow to parents as a sign of respect. In school, pupils learn to write the 1,850 characters in the Japanese language. A favorite sport is *beisuboru*—baseball.

Spectators gather in arenas to watch 300-pound (136 kg) sumo wrestlers. Before a match they clap hands to call the gods, a practice also seen at Buddhist temples and Shinto shrines. Robed Shinto priests sometimes bless boats headed for the ripping currents of the Inland Sea. To the south, on the island of Kyushu, steams the world's largest active volcano crater, Mount Aso.

OFFICIAL NAME: Japan
AREA: 143,000 sq mi (370,300 sq km)
POPULATION: 114,983,000
CAPITAL: Tokyo (pop. 8,544,000)
ETHNIC GROUPS: Japanese. **LANGUAGE:** Japanese. **RELIGION:** Buddhist, Shintoist. **ECONOMY:** chemicals, electronics, engineering, fish, fruit, grains, machinery, motor vehicles, ships, steel, sugar, textiles, vegetables. **CURRENCY:** yen.

North Korea

Baby palaces. That's the name North Koreans give nursery schools run by the government. While mothers work in factories, young voices sing, "We Are the Happiest Children in the World." Pupils attend school six days a week for ten years. Besides learning to read and write, they master other skills such as sewing and auto repair.

Guided by the slogan "Learn while working and work while learning," North Koreans look to mythical Chollima, a statue of a winged horse overlooking the capital city of Pyongyang. Chollima symbolizes efforts to build a strong nation. Pyongyang boasts skyscrapers and a sports stadium that can seat 70,000 people.

Most North Koreans live on the coastal plains that flank the central mountains. From 9,003-foot (2,744 m) Paektu, the highest peak, flows the Yalu River. Cold air from Siberia blows across it in winter, often dropping temperatures to −6° F (−21° C).

OFFICIAL NAME: Democratic People's Republic of Korea
AREA: 47,000 sq mi (121,700 sq km)
POPULATION: 18,134,000
CAPITAL: Pyongyang (pop. 840,000)
ETHNIC GROUPS: Korean. **LANGUAGE:** Korean. **RELIGION:** Buddhist, Confucianist. (Government discourages religion.) **ECONOMY:** cement, chemicals, coal, grains, machinery, metals, textiles, vegetables. **CURRENCY:** won.

South Korea

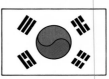

Schoolboys in sneakers and jeans spin tops on a sidewalk in Seoul. Their clothes look like those worn in the United States, and for good reason. South Korea, the southern half of the Korean peninsula, makes and sells much of the clothing worn in the United States. Factories and shops turn out a flood of modern things, from television sets to plastic boots.

In farm villages, by contrast, time has brought little change in recent years. Oxen pull plows through terraced fields. Women in long skirts worn over baggy trousers chop cabbages, turnips, and red peppers for spicy *kimchi*. Older people wear stovepipe hats made of woven horsehair.

City dwellers live in high-rise apartments and tile-roofed houses spiked with television antennas. In winter, coal stoves heat most homes; the warm air circulates through stone-lined pipes under the floor.

OFFICIAL NAME: Republic of Korea
AREA: 38,000 sq mi (98,400 sq km)
POPULATION: 38,869,000
CAPITAL: Seoul (pop. 6,889,000)
ETHNIC GROUPS: Korean. **LANGUAGE:** Korean. **RELIGION:** Buddhist, also Christian, Confucianist, shamanist. **ECONOMY:** chemicals, electronics, fertilizer, fish, grains, machinery, ships, shoes, steel, textiles, wood. **CURRENCY:** won.

1

2

3

Japan

1 *Doll-faced drummer girl performs in a Kyoto geisha house. A geisha—which means "art person"—entertains guests with song, dance, and conversation.*

2 *Blue-coated technicians assemble color television sets at a plant near Osaka. Mass-produced Japanese goods are exported to buyers around the globe.*

3 *Clouds wreathe Mount Fuji's summit. From a distant temple, Buddhist monks pay homage to the sacred mountain.*

4 *From an air-conditioned control booth, a supervisor directs work in a Kobe steel mill. Modern techniques make Japan a world industrial leader.*

5 *Bathed in blues of night, Osaka's shipyards and petrochemical plants crowd shores washed by the Inland Sea. Through Japan's ports pour iron ore, coal, and chemicals, the raw materials for her steel and textile mills.*

South Korea

1 *L-shaped houses of thatch and mud nestle together in a farm village.*

2 *Oil refinery at Ulsan awes a Korean elder wearing a traditional horsehair hat. Factories, power plants, four-lane highways, and new housing projects are changing the rural face of the nation.*

3 *Squid hang out to dry on lines at Sokcho, an east-coast port near the North Korean border. Each year fishermen catch tons of this favorite snack food.*

North Korea

4 *Haze dims ridges of the scenic Diamond Mountains, near Kosong. Much of the country is mountainous, limiting farms to coastal plains and river valleys.*

5 *Accordionists smile while they play at a junior high school near Pyongyang.*

Legend

★ Capital City
✈ International Airport
— Roads
+—+ Railroads
🐫 Camels
🐂 Cattle
🐖 Hogs
🐐 Goats
🐑 Sheep
🌾 Grains
🌱 Soybeans
🍎 Fruit
☁ Cotton
⛏ Mining
🛢 Oil or Natural Gas
🏭 Manufacturing

14,291 FEET
4,356 METERS

Hovsgol Lake
Uvs Lake

WALL of Genghis Khan

MANCHURIA

Hovd

• Darhan
• Choybalsan

Qiqihar •
• Harbin

ALTAI MOUNTAINS

Tsetserleg •

★ ULAANBAATAR

Herlen River

Changchun •
• Jilin

MONGOLIA

INNER MONGOLIA

Shenyang • Fushun

Anshan

• Dandong

Urumqi •

Orhon River

GOBI DESERT

25,340 FEET
7,724 METERS

SINKIANG

• Kashi

• Shache

Tarim River

Turpan Depression
-505 FEET
-154 METERS

Lop Nur Lake

TAKLIMAKAN DESERT

Baotou • Hohhot

PEKING (BEIJING) ★
• Luda

Yumen •

Great Wall

Tientsin •

Yinchuan •

Taiyuan • Shijiazhuang •

• Qingdao

YELLOW SEA

Area claimed by India

Qinghai Lake

Jinan •

Lanzhou •

Luoyang •

CHINA

Zhengzhou •

• Xian

• Wenquan

Yellow River

Grand Canal

Salween River

Yangtze River

Yangtze River

Nanjing • Wuxi •
Suzhou • • Shanghai

• Lhasa

Chengdu •

Wuhan •

Hangzhou •

Brahmaputra River

Mekong River

HIMALAYAS

+ Mount Everest
29,028 FEET
8,848 METERS
Highest point in the world

Chongqing •

Dongting Lake

Poyang Lake

EAST CHINA SEA

Changsha •

Nanchang •

Hengyang •

Fuzhou •

Guiyang •

• Taipei

Guilin •

Xiamen •

Taichung •

TAIWAN

N

Kunming •

Canton (Guangzhou) •

Kaohsiung •

1000

KILOMETERS

0   500

STATUTE MILES

Nanning •

MACAO (PORTUGAL)

HONG KONG (UNITED KINGDOM)

Gulf of Tonkin

• Haikou

HAINAN

SOUTH CHINA SEA

Liao River

Amur River

China

Schoolchildren in holiday dress line Peking's Boulevard of Eternal Peace to greet a foreign official. They clang cymbals, beat drums, and wave red banners. *"Huan ying!"* they shout. "Welcome!"

From walls and buildings hang giant posters announcing public events and urging workers to greater efforts. Under Communist rule since 1949, this ancient land recently has seen many changes, including a new system for writing Chinese words in the English alphabet. It's called Pinyin. In Pinyin, Peking becomes Beijing, a spelling that shows how the name actually sounds.

Crowds in Peking often gather before the 500-year-old Temple of Ancestors to hear speakers in what was once the "Forbidden City"—the emperor's palace grounds where common people could not enter. Now it's a public area of gardens and museums.

Slightly larger than the United States, China is shaped like a huge basin, separated from the rest of Asia by a rim of deserts, mountains, and plateaus. The western two-thirds lie high and dry, capped by 24,000-foot (7,315 m) peaks in Tibet. Irrigation has created oases in the vast Sinkiang region, sparsely settled but rich in metals, coal, and oil. In Manchuria, China's northeast, factories rise beside state-run farms.

With a population of over one billion, China works mostly at farming, though it cultivates only about one-eighth of its land. In the fertile Yangtze and Huang—or Yellow—river valleys, water buffaloes pull plows alongside modern tractors. Women toil elbow to elbow planting rice seedlings. Wheat ripens on terraced hills.

The eastern third of China, where most Chinese live, has a long coast sometimes lashed by fierce storms called typhoons. Ocean liners and Chinese junks crowd industrial Shanghai, China's largest city.

China's language changes from one region to another. The Mandarin dialect of Peking is not understood by people in South China, who speak Cantonese. Near Canton (Guangzhou) a silkworm factory cultivates cocoons. When unwrapped, each cocoon yields up to a thousand yards of silk thread.

Besides silk, China gave the Western world such things as gunpowder, pulp paper, wok cooking, movable type for printing—and pandas. Canton's zoo displays the panda along with elephants, monkeys, and domestic cats. Why cats? Because they are unusual here; the Chinese rarely keep pets.

In 1949, as Communists were winning control of mainland China, many Chinese chose to flee. They picked China's only island province, Taiwan, as their new home. They took their own "Nationalist" government with them, and made Taipei their capital. Taiwan kept its United Nations seat until 1971, when other countries voted it out in favor of the mainland government. Both Taipei and Peking say that Taiwan is part of China, but neither government has had any control over the other's territory.

The first Europeans to visit Taiwan, in 1517, were Portuguese. They called the island Formosa—Beautiful. The name is still heard and fits well: lofty mountains ridge the island, giving birth to swift rivers.

Farmers till every available inch. Rice paddies cut into hillsides like stairsteps. Pineapples ripen in the subtropical sun. Asparagus grows along riverbanks. In the fields farm girls shade themselves by wearing hats as big as parasols. They help the men harvest rice, saving the stalks for fuel, livestock feed, and papermaking.

About 17 million people—some native Taiwanese, some refugees from the mainland—now crowd into Taiwan's 12,400 square miles (32,200 sq km). They have built their island into a manufacturing center; its economy is one of the strongest in the Far East. If you look carefully at the items around your house, you can probably find a few that bear the label "Made in Taiwan."

OFFICIAL NAME: People's Republic of China
AREA: 3,706,500 sq mi (9,600,000 sq km)
POPULATION: 1,003,855,000
CAPITAL: Peking (pop. 4,800,000)
ETHNIC GROUPS: Chinese. **LANGUAGE:** Mandarin Chinese, Cantonese. **RELIGION:** ancestor worship, Buddhist, Confucianist, Taoist. **ECONOMY:** cement, coal, cotton, fruit, grains, iron, livestock, machinery, oil, salt, soybeans, steel, textiles, tin, tungsten. **CURRENCY:** yuan.

Mongolia

In this fenceless land—about the size of Alaska—wandering tribesmen follow trails of Genghis Khan and other ancient warriors.

Now Mongolia has traded the sword for the ballpoint pen. All Mongol children have to learn reading and writing. Most families live in domed tents and dine on mutton and fermented mare's milk. Near Ulaanbaatar tents sprout television antennas, and you may see a motorbike parked at the door.

Mongolia looks much like Wyoming—rugged mountains, grassy plains, rolling hills. On the Gobi Desert two-humped Bactrian camels walk where dinosaurs roamed.

OFFICIAL NAME: Mongolian People's Republic
AREA: 604,100 sq mi (1,564,600 sq km)
POPULATION: 1,587,000
CAPITAL: Ulaanbaatar (pop. 267,400)
ETHNIC GROUPS: Mongolian. **LANGUAGE:** Mongolian. **RELIGION:** Buddhist. (Government discourages religion.) **ECONOMY:** camels, cattle, cement, coal, fluorite, goats, grains, meat, sheep, wool. **CURRENCY:** togrog.

China

1 *Engineering marvel of the ages, the Great Wall zigzags across mountains and valleys for 1,500 miles (2,414 km)—about the distance between Washington, D.C., and Denver, Colorado. Built 22 centuries ago to keep out invaders from the north, it was made wide enough for horses and wagons. Sightseers climb to watchtowers once manned by soldiers. New bricks top 25-foot-high (8 m) restored walls.*

2 *Grandmother baby-sits while parents work. Thanks to the bottomless garment, she does not have to change diapers.*

3 *School begins with a reading lesson in the walled city of Xian, ancient capital of China. Students fold arms behind their backs and pay strict attention.*

4 *Women bundle rice seedlings for transplanting. Three out of four Chinese live in villages and work on farms.*

2

3

4

China

1 *Chopsticks dip into steaming noodles in a Chinese kindergarten. Why chopsticks? Because they work well on food cooked in small pieces—the usual style in the Far East. Chopsticks were around more than a thousand years before knives and forks.*

2 *Terraced paddies pattern hills north of Taipei. Farmers on Taiwan, most of whom own their land, use tractors as well as water buffaloes to plow fields.*

Mongolia

3 *Hard-riding cowboy snares a wild horse with the noose at the end of a pole. On the steppes—the dry plains—a horse is worth 14 goats or half a camel. Some students, eager for an education, travel 40 miles (64 km) a day by horseback.*

4 *Goats and a ger—a collapsible canvas home—cast long shadows at twilight. Mongol girls milk sheep, cows, yaks, camels, and mares as well as goats.*

3

4

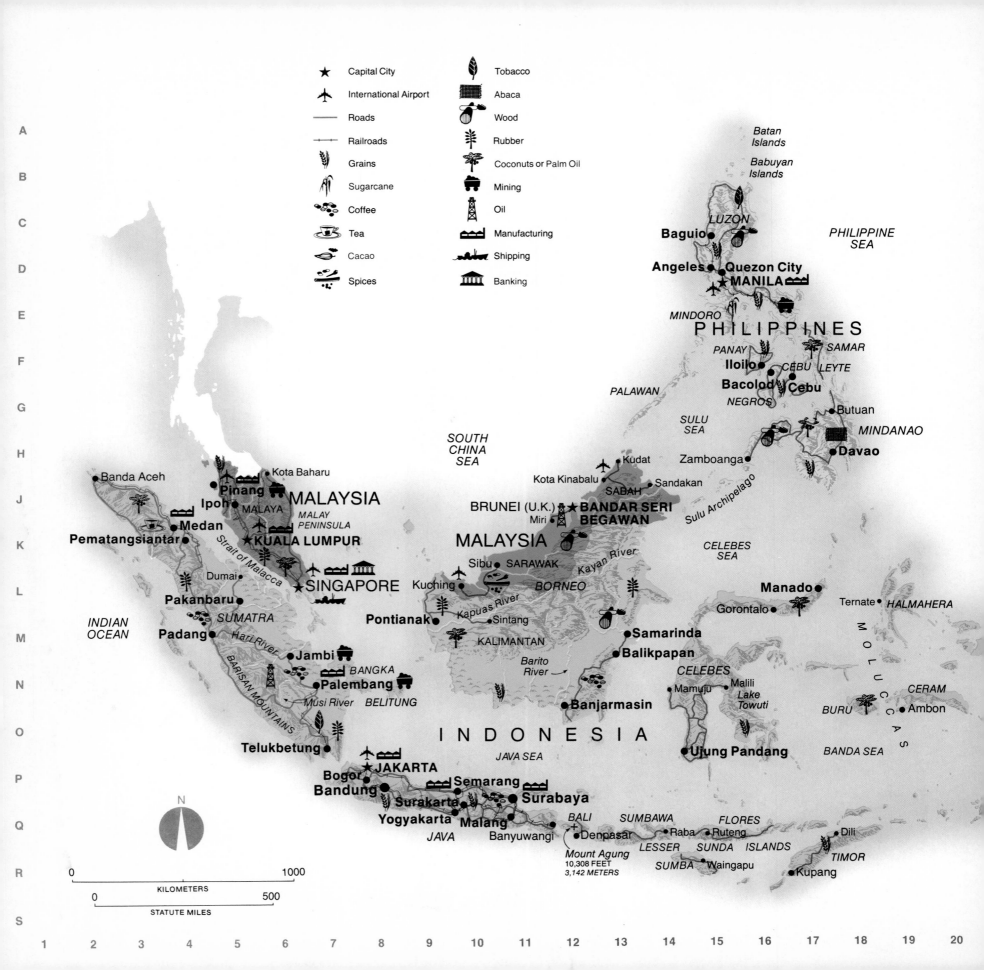

★	Capital City
✈	International Airport
—	Roads
⊢⊢	Railroads
🌾	Grains
🎋	Sugarcane
☕	Coffee
🍵	Tea
🥥	Cacao
🌶	Spices

🍃	Tobacco
▦	Abaca
🪵	Wood
🌿	Rubber
🌴	Coconuts or Palm Oil
🛒	Mining
⛏	Oil
🏭	Manufacturing
⛴	Shipping
🏛	Banking

A
B
C
D
E
F
G
H
J
K
L
M
N
O
P
Q
R
S

Batan Islands

Babuyan Islands

LUZON

Baguio

PHILIPPINE SEA

Angeles **Quezon City**
★ **MANILA**

MINDORO

PHILIPPINES

PANAY *SAMAR*
Iloilo *CEBU* *LEYTE*
Bacolod **Cebu**

PALAWAN *NEGROS*

Butuan

SULU SEA

MINDANAO

Zamboanga

Davao

Banda Aceh

Kota Baharu

Pinang **MALAYSIA**

Ipoh *MALAYA* *MALAY PENINSULA*

Medan

Pematangsiantar

★ **KUALA LUMPUR**

Dumai

Strait of Malacca

SOUTH CHINA SEA

Kudat

Kota Kinabalu Sandakan

BRUNEI (U.K.) ★ **BANDAR SERI BEGAWAN**
Miri

MALAYSIA

SABAH

Sulu Archipelago

CELEBES SEA

Manado

Gorontalo Ternate *HALMAHERA*

✈ ⛴ 🏛 **SINGAPORE**

Pakanbaru

SUMATRA

Padang

Hari River

Sibu *SARAWAK* *Kayan River*

Kuching *BORNEO*

Sintang *Kapuas River*

Pontianak

KALIMANTAN

Barito River

Samarinda

Balikpapan

CELEBES

Mamuju Malili *Lake Towuti*

MOLUCCAS

BURU *CERAM*

Ambon

Jambi

BANGKA

Palembang

BELITUNG

Musi River

Telukbetung

INDONESIA

Banjarmasin

Ujung Pandang

JAVA SEA

BANDA SEA

N

★ **JAKARTA**

Bogor
Bandung

Semarang **Surabaya**

Surakarta

Yogyakarta **Malang**

JAVA Banyuwangi

BALI Denpasar

Mount Agung
10,308 FEET
3,142 METERS

SUMBAWA *FLORES*

Raba Ruteng

LESSER SUNDA ISLANDS

SUMBA Waingapu

Dili

TIMOR

Kupang

INDIAN OCEAN

BARISAN MOUNTAINS

0 ———————————— 1000
KILOMETERS
0 ———————————— 500
STATUTE MILES

1 2 3 4 5 6 7 8 9 10 11 12 13 14 15 16 17 18 19 20

Brunei

Oil and natural gas have made Brunei a tiny pocket of luxury. There's free health care, high salaries, inexpensive gasoline for the many air-conditioned cars, and no income tax. In the backcountry, tribal Ibans watch color television in jungle longhouses.

Brunei is notched into the Borneo coast in two pieces. Long ago the raja of neighboring Sarawak "stole" a river valley, cutting Brunei in two. Brunei's ruler, the sultan, would like the valley back.

Although nearly independent, Brunei has kept close ties to Britain. When Queen Elizabeth came to call, the sultan had 30 turbaned men pull her through the steamy capital in his special golden chariot.

OFFICIAL NAME: State of Brunei
AREA: 2,220 sq mi (5,770 sq km)
POPULATION: 177,000
CAPITAL: Bandar Seri Begawan (pop. 17,500)
ETHNIC GROUPS: Malay, also Chinese, local tribes. **LANGUAGE:** English, Malay, also Chinese. **RELIGION:** Muslim, also animist, Buddhist, Christian. **ECONOMY:** grains, natural gas, oil, pepper, rubber. **CURRENCY:** dollar.

Indonesia

The unexpected is to be expected on Indonesia's 13,000 islands of surprise, the world's largest archipelago. On a beach a boy picks up the family groceries: a newly caught shark half his size. Young men whirl in the traditional Monkey Dance. In the warm wet jungles the largest flower in the world, the rafflesia, displays almost three feet of smelly scarlet bloom.

Indonesia's population speaks 250 dialects and spans the centuries. Tribesmen in loincloths and feathers share their country with business tycoons in three-piece suits. About 65 percent of Indonesia's people live on Java, where smoking volcanoes enrich the soil with lava dust. The Christian Batak people of Sumatra worship in small, wooden country churches—an unusual sight in this Muslim country. In western New Guinea, primitive Dani don't bathe. They rub their bodies with pig fat instead.

Some Balinese believe their island of sunny beaches and terraced rice paddies is the center of the world—and their angry volcano, Mount Agung, the "world's navel."

Indonesia's rich natural resources promise a bright future. On Sumatra, an island almost as long as the distance from Canada to Mexico, rubber trees drip sap: tomorrow's tires and galoshes. Oil has helped change once-sleepy Jakarta into a metropolis of high-rise buildings and traffic jams.

Most Indonesians are farmers who own little more than a wooden plow and a bright, skirtlike sarong. They gather for dances and sport, cheering favorites at bullfights, cockfights, ram fights, even cricket fights.

OFFICIAL NAME: Republic of Indonesia
AREA: 736,000 sq mi (1,906,200 sq km)
POPULATION: 140,680,000
CAPITAL: Jakarta (pop. 4,576,000)
ETHNIC GROUPS: Javanese, also Sundanese, Madurese, Malay. **LANGUAGE:** Indonesian. **RELIGION:** Muslim, also Christian. **ECONOMY:** coconut, coffee, grains, oil, palm oil, rubber, tea, textiles, tin, tobacco, wood. **CURRENCY:** rupiah.

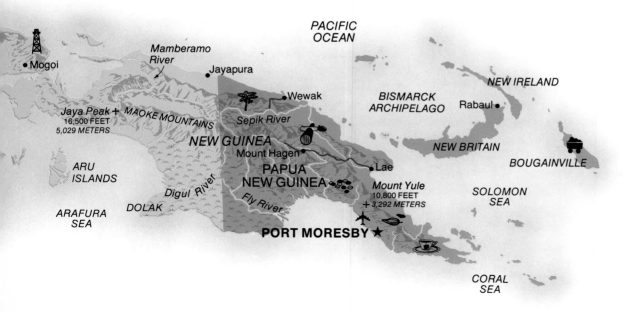

Mogoi

PACIFIC OCEAN

Mamberamo River

Jayapura

Wewak

BISMARCK ARCHIPELAGO

Rabaul

NEW IRELAND

Jaya Peak
16,500 FEET
5,029 METERS

MAOKE MOUNTAINS

Sepik River

NEW GUINEA

Mount Hagen

PAPUA NEW GUINEA

Lae

NEW BRITAIN

BOUGAINVILLE

ARU ISLANDS

Digul River

Fly River

Mount Yule
10,800 FEET
3,292 METERS

SOLOMON SEA

ARAFURA SEA

DOLAK

PORT MORESBY ★

CORAL SEA

Malaysia

Could you play volleyball with your feet as well as your hands? Tap a rubber tree properly? Do long division with the beads of an abacus? Many Malaysian children can.

Their prosperous nation, home to both Malays and Chinese, came into being in 1963 after more than a hundred years of British rule. Centuries earlier the Malay Peninsula was an important stop along the legendary spice route from Asia to Europe.

Today Malaysia is the world's largest producer of rubber, tin, and palm oil. The peninsula's hot, humid jungles hold tigers, butterflies, orchids—and deadly king cobras whose venom can kill an elephant.

In East Malaysia, 400 miles (644 km) across the sea, loggers and oil drillers lead a rugged life. Deep in the rain forests, tattooed Ibans live in giant longhouses, where one thatched roof may shelter more than fifty families. Some tribes own baskets of blackened human skulls. Head-hunting did not end here until the 1940's.

OFFICIAL NAME: Malaysia
AREA: 128,400 sq mi (332,600 sq km)
POPULATION: 12,864,000
CAPITAL: Kuala Lumpur (pop. 452,000)
ETHNIC GROUPS: Malay, Chinese, also East Indian, Pakistani, local tribes. LANGUAGE: Malay, also Chinese, English, Tamil, tribal tongues. RELIGION: Muslim, Buddhist, also Hindu, animist, Christian, Confucianist. ECONOMY: coconut, electronics, grains, oil, palm oil, pepper, rubber, tin, wood. CURRENCY: ringgit.

Papua New Guinea

Papua New Guinea is reaching out to modern times, even though some of its people are barely beyond the Stone Age. Gimi tribesmen hunt with bow and arrow. They use axes to clear the rugged land. Minj girls paint their faces with dots to look like a python's skin.

The country shares the muggy jungles of New Guinea with Indonesia. Rich copper mines help pay for development. The bird of paradise, the national emblem, preens its bright plumage in the trees. Tribal warriors like to wear the colorful feathers, too.

OFFICIAL NAME: Papua New Guinea
AREA: 183,500 sq mi (475,300 sq km)
POPULATION: 2,985,000
CAPITAL: Port Moresby (pop. 77,000)
ETHNIC GROUPS: Melanesian, Papuan. LANGUAGE: pidgin English, tribal tongues. RELIGION: Christian, animist. ECONOMY: cacao, coconut, coffee, copper, wood. CURRENCY: kina.

Philippines

Archipelago. A strange-looking word (it's pronounced ark-uh-PEL-uh-go) that means "a group of islands." And the Philippine archipelago is one of the world's largest: It has more than 7,000 islands. About 700 are inhabited. Some are so small they disappear at high tide. Others have live volcanoes.

Many are covered with jungles where odd creatures live. The rare monkey-eating eagle, found only in the Philippines, is one of them. Another is the tarsier, one of the world's smallest primates. About the size of a squirrel, it lives in trees and makes twisting leaps from branch to branch. It has pop eyes and can turn its head all the way around back, 180° right or left.

On Luzon, the largest island, Manila boils with activity—a city whirl of skyscrapers, discotheques, supermarkets, noisy traffic, mansions with swimming pools, and some of Asia's worst slums.

There's also a touch of America. The years as a United States colony, 1898 to 1946, left the Philippines with non-Asian souvenirs. In Manila, English words mix with Pilipino, and hamburgers share lunch tables with *lumpias,* the local egg rolls.

Another mark of the West, Christianity, came with the Spanish, who ruled the Philippines for more than 300 years. Ferdinand Magellan, sailing under the Spanish flag, landed on Cebu in 1521. He was leading the first expedition around the world.

Most Filipinos are poor. They fish or farm in the sticky climate. In Luzon's rugged interior, farmers grow rice on terraces that their Malay ancestors carved into steep hillsides more than a thousand years ago. On Mindanao, loggers make a living by cutting down mahogany trees. Before a tree falls the lumberjack always shouts a warning so forest spirits can get out of the way.

OFFICIAL NAME: Republic of the Philippines
AREA: 116,000 sq mi (300,400 sq km)
POPULATION: 45,883,000
CAPITAL: Manila (pop. 1,439,000)
ETHNIC GROUPS: Malay. LANGUAGE: Pilipino, English. RELIGION: Roman Catholic, also Protestant. ECONOMY: abaca, chemicals, coconut, copper, grains, nickel, sugar, textiles, tobacco, wood. CURRENCY: peso.

Singapore

Busy, busy, busy. That's Singapore. Shopkeepers, bankers, importers, exporters, shipbuilders—all work hard to make their tiny nation richer.

More a city than a country, crowded Singapore has to depend on the outside world for most things. Even fresh water must be piped in from neighboring Malaysia.

Office towers and heavy traffic are changing Singapore's Oriental flavor. But at sidewalk stalls chopsticks still dig into spicy crabmeat, hot curries, and fried noodles. On poles sticking out from apartment windowsills, laundry dangles in the heat.

OFFICIAL NAME: Republic of Singapore
AREA: 225 sq mi (583 sq km)
POPULATION: 2,339,000
CAPITAL: Singapore (pop. 2,075,000)
ETHNIC GROUPS: Chinese, also Malay, East Indian, Pakistani. LANGUAGE: Malay, Chinese, English, Tamil. RELIGION: Buddhist, also Muslim. ECONOMY: banking, chemicals, electronics, machinery, oil refining, rubber, ship repair, shipping, soft drinks. CURRENCY: dollar.

Indonesia

1 *Largest monument south of the Equator, pyramidlike Borobudur rises higher than an eight-story building. The shrine dates from the ninth century, when Buddhism flowered in Java. Indonesia now follows the Muslim faith. Distant clouds crown one of Java's 61 volcanoes.*

2 *Taxis made like backward tricycles move under pedal power in the cities of Java. This crowded island, no bigger than Florida, holds one-fourth of all the people in the Southern Hemisphere.*

Malaysia

3 *The world's rarest ape, an orangutan, plays with a flower. Malaysia's orangs live in the rain forests of Borneo.*

Papua New Guinea

1 *A landmark in the clouds: Mount Yule's odd, blocky shape makes it easy to spot. It helps pilots find their way across the New Guinea wilderness.*

2 *In their holiday best—face paint, bark skirts, bird of paradise feathers— warriors from the Enga tribe dance at a farming festival. Hundreds of tribes, many still using Stone Age tools, share New Guinea's hilly highlands.*

Philippines

3 *A power saw buzzes into a toppled lauan tree. Lumbering has turned many of Mindanao's forests into plywood.*

4 *A musician's lacy dress and Spanish instrument, a* bandurria, *recall the days when Spain ruled the Philippines.*

5 *What kind of farm village has a river for a main street and water in all the fields? One where people raise fish, of course! Two harvests a year come from the ponds surrounding this Luzon town. The gently curving river holds bamboo fences that trap still more fish.*

3

4

5

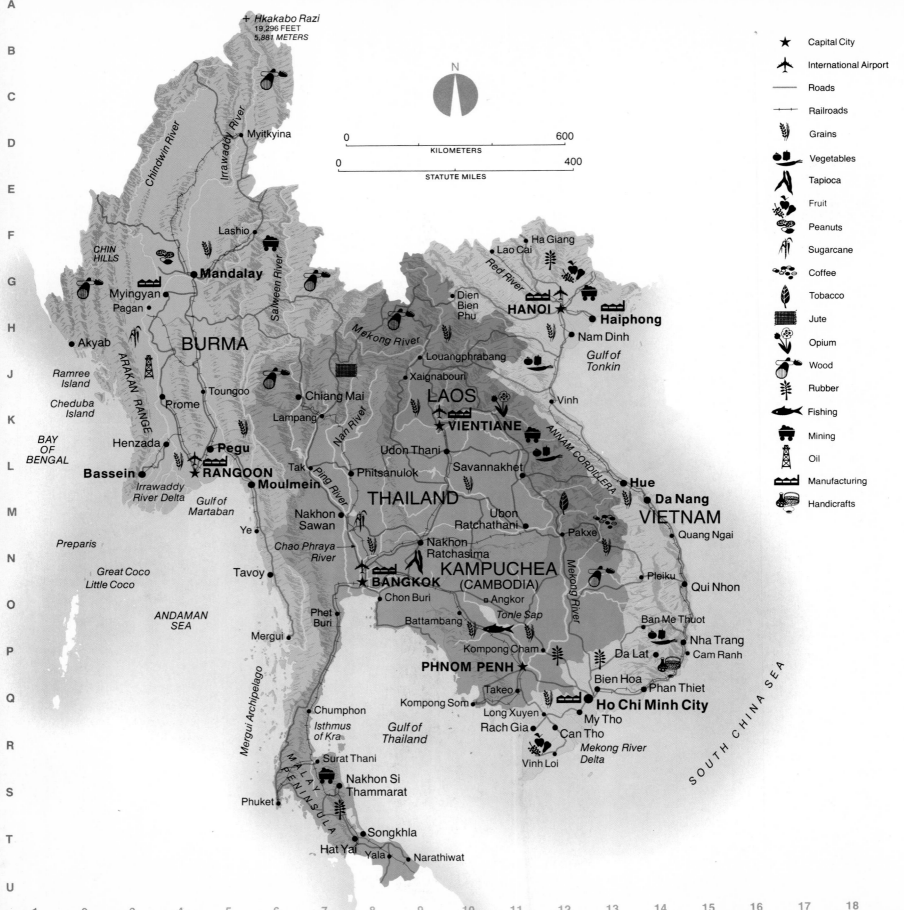

A B C D E F G H J K L M N O P Q R S T U

+ Hkakabo Razi
19,296 FEET
5,881 METERS

N

0   600
KILOMETERS

0   400
STATUTE MILES

Myitkyina

Chindwin River

Irrawaddy River

Lashio

CHIN
HILLS

Myingyan

Mandalay

Pagan

Salween River

Akyab

BURMA

Mekong River

ARAKAN RANGE

Toungoo

Ramree
Island

Prome

Cheduba
Island

Henzada

BAY
OF
BENGAL

Pegu

Bassein

RANGOON

Moulmein

Irrawaddy
River Delta

Gulf of
Martaban

Ye

Chiang Mai

Lampang

Nan River

Ping River

Tak

Phitsanulok

Nakhon
Sawan

Chao Phraya
River

THAILAND

Ha Giang

Lao Cai

Red River

Dien
Bien
Phu

HANOI

Haiphong

Nam Dinh

Gulf of
Tonkin

Louangphrabang

Xaignabouri

LAOS

Vinh

VIENTIANE

Udon Thani

Savannakhet

ANNAM CORDILLERA

Hue

Da Nang

VIETNAM

Ubon
Ratchathani

Quang Ngai

Pakxe

Nakhon
Ratchasima

Preparis

Great Coco
Little Coco

ANDAMAN
SEA

Tavoy

Mergui

Phet
Buri

Chon Buri

BANGKOK

KAMPUCHEA
(CAMBODIA)

Angkor

Tonle Sap

Battambang

Mekong River

Pleiku

Qui Nhon

Ban Me Thuot

Nha Trang

Da Lat

Cam Ranh

Kompong Cham

PHNOM PENH

Bien Hoa

Phan Thiet

Takeo

Ho Chi Minh City

Mergui Archipelago

Isthmus
of Kra

Chumphon

Gulf of
Thailand

Kompong Som

Long Xuyen

Rach Gia

My Tho

Can Tho

Mekong River
Delta

SOUTH CHINA SEA

Surat Thani

MALAY PENINSULA

Phuket

Nakhon Si
Thammarat

Vinh Loi

Songkhla

Hat Yai

Yala

Narathiwat

1 2 3 4 5 6 7 8 9 10 11 12 13 14 15 16 17 18

★ Capital City

✈ International Airport

Roads

Railroads

Grains

Vegetables

Tapioca

Fruit

Peanuts

Sugarcane

Coffee

Tobacco

Jute

Opium

Wood

Rubber

Fishing

Mining

Oil

Manufacturing

Handicrafts

Burma

With a thump, thump, a Mandalay craftsman hammers small squares of gold, beating them into a foil thinner than the layer of ink that forms these words. Such gold leaf glitters atop Burma's Buddhist temples.

These shining spires gleam in much of the hot, green land centered on the Irrawaddy River—the heart of Burma. Farmers grow rice in the surrounding delta.

In the hills and mountains far from the Irrawaddy live many tribes that do not speak Burmese, but one of a hundred other languages instead. Intha boatmen row standing on one leg while guiding an oar with the other. Shan tribesmen sometimes tattoo themselves all over with small blue designs. Some Padaung women still stretch their necks to three times normal length by wearing thick brass coils.

OFFICIAL NAME: Socialist Republic of the Union of Burma
AREA: 262,000 sq mi (678,600 sq km)
POPULATION: 32,205,000
CAPITAL: Rangoon (pop. 2,056,000)
ETHNIC GROUPS: Burman, also Karen, Shan.
LANGUAGE: Burmese, also Karen, Shan. RELIGION: Buddhist, also animist. ECONOMY: grains, lead, oil, peanuts, shoes, soap, sugar, textiles, wood, zinc. CURRENCY: kyat.

Cambodia

Peer through the jungle leaves, and you can see them on silent parade—elephants and dancing girls, gods and kings. They are stone, around 800 years old. These carved ruins at the fabled city of Angkor tell of the Khmer people. Their great empire once included Laos, Thailand, and southern Vietnam. Heir to Khmer glory is today's troubled Cambodia, also known as "Kampuchea" after Communists won a revolution here in the 1970's.

At the heart of this land's rice paddies and rubber-tree forests lies Tonle Sap, the "Great Lake." It supplies both fish and farmland—by changing size! In the wet season the lake floods to more than three times its normal area, and fishermen make large catches. Later on, the waters shrink, leaving rich silt for growing rice.

OFFICIAL NAME: Democratic Kampuchea
AREA: 70,000 sq mi (181,300 sq km)
POPULATION: 8,148,000
CAPITAL: Phnom Penh (pop. 394,000)
ETHNIC GROUPS: Khmer also Chinese. LANGUAGE: Cambodian. RELIGION: Buddhist. ECONOMY: fish, grains, rubber, textiles, wood. CURRENCY: riel.

Laos

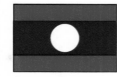

"Land of a Million Elephants," Laos has no seacoast, no railroad, and few roads. Mountain ridges and bamboo jungles separate small valleys strung along the Mekong River. Most of Laos's streams flow into the Mekong. Its waters nourish rice fields and provide a way to travel from village to village in small boats.

Laotians' favorite food is sticky rice, pressed into balls and eaten with bits of vegetable or meat. During their New Year, celebrated in April, girls in striped sarongs buy birds in cages and fish in water-filled plastic bags to set free as good deeds.

Mountain people grow corn and rice, and poppy flowers for opium. A Hmong tribeswoman is a walking treasury; her silver jewels make up the family savings.

OFFICIAL NAME: Lao People's Democratic Republic
AREA: 91,400 sq mi (236,800 sq km)
POPULATION: 3,545,000
CAPITAL: Vientiane (pop. 175,000)
ETHNIC GROUPS: Lao, also Kha, Tai, Meo, Yao.
LANGUAGE: Lao. RELIGION: Buddhist, animist.
ECONOMY: coffee, grains, opium, textiles, tin, tobacco, vegetables, wood. CURRENCY: kip.

Thailand

How would you like to take a bath in the river or paddle a boat to school? Or live in a house surrounded by water so that you could jump out the window for a swim? That's the way children live in much of Thailand, where traditional houses are built on stilts along rivers or small canals called *klongs*. Mothers bathe babies and wash dishes in the klongs.

The Chao Phraya River flows north to south through Thailand, irrigating fields and providing transportation. In the hilly north, teak logs are dragged through the jungles by elephants and floated down the river to market. In the southern panhandle, rubber trees grow in orderly lines, mile after mile. Thais grow rice, their most important crop, in the fertile central plains.

The Buddhist religion is important to Thais. When a boy grows up, by custom he becomes a monk for several months and lives in a temple. He must shave his head, walk barefoot, collect alms, and meditate.

Thailand was called Siam until 1939. Its present name means "free nation."

OFFICIAL NAME: Kingdom of Thailand
AREA: 198,000 sq mi (512,800 sq km)
POPULATION: 45,850,000
CAPITAL: Bangkok (pop. 3,134,000)
ETHNIC GROUPS: Thai, also Chinese. LANGUAGE: Thai. RELIGION: Buddhist. ECONOMY: cement, grains, jute, rubber, sugar, tapioca, textiles, tin, tungsten, wood. CURRENCY: baht.

Vietnam

One of Asia's great "rice bowls," this fertile land has been cracked in two and then made whole again. The change came as the result of conflicts that saw world powers lined up on opposing sides of a war that ended in 1975. All of Vietnam then became Communist, and the former southern capital, Saigon, was renamed Ho Chi Minh City after the late Communist leader.

In the south the Mekong River leaves rich deposits of silt on the rice paddies of the delta. Farmers in cone-shaped straw hats work knee-deep in the muddy waters. Children perch on broad-backed water buffalo that pull the farmers' plows.

In the north much of the farmland lies in another delta, that of the Red River. A network of dikes and busy canals brings water to rice fields. Many Vietnamese do not farm; they work instead in coal and tin mines, and in bustling factories that make chemicals and textiles.

Government clerks and office workers in the cities whisk along the streets on bicycles. When women change out of their work clothes, they like to dress up in the traditional *ao dai*, a high-collared tunic worn over trousers. Vietnamese food includes many kinds of soup, often flavored with a squirt of fish sauce called *nuoc mam*.

Dozens of tribes live in Vietnam's central and northern mountains. Some men keep knives in their long hair. Both sexes file their teeth to sharp points. Tribal villagers make a ceremonial sacrifice of pigs or poultry before eating them. The biggest ceremonies of all call for a whole buffalo.

OFFICIAL NAME: Socialist Republic of Vietnam
AREA: 127,300 sq mi (329,700 sq km)
POPULATION: 51,226,000
CAPITAL: Hanoi (pop. 415,000)
ETHNIC GROUPS: Vietnamese. **LANGUAGE:** Vietnamese, French. **RELIGION:** Buddhist. **ECONOMY:** cement, coal, fertilizer, fruit, glass, grains, handicrafts, machinery, rubber, textiles, tires, vegetables. **CURRENCY:** dong.

1

Burma

1 *Shwe Dagon's golden spire soars 326
feet (99 m) above a cluster of smaller
temples in Rangoon, Burma's capital.
It is said that the huge pagoda was
begun about 2,500 years ago to enshrine
eight hairs from the head of Buddha.*

2 *Loaded with baskets of palm sugar,
a convoy of oxcarts creaks toward the
Irrawaddy River to unload its cargo.*

Cambodia

3 *Stewed stork for dinner? A young boy
force-feeds a tame bird to fatten it
for the family cookpot. Lakeside towns
rise on stilts from Tonle Sap, one
of the world's richest fishing grounds.*

Laos

1 *Monsoon rains bring October grains. A Lao girl carries bundles of newly cut rice by wedging them onto a pole.*

Vietnam

2 *Roads can't reach all of the wet Mekong Delta, so the people use canals instead. Watery highways as straight as bamboo shafts also drain and irrigate the land.*

Thailand

3 *Performers of the* Lakon, *a traditional dance-drama, lock their long brass fingernails in mock battle between good and evil. Embroidered silk costumes imitate those worn by royal dancers.*

4 *In a wonderland of huge plants, boys carry alocasia-leaf umbrellas. Dense forests drip with colorful orchids and other tropical flowers. Water lily and lotus brighten swamps and ponds.*

5 *Buddhist monk from one of Bangkok's 400 monasteries leaves to collect food from donors. Saffron, the sacred color of his robe, symbolizes humility.*

Nepal

Snow leopards roam the Himalaya Mountains that cover nine-tenths of Nepal. You may hear rumors of the *yeti*, the legendary Abominable Snowman. Its "footprints" could be those of a bear, or the shaggy yak that provides the Nepalese with wool, butter, and transportation. But you're sure to see the highest point on earth: Mount Everest, 29,028 feet (8,848 m) above sea level.

OFFICIAL NAME: Kingdom of Nepal
AREA: 54,590 sq mi (141,400 sq km)
POPULATION: 13,680,000
CAPITAL: Kathmandu (pop. 150,000)
ETHNIC GROUPS: Indo-Nepalese, also Tibeto-Nepalese. **LANGUAGE:** Nepali. **RELIGION:** Hindu, also Buddhist. **ECONOMY:** grains, jute, oilseeds, potatoes. **CURRENCY:** rupee.

Sri Lanka

Slurp, swish, spit! A person with no table manners? No, it's a tea taster in Sri Lanka judging samples of tea. This island nation, once called Ceylon, is second only to India in the amount of tea it exports.

Sri Lanka—the name means splendid, brightly shining—is rich in religious celebration. Each summer in the city of Kandy, the Temple of the Tooth blazes with light for the festival honoring Buddha's tooth. Elephants parade in jewels and satin. Dancers whirl through the night to ward off evil. Witch doctors try to cure ills with drumming, chanting, and fire eating.

OFFICIAL NAME: Republic of Sri Lanka
AREA: 25,200 sq mi (65,500 sq km)
POPULATION: 14,283,000
CAPITAL: Colombo (pop. 618,000)
ETHNIC GROUPS: Sinhalese, also Tamil, Moor. **LANGUAGE:** Sinhala, also Tamil, English. **RELIGION:** Buddhist, also Hindu, Christian, Muslim. **ECONOMY:** cement, coconut, grains, rubber, tea, textiles. **CURRENCY:** rupee.

4

India

1 *In a land that loves beautiful ornaments of gold, a bride wears all she owns on her wedding day—gold on every finger, even freckles of gold dust. Her home, Calcutta, is the capital of West Bengal State, known for its skilled goldsmiths.*

2 *Students of the sitar enjoy a class with a master in Calcutta. The stringed, guitarlike instrument of northern India is made from teakwood and a gourd. Drum music often accompanies the sitar.*

3 *Hindu pilgrims crowd Hardwar for a New Year's celebration. On bathing steps called ghats, worshipers bathe in the Ganges, sacred river of India.*

4 *Wild elephants see their last moments of freedom before herders drive them into a stockade in southern India. The elephants will train for a lifetime of labor in the timber industry.*

3

Nepal

1 *Frozen Himalayas, where the gods of the mountain folk dwell, rise to form Kanchenjunga on the border between Nepal and India. At 28,208 feet (8,598 m) the peak ranks third highest in the world, below Everest and K2.*

2 *A mountain god dances at a ceremony. Behind the mask is a lama, a monk in the Himalayan form of Buddhism.*

Sri Lanka

3 *Buddhist monks in traditional robes make offerings of flowers to a giant Buddha at Avukana. Born about 2,500 years ago, Buddha taught that unselfish living could overcome human sorrow.*

Legend:

- ★ Capital City
- ✈ International Airport
- — Roads
- ┼ Railroads
- 🐫 Camels
- 🐂 Cattle
- 🐐 Goats
- 🐑 Sheep
- 🌾 Grains
- 🍇 Fruit
- Nuts
- 🥬 Sugar Beets
- ☕ Tea
- 🌿 Tobacco
- 🌸 Cotton
- 🐟 Fishing
- Mining
- Oil or Natural Gas
- Manufacturing

Khvoy
Lake Urmia
Tabriz · Ardabil
Rezaiyeh
CASPIAN SEA
Rasht · Bandar-e Pahlavi
Zanjan
Atrak River
Bojnurd
Bandar-e Shah
Quchan
Amu Darya River · Feyzabad
Mazar-e Sharif
K2 (Godwin Austen) 28,250 FEET 8,611 METERS
Area in dispute with India
KARAKORAM RANGE
Sanandaj
ELBURZ MOUNTAINS
TEHRAN ★
Mashhad
Baghlan
HINDU KUSH
Meymaneh
Kunar River
Charikar
Mardan
FRONTIER
Indus River
Hamadan
Kermanshah
Qom
Arak
Kashan
Torbat-e Heydariyeh
DASHT-E KAVIR (Salt Desert)
IRAN
Harirud River
Herat
KABUL ★
Khyber Pass
Peshawar
ISLAMABAD ★
Rawalpindi
Karkheh River
ZAGROS MOUNTAINS
Dezful
Esfahan
Birjand
DASHT-E LUT
Farah River
AFGHANISTAN
NORTHWEST
Gujrat
Sialkot
Gujranwala
Karun River
Ahvaz
Yazd
Qandahar
Dera Ismail Khan
Lyallpur
Lahore
Khorramshahr
Abadan
Zabol
DASHT-E MARGOW
Helmand River
Zhob River
Okara
Ravi River
Persepolis
Shiraz
Kerman
Zahedan
Bam
Quetta
Dera Ghazi Khan
Multan
Sutlej River
Bushehr
Persian Gulf
CHAGAI HILLS
PAKISTAN
Bahawalpur
THAR DESERT
Bandar Abbas
Bampur River
CENTRAL MAKRAN RANGE
SIND
Sukkur
Koja River
Hyderabad
Gulf of Oman
Karachi
Indus River

ARABIAN SEA

N

0 ———————— 800
KILOMETERS
0 ———————— 500
STATUTE MILES

A B C D E F G H J K L M N O P

1 2 3 4 5 6 7 8 9 10 11 12 13 14 15 16 17 18 19 20

Afghanistan

A rodeo Afghan style: That's the sport of *buz kashi,* a kind of free-for-all in which riders on madly galloping horses try to grab the "ball"—the carcass of a headless calf—and then race to a goal.

Life itself is almost as rugged as the game in high and dry Afghanistan. Mountains and deserts make the land look like the moon's surface in places. Countless invaders have struck, often while heading for the famous Khyber Pass. They left behind a colorful mix of people and customs. Pushtun nomads move black tents on camels. A veiled Turkmen bride is "kidnapped" to her new home in a make-believe battle. She weaves red and blue rugs prized worldwide. She dreams of the silver jewelry she will get when her carpets are sold at market.

OFFICIAL NAME: Democratic Republic of Afghanistan
AREA: 250,000 sq mi (647,500 sq km)
POPULATION: 14,381,000
CAPITAL: Kabul (pop. 318,000)
ETHNIC GROUPS: Pushtun, also Tajik, Uzbek, Hazara. LANGUAGE: Pushtun, Persian, also Turkic languages, Baluchi, Pashai. RELIGION: Muslim. ECONOMY: carpets, cement, coal, cotton, fruit, grains, hides and skins, livestock, natural gas, nuts, textiles, wool. CURRENCY: afghani.

Iran

In a canal deep underground, workmen wade in knee-high water, inspecting the tunnel for wear. Shafts spaced in the ceiling show pinpoints of daylight far above. At day's end a helper will drop a rope sling down one of these tubes and crank each man to the top, like a bucket from the bottom of a 20-story well.

Called *qanats,* these ancient aqueducts carry water from the mountains to Iran's thirsty farmlands. Some qanats are an incredible 40 miles (64 km) long, yet all were dug by hand—and still are.

Qanats are almost as old as Iran's history, which began about 2,500 years ago when Cyrus the Great ruled one of the world's first empires from here. Ancient Greeks called his land *Persis,* and Persia is a name still heard today. Over the centuries Iran has conquered, and been conquered, often.

Most of Iran lies inside the wishbone shape of two mountain ranges—the towering Elburz in the north, and the long, curving Zagros in the west and south. Moist winds from the world's largest landlocked sea, the Caspian, wash the north slopes of the Elburz in frequent showers, but the rest of the rugged nation rarely sees rain.

To see bright colors in this brown land you must turn to the handiwork of man. Mosques topped with domes of turquoise tile shimmer like mirages. Weavers tie red, gold, and blue threads into as many as 500 knots to make a single square inch of costly Persian carpet. Amid the flashing rainbow colors of the Crown Jewels in Tehran you can find an 18-inch (46 cm) world globe made of 51,366 gems—emerald seas, ruby continents, and a diamond equator!

But Iran's richest treasure is dull black: oil. Oil wealth has bought jet planes, skyscrapers, and university educations—strange new things in a land where some two million nomads still live in goat-hair tents in the desert. Troubled by all the sudden changes, Iranians have argued, sometimes violently, over what course their country's long history should follow next.

OFFICIAL NAME: Iran
AREA: 636,000 sq mi (1,647,200 sq km)
POPULATION: 35,286,000
CAPITAL: Tehran (pop. 3,774,000)
ETHNIC GROUPS: Iranian, also Turk. LANGUAGE: Persian, also Arabic, Kurdish, Turkish. RELIGION: Muslim. ECONOMY: carpets, cement, cotton, fruit, grains, hides and skins, livestock, metals, oil, pistachio nuts, sugar, tea, textiles, tobacco. CURRENCY: rial.

Pakistan

Millions of Muslims in India set up their own independent country in 1947. They named it Pakistan—"land of the pure." (It was in two pieces, and the eastern part later split away to form yet another new nation: Bangladesh.)

Religion plays a daily role in the lives of most Pakistanis. They kneel on small rugs five times a day to pray. On Friday they crowd into mosques whose slender towers and onion-shaped domes dot the land. Some girls and women still wear the traditional *burqa* when they leave home. This tentlike dress covers the body from head to toe, leaving only a small slit for the eyes.

In rugged hills of the Northwest Frontier Province, Pathan tribesmen grow full beards which they sometimes dye bright red. These proud and warlike men carry heavy knives and rifles, as they have for centuries. Sitting beside mud-brick shops in the town of Peshawar, they slurp noisily from cups of steaming sweet tea, and puff on a gurgling water pipe that sounds like its name: "hubble-bubble."

OFFICIAL NAME: Islamic Republic of Pakistan
AREA: 310,000 sq mi (803,000 sq km)
POPULATION: 77,786,000
CAPITAL: Islamabad (pop. 77,000)
ETHNIC GROUPS: Punjabi, also Sindhi, Pushtun, Baluchi. LANGUAGE: Urdu, Punjabi, Sindhi, Pushtun, English. RELIGION: Muslim. ECONOMY: chemicals, cotton, engineering, grains, natural gas, textiles, tobacco. CURRENCY: rupee.

Afghanistan

1 *A super pancake delights a youngster. Afghan mothers cook these whole-wheat wheels on hot griddles over open fires.*

2 *Terraced fields of wheat drop away to the swift Kunar River in northeastern Afghanistan. Beyond rise the Hindu Kush Mountains, their crests dusted with snow. Less than one percent of this rugged country is used for farming.*

Pakistan

3 *Feathery plumes of sugarcane flutter above a field in the dry Sind region. Irrigation from Pakistan's Indus River makes thousands of acres bloom.*

Iran

4 *A Persian rug gets a soaking at a spring near Tehran. Artisans believe that mineral-rich waters brighten the colors.*

5 *Crowds jam a vaulted bazaar in Shiraz. Some of these supermarkets of the Orient stretch for miles. Here Iranians trade ideas as well as merchandise.*

1

3

2

4   5

United Arab Emirates

 When the sheikdom of Abu Dhabi—one of the United Arab Emirates—first struck oil, the ruling sheik had grown so accustomed to the poverty of the desert he didn't want to spend the newfound wealth. So he just stored the money in a room at his old fort. Insects ate some of the paper money.

The ruler's brother finally forced him out and started spending. And Abu Dhabi, now another oil-rich Arab state, replaced its huts with high-rise buildings and broad avenues. Abu Dhabi is the largest and wealthiest of seven sheikdoms that now make up the United Arab Emirates. An emirate is a territory ruled by a chieftain called an emir.

OFFICIAL NAME: United Arab Emirates
AREA: 32,000 sq mi (82,800 sq km)
POPULATION: 656,000
CAPITAL: Abu Dhabi (pop. 50,000)
ETHNIC GROUPS: Arab, also Indian, Iranian, Pakistani. **LANGUAGE:** Arabic. **RELIGION:** Muslim. **ECONOMY:** fish, fruit, oil, pearls, tobacco, vegetables. **CURRENCY:** dirham.

North Yemen

Smells of fast-food hamburgers mingle with the roar of motorcycles and the throbbing beat of disco music in the marketplaces of Sana, capital of North Yemen. Oil money from neighboring Saudi Arabia is sweeping away many of the old ways in this land once ruled by the Queen of Sheba. The camel is giving way to motorbikes and four-wheel-drives.

Unlike Arab countries to the east, North Yemen has no oil. But it does have one thing the others lack—high mountains. Peaks up to 12,000 feet (3,660 m) catch rain from passing clouds. There's enough rain for crops in the valleys and on terraces cut in moun-tainsides. North Yemen is the only country on the Arabian Peninsula not mostly desert. That's why so many people live there. Only Saudi Arabia has more people.

OFFICIAL NAME: Yemen Arab Republic
AREA: 75,000 sq mi (194,200 sq km)
POPULATION: 5,031,000
CAPITAL: Sana (pop. 135,000)
ETHNIC GROUPS: Arab, also blacks. **LANGUAGE:** Arabic. **RELIGION:** Muslim. **ECONOMY:** coffee, cotton, fruit, grains, handicrafts, hides and skins, kat, textiles, vegetables. **CURRENCY:** rial.

South Yemen

Who would live in a five-story house made of mud? Many people do in South Yemen. In the fertile valleys of the arid Hadhramaut mountains—Arabic for "Death is present"—stand cities that are crowded with mud buildings up to 80 feet (24 m) tall. Over the years the desert sun has baked their thick, whitewashed walls hard as rock. You find buildings like this only in the two Yemens.

Two Yemens? "All Yemen is one," the Arabs say. Some want South Yemen to unite with its neighbor, the Yemen Arab Republic. But the south, as the Arabian Peninsula's only Communist state, frequently finds itself at odds with its more tradition-minded neighbors.

OFFICIAL NAME: People's Democratic Republic of Yemen
AREA: 111,000 sq mi (287,400 sq km)
POPULATION: 1,851,000
CAPITAL: Aden (pop. 264,300)
ETHNIC GROUPS: Arab. **LANGUAGE:** Arabic. **RELIGION:** Muslim. **ECONOMY:** coffee, cotton, dates, fish, grains, hides and skins, kat, livestock, oil refining. **CURRENCY:** dinar.

Saudi Arabia

▶ *A sight forbidden by law to all but Muslims—the city of Mecca. White-robed pilgrims come from around the world to visit the holiest shrine of their faith, the Kaaba. It lies beyond this gate.*

Kuwait

1 *Oil! A beaming Kuwaiti holds a pitcher of the liquid that has made his country one of the world's richest. In 1978 oil earned Kuwait about $300 — every second!*

2 *Arab dhows like this one slowly sail into history as diesel-powered boats take their place. Great dhow fleets once crisscrossed the Arabian Sea, and a few still trade with East Africa each year. Kuwaiti shipwrights can make a dhow so well it will last for a century or more.*

North Yemen

3 *A green staircase of terraced fields climbs a Yemeni hillside. These camels follow a caravan route used for centuries. Trucks and airplanes now do most of the hauling. Ancient Romans called this rain-blessed land Arabia Felix — Happy Arabia.*

Oman

4 *Pounding drums help celebrate the Feast of the Sacrifice, a holiday that recalls an important Muslim principle: faith.*

5 *Tired of school buses? Some Omani boys go back and forth to classes on burros.*

1

2

3

4 5

A B C D E F G H J K L M N O P Q R S

BLACK SEA

Edirne • Kirklareli
Istanbul
Bosporus
Sea of Marmara
Izmit
Dardanelles
Bandirma
Bursa
Balikesir
Sakarya River
ANKARA ★
Manisa
ANATOLIA
Izmir
AEGEAN SEA
Denizli
Isparta
Kutahya
Eskisehir
Kizil River
Tuz Lake
Aksehir Lake
Konya
Karaman
Antalya
TAURUS MOUNTAINS
Tarsus
Mersin
Adana
Iskenderun

Zonguldak
Karabuk
Sinop

Samsun

Trabzon
Coruh River
Aras River
Mount Ararat
16,946 FEET
5,165 METERS

Kirikkale
Sivas
Erzincan
Erzurum

TURKEY
Kayseri
CAPPADOCIA
Elazig
Malatya
Diyarbakir
Batman
Van Lake
Van
Murat River
Hakkari
KURDISTAN
Great Zab River

Maras
Gaziantep
Urfa
Al Qamishli
Little Zab River
Tigris River
Mosul
Irbil
Dokan Dam
Al Sulaymaniyah

Aleppo
Tabaqah Dam
Ar Raqqah
Euphrates River
Khabur River
Kirkuk
Diyala River

Latakia
NICOSIA
Famagusta
CYPRUS
Limassol
Tartus
Tripoli
Hamath
Dayr az Zawr
Khanaqin

Homs
Palmyra
Orontes River
SYRIA
Tharthar Basin

BEIRUT ★
Sayda
LEBANON
Tripoli
DAMASCUS ★
SYRIAN DESERT
IRAQ
Ar Ramadi
BAGHDAD ★

MEDITERRANEAN SEA
Haifa
Irbid
Tel Aviv-Yafo
Az Zarqa
JERUSALEM ★
AMMAN ★
Jordan River
Dead Sea
−1,312 FEET, −400 METERS
Lowest point in the world
ISRAEL
NEGEV DESERT
JORDAN

Karbala
Al Hillah
Al Kut
An Najaf
Al Amarah
Tigris River
Euphrates River

An Nasiriyah
Hawr al Hammar
Shatt al Arab
Basra

Elat
Al Aqabah

Gulf of Aqaba

RED SEA

PERSIAN GULF

N

0   400
KILOMETERS
0   300
STATUTE MILES

Legend

★ Capital City

✈ International Airport

— Roads

⊢⊣ Railroads

🐄 Livestock

🐂 Dairy Products

🌾 Grains

🍅 Vegetables

🍇 Fruit

🌴 Dates

🫒 Olives

🌰 Nuts

🌱 Sugar Beets

🍃 Tobacco

☁ Cotton

⛏ Mining

🛢 Oil

🏭 Manufacturing

1 2 3 4 5 6 7 8 9 10 11 12 13 14 15 16 17 18 19 20

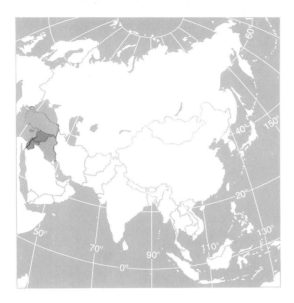

Cyprus

Imagine a house where two quarreling families live. Outsiders interfere. No longer on speaking terms, the opposing sides shut themselves off in different parts of the house. That's the way things worked out on the island of Cyprus in 1974. Greek Cypriots occupied the southern two-thirds of the country. Turkish Cypriots controlled the northern part.

Barbed wire and barricades arose between Greeks and Turks in Nicosia. The divided capital lies in the fertile central plain between two east-west mountain ranges. Houses of mud or stone, painted in soft pastel colors, cling to the hillsides, where wild tulips and poppies grow. Forests of pine and cypress thrive on the upper slopes. In ancient times the island's mines were a leading source of copper, *kypros*—the Greek word shared by mineral and island alike.

OFFICIAL NAME: Republic of Cyprus
AREA: 3,600 sq mi (9,200 sq km)
POPULATION: 641,000
CAPITAL: Nicosia (pop. 51,000)
ETHNIC GROUPS: Greek, also Turk. LANGUAGE: Greek, Turkish, English. RELIGION: Eastern Orthodox, also Muslim. ECONOMY: asbestos, cement, citrus fruit, copper, grapes, pyrites, shoes, vegetables, wine. CURRENCY: pound.

Iraq

A bicycle leans against a mud hut with a roof made of reeds. Inside, a dirt-floored room shelters both people and animals. Here, in the Tigris and Euphrates delta, Iraq's *fellahin* (peasants) harvest dates and herd sheep on the legendary site of the Garden of Eden.

At Baghdad, coppersmiths' hammers ring in the marketplace. But tall office buildings show the effect of new oil wealth. Iraq's largest oil fields lie in the mountainous north, homeland of the fiercely independent Kurds. Muslims but not Arabs, the Kurds also live in nearby sections of Syria, Iran, Turkey, and the U.S.S.R. For centuries they have peopled this realm, a borderless "nation" that they call Kurdistan.

OFFICIAL NAME: Republic of Iraq
AREA: 172,000 sq mi (445,400 sq km)
POPULATION: 12,470,000
CAPITAL: Baghdad (pop. 1,300,000)
ETHNIC GROUPS: Arab, also Kurd. LANGUAGE: Arabic, also Kurdish. RELIGION: Muslim, also Christian. ECONOMY: dates, grains, livestock, oil. CURRENCY: dinar.

Israel

The story of Israel is a story of the old and the new. David, the shepherd hero who slew Goliath in the Bible, ruled Israel 3,000 years ago. In time Israel was crushed, but in 1948 it was reborn.

The national flag carries the six-pointed shield of David. From more than 100 nations, Jewish people have come to live in the homeland. Many were drawn to the *kibbutzim*, cooperative farm settlements where members share the chores and the satisfaction of working together. Jerusalem, David's capital, is Israel's capital too. The city of Jesus' last days, Jerusalem has shrines sacred to Christians, Muslims, and Jews, and all faiths may worship there. Nearby lies Bethlehem, birthplace of Jesus.

With modern science, Israel makes desert land bloom with fruits and vegetables. Factories turn out clothes, cars, television sets, and cut diamonds. Yet Bedouin nomads still wander the Negev Desert. They are among the Arabs who remain in Israel. Others left, in bitterness, and have helped wage war against the new nation.

Peace comes slowly, even though people of the region speak it all the time. In both Hebrew and Arabic the word of greeting—"shalom" and "salaam"—means peace.

OFFICIAL NAME: State of Israel
AREA: 8,000 sq mi (20,700 sq km)
POPULATION: 3,654,000
CAPITAL: Jerusalem (pop. 356,000)
ETHNIC GROUPS: Jewish, also Arab. LANGUAGE: Hebrew, also Arabic. RELIGION: Jewish, also Muslim. ECONOMY: chemicals, dairy products, diamond cutting, fertilizer, fruit, machinery, meat, metals, plastics, potash, poultry, rubber products, textiles, tourism, transportation equipment, vegetables. CURRENCY: pound.

Jordan

The "River Jordan" of the Bible threads a narrow valley carpeted with fields of wheat and barley. Canals carry water to olive groves, orchards, and vegetable plots.

The river flows into the Dead Sea, far below ocean level. With no place to go, the water evaporates, leaving minerals that make the Dead Sea much saltier than the oceans.

Eastward lies the desert. Narrow passes in the mountainous southeast lead between steep cliffs to Saudi Arabia. Nomadic Bedouins often cross such frontiers freely, caring little what country they are in.

OFFICIAL NAME: Hashemite Kingdom of Jordan
AREA: 37,100 sq mi (96,000 sq km)
POPULATION: 2,960,000
CAPITAL: Amman (pop. 607,000)
ETHNIC GROUPS: Arab. LANGUAGE: Arabic. RELIGION: Muslim, also Christian. ECONOMY: cement, fruit, grains, oil refining, olives, phosphates, vegetables. CURRENCY: dinar.

Lebanon

A village potter turns wet clay into a water jug. Weavers hand-tie rugs. A coppersmith hammers out a tray. The land of Lebanon, scourged in recent years by bitter fighting between Christians and Muslims, has been a center of craftsmanship and commerce since the days of ancient seagoing traders called Phoenicians.

Lebanon's warm coastal lowlands bordering the Mediterranean Sea are lush with cotton fields, citrus groves, olive trees, and banana plantations. From there steep roads climb into the Lebanon Mountains. From December to May the mountain peaks are white with snow.

At Jubayl (ancient Byblos) the Egyptians came for cedar wood thousands of years ago. Only a few groves of the giant trees remain. But cedar seedlings promise new forests.

OFFICIAL NAME: Republic of Lebanon
AREA: 4,000 sq mi (10,300 sq km)
POPULATION: 2,540,000
CAPITAL: Beirut (pop. 475,000)
ETHNIC GROUPS: Arab, also Armenian. **LANGUAGE:** Arabic, French. **RELIGION:** Muslim, Christian. **ECONOMY:** cement, chemicals, fruit, grains, metals, oil refining, olives, textiles, tobacco, tourism, vegetables. **CURRENCY:** pound.

Syria

In a Damascus mosque a thousand Arabs kneel and touch their foreheads to carpets. *"Allahu akbar!"* they chorus. "God is great." It is the traditional Muslim way of praying five times a day.

Minarets tower above Damascus, one of the oldest cities in the world. In narrow streets where Paul the Apostle once walked, vendors sell everything from almonds to T-shirts bearing the likeness of the fighter Muhammad Ali.

The Barada River waters orchards and gardens around Damascus. In the dry eastern region the Euphrates, Syria's only navigable river, provides irrigation water for fields that grow cotton and food crops.

OFFICIAL NAME: Syrian Arab Republic
AREA: 72,000 sq mi (186,400 sq km)
POPULATION: 8,124,000
CAPITAL: Damascus (pop. 1,054,000)
ETHNIC GROUPS: Arab, also Kurd, Armenian. **LANGUAGE:** Arabic, English, French, Kurdish, Armenian. **RELIGION:** Muslim, also Christian. **ECONOMY:** cotton, fruit, grains, livestock, oil, textiles, tobacco, vegetables. **CURRENCY:** pound.

Turkey

A Gypsy with a dancing bear. A man selling balloons on a bridge. A blind musician singing folksongs of his boyhood village. A shoeshine vendor whose tools nestle in an ornate brass chest. You can meet them all in jam-packed Istanbul.

Known for 16 centuries as Constantinople, Turkey's largest city links Europe and Asia—and its own two halves—with both ferries and a long suspension bridge over the Bosporus, the strait that joins the Black Sea and the Sea of Marmara. Cross it, heading east, and you enter Anatolia, a peninsula of high plains and swift rivers walled by mountains. In eastern Anatolia, early Christians carved rooms in the volcanic rock cones of Cappadocia. Some of these caves still serve as homes for farmers. Men and women work in the fields, harvesting wheat and barley by hand.

Along the Aegean and Black Sea coasts, Turkey grows tobacco, olives, and tea. Villagers weave mohair rugs, raise silkworms, and make brass and copper pots. Miners dig coal, chrome ore, and tungsten.

OFFICIAL NAME: Republic of Turkey
AREA: 296,000 sq mi (766,600 sq mi)
POPULATION: 43,059,000
CAPITAL: Ankara (pop. 1,702,000)
ETHNIC GROUPS: Turk, also Kurd. **LANGUAGE:** Turkish, Kurdish, Arabic. **RELIGION:** Muslim. **ECONOMY:** boron, chromite, coal, copper, cotton, fruit, grains, iron, livestock, nuts, oil, steel, sugar, textiles, tobacco. **CURRENCY:** lira.

Jordan

1 *The Jordan River turns desert to green as it snakes through its valley west of Amman. Irrigation and a hot climate produce fruits and vegetables for export.*

Israel

2 *Farm workers harvest Jaffa oranges, famous around the world for their size and flavor. Citrus fruits, first planted in the Holy Land around the time of Jesus, are a major export crop.*

Lebanon

3 *"Cedar trees out of Lebanon" went into King Solomon's temple, says the Bible. The trees also made ships and houses.*

Turkey

1 *Beyond a horse-drawn carriage floats the silent cone of Ararat, long-dormant volcano in eastern Turkey. Noah's Ark is said to have come to rest in a mountainous region called Ararat after the great flood of Bible times.*

2 *Galata Bridge connects two sections of European Istanbul over an inlet called the Golden Horn. Istanbul spreads into two continents, the only big city that does so. Ferries cross the Bosporus to Asia, off the picture to the right.*

Iraq

3 *Ready for reading among the reeds? A visiting teacher gives an English lesson to pupils who live in reed houses in the marshes of southern Iraq.*

Syria

4 *Day care center for a working mother in a cotton field is on her back. Women, mainly in farming, make up a third of the labor force. Syria was the first Arab nation to give women the vote.*

2

Africa

Sunlight washes over the Serengeti Plain in northern Tanzania. A far-off rumble, like thunder, rolls across the ocean of grass. The rumble gets louder, closer. The ground trembles. A stampede! Heavy, hairy antelopes called wildebeests, thousands of them, gallop by. Perhaps hyenas or cheetahs scared them. The grassland seems solid wildebeests. At last they pass, and the silence of the Serengeti returns.

Only here, in Tanzania's great national park, can such huge herds of wild animals still be seen. Today Africa is changing. Skyscrapers rise, highways and railroads push into the wilderness, and cotton grows where elephants once roamed. Boys and girls whose fathers learned only tribal duties now go to school to learn French and arithmetic.

Africa's countries number among the world's youngest and poorest. Most have gained their freedom since 1960. Before then, a handful of European nations ruled almost all of Africa. They sliced it up to suit themselves. That's why some of today's African countries have peculiar shapes, like skinny Togo or ragged Mozambique.

Some of these borders have caused

The majestic lion symbolizes Africa's varied wildlife. The continent's mightiest hunters, lions range over the central grasslands as they stalk zebras, buffalo, deer, antelopes, and other grazing animals. Lionesses do most of the hunting, sometimes working together in groups. A large lion can eat 75 pounds (34 kg) of meat in one day.

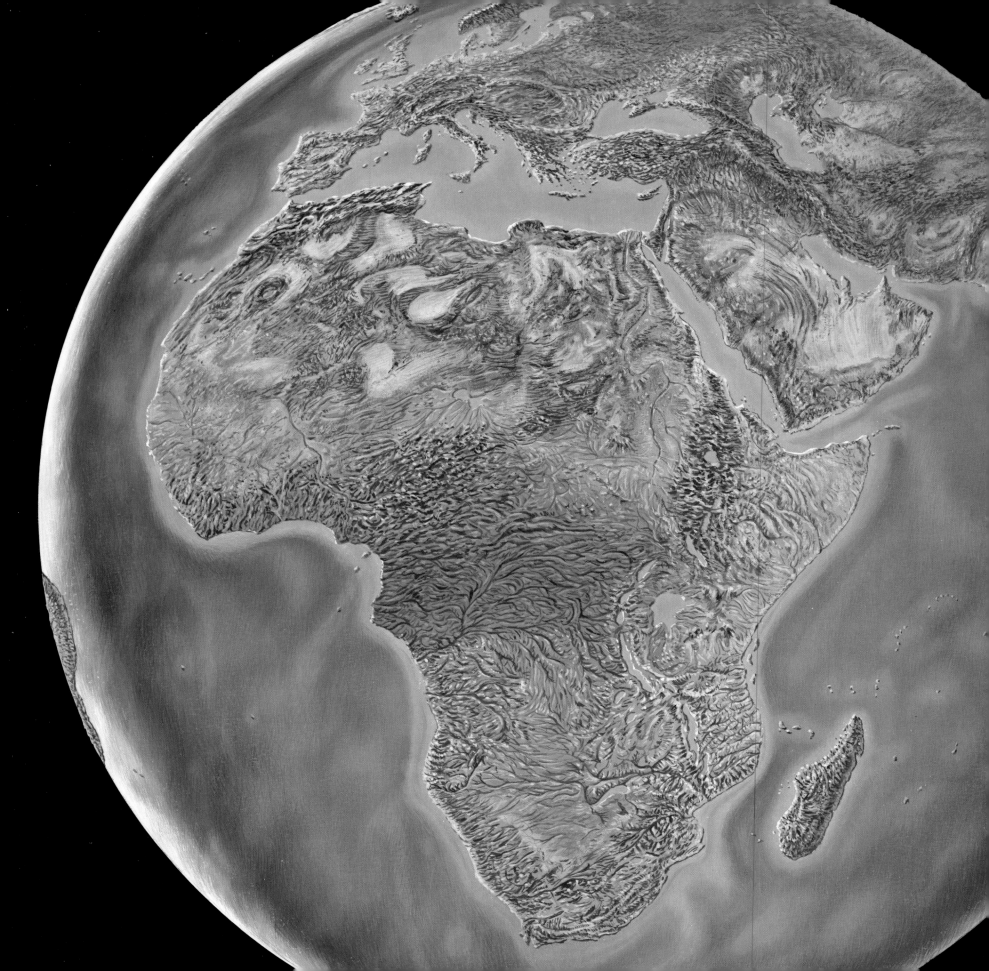

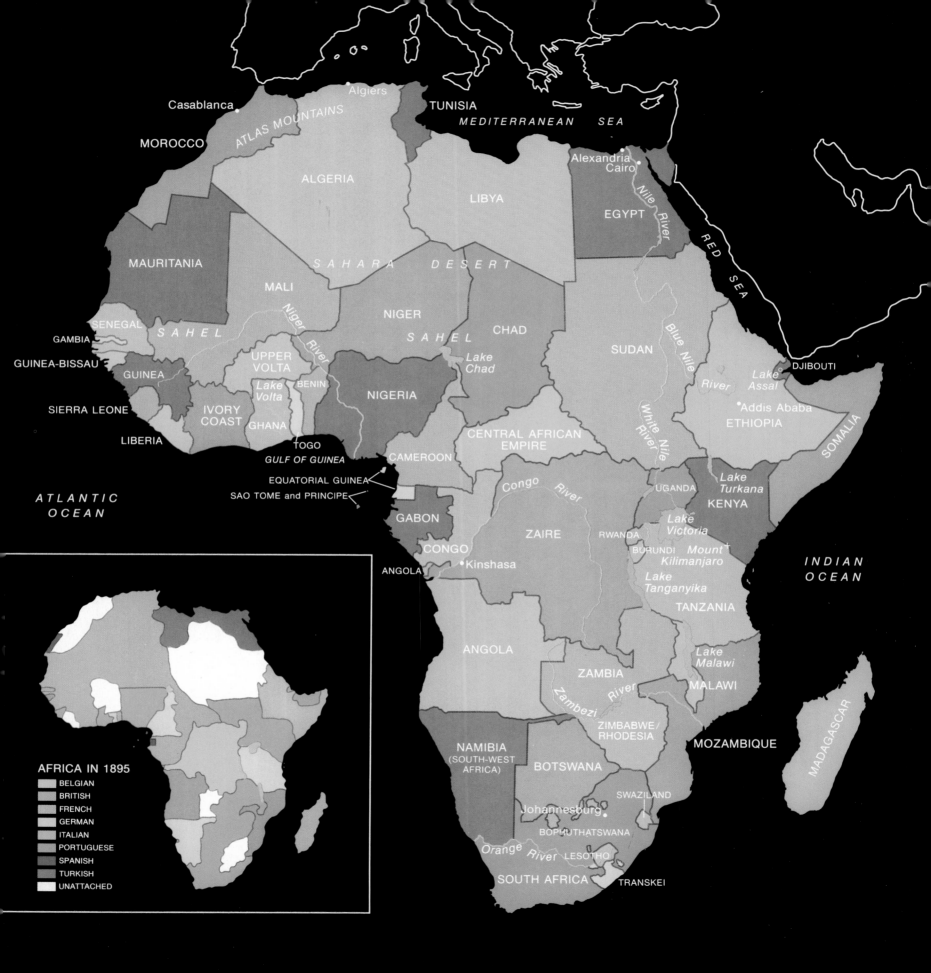

Casablanca

Algiers

TUNISIA

MEDITERRANEAN SEA

MOROCCO

ATLAS MOUNTAINS

ALGERIA

LIBYA

Alexandria
Cairo

EGYPT

Nile River

RED SEA

MAURITANIA

SAHARA DESERT

MALI

SAHEL

NIGER

SAHEL

CHAD

SUDAN

Blue Nile River

SENEGAL

Niger River

Lake
Chad

Lake
Assal

DJIBOUTI

GAMBIA

GUINEA-BISSAU

UPPER
VOLTA

BENIN

GUINEA

Lake
Volta

NIGERIA

White Nile River

Addis Ababa

SIERRA LEONE

IVORY
COAST

GHANA

ETHIOPIA

SOMALIA

LIBERIA

TOGO

GULF OF GUINEA

CAMEROON

CENTRAL AFRICAN
EMPIRE

EQUATORIAL GUINEA

Congo River

UGANDA

Lake
Turkana

SAO TOME and PRINCIPE

GABON

ZAIRE

KENYA

ATLANTIC
OCEAN

CONGO

RWANDA

Lake
Victoria

ANGOLA

Kinshasa

BURUNDI

Mount
Kilimanjaro

Lake
Tanganyika

INDIAN
OCEAN

TANZANIA

ANGOLA

Lake
Malawi

ZAMBIA

MALAWI

Zambezi River

NAMIBIA
(SOUTH-WEST
AFRICA)

ZIMBABWE/
RHODESIA

MOZAMBIQUE

MADAGASCAR

BOTSWANA

SWAZILAND

Johannesburg

BOPHUTHATSWANA

Orange River

LESOTHO

SOUTH AFRICA

TRANSKEI

AFRICA IN 1895

BELGIAN
BRITISH
FRENCH
GERMAN
ITALIAN
PORTUGUESE
SPANISH
TURKISH
UNATTACHED

problems for the Africans. Many black Africans still belong to tribes with their own languages and customs. Some tribes have only a few hundred members. But others, like the Yoruba of West Africa, live in cities and count their number in the millions. The Europeans' mixed-up borders have split the Yoruba into three different countries— Togo, Benin, and Nigeria—which the Yoruba share with other tribes. The same kind of problem troubles other parts of Africa, and even leads to war.

The northern third of Africa is Arabic in culture. Many Arabs live near the Mediterranean Sea, north of the Atlas Mountains. There along the seacoast enough rain falls for farming. To the south and east, sun and wind rule the thirsty waste of the Sahara, the world's largest desert. The area of rock, sand, and dust that reaches from the Atlantic to the Red Sea is large enough to swallow most of the United States.

Black Africa begins south of the Sahara. In the Sahel, a strip of land from Senegal to southern Chad, Africans graze their cattle on the dry plains. Sometimes, when the rains don't come and the herds have stripped away too much grass, the Sahel turns to desert. Then both animals and people starve.

What could be more African than lions roaring in the bush? Many things. One is the steamy rain forest that dampens Zaire and the countries along the Gulf of Guinea. But that's only a tenth of Africa! And lions don't live there; they like tree-dotted grasslands called savannas. Like a big, backwards "Ɔ," Afri-

ca's savannas sweep from the Sahel, up into the southern Sudan and down through East Africa and the south. Most of the large African animals—lion, elephant, Cape buffalo, wildebeest, rhinoceros, giraffe—live on the savanna. But people and their cattle take up ever more room, and wild animals find safety in parks like the Serengeti.

Underground forces are also changing Africa. Currents in the earth's molten insides slowly tear the continent in two. One of the tears can be seen on the map—it's the line of lakes between East Africa and Zaire. Here a "rift valley" has formed, catching water in long, deep lakes. A line drawn from Lake Malawi to Lake Turkana in Kenya traces another rift, where the land has fallen thousands of feet. The gap grows four inches wider every century. Beyond Ethiopia the Great Rift Valley is already filled with ocean—the Red Sea.

In places the restless rock of the rift has laid bare bits of fossil bone almost three million years old. They belong to a manlike creature, *Homo habilis*, the oldest ancestor of the human family that scientists have found.

Africa's many peoples show how large that family has grown. Tutsi, seven feet tall, rule Burundi, not far from where four-and-a-half foot Pygmies hunt in the Zaire jungle. White Afrikaners in the south, Arabs in the north, Malays in Madagascar, even some Asian Indians in the cities—all call Africa home. With such a mixture of people and cultures, it is no wonder this continent has given us both our oldest ancestors and our youngest countries.

Facts About Africa

SIZE: 11,586,000 sq mi (30,009,000 sq km)

POPULATION: 437,000,000

DENSITY: 38 persons for every sq mi (15 per sq km)

HIGHEST POINT: Mount Kilimanjaro, Tanzania, 19,340 ft (5,895 m) above sea level

LOWEST POINT: Lake Assal, Djibouti, 512 ft (156 m) below sea level

LARGEST COUNTRY: (by area) Sudan 967,000 sq mi (2,504,500 sq km)

LARGEST COUNTRY: (by population) Nigeria 68,486,000

LARGEST METROPOLITAN AREAS:
(by population)

Cairo	8,000,000
Johannesburg	2,600,000
Alexandria	2,500,000
Kinshasa	2,100,000
Algiers	1,800,000
Casablanca	1,600,000

LONGEST RIVERS: (mi and km)

*Nile	4,100	6,500
Congo	2,700	4,300
Niger	2,600	4,100
Zambezi	1,700	2,700
Orange	1,300	2,000

LARGEST LAKES: (sq mi and sq km)

Victoria	26,800	69,400
Tanganyika	12,700	32,800
Malawi	11,400	29,500
Chad	6,300	16,300
Volta	3,200	8,200
Turkana	2,400	6,200

*World Record

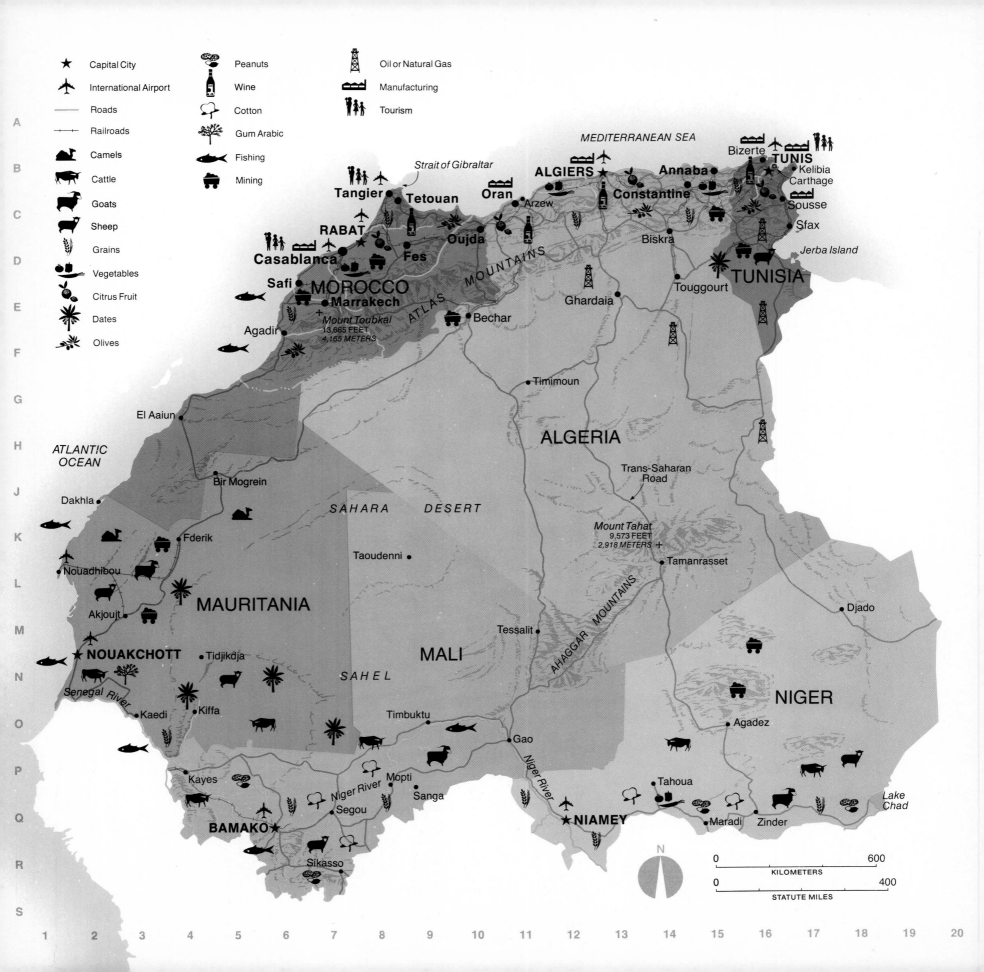

Legend:

- ★ Capital City
- ✈ International Airport
- Roads
- +++ Railroads
- Camels
- Cattle
- Goats
- Sheep
- Grains
- Vegetables
- Citrus Fruit
- Dates
- Olives
- Peanuts
- Wine
- Cotton
- Gum Arabic
- Fishing
- Mining
- Oil or Natural Gas
- Manufacturing
- Tourism

Map labels:

MEDITERRANEAN SEA

Strait of Gibraltar

Bizerte
TUNIS
ALGIERS
Annaba
Kelibia
Carthage
Oran
Arzew
Constantine
Sousse
Tangier
Tetouan
Sfax
RABAT
Oujda
Biskra
Jerba Island
Casablanca
Fes
MOROCCO
ATLAS MOUNTAINS
TUNISIA
Safi
Ghardaia
Touggourt
Marrakech
Bechar
Mount Toubkal
13,665 FEET
4,165 METERS
Agadir
Timimoun

ATLANTIC
OCEAN

El Aaiun

ALGERIA

Bir Mogrein

SAHARA DESERT
Trans-Saharan
Road

Dakhla

Fderik

Taoudenni

Mount Tahat
9,573 FEET
2,918 METERS

Nouadhibou

Tamanrasset

Djado

Akjoujt

MAURITANIA

MALI

AHAGGAR MOUNTAINS

Tessalit

NOUAKCHOTT
Tidjikdja
SAHEL
NIGER

Senegal River

Kaedi
Kiffa
Timbuktu
Agadez

Gao

Kayes
Niger River
Mopti
Tahoua
Lake Chad
Segou
Sanga
Niger River
Maradi
Zinder
BAMAKO
NIAMEY
Sikasso

N

0 — 600
KILOMETERS

0 — 400
STATUTE MILES

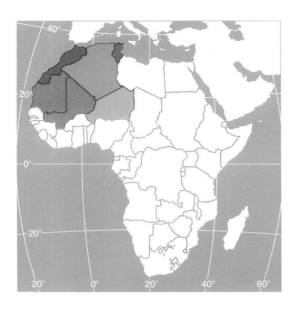

Algeria

Three states the size of Texas could be fitted into Algeria's part of the vast Sahara Desert. But only half a million people, mostly tribes of Arab and Berber Muslims, live in this part of the nation. Of these, many are robed Tuareg nomads famed for the endurance of their camels and for the fact that men — not women — wear the veil.

In camel caravans the hardy Tuareg plod through blistering heat and sudden sandstorms. They trade camels, goats, sheep, and salt for cloth, wheat, dates, and tea. Camped in tents, children learn the Koran from a *marabout,* or holy man. Boys also tend the herds; girls spin wool into yarn and help make leather bags and wallets.

Tuareg life seems a thousand years away from modern Algeria, which gained its independence from France in 1962. From beneath the eastern sands, the nation pumps a wealth of oil and gas. Along a fertile coastal strip — home to 95 percent of the population — grain, grapes, olives, and oranges flourish. In Algiers, freighters and fishing boats crowd the docks. Noisy market stalls line narrow and shadowy streets in the old section called the Casbah.

East of the city, a factory makes giant trucks. Each can carry as much as 100 camels can. One day, trucks rolling down the trans-Saharan road may replace camels.

OFFICIAL NAME: Democratic and Popular Republic of Algeria
AREA: 950,000 sq mi (2,460,500 sq km)
POPULATION: 17,639,000
CAPITAL: Algiers (pop. 1,504,000)
ETHNIC GROUPS: Arab, Berber. **LANGUAGE:** Arabic, French, also Berber. **RELIGION:** Muslim.
ECONOMY: citrus fruit, grains, iron, natural gas, oil, olives, vegetables, wine. **CURRENCY:** dinar.

Mali

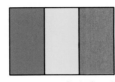

Don't say "Get lost!" Say "Go to Timbuktu!" the next time you want a person out of sight. This faraway trading post was thought to be a city of gold, and many an explorer lost his life trying to reach it. Others found not gold but sand — sand in the millet mush, and sand in the honey cakes sold on the streets in the cool of evening. Mud homes and mosques bristle with sticks that hold the mud together; rare rains may wash away part of their walls.

Beyond the city lies the Sahara. Proud Tuareg nomads wander this realm. Like knights of old, warriors sharpen their spears and skills in mock battles.

South of Timbuktu stretch mile upon mile of grasslands and grainfields watered by the Niger River. Yearly the Niger floods its banks, layering the land with silt and sowing fish in lakes and ponds. Wandering Fulani herdsmen drive their cattle from open range into harvested fields. The farmers get milk and fertilizer; the cattle fatten on stubble. But some years the Niger doesn't play its part. It dries to a stream, and people and cattle starve.

OFFICIAL NAME: Republic of Mali
AREA: 465,000 sq mi (1,204,300 sq km)
POPULATION: 6,284,000
CAPITAL: Bamako (pop. 237,000)
ETHNIC GROUPS: Berber, blacks. **LANGUAGE:** French, Mande. **RELIGION:** Muslim, animist.
ECONOMY: cotton, fish, grains, hides and skins, livestock, peanuts. **CURRENCY:** franc.

Mauritania

The baby's small head is shaved, leaving only a topknot. This hairstyle isn't for beauty; a Moorish mother believes the tuft is a handle that helps Allah lift the body to heaven if the baby dies.

In Mauritania, most people are Moors, a mixture of Arab-Berber folk. They wander the scrubby grassland of the Sahel and the Sahara beyond.

In the northwest, iron is mined near a once-disputed territory, the former Spanish Sahara, part of which now belongs to Mauritania. On the Atlantic coast, fishermen swim out with nets in view of modern trawlers reaping the rich fishing grounds.

Blacks farm along the Senegal River. These people once were slaves of the Moors, but they received a modern education under the former French rulers. Now many work in government and teach.

OFFICIAL NAME: Islamic Republic of Mauritania
AREA: 419,000 sq mi (1,085,200 sq km)
POPULATION: 1,542,000
CAPITAL: Nouakchott (pop. 35,000)
ETHNIC GROUPS: Moor, blacks. **LANGUAGE:** Arabic, French. **RELIGION:** Muslim. **ECONOMY:** copper, dates, fish, grains, gum arabic, iron, livestock. **CURRENCY:** ouguiya.

Morocco

Rock music from Rabat beats into the ear of a Berber chieftain in the mountains of northern Morocco. In Casablanca, his daughter Rhima shops at a boutique and wears jeans at college. But when she goes home to the mountains, she changes into a burnoose, a shapeless cloak. To expose arms or legs in public would be frowned on in her Muslim village.

In Moroccan cities, to step through an arch in a wall is to pass through Alice's looking glass. You go from modern, palm-shaded suburbs into the maze of the old city, the *medina* . . . from courtyards cooled by fountains to richly decorated rooms.

Most Moroccans make their living by farming. They tend orchards of citrus, olives, and almonds on the coastal plains, or they herd sheep and goats in the mountains. But they are also superb craftsmen. In the bazaars, or markets, they spread out articles of copper and fine leather, carpets, and hand-embroidered slippers. In his stall a brass worker taps perfect patterns into the metal, carrying on a skill passed down through the generations from father to son.

OFFICIAL NAME: Kingdom of Morocco
AREA: 158,000 sq mi (409,200 sq km)
POPULATION: 18,915,000
CAPITAL: Rabat (pop. 368,000)
ETHNIC GROUPS: Arab, Berber. **LANGUAGE:** Arabic, also Berber, French. **RELIGION:** Muslim.
ECONOMY: carpets, citrus fruit, fish, grains, olives, phosphates, textiles, tourism, vegetables, wine. **CURRENCY:** dirham.

Niger

When Kabo calls, his cattle come running. They lick him on the arm and face. He's helped care for them since he was six—and also his sweaty skin is salty. Cattle like salt.

The Fulani people of Niger's central semidesert get much in return from their long-horned cattle. What's for breakfast, lunch, snack, and supper? Milk, buttermilk, curdled milk, and more milk. At yearly reunions the people dance for days and share their cattle with families who have lost herds to drought.

In the dry season, when water has to be dug from beneath the sand, the herders move into the Niger River area to trade for millet from the Hausa people. Farmers and traders, the Hausa make up the largest tribe in the country.

The Sahara dunes that ripple across most of Niger are left to the "Blue Men." These Tuareg nomads wrap all but their eyes in indigo-dyed cloth; the blue rubs off on their faces. As modest as women in most other Muslim lands, men sip hot mint tea beneath the veils and kiss wives with noses. They travel in caravans across a desert so barren that a single tree may be marked on a map.

OFFICIAL NAME: Republic of Niger
AREA: 489,000 sq mi (1,266,500 sq km)
POPULATION: 4,995,000
CAPITAL: Niamey (pop. 131,000)
ETHNIC GROUPS: Hausa, also Djerma, Songhai, Fulani, Tuareg. **LANGUAGE:** French, Hausa. **RELIGION:** Muslim, animist. **ECONOMY:** cotton, grains, hides and skins, livestock, peanuts, uranium, vegetables. **CURRENCY:** franc.

Tunisia

Where is everybody? It's possible to stand on the edge of a Tunisian village and see nothing but date palms and dips in the earth. No mud huts, no tents, maybe a few girls drawing water at the well. But look over the edge of those steep-walled craters and you see doors leading into the earth. Here on the rim of the Sahara the Tunisians know the advantage of such a cool, dug-in community.

Here only one crop every seven years may survive. But the northern valleys get rain enough for wheat and barley, and olive groves dot the coastal plains in the east. Almost every family in a village is related; uncles and aunts abound. At the end of Ramadan, the Muslim month of fasting, children receive gifts and everyone feasts. Centuries of conquerors have known busy Tunis as a key to the Mediterranean world. Perched near a peninsula that narrows the sea to a bottleneck, the city is in a good position to control who sails where.

OFFICIAL NAME: Republic of Tunisia
AREA: 63,400 sq mi (164,200 sq km)
POPULATION: 6,242,000
CAPITAL: Tunis (pop. 551,000)
ETHNIC GROUPS: Arab. **LANGUAGE:** Arabic, French. **RELIGION:** Muslim. **ECONOMY:** citrus fruit, dates, fertilizers, grains, leather, livestock, oil, olives, phosphates, textiles, tourism, vegetables, wine. **CURRENCY:** dinar.

1

2

Algeria

1 *Blown by wind, dunes 150 feet (46 m) high shift constantly in the Sahara. Sand cloaks less than a fifth of the world's largest desert. Gravelly plains and stark mountains cover the rest.*

2 *A road grader churns the earth near an oil refinery at Arzew, a coastal terminal for pipelines from the Sahara. A painting of wavy colors symbolizing oil's fiery energy decorates the refinery.*

3 *Tuareg nomads brew tea in their shelter near Tamanrasset. Unlike many Muslims, Tuareg men mask their faces, while the women go unveiled.*

4 *Twisting lanes, closed doors, and veiled women lend an air of mystery to the famous Casbah, French for a North African fortress. Here in old Algiers, Islamic culture survived during more than a hundred years of French rule.*

Morocco

1 *Gleaming buildings keep alive the meaning of Casablanca, Spanish for "white house." Skyscrapers, boutiques, and factories give the city its European flavor. With more than a million residents, the city holds half of the country's industrial force. Its port handles most of the nation's shipping.*

2 *Climbers get a downhill breather on a Grand Atlas peak near Marrakech. The craggy, often snowcapped peaks border the burning Sahara. They are the highest of the Atlas chain, which stretches across Algeria into Tunisia.*

3

Morocco

3 *Green ribbons of young wheat separate rows of fruit trees in the fertile coastal plain between Rabat and Fes. Hot, dry winds of August will parch these hills to brown, but irrigation ditches will keep the trees growing.*

Tunisia

4 *Fishermen unload their catch in the port of Kelibia. Nearby stood ancient Carthage, a stronghold of the seafaring Phoenicians. Romans destroyed Carthage in the middle of the second century B.C.*

4

Mali

1 *Famed for colorful displays, foot-stomping Dogon dancers perform in the cliffside village of Sanga. Masquerading as women, these men wear fiber skirts and masks made of cowrie shells. The shells once were West Africa's most common currency.*
2 *Harvesters stack spikes of millet grain for drying south of Timbuktu.*

Niger

3 *Thump, thump, thump echoes across the savanna as Fulani women pound sorghum into flour. Women also cook meals, gather firewood, fetch water, build huts, and milk cows. The Fulani treat their cattle almost like pets, giving each one a name.*
4 *Donkeys haul water to a Tuareg camp in bags made from goatskins and inner tubes.*

Mauritania

5 *Nouakchott, the capital of this iron-rich nation, invades the desert. Elsewhere the Sahara gets even by devouring thousands of acres of once-productive farmland.*

Sudan

If you have a sweet tooth, you're likely to pop a bit of the Sudan into your mouth soon. Gooey goodies from marshmallows to gumdrops often contain gum arabic. This sticky sap, also used in adhesives, perfumes, and medicines, comes from acacia trees that grow in the Sudan, the largest country in Africa.

Sudan's great area takes in extremes of climate and ways of life. In the desert land of the north, little or no rain falls. Arab nomads wander in search of water and grass for camels and sheep. In steamy forests of the south, some 57 inches of rain falls during the nine-month wet season.

Between desert and forest lies the Sudd, one of the largest marshes in the world. It drains into the White Nile, which meets the Blue Nile at Khartoum. The Nile, longest of all rivers, flows more than 4,000 miles from its headwaters in Rwanda to its delta on the Mediterranean Sea. Cotton fields stretch along its banks.

Among low hills in the Sudan's grassy midlands live the Nuba, tall, black-skinned tribal folk. They build round, thatch-roofed houses with mud walls. Tobacco is raised for cash to buy tools from the Arabs. In centuries past, the Nuba hid in the hills to escape the Arab slave-raiders. The Nuba wear little or no clothes. For decoration women cut scar patterns on their bodies.

Nuba men love to wrestle. A wrestler first smears himself with ashes, held sacred in a region where wood is scarce. The winner is awarded the ash of an acacia tree—buried with him when he dies.

OFFICIAL NAME: Democratic Republic of the Sudan
AREA: 967,000 sq mi (2,504,500 sq km)
POPULATION: 16,740,000
CAPITAL: Khartoum (pop. 334,000)
ETHNIC GROUPS: Arab, Nilotic tribes. **LANGUAGE:** Arabic, English. **RELIGION:** Muslim.
ECONOMY: beans, beer, cement, cotton, edible oils, grains, gum arabic, peanuts, medicines, sesame, shoes, soap, textiles. **CURRENCY:** pound.

1

2

3

4

Egypt

1 *Funeral mask of solid gold recalls the features of boy-king Tutankhamun. The young pharaoh's tomb contained nearly 5,000 pieces of treasure.*

2 *Skilled hands shape a fancy brass tray in Cairo's Khan el Khalili bazaar. Here dozens of tiny shops offer everything from savory spices to Oriental carpets.*

3 *Pyramids of Giza cradle the setting sun and look down on fields of grain. Peasants called* fellahin *turn the soil with wooden plows and reap with sickles.*

4 *Modern buildings of concrete and steel rise from the banks of the Nile. Cairo, Africa's largest city, grows at the rate of a thousand people a day.*

Libya

1 *Silent reminder of the Roman empire, the ruins of an ancient theater stand near the Mediterranean port of Al Khums. In Roman times this region paid Caesar a tax of olive oil. People still make it here today, by squeezing the fruit pulp in presses to extract the oil.*

2 *Mountains blasted by sand and creased by* wadis—*dry stream beds*—*rumple the sunbaked desert. Wells pump abundant water and oil from under the Sahara.*

Sudan

3 *Stalwart tribesmen gaze down on their village in the Nuba Mountains. Each family's cluster of castlelike mud huts boasts a shower—a water jug cradled in wall brackets made of antelope horns.*

Chad

4 *Seen in dawn's light, island-studded Lake Chad seems to spill across the land like a giant puddle of milk chocolate. Because it has no surface outlet, the lake fills with Sahara sand and river silt. Its average depth—four feet—makes the lake a water hole for hippos and cattle. At times as big as Lake Ontario, it can shrink by half during a dry winter.*

5 *Sky-blue at midday, Lake Chad presents a calm surface to fishermen in reed boats. Chadians dam narrow shallows and pump them dry, uncovering rich land good for growing millet and sorghum.*

Liberia

A small colony of freed slaves from America came to west Africa in the early 1800's. They settled on land bought from tribal chiefs by the American Colonization Society. In 1847 Liberia—"Land of Freedom"—became Africa's first black republic. Many descendants of former slaves live in coastal cities like Monrovia, named after U.S. President James Monroe. They speak English and wear American-style clothes.

Inland, Liberians usually live in villages, speak tribal languages, and wear flowing, colorful clothes. Farm families share the work. Men clear the fields. Women plant and harvest crops. Boys chase away baboons. Girls help winnow the rice. Many people work on rubber plantations and in open-pit iron mines.

Liberia's flag is one of the best known on the high seas. Foreign companies often register their ships in Liberia in order to take advantage of its low taxes.

OFFICIAL NAME: Republic of Liberia
AREA: 42,900 sq mi (111,300 sq km)
POPULATION: 1,733,000
CAPITAL: Monrovia (pop. 100,000)
ETHNIC GROUPS: Bassa, Gola, Grebo, Kissi, Kpelle, Kran, Kru, Mandingo. LANGUAGE: English, also many tribal tongues. RELIGION: animist, also Muslim, Christian. ECONOMY: cacao, cassava, coffee, diamonds, iron, oil refining, palm oil, rubber, wood. CURRENCY: dollar.

Senegal

On Cape Verde Peninsula, westernmost point of the African continent, sprawls Dakar, Senegal's capital city. Traders have known its fine harbor for five centuries. It was an important military base for the Allies in World War II. Now an air-traffic center, Dakar also has rail transport, fish canneries, and a shipyard.

From its 310-mile (499 km) Atlantic coastline fringed with marshes, Senegal rises to grassy plains and then to a dry region called the Sahel. The edge of the Sahara, the Sahel is lashed by sandstorms and seared by hot winds. Drought withers crops. But in the south, along the Casamance River, plenty of rain falls—five feet or more a year, despite a dry season. Peanuts, Senegal's leading export, thrive in its sandy soil. The Senegalese people have a saying: "When peanuts do well, we all do well."

OFFICIAL NAME: Republic of Senegal
AREA: 76,000 sq mi (196,800 sq km)
POPULATION: 5,380,000
CAPITAL: Dakar (pop. 667,000)
ETHNIC GROUPS: Wolof, also Fulani, Serer, Tukulor, Diola, Malinke. LANGUAGE: French, Wolof. RELIGION: Muslim, also animist, Christian. ECONOMY: beer, cassava, cement, fish, grains, peanuts, phosphates. CURRENCY: franc.

Sierra Leone

June is a hungry month for families who farm in Sierra Leone. When last year's rice is almost gone, other food must be found until new harvests begin in November. That's not easy, for crops grow poorly in the worn-out soil. Many workers find jobs in bauxite mines or dig for diamonds. New factories employ people to make paint, furniture, textiles, and soap.

Sierra Leone supposedly got its name in 1462 when Portuguese explorers heard thunder in the hills near a deep harbor. They called the land *Serra Lyoa*—Lion Mountain. Britain in 1787 founded Freetown as a colony for freed American slaves. The nation won independence in 1961.

OFFICIAL NAME: Republic of Sierra Leone
AREA: 27,900 sq mi (72,200 sq km)
POPULATION: 3,256,000
CAPITAL: Freetown (pop. 274,000)
ETHNIC GROUPS: Mende, Temne. LANGUAGE: English, also Krio, Mende, Temne. RELIGION: animist, also Muslim, Christian. ECONOMY: bauxite, beer, cacao, cassava, cigarettes, coffee, diamonds, ginger, grains, oil refining, palm kernels, rutile, textiles, yams. CURRENCY: leone.

1

2

Ivory Coast

1 *Abidjan's modern skyline reflects the nation's skyrocketing growth. One of Africa's busiest ports, the capital handles cargo from the Ivory Coast as well as from its neighbor, Upper Volta. New roads cut into the interior, where tribal drums beat, witch doctors chant, and elephants crash through rain forests.*

2 *Headdress of bananas crowns a woman on her way to market. Foutou, the national dish, is based on bananas or yams and topped with peanut or palm-seed sauce.*

3 *Workers from neighboring Mali cut wood into lumber at Bingerville, near Abidjan. Hardwood forests and mills like this make the nation Africa's top exporter of wood.*

3

1

3

2

The Gambia

1 Burlap masks filter the dust-choked
air aboard a Gambia River peanut boat.
Gambians have experimented with shark
oil, rice, and poultry production, but
peanuts remain the best money-maker.

Guinea

2 It's a short hop from home to work for
high-rise apartment dwellers in the
town of Fria. They process bauxite in one
of Africa's largest alumina plants.

4

Senegal

3 *From stacks to sacks go peanuts bound for a factory near Dakar. There the peanuts will be turned into golden peanut oil. The oil is used to make soap, shampoo, face powder, paint, and even explosives.*

Liberia

4 *Milky drops of latex fill a cup on a rubber tree. Each year a full-grown tree produces enough sap for 11 pounds (5 kg) of rubber, a leading export.*

breathe in Kano when a hot, dusty wind, the *harmattan,* blows in from the Sahara Desert for six months of the year.

Yorubas (who live in the southwest) and Ibos are both farmers and factory workers. Some build autos in modern plants while neighbors grow yams, cassava, and grain in jungle clearings. When the soil is worn out, the jungle returns as the farmer burns off a patch elsewhere for a new plot.

Oil has brought wealth to some Nigerians, but not to most. So Nigeria struggles to grow more food, build more schools, houses, roads—and unify the nation. To help reach this goal, a new capital city is planned, to be built in the center of the country.

OFFICIAL NAME: Federal Republic of Nigeria
AREA: 357,000 sq mi (924,600 sq km)
POPULATION: 68,486,000
CAPITAL: Lagos (pop. 1,061,000)
ETHNIC GROUPS: Fulani, Hausa, Ibo, Yoruba.
LANGUAGE: English, also Hausa, Ibo, Yoruba.
RELIGION: Muslim, also Christian, animist.
ECONOMY: cacao, cassava, cement, chemicals, coal, columbite, cotton, grains, livestock, natural gas, oil, palm products, peanuts, rubber, textiles, tin, wood, yams. **CURRENCY:** naira.

Togo

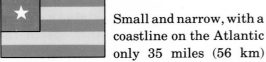

Small and narrow, with a coastline on the Atlantic only 35 miles (56 km) long, Togo is about the size of West Virginia. As in that state, mountains dominate the landscape, and mining provides a living for many families. Workers quarry phosphate, a mineral used to make fertilizer. It comes from one of the largest phosphate beds in the world, northeast of Lome.

The Togo Mountains divide the country into two different regions. Mountain people include the Kabre, or "people of the stones." These villagers build stone terraces on the hillsides to fight erosion. There they tend rocky garden plots that reach almost to the tops of the mountains.

In the swampy coastal region, the Ewe people cultivate coconut palms, coffee, and cacao, or work in Lome's food processing plants. Almost all boys and girls on the coast go to school, but in the mountains fewer than one in five have that chance.

OFFICIAL NAME: Republic of Togo
AREA: 21,900 sq mi (56,900 sq km)
POPULATION: 2,458,000
CAPITAL: Lome (pop. 145,000)
ETHNIC GROUPS: Kabre, Ewe, Mina. **LANGUAGE:** French, also Dagomba, Ewe, Kabie, Mina. **RELIGION:** animist, also Christian, Muslim. **ECONOMY:** beans, cacao, cassava, coffee, cotton, fish, grains, handicrafts, palm oil, phosphates, textiles, yams. **CURRENCY:** franc.

Upper Volta

Snake heads, lion tails, squares of elephant hide —sidewalk vendors sell such folk remedies at the bustling outdoor market of Ouagadougou, capital of Upper Volta. (It's easy to pronounce the city's name if you think of it as "Wagadugu.")

One of the poorest nations in West Africa, Upper Volta suffers with rocky soil and sudden drought. It sits on the edge of the Sahel, a region where the desert meets the grasslands. Nine of every ten families scratch out a living by growing millet, sorghum, corn, and rice. Only one person in ten can read.

Summer months may bring 40 inches (102 cm) of rain. Then crops turn the land green around the small huts in which most Upper Voltans live. But if—as often happens—the rains don't come, or they are too heavy and sweep the soil and seeds into flooded streambeds, the people go hungry. Then fathers seek farm or factory jobs in neighboring Ghana and the Ivory Coast.

OFFICIAL NAME: Republic of Upper Volta
AREA: 105,900 sq mi (274,500 sq km)
POPULATION: 6,508,000
CAPITAL: Ouagadougou (pop. 173,000)
ETHNIC GROUPS: Mossi, also Bobo, Mande. **LANGUAGE:** French, Mossi, also Gourounsi, Lobi, Samo. **RELIGION:** animist, also Muslim, Christian. **ECONOMY:** beer, bricks, cotton, grains, hides and skins, livestock, peanuts, sesame, shea nuts. **CURRENCY:** franc.

Nigeria

1 *Thousands of nets and floating balls suggest a kind of game. So it is. Participants score by catching fish in a shallow tributary of the Niger River. Clinging to gourd floats the size of basketballs, tribesmen dip their nets and hope for a big fish. Prize catch of this competition was a Nile perch weighing 121 pounds (55 kg).*

2 *An open-air market beside a street in Ibadan displays produce of Yoruba farmers. Other members of this tribe, one of Nigeria's biggest, grow cacao trees or work at trades and crafts.*

3 *The port of Warri on the Niger Delta prospers from rich strikes of oil. With Africa's largest population—some 68 million—Nigeria can use the money.*

Benin

1 *A brightly clad woman paddles her canoe past houses built on wood stilts. Saltwater lagoons serve as streets in the coastal village of Ganvie.*

2 *Sprouting like mushrooms, Ganvie's long-stemmed dwellings stand on bushy sandbars. A house at lower right awaits bamboo floor and thatched roof. Curving weirs (screens) stretch across a main channel to trap fish, which are then smoked in indoor earthen ovens.*

Ghana

3 *Pods dangle from a cacao tree trunk. These evergreens grow well in southern Ghana's rich soil and wet climate.*

4 *Slashed open by a machete, a pod spills pulp-covered beans. Dried and roasted, they will be ground into chocolate. Ghana grows much of the world's cacao.*

1

2

3

4

5

6

Togo

5 *Beyond lush tropical slopes loom the Togo Mountains. To the north lie dusty plains and well-watered grasslands.*

Cameroon

6 *Hardwood logs harvested from southern rain forests are readied for export. They travel first by rail to the busy port of Douala, then by ocean freighters.*

Upper Volta

7 *Using her head instead of a shopping bag, a young woman strolls through a market. She holds a ring like those that cradle the bowls on her head. The Ouagadougou market devotes a whole section to flavorings for soups and stews.*

7

AFRICA 237

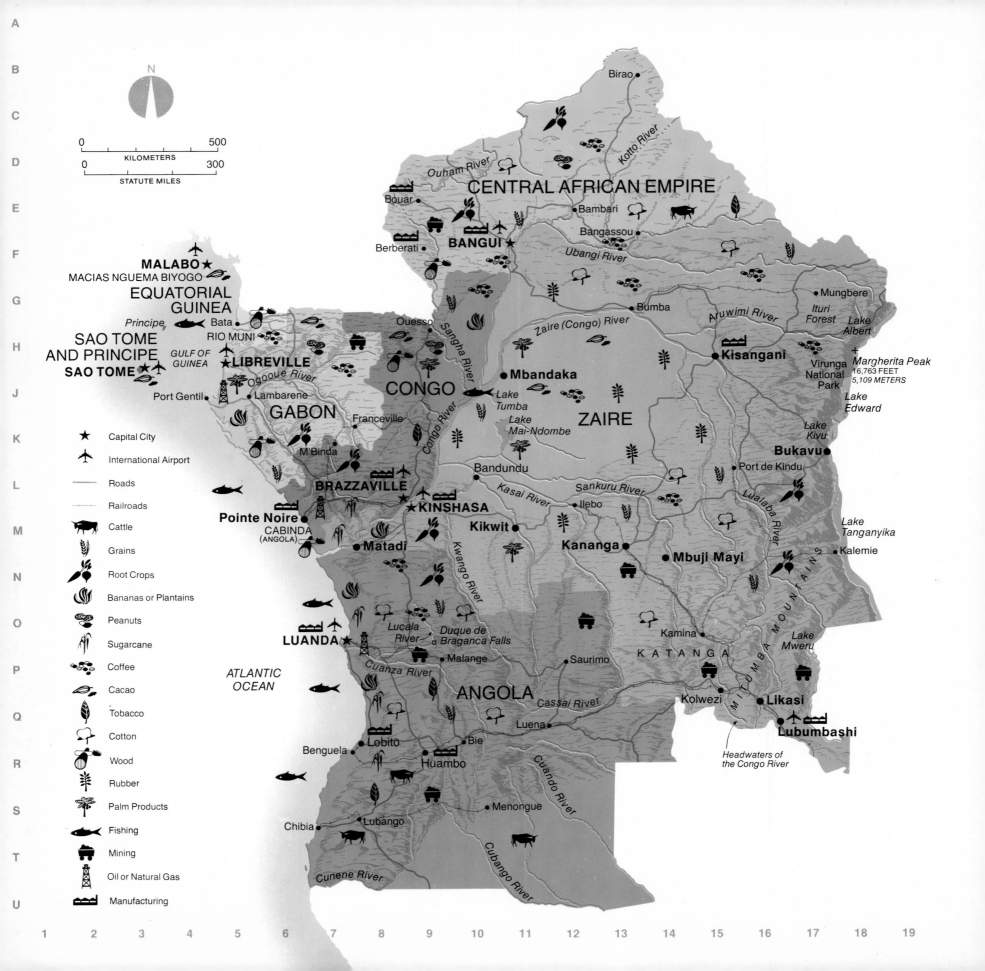

A B C D E F G H J K L M N O P Q R S T U

1 2 3 4 5 6 7 8 9 10 11 12 13 14 15 16 17 18 19

N

0 500
KILOMETERS
0 300
STATUTE MILES

CENTRAL AFRICAN EMPIRE

Birao

Ouham River
Kotto River

Bouar
Bambari

Bangassou
BANGUI

Berberati
Ubangi River

MALABO ★
MACIAS NGUEMA BIYOGO
EQUATORIAL
GUINEA

Principe
Bata
RIO MUNI

SAO TOME
AND PRINCIPE
GULF OF
GUINEA
SAO TOME ★

Port Gentil

Ogooue River

Lambarene

GABON
Franceville

M'Binda

Ouesso

Sangha River

Zaire (Congo) River

Mungbere

Aruwimi River

Ituri
Forest

Lake
Albert

Bumba

CONGO

Mbandaka

Kisangani

Virunga
National
Park

+ Margherita Peak
16,763 FEET
5,109 METERS

Lake
Edward

Lake
Tumba

Lake
Mai-Ndombe

ZAIRE

Lake
Kivu

BUKAVU

Port de Kindu

LIBREVILLE ★

Congo River

Bandundu

Kasai River
Sankuru River

Ilebo

Lualaba River

Lake
Tanganyika

BRAZZAVILLE

KINSHASA ★

Kikwit

Kanga

Kananga

Mbuji Mayi

Kalemie

Pointe Noire
CABINDA
(ANGOLA)

Matadi

Kwango River

Kamina

KATANGA

Lake
Mweru

ATLANTIC
OCEAN

Lucala
River
Duque de
Braganca Falls

LUANDA ★

Cuanza River
Malange

ANGOLA

Saurimo

Cassai River

MITUMBA MOUNTAINS

Kolwezi

Likasi

Lubumbashi

Benguela
Lobito
Bie

Huambo

Luena

Cuando River

Headwaters of
the Congo River

Chibia
Lubango

Menongue

Cubango River

Cunene River

Capital City
International Airport
Roads
Railroads
Cattle
Grains
Root Crops
Bananas or Plantains
Peanuts
Sugarcane
Coffee
Cacao
Tobacco
Cotton
Wood
Rubber
Palm Products
Fishing
Mining
Oil or Natural Gas
Manufacturing

Angola

Beyond Angola's coastal plain lies "staircase" country, where the land rises in broad steps to high plateaus. Rivers rush down the slopes in every direction, like the spokes of a wheel, draining an area almost twice the size of Texas.

Some rivers in the eastern region are alive with crocodiles and hippos. The Cuanza spins generators at a hydroelectric dam as it flows west to the Atlantic. The Cassai, bordering Zaire, is one of the main streams flowing through the humid north, where Bantu tribesmen harvest coffee and mine diamonds. The Cubango wends through dry southern regions former Portuguese rulers called the "end of the world." Herdsmen live in round huts. Cattle corrals are ringed with thorns to keep out lions.

OFFICIAL NAME: People's Republic of Angola
AREA: 481,000 sq mi (1,245,700 sq km)
POPULATION: 6,449,000
CAPITAL: Luanda (pop. 475,000)
ETHNIC GROUPS: Bantu, also European. **LANGUAGE:** Bantu dialects, also Portuguese. **RELIGION:** animist, also Christian. **ECONOMY:** bananas, beer, cassava, cement, coffee, cotton, diamonds, fish, grains, iron, oil, plantains, sisal, sugar, textiles, tobacco, vegetables, wood. **CURRENCY:** kwanza.

Central African Empire

This landlocked country lies in the middle of equatorial Africa. Since the nation has few paved roads and no railways, rivers tie it together. Southern streams join the Ubangi, where boats carry exports such as coffee and cotton from the capital city of Bangui to the Congo. To the north flow the tributaries of the Chari River, which empties into the Lake Chad basin. Under French rule — which ended in 1960 — the nation was known as Ubangi-Shari (Chari).

Fishing and hunting occupy black tribespeople scattered over rolling grasslands and in dense rain forests. Desert sands blow in the northeast. Farmers grow cassava, corn, and peanuts and raise some livestock. But production is limited because of tsetse flies, which transmit sleeping sickness. Most of the families live in the countryside, and less than half the children attend school.

OFFICIAL NAME: Central African Empire
AREA: 242,000 sq mi (626,700 sq km)
POPULATION: 1,912,000
CAPITAL: Bangui (pop. 187,000)
ETHNIC GROUPS: Banda, Baya, Manja, Ubangi. **LANGUAGE:** French, Sango. **RELIGION:** Christian, also animist, Muslim. **ECONOMY:** beer, cassava, coffee, cotton, diamonds, grains, meat, peanuts, sesame seeds, sweet potatoes, textiles, wood. **CURRENCY:** franc.

Congo

Young Mbaka paddles his canoe down the Congo River, hurrying back to his village with a catch of fish for his mother to cook. He stays close to the bank, away from large river steamers carrying imported machinery, iron and steel, and foodstuffs upstream from Brazzaville, port city on the mighty Congo.

Below Brazzaville, the Congo plunges into rapids and waterfalls on its way to the Atlantic Ocean. The tribal group that Mbaka belongs to, the Teke, mainly hunts and fishes in the dense jungle and crocodile-infested streams.

Most other Congolese are farmers who raise just enough cassava, yams, and beans for their own families. Roaring Congo waterfalls may change this way of life by bringing electric power for more factories, railroads, and other industry.

OFFICIAL NAME: People's Republic of the Congo
AREA: 135,000 sq mi (349,600 sq km)
POPULATION: 1,464,000
CAPITAL: Brazzaville (pop. 175,000)
ETHNIC GROUPS: Kongo, Sangha, other Bantu. **LANGUAGE:** French, also Kikongo, Lingala. **RELIGION:** animist, Christian. **ECONOMY:** bananas, beer, cacao, cigarettes, coffee, fish, grains, oil, palm oil, peanuts, root crops, soap, sugar, tobacco, wood. **CURRENCY:** franc.

Equatorial Guinea

Imagine a country in two parts, separated by a hundred miles of ocean. That's Equatorial Guinea. One part is Rio Muni, a tropical rain forest on Africa's mainland. Here, people of the Fang tribe earn a living by cutting trees, making lumber, and growing coffee.

The other part is Macias Nguema Biyogo, a volcanic island in the Gulf of Guinea, just below Africa's western bulge. Here, people of the Bubi tribe grow not only coffee but also bananas and cacao beans of unusually high quality. Because Spain once ruled this nation, Spanish has remained as the language of government and business.

OFFICIAL NAME: Republic of Equatorial Guinea
AREA: 10,800 sq mi (27,900 sq km)
POPULATION: 336,000
CAPITAL: Malabo (pop. 17,500)
ETHNIC GROUPS: Bubi, Fang. **LANGUAGE:** Spanish, also Bubi, Pidgin English, Fang. **RELIGION:** Roman Catholic. **ECONOMY:** bananas, cacao, cassava, coffee, fish, grains, livestock, palm oil, wood, yams. **CURRENCY:** ekuele.

Gabon

A Roman Catholic nun threads her motorbike through the modern city of Libreville in Gabon. She passes white sand beaches shaded by coconut palms, tall office buildings gleaming in the sun, and outdoor markets bright with bananas, pineapples, and avocados. Those fruits were picked earlier by a woman in the tropical rain forest that covers most of Gabon. She carried them to market on her back.

Oil and other minerals have been discovered in this land once ruled by France, but the forest is still an important source of wealth. Logs of okoume, used to make plywood, and of mahogany are floated down the many rivers to seaports. From there the wood is shipped all over the world.

OFFICIAL NAME: Gabonese Republic
AREA: 102,000 sq mi (264,100 sq km)
POPULATION: 571,000
CAPITAL: Libreville (pop. 73,000)
ETHNIC GROUPS: Bantu. LANGUAGE: French, also Fang, other Bantu tongues. RELIGION: Christian, animist. ECONOMY: bananas, cacao, coffee, gold, grains, iron, manganese, natural gas, oil, palm oil, peanuts, root crops, uranium, wood. CURRENCY: franc.

Sao Tome and Principe

Can you picture two big chocolate mountains rising out of the ocean? The two islands that make up the country of Sao Tome and Principe are the tips of mountains that start at the bottom of the Gulf of Guinea. And though the islands aren't really made of chocolate, their steep slopes are covered with millions of cacao trees.

The small evergreen trees bear big pods swollen with cacao beans. The beans are fermented, dried, and roasted before being turned into cocoa and candy bars. Former colonies of Portugal, this pair of islands became one independent nation in 1975.

OFFICIAL NAME: Democratic Republic of Sao Tome and Principe
AREA: 370 sq mi (960 sq km)
POPULATION: 75,000
CAPITAL: Sao Tome (pop. 17,400)
ETHNIC GROUPS: Bantu, Portuguese. LANGUAGE: Portuguese. RELIGION: Christian. ECONOMY: bananas, cacao, coconut, coffee, palm oil, wood. CURRENCY: escudo.

Zaire

What would it be like if Americans in the area east of the Mississippi River spoke more than 200 different languages? It would be something like Zaire, the third largest country in Africa.

Although members of Zaire's different tribes can't speak each other's language, many of them speak French, the official language of the country. Why French? Because until 1960 Zaire was a colony of Belgium, where French also is the language of many of the people.

Most of Zaire's people are farmers. Every morning, families walk from their mud-and-thatch huts to jungle clearings. There bananas, cassava, and corn ripen in the soaking rains and hot sun of this land along the Equator. But a greater treasure lies underfoot. From mines in the Katanga region come some of the world's largest deposits of cobalt, copper, and diamonds.

In the Ituri forest of northeast Zaire live the Pygmies, about four and a half feet tall. Hunters and gatherers of food, rather than farmers, they build no houses—just temporary shelters of saplings and leaves.

OFFICIAL NAME: Republic of Zaire
AREA: 905,000 sq mi (2,343,900 sq km)
POPULATION: 27,080,000
CAPITAL: Kinshasa (pop. 2,202,000)
ETHNIC GROUPS: Bantu. LANGUAGE: French, also English, many tribal tongues. RELIGION: Christian, animist. ECONOMY: bananas, cement, cobalt, coffee, copper, cotton, diamonds, grains, palm oil, root crops, rubber. CURRENCY: zaire.

1

2

Angola

1 *Waters of the Lucala River plunge 344 feet (105 m) over a falls north of Malange. Spray supports lush plant life.*

2 *Tattoo design on a wooden mask echoes the old tribal custom of scarring. Now paint decorates faces for ceremonies.*

3 *A woman worker bundles sisal, strung up to dry. The fibers are woven into rope.*

Equatorial Guinea

4 *The world's largest frog lurks in the streams of Rio Muni. Tribesmen call it "mother's son" because its size and its limbs remind them of a small child. This one weighed almost seven pounds.*

Zaire

1 *A Mbuti bowman, slightly more than four feet tall, takes aim at a monkey in Ituri Forest. Zaire's Pygmies trade meat to taller Bantu neighbors for food, such as bananas and peanuts, as well as spears, knives, and other metal tools.*

2 *Friendly elephant accepts a handout at a village in Virunga National Park. Within the refuge, stretching for 190 miles (306 km) along the Uganda border, vast herds of wildlife roam the land.*

2

1

3

Zaire

3 *Lovesick hippopotamus bulls roar their toothy threats over a sausage-shaped female. She refuses to take sides, turning away instead. The largest hippo population in the world—about 25,000 animals—finds protection from hunters in the safety of Virunga National Park.*

4 *Cone baskets trap fish in the rushing Zaire River, as the Congo is called here. Tribesmen scramble down scaffolds to gather their catch. Steamers bound for Kinshasa provide a ready market for vendors plying their trade in small boats.*

4

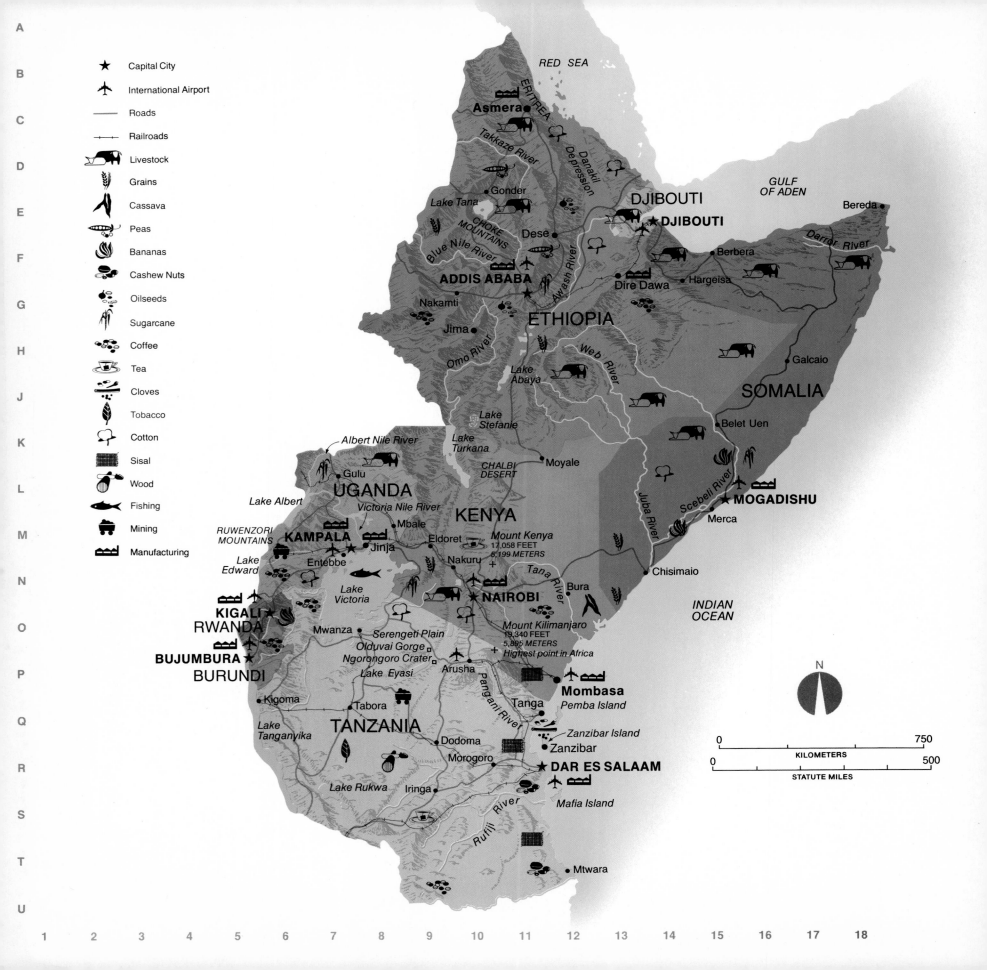

Capital City
International Airport
Roads
Railroads
Livestock
Grains
Cassava
Peas
Bananas
Cashew Nuts
Oilseeds
Sugarcane
Coffee
Tea
Cloves
Tobacco
Cotton
Sisal
Wood
Fishing
Mining
Manufacturing

RED SEA

GULF
OF ADEN

Bereda

ERITREA

Asmera

Takkaze River

Danakil
Depression

Gonder

DJIBOUTI

Lake Tana

CHOKE
MOUNTAINS

Dese

DJIBOUTI

Blue Nile River

Berbera

Awash River

Dire Dawa

Hargeisa

ADDIS ABABA

Nakamti

ETHIOPIA

Darror River

Jima

Omo River

Web River

Galcaio

Lake
Abaya

SOMALIA

Lake
Stefanie

Belet Uen

Lake
Turkana

Albert Nile River

Gulu

CHALBI
DESERT

Moyale

UGANDA

KENYA

MOGADISHU

Lake Albert

Victoria Nile River

Mbale

Merca

Juba River

Scebeli River

RUWENZORI
MOUNTAINS

KAMPALA

Jinja

Eldoret

Mount Kenya
17,058 FEET
5,199 METERS

Entebbe

Nakuru

Lake
Edward

Tana River

INDIAN
OCEAN

Lake
Victoria

NAIROBI

Bura

KIGALI

RWANDA

Mwanza

Serengeti Plain

Mount Kilimanjaro
19,340 FEET
5,895 METERS
Highest point in Africa

Chisimaio

Olduvai Gorge
Ngorongoro Crater

BUJUMBURA

Arusha

N

BURUNDI

Lake Eyasi

Mombasa

Kigoma

Tabora

Pemba Island

Tanga

Pangani River

TANZANIA

Lake
Tanganyika

Dodoma

Zanzibar Island

Morogoro

Zanzibar

Lake Rukwa

Iringa

DAR ES SALAAM

Rufiji River

Mafia Island

0   750
KILOMETERS
0   500
STATUTE MILES

Mtwara

Burundi

If the people of Burundi stood in a row in order of height, the lineup would slope much as the country itself does.

From western mountains the land steps down eastward in a series of flat plateaus. And Burundi's tribes range from towering seven-foot Tutsi (also known as Watutsi) through stocky Hutus of average height to Twa Pygmies, four and a half feet tall.

Burundi is one of the smallest, most crowded countries in Africa. But its highlands are free of the dreaded tsetse fly, whose bites bring sleeping sickness to both humans and cattle.

Tutsi herdsmen view long-horned Zebu cattle as wealth rather than food. So they tend to raise too many, resulting in overgrazed land and skinny cattle. Hutus are farmers. In the mountains live the Twa Pygmies, known for their pottery.

OFFICIAL NAME: Republic of Burundi
AREA: 11,000 sq mi (28,500 sq km)
POPULATION: 4,212,000
CAPITAL: Bujumbura (pop. 79,000)
ETHNIC GROUPS: Hutu, Tutsi, also Twa. **LANGUAGE:** French, Kirundi, Swahili. **RELIGION:** Christian, also animist. **ECONOMY:** bananas, beans, beer, blankets, coffee, cotton, grains, shoes, soap, tea, yams. **CURRENCY:** franc.

Djibouti

It's too hot here for the Devil himself. Or so they brag in Djibouti. Blistered by the sun, this tiny country is a desert with less than one square mile of farmland. Goats nibble at desert scrub and supply milk, the main food.

Tribes of Afars and Issas herd their goats from one water hole to the next, pitching hide tents and harvesting salt from surface deposits. An Afar bride may be given goats or chickens for a wedding gift.

The city of Djibouti, near the strait between the Red Sea and the Gulf of Aden, has a deep harbor and is a major fuel stop for freighters and oil tankers. About 70 ships pass through the strait each day.

OFFICIAL NAME: Republic of Djibouti
AREA: 9,000 sq mi (23,300 sq km)
POPULATION: 180,000
CAPITAL: Djibouti (pop. 62,000)
ETHNIC GROUPS: Issa, Afar. **LANGUAGE:** Afar, Arabic, French, Somali. **RELIGION:** Muslim, also Christian. **ECONOMY:** hides and skins, livestock. **CURRENCY:** franc.

Ethiopia

To reach the cool highlands where most Ethiopians live, a traveler by land must cross a strip of hot desert wastes bordering the Red Sea—the land of the warlike Danakil.

Better get protection from a local sultan before you enter there. These wandering tribesmen of Eritrea carry curving knives as long as a man's arm and have no use whatever for strangers.

Visitors usually ride airliners into the high country where Addis Ababa stands. West of the capital rise wild, beautiful mountains that cradle Lake Tana, source of the Blue Nile. The famed river tumbles down a canyon 20 miles (32 km) wide, two miles (3.2 km) wider than the Grand Canyon. The Amhara people, rulers here for the past 3,000 years, came into these once-remote mountains from Arabian lands across the Red Sea.

The Amharas and most other Ethiopians raise cattle, goats, and food crops on small farms. Early Greek explorers gave this ancient country its name, which means "the land of sunburned faces."

OFFICIAL NAME: Ethiopia
AREA: 454,900 sq mi (1,178,400 sq km)
POPULATION: 29,679,000
CAPITAL: Addis Ababa (pop. 1,162,000)
ETHNIC GROUPS: Galla, Amhara, Tigrai, Sidamo, Shankella, Somali. **LANGUAGE:** Amharic, English, also Arabic, Galla, and Tigrai. **RELIGION:** Muslim, Eastern Orthodox, also animist. **ECONOMY:** cement, coffee, cotton, grains, livestock, oil refining, oilseeds, peas, sugar, textiles. **CURRENCY:** birr.

Kenya

On the dusty plains of southwestern Kenya, a 16-year-old Masai *moran,* or warrior, wanders with his cattle in search of grass. He glances anxiously at a clump of bushes. If a lion jumps out and attacks the herd, the young warrior may try to kill the lion with his spear.

The Masai dwell in huts plastered with cow dung and live on a diet of ox blood, milk, and meat. They are one of more than 40 tribes in Kenya.

The Kikuyus are Kenya's largest tribe. They tell the legend of Ngai, Divider of the Universe, who created lofty Mount Kenya and gave the surrounding highlands to the Kikuyus. To this day most of Kenya's people dwell in this fertile region, or among the hills near Lake Victoria's shores, or along the Indian Ocean coast.

The rest of Kenya, dry scrubland and searing desert, is home mainly to wild animals and hardy tribes such as the Masai, Turkana, and Somali.

Farming is Kenya's chief occupation. But money also is earned through the many thousands of animals—including lions, zebras, and elephants—that roam, protected from hunters, in 16 wildlife parks.

Every day, planeloads of tourists arrive in Kenya and head for the parks on guided safaris. Safe in a Land-Rover, a group of visitors stops near a clump of bushes. If a lion jumps out, the visitors will try to shoot it—with their cameras.

OFFICIAL NAME: Republic of Kenya
AREA: 225,000 sq mi (582,700 sq km)
POPULATION: 14,837,000
CAPITAL: Nairobi (pop. 736,000)
ETHNIC GROUPS: Bantu. **LANGUAGE:** English, Swahili, also Kikuyu, Luo. **RELIGION:** Christian, animist, also Muslim. **ECONOMY:** beer, cassava, cement, coffee, cotton, grains, hides and skins, livestock, meat, oil refining, pyrethrum, sisal, soda ash, tea. **CURRENCY:** shilling.

Rwanda

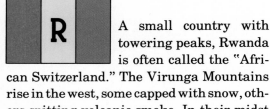 A small country with towering peaks, Rwanda is often called the "African Switzerland." The Virunga Mountains rise in the west, some capped with snow, others spitting volcanic smoke. In their midst lies Lake Kivu—beautiful, largely unspoiled, and fringed with narrow inlets.

Grassy, rolling plateaus slope eastward across Rwanda. Once covered by forests, the plateaus were cleared for farming. Now erosion scars the land. Rwanda is a crowded country, and growing numbers of Hutu farmers and cattle-raising Tutsi tribes overuse the fields and pastures. But some areas still bloom like a florist's shop. Geraniums are grown for perfume and pyrethrum, another flower, makes insecticides.

A few Pygmies, the original Rwandans, hunt in the forests; others work in town.

OFFICIAL NAME: Republic of Rwanda
AREA: 10,000 sq mi (25,900 sq km)
POPULATION: 4,444,000
CAPITAL: Kigali (pop. 59,100)
ETHNIC GROUPS: Hutu, also Tutsi. **LANGUAGE:** French, Kinyarwanda, also Swahili. **RELIGION:** Christian, animist. **ECONOMY:** bananas, cassava, coffee, livestock, pyrethrum, tea, tin. **CURRENCY:** franc.

Somalia

 In Somalia, the camel is boss. Wealth, power, and damages for injury are measured in camels. Relatives of a Somali man killed by accident, or murdered, may demand 100 camels in payment. For a woman's life, 50 will do.

Nomad Somali families follow their herds of camels, sheep, and goats over sandy wilds that may be desert one week, then pasture the next—when the scant rains fall. Without the rain, Somalia would be an extension of the Sahara Desert.

This country forms most of the "Horn of Africa." Look at a map and you can see how this part of Africa got that name.

When days are hotter and drier than usual, Somalis may get as bad-tempered as their camels. Deadly fights break out at water wells. (And may result in a 100-camel penalty.) Somali herdsmen look down on the few farmers who raise grains. Milking camels is what "real men" do here. Women are only allowed to load the animals for travel.

OFFICIAL NAME: Somali Democratic Republic
AREA: 246,000 sq mi (637,100 sq km)
POPULATION: 3,388,000
CAPITAL: Mogadishu (pop. 230,000)
ETHNIC GROUPS: Somali, also Bantu, Arab. **LANGUAGE:** Somali, also Arabic, English, Italian. **RELIGION:** Muslim. **ECONOMY:** bananas, cotton, grains, hides and skins, livestock, meat, sugar. **CURRENCY:** shilling.

Tanzania

 Ngorongoro Crater in northern Tanzania is one of nature's great zoos. But it's the people who are caged here, in vehicles, while hyenas, hippos, wildebeests, and other animals freely roam the 11-by-13 mile (18-by-21 km) grassy bowl, shaped long ago when a volcano collapsed inward. Not far away from this wildlife

preserve, tourists may also visit Olduvai Gorge, where Dr. Mary Leakey has discovered what may be the fossilized bones of some of man's earliest relatives.

The "Tan" in Tanzania stands for the mainland, called Tanganyika; the "zan" represents the island of Zanzibar, once a separate country. Zanzibar and nearby Pemba provide most of the world's cloves.

OFFICIAL NAME: United Republic of Tanzania
AREA: 362,800 sq mi (939,700 sq km)
POPULATION: 16,838,000
CAPITAL: Dar es Salaam (pop. 517,000)
ETHNIC GROUPS: Bantu. **LANGUAGE:** Swahili, English, also Bantu dialects. **RELIGION:** Muslim, Christian, animist. **ECONOMY:** beer, cashew nuts, cement, cloves, coffee, cotton, diamonds, meat, oil refining, shoes, sisal, tea, textiles, tobacco, wood. **CURRENCY:** shilling.

Uganda

 When the sun hangs nearly overhead, Ugandan farmers put down their hoes. After working in the peanut fields for five hours, they are ready to troop back to the family hut for a meal of *matoke*—steamed mashed bananas.

Clans (large families) stick together in Uganda, a mid-African nation flanked on the southeast by Lake Victoria, largest lake in Africa, and on the west by the rainy Ruwenzori—the "Mountains of the Moon," so high that glaciers form at the top.

When a young Ugandan gets a job in a copper mine or cotton mill, he shares his pay with relatives. Many young people work in cities around Lake Victoria. From it flows the Victoria Nile, which winds northward through lakes and over waterfalls.

OFFICIAL NAME: Republic of Uganda
AREA: 91,000 sq mi (235,700 sq km)
POPULATION: 12,780,000
CAPITAL: Kampala (pop. 330,700)
ETHNIC GROUPS: Baganda, Banyankore, Basoga, Iteso. **LANGUAGE:** English, Swahili, also Luganda. **RELIGION:** Christian, also animist, Muslim. **ECONOMY:** beer, cement, coffee, copper, cotton, fertilizer, fish, livestock, shoes, sugar, tea, textiles, tobacco, wood. **CURRENCY:** shilling.

Ethiopia

1 *Salt miners pry a living from lakebeds in the Danakil Depression. Seasonal rains in hills wash salt to the valley, where scorching heat dries up the salty water. The shrinking lakes leave behind white cakes to be harvested and sold.*

2 *A patchwork of fields tops Ethiopia's broken tableland. In thousands of years only three foreign invasions—Muslim, British, and Italian—have succeeded in penetrating these fortress highlands.*

Kenya

1 Mount Kenya's rocky spires loom behind top-heavy plants called giant groundsels, found only in uplands above 11,000 feet.

2 Somali women, at a Mombasa celebration, go without the veils many other Muslim women wear. Some Somalis are Kenyans, but most live in neighboring Somalia.

3 Safe in a national park, giraffes browse in sight of Nairobi's rising skyline. Many safaris start at this mile-high city.

Burundi

▶ Graceful dancers from Burundi's ruling Tutsi tribe honor bygone battles.

1

Tanzania

1 *Wildebeests speckle grasslands of the Serengeti Plain. A fifth of Africa's ten million or so large mammals live in this part of northern Tanzania.*

2 *Atop mighty Kilimanjaro's slumbering crater, glaciers turn a cold shoulder to the hot equatorial sun. Africa's tallest peak, 19,340 feet (5,895 m), rises from a base big enough to cover Rhode Island.*

Rwanda

3 *Fierce in folktales, gorillas seem to lead gentle lives in Rwanda's mountain forests. When only hours old, a baby can keep a firm, hairy grip on its mother.*

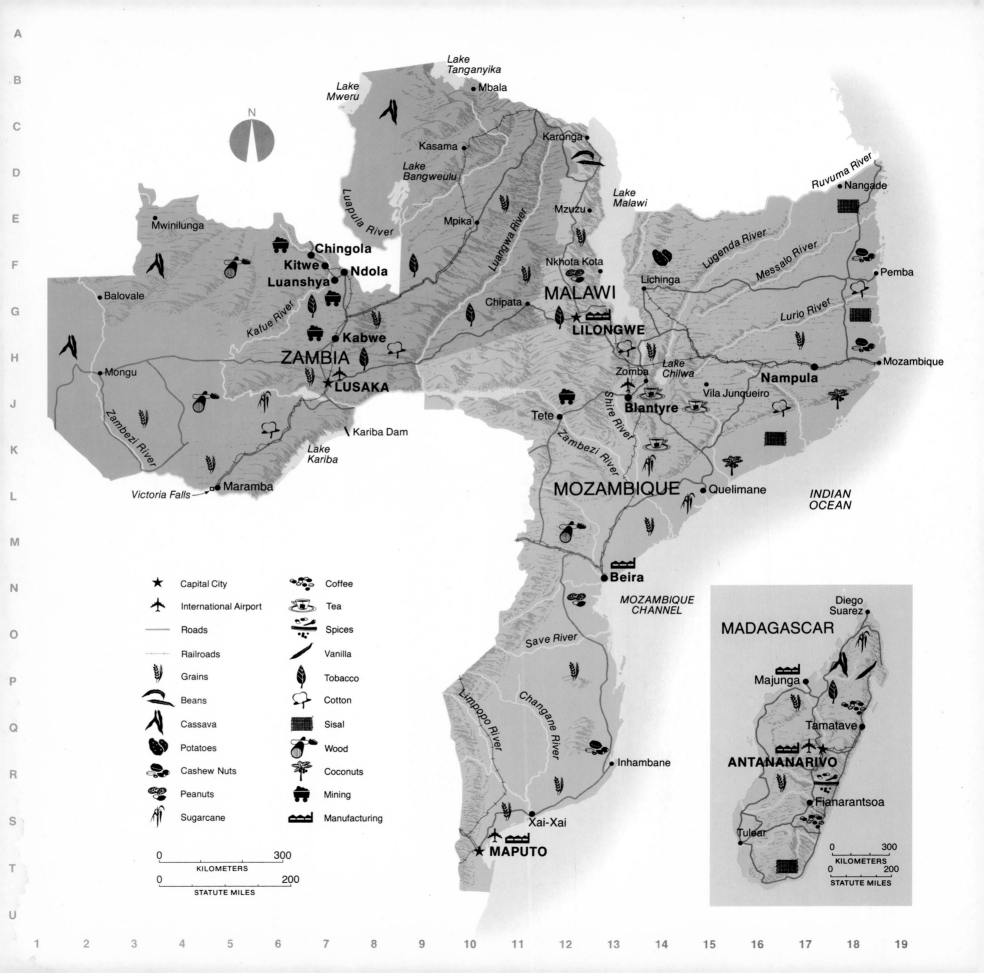

Lake Tanganyika

Lake Mweru

• Mbala

Karonga •

Kasama •

Lake Bangweulu

Luapula River

Ruvuma River

• Nangade

Mwinilunga •

Mpika •

Mzuzu •

Lake Malawi

Chingola

Kitwe **Ndola**

Luanshya

Nkhota Kota

Lichinga •

Lugenda River

Messalo River

• Pemba

Balovale •

Kafue River

Luangwa River

Chipata •

MALAWI

Lurio River

Kabwe

LILONGWE

ZAMBIA

Mozambique •

Mongu •

LUSAKA

Zomba •

Lake Chilwa

Vila Junqueiro •

Nampula

Zambezi River

Shire River

Blantyre

Tete •

Kariba Dam

Lake Kariba

Zambezi River

MOZAMBIQUE

• Quelimane

INDIAN OCEAN

Victoria Falls → • Maramba

N

Beira

MOZAMBIQUE CHANNEL

Save River

Changane River

Limpopo River

• Inhambane

Xai-Xai

MAPUTO

Legend

★ Capital City
✈ International Airport
— Roads
— Railroads
Grains
Beans
Cassava
Potatoes
Cashew Nuts
Peanuts
Sugarcane

Coffee
Tea
Spices
Vanilla
Tobacco
Cotton
Sisal
Wood
Coconuts
Mining
Manufacturing

0 _____ 300
KILOMETERS
0 _____ 200
STATUTE MILES

MADAGASCAR

Diego Suarez •

Majunga •

Tamatave •

ANTANANARIVO

Fianarantsoa •

Tulear •

0 _____ 300
KILOMETERS
0 _____ 200
STATUTE MILES

Madagascar

An ideal base for pirates, thought Capt. William Kidd. From Madagascar's mountains one could spy merchant ships in the Mozambique Channel, which separates this fourth largest island in the world from mainland Africa.

Madagascar seems to have borrowed from everywhere else. From France, once ruler of this island, come sidewalk cafes. The dark-skinned Malagasy people, part African and part Indonesian, speak a language related to those heard in the East Indies. Madagascar's Oriental roots are also seen in rice terraces and outrigger canoes. Some animal life appears almost South American. One creature, the monkeylike lemur, has a tail like a fox's and ears like a bat's.

"Don't disturb the dead!" Western custom warns. But Malagasians often dig up their dead to wrap the bodies in fresh shrouds.

Madagascar grows more than half the world's vanilla. The vanilla bean, from which the flavor comes, is the seed pod of a climbing orchid. After harvesting, the beans must dry for weeks. Sometimes they are "branded" with pinpricks to stop bean rustlers. Can you tell a place by its smell? Of course! Parts of Madagascar smell like an old-fashioned ice-cream parlor.

OFFICIAL NAME: Democratic Republic of Madagascar
AREA: 230,000 sq mi (595,700 sq km)
POPULATION: 8,158,000
CAPITAL: Antananarivo (pop. 367,000)
ETHNIC GROUPS: Merina, Betsimisaraka. **LANGUAGE:** French, Malagasy (Merina dialect).
RELIGION: animist, Christian, also Muslim.
ECONOMY: cassava, cloves, coffee, grains, livestock, oil refining, raffia, sisal, soap, sugar, textiles, tobacco, vanilla. **CURRENCY:** franc.

Malawi

All of Malawi could be a national park. Its green mountains and grassy plateaus, part of the Great Rift Valley system, make the country one of Africa's most scenic. Small hotels and fishing villages dot the shores of glittering Lake Malawi.

Beautiful but poor, Malawi has no mineral treasures and few factories. Many of the men must leave home for months or years to work in the mines of Zambia and South Africa. At home, women run the farms that feed their families. Most Malawians trace their ancestors through the mother's side of the family only.

OFFICIAL NAME: Republic of Malawi
AREA: 36,700 sq mi (95,000 sq km)
POPULATION: 5,694,000
CAPITAL: Lilongwe (pop. 102,000)
ETHNIC GROUPS: Bantu. **LANGUAGE:** Chichewa, English, Lomwe, also many tribal tongues. **RELIGION:** animist, also Christian, Muslim. **ECONOMY:** beans, cement, cotton, fruit, grains, peanuts, peas, sugar, tea, tobacco, tung nuts, vegetables, wood. **CURRENCY:** kwacha.

Mozambique

Don't be confused by the rickshas bouncing along the harbor boulevard. This is not Hong Kong, but a town in Mozambique. For centuries traders brought foreign culture—rickshas, mosques, soccer. They took away ivory and slaves—and gold from what some say were King Solomon's mines. Portuguese colonists cleared land for tea and sugar plantations.

But railroads and harbors are now Mozambique's chief source of wealth. Landlocked countries west of the mountains depend on them for a way to reach the sea.

Little of the coastal bustle spreads to the interior. There Makonde girls cut their faces to leave beauty scars, and Makua dancers prance about on six-foot (2 m) stilts.

OFFICIAL NAME: People's Republic of Mozambique
AREA: 303,700 sq mi (786,700 sq km)
POPULATION: 9,866,000
CAPITAL: Maputo (pop. 342,000)
ETHNIC GROUPS: Makua-Lomue, Tsonga, other Bantu. **LANGUAGE:** Portuguese, also many tribal tongues. **RELIGION:** animist, also Christian, Muslim. **ECONOMY:** beer, cashew nuts, cement, chemicals, coal, coconut, cotton, grains, oil refining, peanuts, potatoes, sisal, sugar, tea, textiles, wood. **CURRENCY:** escudo.

Zambia

From 25 miles (40 km) away the thundering roar can be heard: Victoria Falls, where the Zambezi River dives into a mist-filled gorge. Downstream, the huge Kariba Dam pumps electric power to Zambia and its neighbor Rhodesia.

Copper and corn—most Zambians live off one or the other. The busy Copperbelt north of Lusaka holds one of the world's richest deposits. In the bush, families grow corn for *nshima,* a stiff mush. Balls of nshima, rolled by hand straight from the pot, go well with a relish of dried buffalo meat.

OFFICIAL NAME: Republic of Zambia
AREA: 288,000 sq mi (745,900 sq km)
POPULATION: 5,471,000
CAPITAL: Lusaka (pop. 483,000)
ETHNIC GROUPS: Bantu. **LANGUAGE:** English, also many tribal tongues. **RELIGION:** animist, also Christian. **ECONOMY:** cassava, cobalt, copper, cotton, grains, lead, sugar, tobacco, wood, zinc. **CURRENCY:** kwacha.

Mozambique

1 *High-kicking Makua tribesmen strap on long stilts and do acrobatic dances. The men make their own masks and costumes—and the sillier the better!*

2 *Waist-deep in tea plants, workers pluck leaves from terraced slopes above Vila Junqueiro. Portuguese settlers brought in crops such as corn, peanuts, cassava, and cashew nuts. Mozambique Island exports much of the world's cashew nuts.*

3 *Portuguese colonists named this busy port Lourenco Marques for a trader who explored here in 1544. With independence the country's new leaders gave the city, their national capital, a new African name—Maputo, same as a nearby river.*

4

5

6

Malawi

4 *Teamwork on the Shire River: A Malawi boy gets set to lower a fish trap while another poles the canoe. Boats made of wood planks and fitted with outboard motors are now replacing these dugouts.*

5 *A young marketplace musician fingers his flute. Schoolchildren attend classes taught by teachers from Great Britain who teach them to speak English.*

6 *Baby rides piggyback as mother sifts rice. Behind them sparkles Lake Malawi, the third largest lake in Africa.*

1

2

3

Madagascar

1 A highland girl picks wild yellow cosmos.
Some plants native to Madagascar, like
the crown-of-thorns and flamboyant tree,
can be found in Florida and California.

2 Bottle-shaped baobab trees seem to wave
leafy roots instead of branches. The
spongy trunks store water as cacti do.

3 A chameleon opens wide, perhaps ready
to flick out its long tongue to catch
a tasty fly. This lizard can blend into
the background by changing color. That
way it is invisible both to enemies and
to any careless dinners that come near.

4 Nimble fingers bundle vanilla bean pods.
Juice from crushed beans is exported
to flavor foods such as ice cream.

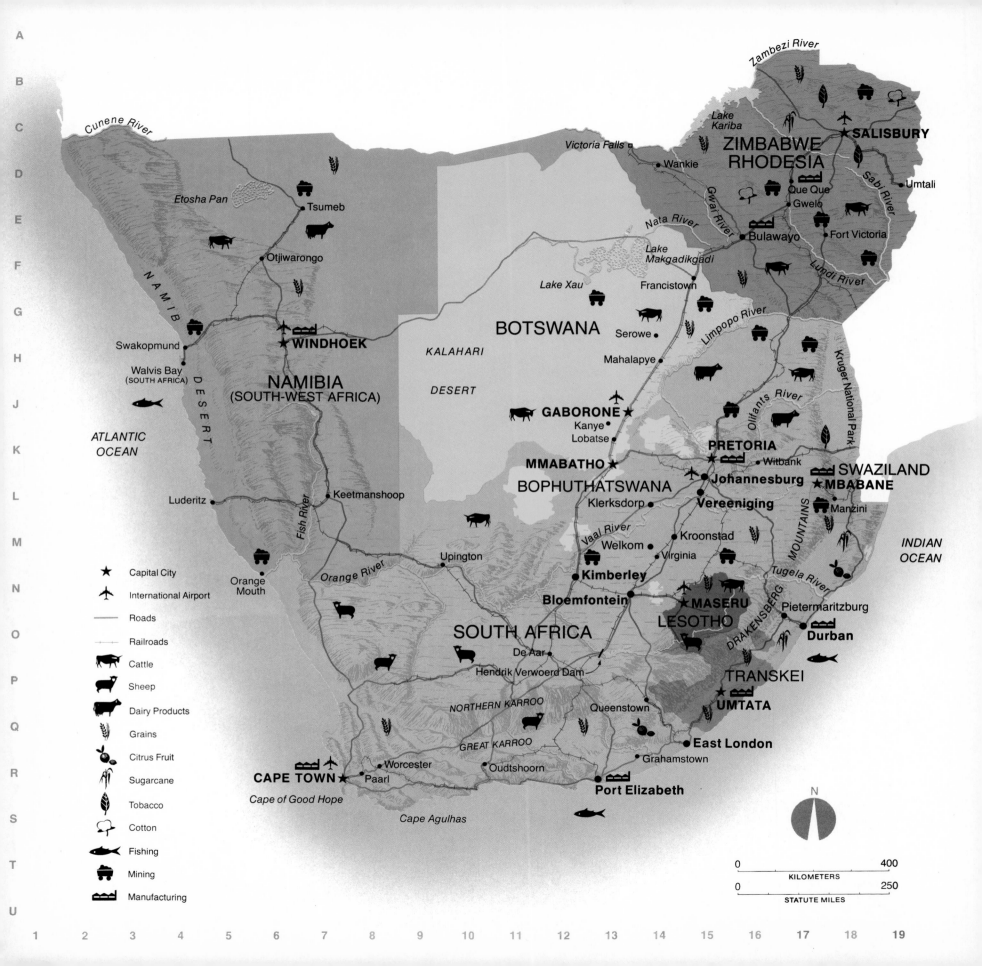

Botswana

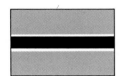

While a Bushman hunts antelope, his wife hunts for water in the Kalahari Desert, which covers three-fourths of Botswana. Seeing a plant in damp sand, she digs a deep hole and places a hollow reed in it. Patiently she sucks on the straw. When the water rises, she sends it from her mouth through another straw into a hollow ostrich egg. She will seal the egg with clay and bury it for future use.

The great majority of Botswana's population—the Tswana people—raises cattle and grain along the country's wetter eastern border. Now that diamonds and other minerals have been discovered, Botswana's economy no longer depends so heavily on the size of the yearly cattle herd. But the country still does depend on South Africa for jobs and a lifeline to the outside world.

OFFICIAL NAME: Republic of Botswana
AREA: 220,000 sq mi (569,800 sq km)
POPULATION: 750,000
CAPITAL: Gaborone (pop. 17,700)
ETHNIC GROUPS: Tswana, also Bushman. **LANGUAGE:** Tswana, English. **RELIGION:** animist, also Christian. **ECONOMY:** coal, copper, diamonds, grains, hides and skins, livestock, meat, nickel. **CURRENCY:** pula.

Lesotho

When the sun is barely up, Thoka leaves her mud hut for the long walk to school. About three-fourths of Lesotho's children go to school, more than in most other African countries. Most students are girls. Boys—even at age five—must often herd cattle instead.

People of Lesotho—the Sotho—count their wealth in cattle. People who commit crimes may even pay their fines in cattle. Very little grows in the red earth of this dry and mountainous country. Its steeply eroded canyons look like northern Arizona. Because soil is so poor and resources so few, many Sotho must spend at least half the year working in the mines, factories, and farms of neighboring South Africa.

OFFICIAL NAME: Kingdom of Lesotho
AREA: 11,700 sq mi (30,300 sq km)
POPULATION: 1,277,000
CAPITAL: Maseru (pop. 17,000)
ETHNIC GROUPS: Sotho. **LANGUAGE:** Sotho, English. **RELIGION:** Christian, also animist. **ECONOMY:** diamonds, grains, livestock, mohair, wool. **CURRENCY:** rand.

Namibia

Deserts can't get much drier than the Namib. With only about an inch of rain each year, little grows. One of the few things that can survive: a unique, low-lying plant called *Welwitschia mirabilis*. Its green fronds may reach as long as 20 feet (6 m). It can live for hundreds of years.

These old, old plants grow in what soon may be a new country—Namibia. Once called South-West Africa, Namibia has been controlled by South Africa for 60 years and depends heavily on its neighbor for commerce. A treasure in diamonds lies along the southwest coast. Uranium, copper, and other minerals are mined in the north.

As large as Texas and Louisiana put to-gether, Namibia has only about as many people as the tiny state of Rhode Island.

OFFICIAL NAME: Namibia
AREA: 318,000 sq mi (823,600 sq km)
POPULATION: 964,000
CAPITAL: Windhoek (pop. 61,300)
ETHNIC GROUPS: Bantu, Bushman, Hottentot, also European, mulattos. **LANGUAGE:** Afrikaans, German, also English, tribal tongues. **RELIGION:** Christian, animist. **ECONOMY:** copper, dairy products, diamonds, fish, grains, lead, livestock, meat, pelts, uranium. **CURRENCY:** rand.

South Africa

South Africans have a word. It stands for an idea, perhaps the most important idea in the country. Laws based on the word tell people where they may live, what work they may do, what schools they may go to, whom they may marry. The word has brought South Africa rebellion at home and criticism from abroad.

The word is *apartheid,* pronounced a-PART-hite. It means "apartness" and stands for the policy of the white-controlled government that South Africa's non-white peoples, including 19 million blacks, and its 5 million whites must stay separate. Each race has its own neighborhoods, schools, jobs, parks, and beaches. Blacks complain that these divisions are unfair, and their anger has often given birth to strikes and riots.

Such trouble seems out of place in a land with South Africa's blessings. Mines rich in diamonds and uranium add to a national fortune in gold, some of it mined from tunnels more than *two miles* (3.2 km) deep.

South Africa is rich in beauty, too. Sunny beaches dot the rugged coast. The Drakensberg Mountains loom like a castle wall over the eastern side of the country. Herds of Cape buffalo thunder across a grassy plain called the *veld* in Kruger National Park.

The Great Karroo, a drab desert, turns into a rainbow of wild flowers at the magic touch of a spring shower. Pieter Bosch lives on a farm west of the Great Karroo. In these rolling hills near Cape Town his family grows grapes for wine. Pieter is an Afrikaner whose ancestors came here from Holland 300 years ago.

In an all-black suburb of Johannesburg, Stella Mbele lives in a crowded three-room house. Every day her father takes a long bus ride to his job in a white-owned factory. Like all black adults, he must carry a passbook to prove that he has permission to live and work where he does. Otherwise he would be sent to a "homeland." The government has set aside ten such areas, called Bantustans, in the countryside for black tribes.

South Africa has started giving these homelands independence. Some blacks like this idea, but many others do not. They say that the homelands have too few resources and that too few blacks actually live in them. Other countries agree that the homelands are not "real" nations. Even so, South Africa has already declared two of these Bantustans to be independent:

Bophuthatswana. To see all of this homeland you must cross the border twelve times. Six separate pieces make Bophuthatswana a country of islands surrounded by South African land. Its long name is pronounced Bo-pu-to-swa-na and means "place of the Tswanas."

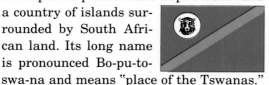

Yet many Tswanas who live here do not work here. Some towns in the flat, dusty countryside are really suburbs of nearby South African cities. Many residents spend their days working in South Africa and their nights sleeping in Bophuthatswana.

Transkei. Round, white huts dot the rolling green hills of Transkei, the "land across the Kei River." In this 16,329-square-mile (42,292 sq km) homeland, which is made of one large area and two smaller ones, most people speak the Xhosa language, with its popping, clicking sounds.

Lacking jobs at home, about 300,000 Transkeians must work in South Africa. Transkei's government hopes foreigners will come here to build factories, where Transkeians can work, and to stay in

vacation hotels perched among the cliffs and waterfalls along the wild, rocky coast.

OFFICIAL NAME: Republic of South Africa
AREA: 472,000 sq mi (1,223,000 sq km)
POPULATION: 27,432,000
CAPITAL: Cape Town, legislative (pop. 698,000)
    Pretoria, administrative (pop. 545,500)
    Bloemfontein, judicial (pop. 150,000)
ETHNIC GROUPS: Bantu, also European, mixed.
LANGUAGE: Afrikaans, English, also Bantu dialects. **RELIGION:** Christian. **ECONOMY:** chemicals, citrus fruit, dairy products, diamonds, fish, gold, grains, iron, machinery, metals, motor vehicles, steel, sugar, textiles, tobacco, uranium, wool. **CURRENCY:** rand.

Swaziland

Watering the cattle is a favorite chore of seven-year-old Bunu. When the cattle are driven into a stream, he and his friends get to swim too. Bunu belongs to the Swazi people, who make up 96 percent of the population. In this strongly traditional society, many boys at age six have their earlobes slit in a ceremony. They then leave their mothers' huts to live in dormitories.

Bunu's little brother scares monkeys and birds out of the cornfields. His sisters help their mother grind corn into meal with a heavy stone. Cornmeal cooked with vegetables is the main dish at most meals.

Bunu lives on a low plain in eastern Swaziland. High mountains covered with pine forests rise along the western border. In between are grassy hills where citrus fruit, sugarcane, and cotton grow on large farms. More and more Swazis now work in factories and in mines that produce iron, asbestos, and coal. Beautiful scenery and a large wildlife preserve attract many tourists.

OFFICIAL NAME: Kingdom of Swaziland
AREA: 6,718 sq mi (17,400 sq km)
POPULATION: 526,000
CAPITAL: Mbabane (pop. 22,000)
ETHNIC GROUPS: Swazi. **LANGUAGE:** English, siSwati. **RELIGION:** Christian, animist. **ECONOMY:** asbestos, citrus fruit, cotton, grains, iron, meat, sugar, wood. **CURRENCY:** lilangeni.

Zimbabwe Rhodesia

The name Zimbabwe belongs to a mystery: a thick-walled ruin made of stone, near Fort Victoria. Stones are rare in the bush country. People here think Zimbabwe was once center of a great empire. So they named the country after it.

In recent times the nation has also been known as Rhodesia. That name honored Cecil Rhodes, an Englishman who wanted to plant the British flag all over Africa. He sent white settlers to farm the grasslands. The colonists built huge estates on which they grew tobacco, cotton, wheat, and sugarcane. They also found great wealth in minerals—copper, gold, iron, and the chromium that is so important in making stainless steel. This land is believed to hold the world's largest reserves of chrome ore.

Zimbabwe stands for a struggle as well as a country. Whites, with only 4 percent of the population, controlled the government. Blacks wanted a full say. As the contest goes on, white Rhodesia slowly gives way.

Even in the painful time of change the bright spots stand out. There are the fine cities of Salisbury and Bulawayo. A dam across the Zambezi River created Lake Kariba, a big blue jewel the size of Delaware. Its waters irrigate farms, drive generators that supply electricity to homes and factories, and delight boaters.

Wankie National Park, bigger than Connecticut, is called tusker territory—home to 10,000 elephants. To the north of Wankie the Zambezi roars over one of the mightiest waterfalls on earth: Victoria Falls.

OFFICIAL NAME: Zimbabwe Rhodesia
AREA: 151,000 sq mi (391,100 sq km)
POPULATION: 6,972,000
CAPITAL: Salisbury (pop. 107,000)
ETHNIC GROUPS: Bantu, also whites. **LANGUAGE:** English, also Chishona, Sindebele. **RELIGION:** animist, Christian. **ECONOMY:** asbestos, chrome, copper, cotton, gold, grains, livestock, meat, nickel, steel, tobacco. **CURRENCY:** dollar.

Zimbabwe Rhodesia

1 *"I felt a little tremor," wrote the explorer David Livingstone as he approached Victoria Falls, which he named in honor of Britain's Queen Victoria. His guides called the falls* Mosi oa Tunya *(Smoke that Thunders) after its mighty roar and cloud of mist. The spray bounces higher than a thousand feet into the air and can sometimes be seen 40 miles (64 km) away. Stretching a mile across the entire width of the Zambezi River, the falls tumble down sheer walls as high as a 35-story building.*

2 *Ever on the lookout, a fish eagle perches above a river. This powerful bird of prey snatches fish out of the water with sharp talons—long, curved claws. When the fish eagle calls out, it throws back its head until its crown touches its back.*

South Africa

1 *Grapes for excellent wines pour forth from the Cape region, blessed with sandy soil. Huguenots introduced vine cuttings from their native France.*

2 *Fort Knox? No, a bank vault in Pretoria glimmers with $27\frac{1}{2}$-pound (12.5 kg) bars of gold. It takes about 3 tons of rock to produce an ounce of gold.*

3 *Shoulder to shoulder with their mothers, Zulu girls prepare to plant grain near their village. Men take care of cattle, the standard used to measure wealth.*

4 *In steaming mines 8,000 feet (2,438 m) deep, Bantu-speaking tribesmen drill for gold. In 1977 over half of the nearly 500,000 black workers in the mines came from outside of South Africa.*

5 *Cape Town, the seat of Parliament, curls around flat-topped Table Mountain and its neighboring peaks. Pretoria, lying 800 miles (1,287 km) to the northeast, serves as the administrative capital.*

Namibia

1 *Of the 18 countries producing diamonds, Namibia supplies the most valuable.*

2 *Man-made dunes line Namibia's desert coast. Machines digging for diamonds dump a hundred million pounds of sand and gravel for each pound of gems.*

3 *Fleeing ostriches leave their prints in the clay pan of Etosha Game Reserve. Wild animals range over much of Namibia's scrub desert and grassy plains.*

Swaziland

4 *Grapefruit for overseas markets tumble into a wagon. Irrigation has turned grazing lands into lush citrus groves.*

5 *A mountain of iron-rich hematite near Mbabane is sliced up and hauled away. Stone Age Africans mined ore 43,000 years ago, probably for body paint.*

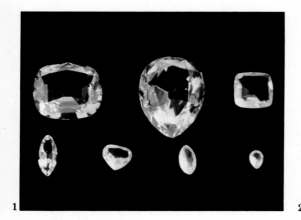

Lesotho

6 A Sotho cowboy's hat, shaped like a church bell, has become the country's symbol. It decorates Lesotho's flag. The blanket gives protection from mountain cold. Many families measure their wealth by the number of cattle they own.

Botswana

7 Stately in Victorian dress, Herero women borrowed styles from missionaries. By tradition, Hereros pay little heed to boundaries. They follow their cattle over grazing lands in corners of Angola and Botswana as well as in Namibia.

Australia

The flat, L-shaped piece of wood whirls down like a helicopter into the desert dust, right at the feet of the man who threw it. He picks it up and grins — most Australians don't know how to throw a returning boomerang. But this man's ancestors invented them. He is an Aborigine, one of a dark-skinned race that lives on earth's smallest continent. Aborigines probably crossed an Ice Age land bridge from Asia.

Aborigines were the first of three peoples to move into the region "down under" the Equator. Later came the Maori, Polynesian warriors in giant outrigger canoes. In the 1300's, or perhaps before, they settled New Zealand.

The late 1700's brought the third colonizers, the English. They soon outnumbered the other two groups. Today's nations — big, flat, brown Australia and small, hilly, green New Zealand — stand as outposts of a European people on Asia's side of the world.

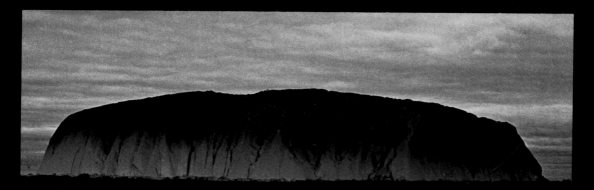

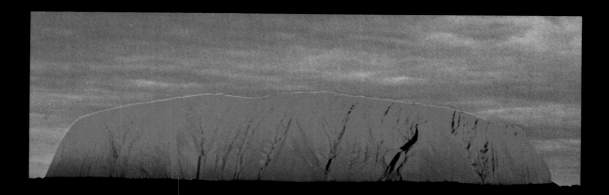

Lonely lump on a pancake landscape, Ayers Rock in Australia's Northern Territory catches the sunset's fire in photos taken minutes apart. The huge boulder, a mile and a half long, catches the sun's heat, too — then gives it off by night in an invisible fountain of hot air. Raging winds sucked up from the plain carve gullies in its flanks.

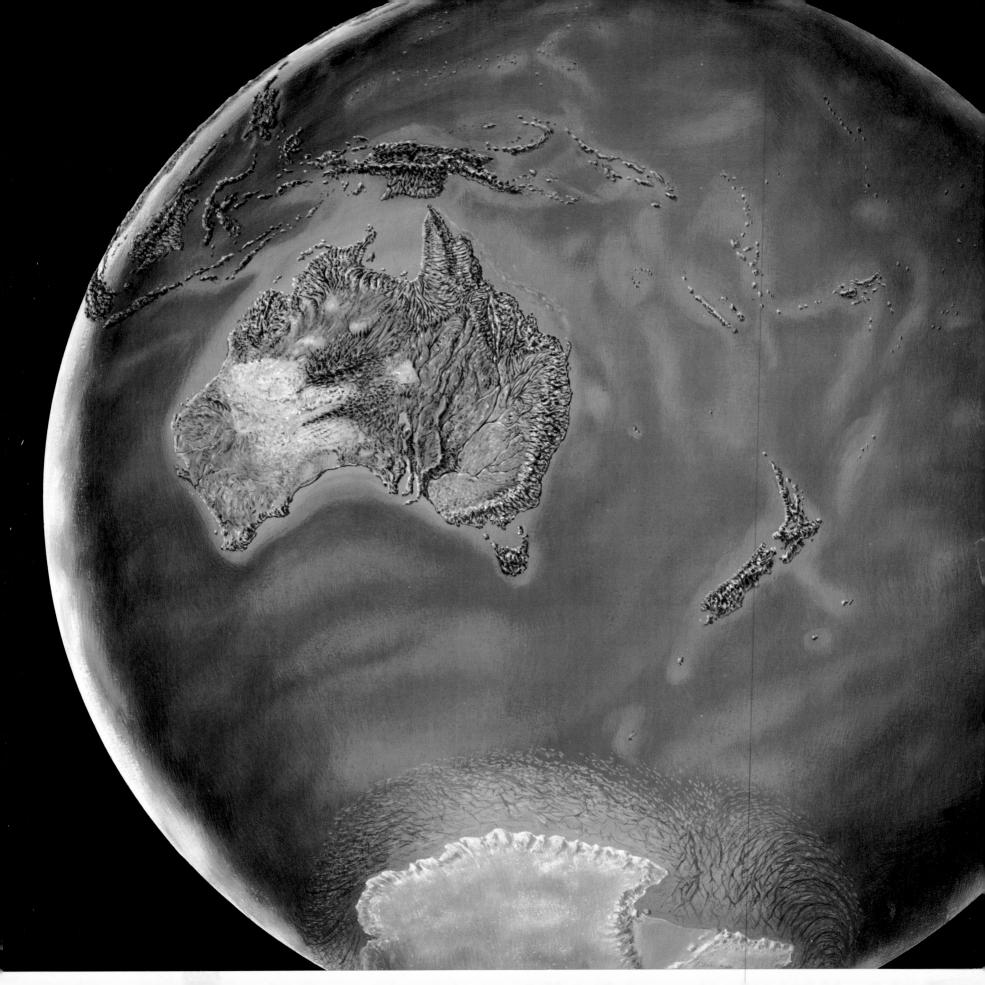

Australia

1 *Two koalas peer at the world from a preserve near Brisbane. A taste for eucalyptus leaves keeps them climbing.*

2 *Richly colored opals lure miners to South Australia. In sweltering heat men dig some $4 million worth a year.*

3 *Male harlequin tuskfish splash their brilliant hues over the Great Barrier Reef, a coral wonderland that guards Australia's northeastern coastline.*

4 *Lost in billows of fleece, Merino sheep await the judges' nod of approval at the annual Sydney Sheep Show.*

5 *Sydney's skyscrapers—and modern Opera House—line Port Jackson inlet. The harbor is Australia's busiest.*

6 *Young kangaroo, called a "joey," hangs in there. These great gray kangaroos are one of 56 species in Australia.*

1

2

4

3

5

6

1

Australia

1 *Flat as a griddle and nearly as hot, the outback is home to cattle. Australia exports some 150,000 tons of beef a year.*

2 *Outsmarting the outback south of Darwin, an Australian chops open a tree knot and drinks the water stored inside.*

New Zealand

3 *Milford Sound twists around the feet of mountain majesties on South Island's southwestern coast. Wilderness here is preserved in Fiordland National Park.*

4 *Maori children frolic in a tub warmed by the earth's inner furnace. North Island's unstable crust gives birth to hot springs, geysers, bubbling mud pools—and earth tremors.*

5 *Bizarre bird of the New Zealand night, the kiwi sniffs for earthworms through nostrils at the end of its long beak. Grounded by its tiny wings, the species quit flying thousands of years ago. Like a Noah's ark adrift alone, these islands hold animals found nowhere else.*

2   3

4

5

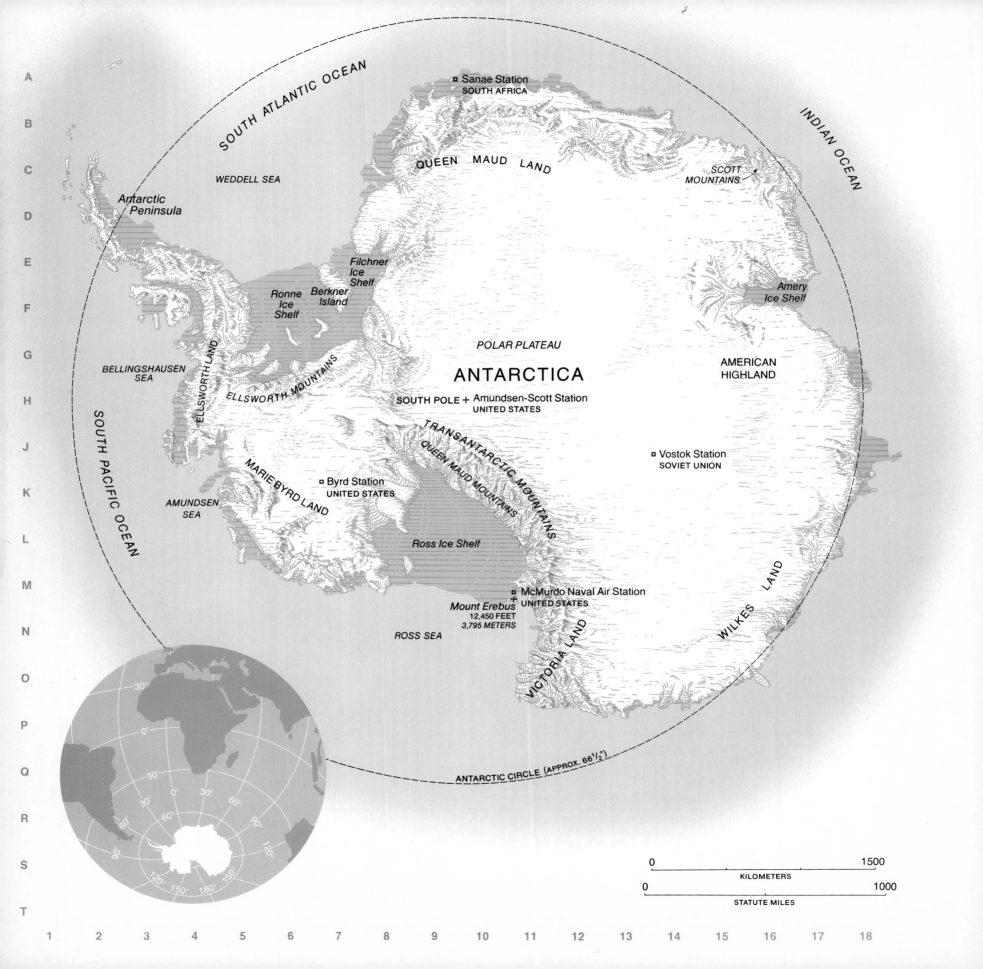

SOUTH ATLANTIC OCEAN

□ Sanae Station
SOUTH AFRICA

INDIAN OCEAN

QUEEN MAUD LAND

WEDDELL SEA

SCOTT
MOUNTAINS

Antarctic
Peninsula

Filchner
Ice
Shelf

Ronne
Ice
Shelf

Berkner
Island

Amery
Ice Shelf

POLAR PLATEAU

ANTARCTICA

AMERICAN
HIGHLAND

BELLINGSHAUSEN
SEA

ELLSWORTH LAND

ELLSWORTH MOUNTAINS

SOUTH POLE +

Amundsen-Scott Station
UNITED STATES

□ Vostok Station
SOVIET UNION

TRANSANTARCTIC MOUNTAINS

QUEEN MAUD MOUNTAINS

SOUTH PACIFIC OCEAN

MARIE BYRD LAND

□ Byrd Station
UNITED STATES

AMUNDSEN
SEA

Ross Ice Shelf

WILKES LAND

McMurdo Naval Air Station
□ UNITED STATES

Mount Erebus
12,450 FEET
3,795 METERS

VICTORIA LAND

ROSS SEA

ANTARCTIC CIRCLE (APPROX. 66½°)

0   1500
KILOMETERS
0   1000
STATUTE MILES

Antarctica

Blizzards of hurricane force shriek for days. Temperatures plunge more than 100° below zero F (–73° C). Surrounded by three oceans, buried under ice two miles (3.2 km) thick in places, Antarctica has been described as "the most remote, the most inaccessible, and the most inhospitable land on earth."

The size of the United States and Europe combined, this continent serves as an ice-age laboratory for explorers and scientists. No nation owns land in Antarctica. But the United States, the Soviet Union, Australia, and other countries have set up scientific research stations to solve such mysteries as how the creeping movement of the polar ice cap affects the world's weather. Scientists probe the frozen landscape. Nine-tenths of the world's ice lies locked beneath their feet — enough fresh water to fill the North Atlantic Ocean. If all the ice melted, oceans would rise 200 feet (61 m) and drown every coastal city in the world.

Along Antarctica's coastline, giant icebergs break off and drift out to sea. One that split off measured 208 miles (335 km) long and 60 miles (97 km) wide — an area as large as Belgium.

Beneath Antarctic ice lie untapped pools of oil, rich seams of coal, and deposits of manganese, iron, copper, and other minerals. Coastal waters, stained brown with tiny marine organisms called plankton, are enormously rich in nutrients. These support a dense population of shrimp-like krill, believed to be the world's largest source of animal protein. Finback and blue whales, the largest creatures on earth, gulp krill by the ton. Killer whales and leopard seals smash through pack ice to grab penguins and seals.

Fur seals, almost hunted to extinction in the 19th century, led to the discovery of Antarctica. Sealer Nathaniel Palmer of Connecticut may have been the first to sight the mainland when sailing near the Antarctic Peninsula in November 1820. A fellow sealer from Connecticut, John Davis, made history several months later — he was the first person to set foot on the continent.

When he landed he might have seen Antarctica's largest land animal, but he would have needed sharp eyes. It's no bigger than a gnat — the wingless fly *Belgica antarctica*. It feeds on the algae and fungi that grow where melting snow has formed pools.

Southward across deep crevasses and wavy ridges of ice lies the South Pole, first reached by the Norwegian explorer Roald Amundsen in 1911. His dog teams gave way to mechanized expeditions led by such men as Admiral Richard E. Byrd and Sir Vivian Fuchs. In tracked vehicles they blazed trails across a vast white desert. In Antarctica annual precipitation averages only about four to six inches. But millions of years ago this desert bloomed. Fossil ferns and tree trunks have turned up in the Queen Maud Mountains and other ranges. Antarctica was once a lush rain forest.

Arctic Regions

Unlike the Antarctic, a body of land surrounded by water, the Arctic is a body of water encircled by land. Nor is the Arctic as cold. Winter temperatures around the North Pole average about 30° below zero F. Parts of inland Siberia, more than one thousand miles to the south, can easily get much colder — as low as minus 96° F (–71° C).

The Arctic Ocean is warmed by currents from the Atlantic. Pack ice, ribboned with channels of open water called leads, wheels clockwise around the North Pole. On drifting ice-islands up to six miles (9.6 km) long and 200 feet (61 m) thick, research teams set up laboratories after World War II. Through holes in the ice they explored the mysteries of the Arctic Ocean. Core samples of sea-floor sediment indicated a warm-weather past. Undersea mountain ranges were charted. Nets yielded abundant sea life.

Sometimes polar bears hitchhike on the floating islands. Seals and whales also roam Arctic waters. But not penguins, which live only in Antarctic regions, nor their northern relatives, the extinct great auks.

The North Pole has long challenged explorers. Men in wooden ships tried to drift across the top of the world. Norway's Fridtjof Nansen in *Fram* came closest in 1896. He reached 85° N. In the early 1900's daring men drove sledges over the ice. Robert E. Peary and Dr. Frederick A. Cook both claimed to have reached the Pole first, a controversy that still lingers. In 1978 Japan's Naomi Uemura became the first man to sledge to the North Pole alone.

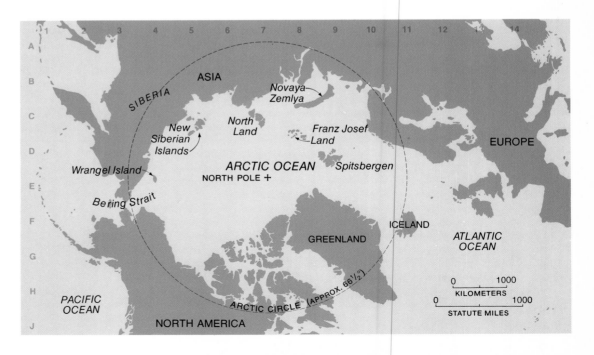

Antarctica

1 *A skua, hungry pirate of the penguin rookery, steals an egg as a mother penguin flaps flightless wings in protest. Despite skuas on land and leopard seals off shore, penguin colonies thrive.*

2 *"Scram!" an elephant seal seems to be telling the cameraman. Is it bluffing? Probably, though bulls sometimes bloody each other in battles for the females.*

3 *Penguins and blue-eyed shags share nest space on the Antarctic Peninsula.*

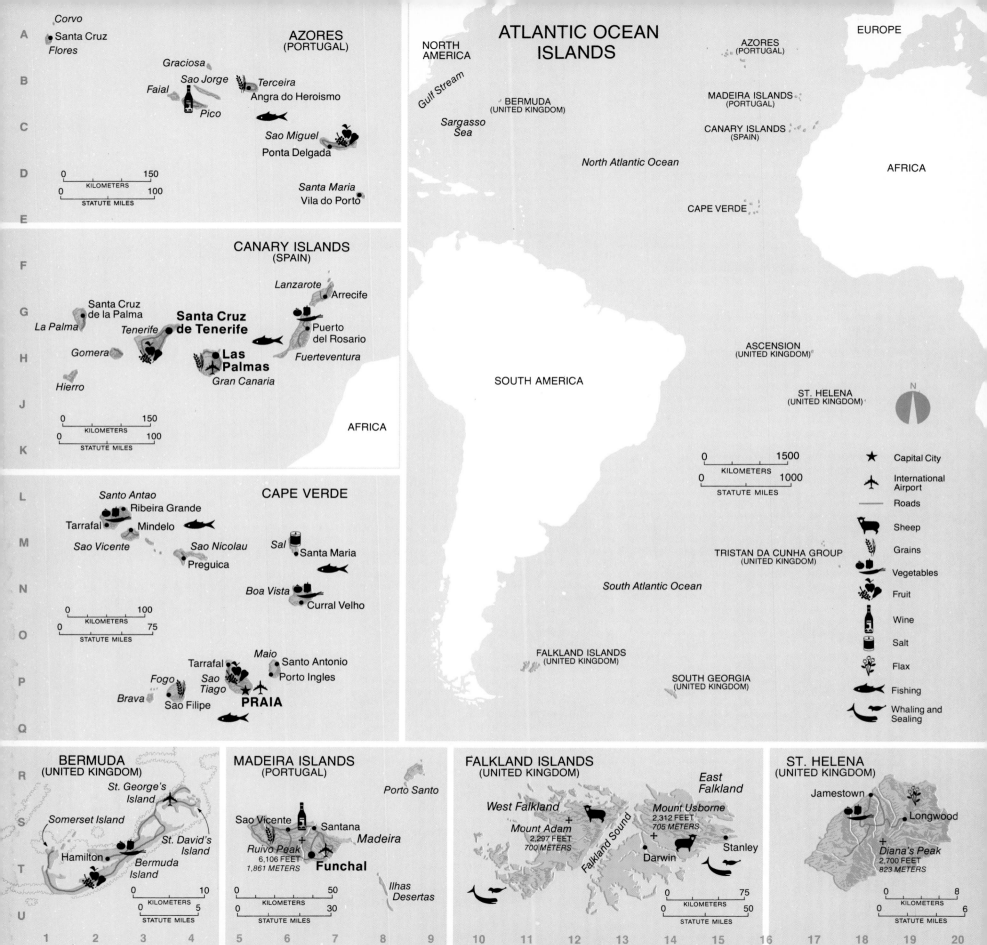

ATLANTIC OCEAN ISLANDS

AZORES (PORTUGAL)

Corvo
Santa Cruz
Flores

Graciosa
Sao Jorge
Faial
Terceira
Angra do Heroismo
Pico

Sao Miguel
Ponta Delgada

Santa Maria
Vila do Porto

0   150
KILOMETERS
0   100
STATUTE MILES

CANARY ISLANDS (SPAIN)

Lanzarote
Arrecife

Santa Cruz
de la Palma
La Palma
**Santa Cruz
de Tenerife**
Tenerife
Gomera
Puerto
del Rosario
**Las
Palmas**
Fuerteventura
Hierro
Gran Canaria

AFRICA

0   150
KILOMETERS
0   100
STATUTE MILES

CAPE VERDE

Santo Antao
Ribeira Grande
Tarrafal
Mindelo
Sao Vicente
Sao Nicolau
Preguica
Sal
Santa Maria

Boa Vista
Curral Velho

Maio
Tarrafal
Santo Antonio
*Sao
Tiago*
Porto Ingles
Fogo
Brava
Sao Filipe
PRAIA

0   100
KILOMETERS
0   75
STATUTE MILES

Overview map labels

NORTH AMERICA

EUROPE

AZORES (PORTUGAL)

Gulf Stream

BERMUDA (UNITED KINGDOM)

MADEIRA ISLANDS (PORTUGAL)

Sargasso Sea

CANARY ISLANDS (SPAIN)

North Atlantic Ocean

AFRICA

CAPE VERDE

ASCENSION (UNITED KINGDOM)

SOUTH AMERICA

ST. HELENA (UNITED KINGDOM)

N

0   1500
KILOMETERS
0   1000
STATUTE MILES

TRISTAN DA CUNHA GROUP (UNITED KINGDOM)

South Atlantic Ocean

FALKLAND ISLANDS (UNITED KINGDOM)

SOUTH GEORGIA (UNITED KINGDOM)

★ Capital City
✈ International Airport
— Roads
🐑 Sheep
🌾 Grains
Vegetables
Fruit
Wine
Salt
Flax
Fishing
Whaling and Sealing

BERMUDA (UNITED KINGDOM)

St. George's Island
Somerset Island
St. David's Island
Hamilton
Bermuda Island

0   10
KILOMETERS
0   5
STATUTE MILES

MADEIRA ISLANDS (PORTUGAL)

Porto Santo
Sao Vicente
Santana
Madeira
Ruivo Peak
6,106 FEET
1,861 METERS
Funchal
Ilhas Desertas

0   50
KILOMETERS
0   30
STATUTE MILES

FALKLAND ISLANDS (UNITED KINGDOM)

East Falkland
West Falkland
Mount Adam
2,297 FEET
700 METERS
Mount Usborne
2,312 FEET
705 METERS
Falkland Sound
Darwin
Stanley

0   75
KILOMETERS
0   50
STATUTE MILES

ST. HELENA (UNITED KINGDOM)

Jamestown
Longwood
Diana's Peak
2,700 FEET
823 METERS

0   8
KILOMETERS
0   6
STATUTE MILES

Azores

Bold seafarers sent by Prince Henry the Navigator in the 15th century were the first Europeans to see the nine Azores Islands and claim them for Portugal.

The location of the Azores part way between North America and Europe has long made them an important stop for Atlantic travelers. Columbus rested here in 1493. New England whaling ships picked up supplies and crew members in colonial days. Today the U. S. Navy and Air Force have a base on Terceira Island, where they refuel planes and launch anti-submarine patrols.

Azoreans still cast their fishing nets and plant corn, sugar beets, tea, and citrus fruits the way their grandfathers did. The whalers of Pico hunt sperm whales in small *canoa,* using hand-held harpoons.

The Gulf Stream's warm waters protect the chain of islands, 400 miles (644 km) long, from temperature extremes. That brings a pleasant climate and a wealth of flowers. Buildings made of lava remind you the Azores rose from the sea as volcanoes.

OFFICIAL NAME: Azores
AREA: 900 sq mi (2,330 sq km)
POPULATION: 291,000
CAPITAL: Ponta Delgada (pop. 21,000)
ETHNIC GROUPS: Portuguese. **LANGUAGE:** Portuguese. **RELIGION:** Roman Catholic. **ECONOMY:** fish, fruit, grains, grapes. **CURRENCY:** escudo.

Bermuda

Beaches of pink sand, gaily-colored cottages, masses of flowers, balmy breezes — all help to draw visitors to Bermuda, home of the famous Easter lily.

Throngs of tourists shop in Hamilton and explore twisting lanes in 370-year-old St. George. Bridges link the seven largest islands in the 300-island group.

Juan de Bermudez, a Spaniard, discovered the Bermudas in the early 1500's. England took possession in 1609. Two hours from New York by plane, the Bermudas are the northernmost coral islands in the world. Yet they have semitropical weather, thanks to the warm Gulf Stream.

OFFICIAL NAME: Colony of Bermuda
AREA: 20 sq mi (54 sq km)
POPULATION: 57,000
CAPITAL: Hamilton (pop. 2,500)
ETHNIC GROUPS: blacks, also British. **LANGUAGE:** English. **RELIGION:** Protestant, also Roman Catholic. **ECONOMY:** bananas, banking, citrus fruit, dairy products, Easter lilies, tourism, vegetables. **CURRENCY:** dollar.

Canary Islands

Romans called them the "Fortunate Islands." A visitor to the 13 Canary Islands can easily see why. Roses, lilies, and other flowers grow so abundantly that their petals carpet the streets of Santa Cruz and Las Palmas at festival time. Fruits and vegetables thrive the year round in the fertile soil and mild climate. Grapevines flourish even on rocky Lanzarote, where they are shielded from the wind in lava-walled pits.

Named by the Romans for the islands' wild dogs (*canis* means "dog"), the Canaries are home to wild Canary birds, first discovered here. The Spanish, who landed in 1402, conquered the natives — Stone Age people called the Guanches — in 1496. The islands remain a province of Spain.

OFFICIAL NAME: Canary Islands
AREA: 2,800 sq mi (7,250 sq km)
POPULATION: 1,170,000
CAPITAL: Santa Cruz de Tenerife (pop. 54,000)
ETHNIC GROUPS: Spanish. **LANGUAGE:** Spanish. **RELIGION:** Roman Catholic. **ECONOMY:** fish, fruit, grains, wine. **CURRENCY:** peseta.

Cape Verde

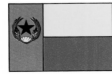 Islands that have sandstorms? And water shortages? That seems highly unlikely, yet it's often the situation in Cape Verde. Located nearly 400 miles off western Africa, the dozen or so islands that make up this country share the windstorms and droughts of the Sahara Desert.

About every 20 to 30 years, rainfall becomes scarce. Drought sears the islands, though deep wells may ease the pain. Then winds that sweep off the Sahara hit with destructive force, blowing soil away. The result: famine, unless the outside world ships in grain and other food.

Farms are tiny and most people are poor. When the weather behaves, Cape Verdians grow corn, beans, and sweet potatoes. Nearby ocean fishing grounds yield good catches. Settled by Portuguese and their African slaves in 1462, Cape Verde became independent in 1975.

OFFICIAL NAME: Republic of Cape Verde
AREA: 1,500 sq mi (4,000 sq km)
POPULATION: 315,000
CAPITAL: Praia (pop. 21,500)
ETHNIC GROUPS: mulattos, also blacks. **LANGUAGE:** Portuguese, also Crioulo. **RELIGION:** Roman Catholic, also animist. **ECONOMY:** bananas, beans, cassava, fish, grains, salt, sweet potatoes. **CURRENCY:** escudo.

Falkland Islands

Penguins, seals, and albatrosses (large seabirds) live in abundant numbers on the 200 Falkland Islands. By contrast, only about two thousand people brave the cold and windy climate near the Antarctic Circle.

Trees can't grow here, yet grass and low shrubs provide ideal grazing for sheep. So most of the islanders are sheep farmers who export the wool and hides. Some are fishermen and whalers. France, Spain, and Argentina all claimed the islands, but Britain has ruled them since 1833 and still keeps an important naval base here.

OFFICIAL NAME: Colony of the Falkland Islands
AREA: 4,700 sq mi (12,100 sq km)
POPULATION: 2,000
CAPITAL: Stanley (pop. 1,500)
ETHNIC GROUPS: British. **LANGUAGE:** English. **RELIGION:** Protestant. **ECONOMY:** hides and skins, sealing, sheep. **CURRENCY:** pound.

Madeira

Famed for fine embroidery and a special kind of wine — called Madeira — Portugal's Madeira Islands have feasts for both the eye and the tongue. Temperatures stay between 60° and 70° F (16° and 21° C) the year round, so fruits and flowers abound here. Volcanic hills and cliffs provide striking scenery — and scary roads as well.

Visitors to Madeira can swim at Porto Santo's beach and slide down snowless hillsides in wicker "sleds." On New Year's Day, fabulous fireworks light up the skies above the harbor at Funchal, the capital.

OFFICIAL NAME: Madeira
AREA: 300 sq mi (777 sq km)
POPULATION: 270,000
CAPITAL: Funchal (pop. 100,000)
ETHNIC GROUPS: Portuguese. **LANGUAGE:** Portuguese. **RELIGION:** Roman Catholic. **ECONOMY:** fruit, handicrafts, sugar, wicker furniture, wine. **CURRENCY:** escudo.

St. Helena

St. Helena, a speck of land near the center of the South Atlantic Ocean, has a major claim to fame. In 1815 England sent Napoleon Bonaparte, the emperor of France, into exile here after defeating him in several wars. His modest house still stands.

Rugged volcanic wasteland covers much of St. Helena. Charles Darwin, the naturalist, said the island's 1,000-foot (300 m) cliffs rose "like a huge black castle from the ocean." Islanders use fertile areas to raise flax and graze sheep and cattle in the temperate climate. Jamestown, the only village and port, serves as capital of several British islands in the South Atlantic.

OFFICIAL NAME: St. Helena (Data includes Ascension, Tristan da Cunha, other islands.)
AREA: 160 sq mi (414 sq km)
POPULATION: 6,500
CAPITAL: Jamestown (pop. 2,000)
ETHNIC GROUPS: mixed. **LANGUAGE:** English. **RELIGION:** Protestant. **ECONOMY:** flax, fodder, vegetables. **CURRENCY:** dollar.

St. Helena

1 *In a majestic setting of sea and hills, an old plantation raises flax for export. Flax fiber can be turned into products as coarse as rope or as fine as lace.*

2 *A scrubwood tree leans toward Atlantic breakers far below. Steep slopes attest to the volcanic origin of the tiny island.*

3 *With the skill he learned from his father, a craftsman "paints" pictures on boxes by piecing together many fragile slices of wood—a technique called inlay.*

Bermuda

1 *Bathed in the day's last light, the isles of Bermuda dapple the sea. Settlers found flowering trees and plants — nearly 1,000 kinds bloom today — but no mammals and only one reptile, a lizard.*

2 *A swimmer strolls along a sunny beach — actually part of the flattened summit of an undersea volcano rising some 14,000 feet from the ocean floor.*

Azores

3 *Roadside homes stitch together a quilt of fields on Terceira. Crops cling even to the cliffsides, wasting little of the land.*

4 *A self-reliant farmer of Pico makes wine for his table out of grapes from his vines.*

Madeira

5 *Elves in a dollhouse garden? No — but these women do seem to have magic in their fingers as they create Madeira's famous needlework. Years of training await the little girl who watches them.*

1   2

3

5

4

PACIFIC OCEAN ISLANDS

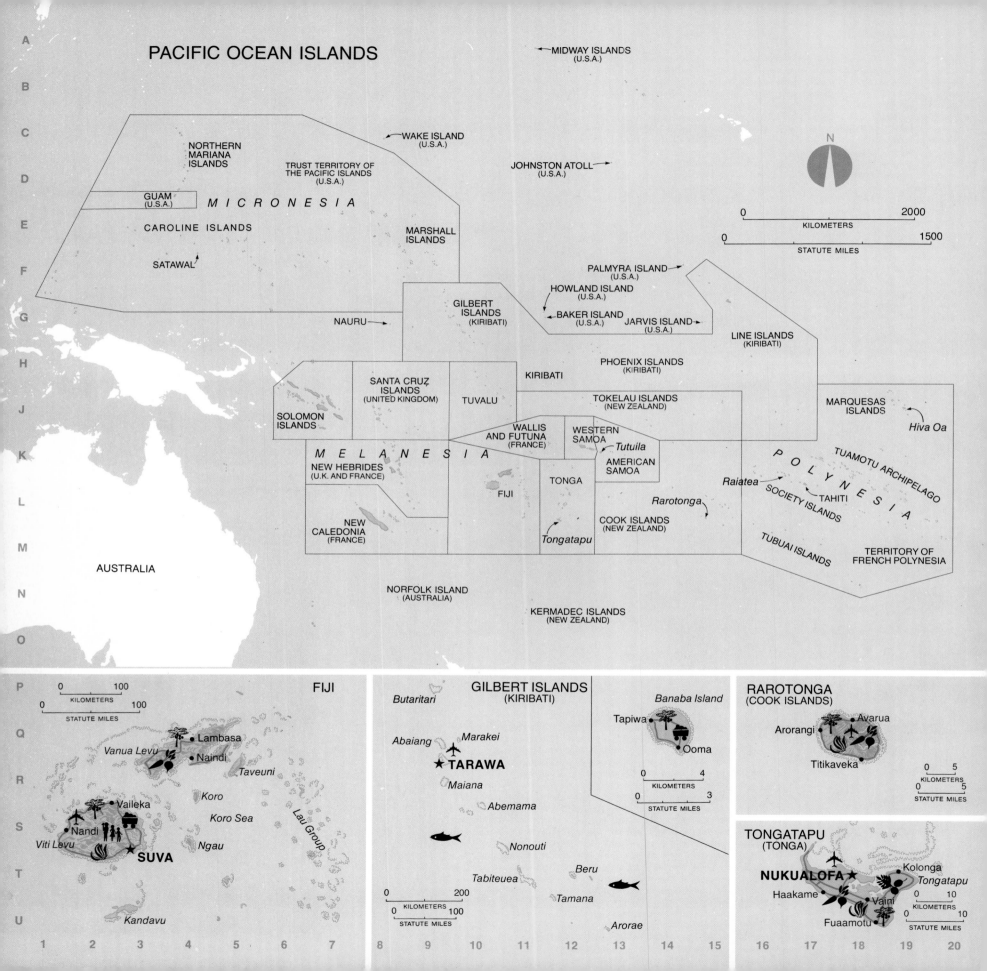

→ MIDWAY ISLANDS (U.S.A.)

→ WAKE ISLAND (U.S.A.)

JOHNSTON ATOLL (U.S.A.) →

N

NORTHERN MARIANA ISLANDS

TRUST TERRITORY OF THE PACIFIC ISLANDS (U.S.A.)

GUAM (U.S.A.)

MICRONESIA

CAROLINE ISLANDS

SATAWAL ↗

MARSHALL ISLANDS

0 ——————— 2000
KILOMETERS

0 ——————— 1500
STATUTE MILES

PALMYRA ISLAND (U.S.A.) →

HOWLAND ISLAND (U.S.A.)

NAURU →

GILBERT ISLANDS (KIRIBATI)

← BAKER ISLAND (U.S.A.)

JARVIS ISLAND → (U.S.A.)

LINE ISLANDS (KIRIBATI)

PHOENIX ISLANDS (KIRIBATI)

KIRIBATI

SANTA CRUZ ISLANDS (UNITED KINGDOM)

TUVALU

TOKELAU ISLANDS (NEW ZEALAND)

MARQUESAS ISLANDS

← *Hiva Oa*

SOLOMON ISLANDS

WALLIS AND FUTUNA (FRANCE)

WESTERN SAMOA

Tutuila

AMERICAN SAMOA

POLYNESIA

TUAMOTU ARCHIPELAGO

MELANESIA

NEW HEBRIDES (U.K. AND FRANCE)

FIJI

TONGA

Raiatea ↘ SOCIETY ISLANDS

Rarotonga

TAHITI

NEW CALEDONIA (FRANCE)

COOK ISLANDS (NEW ZEALAND)

TUBUAI ISLANDS

TERRITORY OF FRENCH POLYNESIA

Tongatapu

AUSTRALIA

NORFOLK ISLAND (AUSTRALIA)

KERMADEC ISLANDS (NEW ZEALAND)

FIJI

0 ——————— 100
KILOMETERS

0 ——————— 100
STATUTE MILES

• Lambasa

Vanua Levu

• Naindi

Taveuni

• Vaileka

Koro

• Nandi

Koro Sea

SUVA

Viti Levu

Ngau

Lau Group

Kandavu

GILBERT ISLANDS (KIRIBATI)

Butaritari

Banaba Island

Tapiwa

Abaiang   *Marakei*

✈ ★ **TARAWA**

Ooma

0 ——————— 4
KILOMETERS

0 ——————— 3
STATUTE MILES

Maiana

Abemama

Nonouti

Beru

Tabiteuea

Tamana

0 ——————— 200
KILOMETERS

0 ——————— 100
STATUTE MILES

Arorae

RAROTONGA (COOK ISLANDS)

Arorangi • • Avarua

Titikaveka •

0 —— 5
KILOMETERS

0 —— 5
STATUTE MILES

TONGATAPU (TONGA)

✈ ★ **NUKUALOFA**   • Kolonga

Tongatapu

Haakame •   • Vaini

0 —— 10
KILOMETERS

Fuaamotu •

0 —— 10
STATUTE MILES

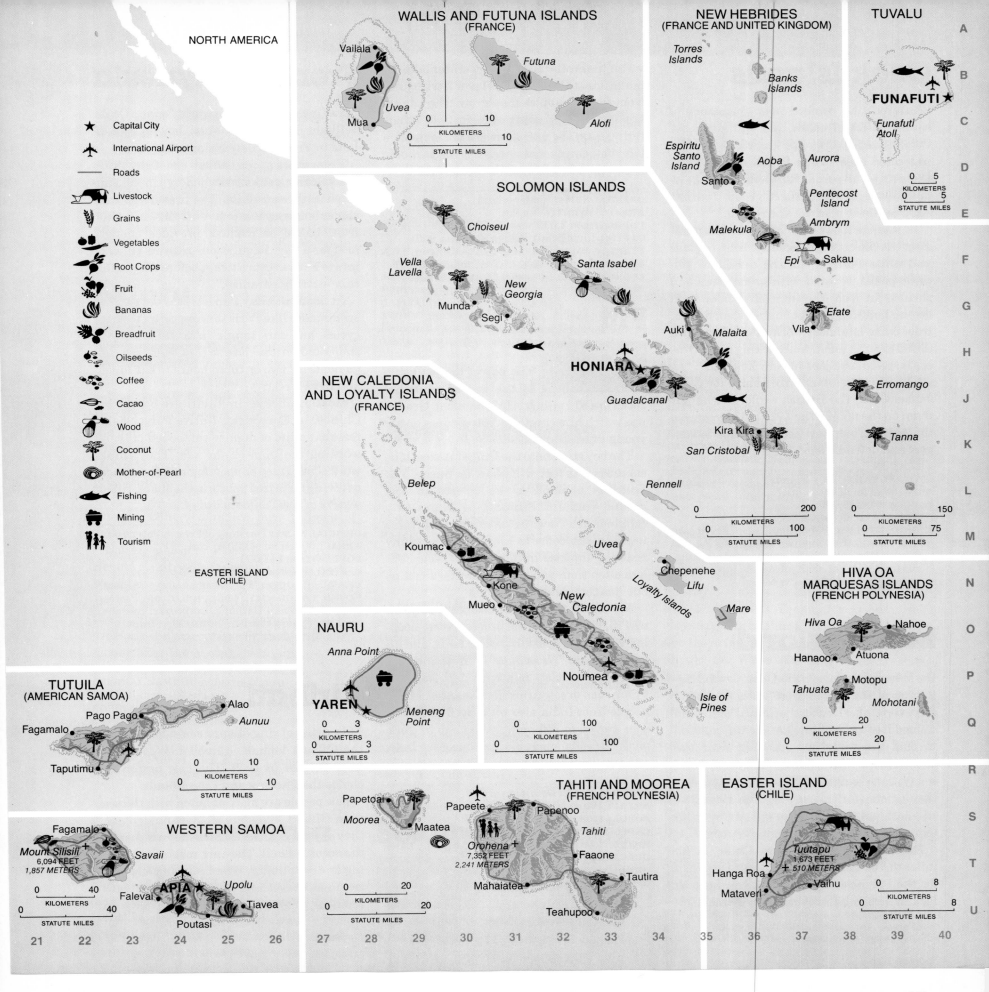

NORTH AMERICA

WALLIS AND FUTUNA ISLANDS
(FRANCE)

Vailala
Futuna
Uvea
Mua
Alofi

0   10
KILOMETERS
0   10
STATUTE MILES

NEW HEBRIDES
(FRANCE AND UNITED KINGDOM)

Torres
Islands
Banks
Islands
Espiritu
Santo
Island
Aoba   Aurora
Santo
Pentecost
Island
Malekula   Ambrym
Epi   Sakau
Efate
Vila
Erromango
Tanna

TUVALU

FUNAFUTI ★

Funafuti
Atoll

0   5
KILOMETERS
0   5
STATUTE MILES

★ Capital City
✈ International Airport
— Roads
🐄 Livestock
🌾 Grains
🥬 Vegetables
🌱 Root Crops
🍒 Fruit
🍌 Bananas
🌰 Breadfruit
🫘 Oilseeds
☕ Coffee
🥜 Cacao
🪵 Wood
🌴 Coconut
🦪 Mother-of-Pearl
🐟 Fishing
⛏ Mining
👫 Tourism

SOLOMON ISLANDS

Choiseul
Vella
Lavella
Santa Isabel
New
Georgia
Munda
Segi
Auki   Malaita
HONIARA ★
Guadalcanal
Kira Kira
San Cristobal
Rennell

0   200
KILOMETERS
0   100
STATUTE MILES

0   150
KILOMETERS
0   75
STATUTE MILES

**NEW CALEDONIA
AND LOYALTY ISLANDS**
(FRANCE)

Belep
Koumac
Kone
Mueo
New
Caledonia
Noumea
Uvea
Chepenehe
Lifu
Loyalty Islands
Mare
Isle of
Pines

EASTER ISLAND
(CHILE)

HIVA OA
MARQUESAS ISLANDS
(FRENCH POLYNESIA)

Hiva Oa   Nahoe
Hanaoo   Atuona
Tahuata   Motopu
Mohotani

0   20
KILOMETERS
0   20
STATUTE MILES

TUTUILA
(AMERICAN SAMOA)

Alao
Pago Pago
Fagamalo
Aunuu
Taputimu

0   10
KILOMETERS
0   10
STATUTE MILES

NAURU

Anna Point
YAREN ★
Meneng
Point

0   3
KILOMETERS
0   3
STATUTE MILES

0   100
KILOMETERS
0   100
STATUTE MILES

WESTERN SAMOA

Fagamalo
Mount Silisili
6,094 FEET
1,857 METERS
Savaii
Falevai
APIA ★
Upolu
Tiavea
Poutasi

0   40
KILOMETERS
0   40
STATUTE MILES

TAHITI AND MOOREA
(FRENCH POLYNESIA)

Papetoai
Papeete
Papenoo
Moorea
Maatea
Tahiti
Orohena
7,352 FEET
2,241 METERS
Faaone
Mahaiatea
Tautira
Teahupoo

0   20
KILOMETERS
0   20
STATUTE MILES

EASTER ISLAND
(CHILE)

Tuutapu
1,673 FEET
510 METERS
Hanga Roa
Vaihu
Mataveri

0   8
KILOMETERS
0   8
STATUTE MILES

A B C D E F G H J K L M N O P Q R S T U

21 22 23 24 25 26 27 28 29 30 31 32 33 34 35 36 37 38 39 40

Tuvalu

Tuvalu is all atolls. What's an atoll? It's an island created when a coral reef builds up, sometimes on the rim of an old undersea volcano, and makes a ring around a lagoon. Nine atolls form Tuvalu—nine freckles on the vast face of the Pacific. They barely poke up above the sea—no more than 14 feet (4 m) high. Britain ruled Tuvalu under the name "Ellice Islands" until the colony won independence in 1978.

Tuvalu's houses stand on stilts to keep out rats and dampness. Pet frigate birds sometimes fly out to sea and back. Because rain quickly seeps through the thin soil to the coral below, Tuvaluans grow their crops in earth-filled pits that will hold water.

OFFICIAL NAME: Tuvalu
AREA: 10 sq mi (26 sq km)
POPULATION: 6,000
CAPITAL: Funafuti (pop. 1,500)
ETHNIC GROUPS: Polynesian. **LANGUAGE:** English, Polynesian. **RELIGION:** Protestant. **ECONOMY:** coconut, fish, handicrafts, vegetables. **CURRENCY:** dollar.

U.S. Territories

United States possessions lie scattered over a vast area of the Pacific, from Midway Islands in the north to American Samoa in the south; from Palmyra Island in the east to the westernmost Caroline Islands. Some islands—narrow coral reefs—barely break above the waves. Kingman Reef has less land area than two normal-size city blocks.

Island governments rule in many different ways. Guam's people are self-governed U. S. citizens. The U. S. Navy runs Midway Islands, and the Air Force is in charge of Wake Island, where only 400 people live.

Unlike Wake, American Samoa faces problems of crowding. Here are scenes from an American suburb: A proud owner washes his car while watching his portable television. The show? Football, broadcast from the mainland. A housewife opens a can of corned beef. Only on Sunday might you find a Polynesian luau—fish, pork, and sweet potatoes wrapped in banana leaves and baked in an earth pit lined with hot stones.

People in Micronesia, the islands of the Trust Territory of the Pacific, seem less touched by tourism and technology than the Samoans. Micronesian boys still learn how to cross empty reaches of ocean as their ancestors did. Those early people used stars, birds, and the feel of unseen ocean swells and currents to guide their outrigger canoes. By reflecting the color of a green lagoon, clouds could show an island's location from afar. Even today a youth may launch his outrigger on a five-day journey, just to buy chewing gum or soft drinks.

Many Pacific islands suffered from battles between Americans and Japanese in World War II. The broken machinery of war still rusts in the sand.

U. S. armed forces keep up bases on islands such as Johnston Atoll. Atomic bomb testing on Bikini in the Marshall Islands ended in 1958, but radioactivity there can still bring a Geiger counter to life.

In the 1800's businessmen feuded over the right to mine guano on Baker, Howland, and Jarvis Islands. Now uninhabited, the islands once again belong to the seabirds.

Wallis and Futuna Islands

It took sharp-eyed sailors to sight the Wallis Islands. Uvea, main island in the group, measures only seven by four miles (11 by 6 km) and less than 500 feet (152 m) above sea level. The islands are named for Capt. Samuel Wallis, who came upon them after his discovery of Tahiti in 1767. The Futuna Islands, the other part of this French colony, bear their Polynesian name.

Coconut palms once spread from shore to shore on Uvea, and many people worked in a thriving copra trade. The oil taken from this dried coconut meat is used in cosmetics, soaps, and explosives. Skirts of tin around palm-tree trunks protected the nuts from rats and tree-climbing crabs. In the 1960's a foreign invader, the rhinoceros beetle, destroyed most of the palms, just as early European explorers brought foreign diseases that devastated many Pacific peoples. Scientists have now stopped the beetle, and the coconuts are returning.

OFFICIAL NAME: Territory of the Wallis and Futuna Islands
AREA: 80 sq mi (207 sq km)
POPULATION: 9,000
CAPITAL: Matu Utu (pop. 600)
ETHNIC GROUPS: Polynesian. **LANGUAGE:** French. **RELIGION:** Roman Catholic. **ECONOMY:** bananas, coconut, taro, yams. **CURRENCY:** franc.

Western Samoa

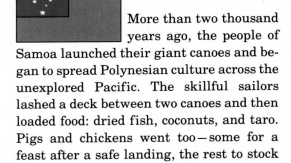

More than two thousand years ago, the people of Samoa launched their giant canoes and began to spread Polynesian culture across the unexplored Pacific. The skillful sailors lashed a deck between two canoes and then loaded food: dried fish, coconuts, and taro. Pigs and chickens went too—some for a feast after a safe landing, the rest to stock the new settlement.

Some believe these hard journeys helped shape Polynesians into the tallest and most powerful of all Pacific people. The travelers developed strong arms from rowing, and layers of fat to guard against cold.

Living seems open and easy in Western Samoa. Large families live in palm-thatched huts with no walls. When the father has been too strict, a child can avoid him by staying with relatives for a while.

OFFICIAL NAME: Independent State of Western Samoa
AREA: 1,100 sq mi (2,800 sq km)
POPULATION: 155,000
CAPITAL: Apia (pop. 33,000)
ETHNIC GROUPS: Polynesian, also Euronesian. **LANGUAGE:** English, Samoan. **RELIGION:** Protestant, also Roman Catholic. **ECONOMY:** bananas, cacao, coconut, oilseeds, taro, wood, yams. **CURRENCY:** tala.

Pacific Ocean Islands

1 *"Cut with great arte, and cunning," said Sir Francis Drake's seamen as they watched outriggers called* popos *in 1579. Sailors of Satawal, an island in the Carolines, still dare to ride such craft across 550 miles (885 km) of open sea.*

2 *How's fishing off Nauru? Great! These beauties were speared in half an hour.*

3 *Volcanic bloom: This splashy* Medinilla *blossom on the Fijian island of Taveuni owes its health partly to a nearby volcano. Eruptions over the years have formed soil so rich the island earned the nickname "Garden of Fiji."*

Pacific Ocean Islands

1 *A boy compares his reach with a bat on Tonga. The crow-size fruit bats damage mango and papaya crops, yet Tongans protect some bats as royal property.*

2 *Surf and reef circle Raiatea in French Polynesia. From this island, tradition says, canoes of bold Polynesian colonists long ago set forth to Hawaii and New Zealand, more than 2,000 miles away.*

3 *Fighting? No, dancing. But the stick dance performed by these Truk schoolboys may re-enact ancient war games. Girls, too, enjoy the swishing, whacking dance.*

4 *A small boy learns a grater lesson as he watches skilled hands shred coconut meat for a cooking sauce on Satawal Island.*

5 *If stones could speak, what stories these could tell! For centuries some 600 of these huge stones have stood over Easter Island. Why were they carved? How were they moved? How did early islanders stand them up? Scholars think they were dragged with ropes and sledges, then erected with levers and mounds of stones as props. But to this day no one knows exactly why.*

4

5

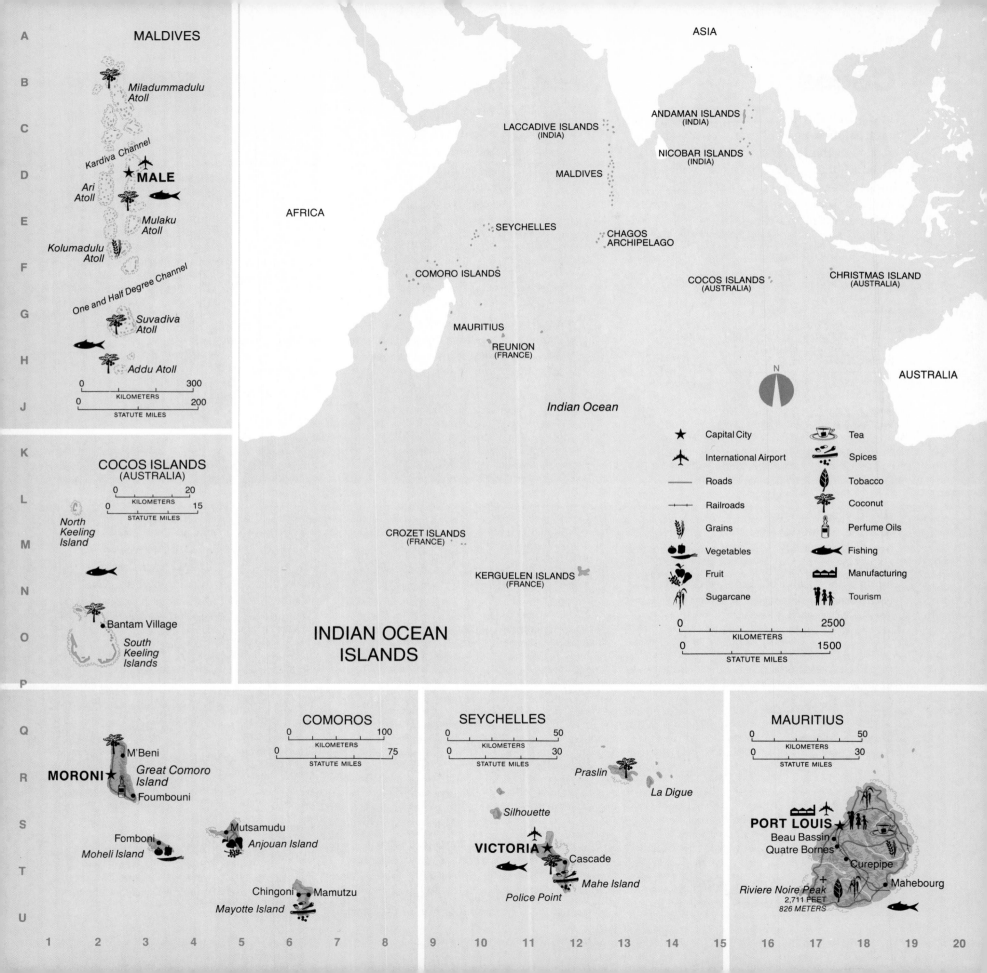

INDIAN OCEAN ISLANDS

MALDIVES

- Miladummadulu Atoll
- Kardiva Channel
- ★ **MALE**
- Ari Atoll
- Mulaku Atoll
- Kolumadulu Atoll
- One and Half Degree Channel
- Suvadiva Atoll
- Addu Atoll

0		300
KILOMETERS		
0		200
STATUTE MILES		

ASIA

LACCADIVE ISLANDS (INDIA)

ANDAMAN ISLANDS (INDIA)

NICOBAR ISLANDS (INDIA)

MALDIVES

AFRICA

SEYCHELLES

CHAGOS ARCHIPELAGO

COMORO ISLANDS

COCOS ISLANDS (AUSTRALIA)

CHRISTMAS ISLAND (AUSTRALIA)

MAURITIUS

REUNION (FRANCE)

AUSTRALIA

Indian Ocean

N

COCOS ISLANDS (AUSTRALIA)

0		20
KILOMETERS		
0		15
STATUTE MILES		

- North Keeling Island
- Bantam Village
- South Keeling Islands

CROZET ISLANDS (FRANCE)

KERGUELEN ISLANDS (FRANCE)

INDIAN OCEAN ISLANDS

★	Capital City		Tea
✈	International Airport		Spices
—	Roads		Tobacco
+++	Railroads		Coconut
	Grains		Perfume Oils
	Vegetables		Fishing
	Fruit		Manufacturing
	Sugarcane		Tourism

0		2500
KILOMETERS		
0		1500
STATUTE MILES		

COMOROS

0		100
KILOMETERS		
0		75
STATUTE MILES		

- M'Beni
- **MORONI** ★
- Great Comoro Island
- Foumbouni
- Fomboni
- Moheli Island
- Mutsamudu
- Anjouan Island
- Chingoni Mamutzu
- Mayotte Island

SEYCHELLES

0		50
KILOMETERS		
0		30
STATUTE MILES		

- Praslin
- La Digue
- Silhouette
- **VICTORIA** ★
- Cascade
- Mahe Island
- Police Point

MAURITIUS

0		50
KILOMETERS		
0		30
STATUTE MILES		

- **PORT LOUIS** ★
- Beau Bassin
- Quatre Bornes
- Curepipe
- Mahebourg
- Riviere Noire Peak
  2,711 FEET
  826 METERS

Cocos

In the Indian Ocean lies an atoll, a ring of coral islets typical of many remote island groups in the Indian and Pacific oceans. A coconut plantation nestles on one palm-shaded isle, and there most of the islanders live and work. Long under the authority of Great Britain, the Cocos—once called the Keeling Islands after their British discoverer—are now governed by Australia.

OFFICIAL NAME: Territory of Cocos (Keeling) Islands
AREA: 5.5 sq mi (14 sq km)
POPULATION: 1,100
ETHNIC GROUPS: Malay, also European. **LANGUAGE:** Malay, English. **RELIGION:** Muslim. **ECONOMY:** coconut, fish. **CURRENCY:** dollar.

Comoros

The Comoro Islands form an archipelago between the island of Madagascar and the southeastern coast of Africa. On Great Comoro, largest of the Comoros, a hundred volcanoes rise from the sea. At least one, Mount Kartala, is still active. In many places, fields of hardened lava stretch to the ocean's edge. In the volcanic soil grow citronella, jasmine, and other plants that yield oils used to make perfume.

Another feature: lemurs. Big-eyed animals that resemble monkeys, lemurs feed and travel at night. They got their name from the Latin word *lemures,* ghosts.

Of the four main Comoro Islands, only Mayotte remains a territory of France. Great Comoro, Anjouan, and Moheli declared their independence in 1975.

OFFICIAL NAME: Federal and Islamic Republic of the Comoros
AREA: 850 sq mi (2,200 sq km)
POPULATION: 317,000
CAPITAL: Moroni (pop. 12,000)
ETHNIC GROUPS: Arab, blacks, Malay. **LANGUAGE:** Arabic, French, Swahili. **RELIGION:** Muslim. **ECONOMY:** cloves, coconut, fruit, perfume oils, vanilla, vegetables. **CURRENCY:** franc.

Maldives

About 2,000 tiny coral islands off the southern tip of India—that's Maldives, one of the smallest republics in the world. Only about 215 of the atolls have enough usable land to support settlements of Maldivians. Most of the people are Muslims who live simply in centuries-old ways.

On some islands the people barter for goods rather than use modern money. Islanders practice another old custom: They banish criminals to the most remote atolls.

Maldivians usually have few possessions. Most families depend on fishing for a living. Fish and coconut meat provide the main part of meals. Male, the capital, offers the only regular contact with the outside world by means of radiotelephone and a small airport. Increasingly, tourists come here seeking refuge in this coral empire of lonely beaches, blue lagoons, and friendly people.

OFFICIAL NAME: Republic of Maldives
AREA: 115 sq mi (298 sq km)
POPULATION: 141,000
CAPITAL: Male (pop. 14,000)
ETHNIC GROUPS: Arab, blacks, East Indian, Sinhalese. **LANGUAGE:** Divehi. **RELIGION:** Muslim. **ECONOMY:** coconut, fish, grains, root crops. **CURRENCY:** rupee.

Mauritius

"What there is of Mauritius is beautiful," wrote Mark Twain in 1896. Deserted beaches as soft as powder, misty volcanic peaks, and fertile plains lured settlers from many different countries. Walking along the streets of Port Louis, the capital, one sees Muslims in fezzes, Chinese in khaki shorts, Indian women in colorful saris, French women in high fashion.

Irish settlers introduced horse racing. Now Mauritians flock each Saturday to the races. The island staggers under the burden of its people, however. It is one of the most densely crowded countries in the world.

Mauritius' most famous native—the dodo—vanished almost 300 years ago. Dutch explorers first spotted the flightless bird in 1598. One hundred years later the dodo became extinct, a victim of man and the predatory animals that he brought with him to the once-uninhabited island.

OFFICIAL NAME: Mauritius
AREA: 690 sq mi (1,800 sq km)
POPULATION: 927,000
CAPITAL: Port Louis (pop. 141,000)
ETHNIC GROUPS: East Indian, also Creole. **LANGUAGE:** English, also Chinese, Creole, Hindi. **RELIGION:** Hindu, also Christian, Muslim. **ECONOMY:** electronics, fish, diamond cutting, grains, molasses, sugar, tea, textiles, tobacco, tourism. **CURRENCY:** rupee.

Seychelles

With a single slash of her machete a woman slices a coconut neatly in two. She can split 2,000 each hour. In the Seychelle Islands, coconuts are important. This is the only place where the giant coconut grows wild.

From dried coconut meat, called copra, comes cooking oil, margarine, and soap. Husks are woven into rope and mats. The milk fattens pigs. Islanders even use coconut oil to polish floors—by skating around the floor on a half shell.

The Seychelles are one of the last places in the world where giant tortoises live in the wild. Some grow more than three feet high and weigh 600 pounds (272 kg). Tortoises can live as long as 200 years.

Britain ruled the French-discovered islands for 162 years. Yet many Seychellois still speak 18th-century French.

OFFICIAL NAME: Republic of the Seychelles
AREA: 156 sq mi (404 sq km)
POPULATION: 62,000
CAPITAL: Victoria (pop. 13,700)
ETHNIC GROUPS: Asian, blacks, European. **LANGUAGE:** English, Creole. **RELIGION:** Roman Catholic, also Protestant. **ECONOMY:** cinnamon, coconut, fish, guano, patchouli, rope, tea, vanilla. **CURRENCY:** rupee.

1

2

3

Comoros

1 *A cat-size mongoose lemur seems to be amazed at its treetop view. Night holds few surprises for this fruit-eater whose wide eyes let it see well in the dark.*

Seychelles

2 *Small islands grow the world's largest tree fruit—the sea coconut, 40 pounds (18 kg) of green skin, husk, and edible jelly. Each takes seven years to ripen on palms as tall as 100 feet (30 m).*

Mauritius

3 *Palm trees tower over man and donkeys. Sacks bulge with coconuts, a minor crop overshadowed by the island's sugarcane.*

Cocos

4 *Flowers brighten hearts and hairstyles on the tiny Cocos Islands, one of earth's most remote spots. The nearest land is Christmas Island, some 600 miles east.*

5 *Coconut crab scuttles up a tree. Until settlers came, no mammals lived here.*

Maldives

6 *As if sailing on sand, twin-masted outriggers hold up cotton sails to dry.*

Illustration Credits

Maps by the Geographic Art Division;
Country flags by the Cartographic Division,
National Geographic Society.

The following abbreviations are used in this list:
NGP - National Geographic Photographer
NGS - National Geographic Staff

Cover: Isadore Seltzer. 2,3-Fabric Sculpture by Carol Inouye. Photograph by Joseph D. Lavenburg and Robert S. Oakes, both NGS.

THE GLOBE BENEATH OUR FEET
6-Lloyd K. Townsend, Jr. 7-D. W. Reeser, National Park Service. (right) Lloyd K. Townsend, Jr. 8,9-Lloyd K. Townsend, Jr. 10-Courtesy the Bancroft Library. 11-Bill and Mary Lou Stackhouse. (bottom) Lloyd K. Townsend, Jr. 12-Lloyd K. Townsend, Jr. 12,13-Walter Romanes. 14-Steve Raymer, NGP. 15-George Billingsley. (bottom) William A. Garnett. 16-Lloyd K. Townsend, Jr. 17-Dick Durrance II. (bottom) Winfield Parks. 18,19-Reynold Ruffins.

AT HOME ON PLANET EARTH
21,22,23-Reynold Ruffins. 26-Lloyd K. Townsend, Jr. 27-Reynold Ruffins.

MAPPING OUR ROUND WORLD
28-Louis S. Glanzman. 29-Naval Museum, Madrid. (right) W. Robert Moore. 30-James Calvert. (bottom) Ludek Pesek. (right) Lloyd K. Townsend, Jr. 30,31-Heinrich C. Berann and Bruce C. Heezen, © NGS. 32-Lloyd K. Townsend, Jr. 33-Drawings by Reynold Ruffins. 34-Maps by Lloyd K. Townsend, Jr. Drawing by Reynold Ruffins.

NORTH AMERICA
38-Robert O. Binnewies. 39-Howard S. Friedman. 44-Frederick Kent Truslow. (bottom left) Robert W. Madden, NGP. (right) Ted Speigel, Black Star. 45-James P. Blair, NGP. (bottom) Jodi Cobb, NGP. 46-Rick McIntyre. (bottom) Gordon W. Gahan, NGP. (right) J. R. Eyerman. 47-Declan Haun. 50-(top) Lowell Georgia. 50,51-Joseph J. Scherschel, NGS. 51-(top) Fred Ward, Black Star. (right) Ted Speigel, Black Star. (bottom) Winfield Parks. 52-William R. Curtsinger. (bottom) Robert W. Madden, NGP. 52,53-George F. Mobley, NGP (bottom left) Thomas Nebbia. 56-(top & left) Thomas Nebbia. (bottom) Guillermo Aldana E. (right) Charles O'Rear. 57-Thomas Nebbia. 61-W. E. Garrett, NGS. 62-Bruce Dale, NGP. (right) Albert Moldvay. 63-Bruce Dale, NGP. (bottom left) Joseph J. Scherschel, NGS. (right) Michael E. Long, NGS. 69-(top & bottom right) John Launois, Black Star. (left) Thomas Nebbia. 70-Emory Kristof, NGP. (bottom) Fred Ward, Black Star. 71-(top & bottom right) Thomas Nebbia. (left) Martin Rogers.

SOUTH AMERICA
72-W. Jesco Von Puttkamer. 73-Howard S. Friedman. 78-Adam Woolfitt. (right) Loren McIntyre. 79-(top & bottom left) Loren McIntyre. (right) Gordon W. Gahan, NGP. 80,81-Robert W. Madden, NGP. 84 & 85-Nicholas DeVore III. 85-Winfield Parks. (bottom left) Helen and Frank Schreider. 86-(top & left) Loren McIntyre. (bottom) Nicholas DeVore III. 87-(top & bottom) Robert W. Madden, NGP. (right) Joseph J. Scherschel, NGS. 90-Loren McIntyre. (bottom) James L. Stanfield, NGP. (right) Alan Root. 91-Loren McIntyre. (bottom) James L. Stanfield, NGP. 92-James Holland. 93-(top left & bottom) Loren McIntyre. (right) Helen and Frank Schreider. 96-Loren McIntyre. 97-Paul A. Zahl. 100,101-Loren McIntyre. 101-(top & bottom) Winfield Parks. (center) Gordon W. Gahan, NGP. 102,103-George F. Mobley, NGP. 103-James L. Stanfield, NGP.

EUROPE
104-George F. Mobley, NGP. 105-Howard S. Friedman. 110, 111-Albert Moldvay. (bottom & right) George F. Mobley, NGP. 112-(top & bottom right) James A. Sugar. (left) Gilbert M. Grosvenor, NGS. 113-George F. Mobley, NGP. 116-Ted Speigel, Black Star. 116,117-(bottom) & 117 (top) Steve Raymer, NGP. (bottom) James P. Blair, NGP. 118,119 & 118-(bottom left) Adam Woolfitt. (right) Robert B. Goodman. 119-Patrick Thurston. (bottom left) Thomas Nebbia. (right) Winfield Parks. 122-Farrell Grehan. (bottom) Walter Meayers Edwards. 123-Flip Schulke, Black Star. (right) Farrell Grehan. 124-Gordon W. Gahan, NGP. (bottom) Richmond Crawford, Jr. 124, 125-(bottom) Bruce Dale, NGP. 125-(top) Robert W. Madden, NGP. 128,129-James P. Blair, NGP. 132,133-James P. Blair, NGP. (bottom) James A. Sugar. 133-(bottom) Dick Durrance II. 136-Winfield Parks. (bottom) Dick Durrance II. 137-(top left & bottom) Winfield Parks. (top right) Robert L'Hommedieu. 140, 141-William Albert Allard. 141-Albert Moldvay. 144,145-Thomas J. Abercrombie, NGS. 146-Thomas Nebbia. (bottom) Walter Meayers Edwards. 147-Joseph J. Scherschel, NGS. (center & bottom) Robert Freson. (top right) Peter Klose, Photo Researchers. 150-Michael Kuh. (bottom & right) David Alan Harvey, NGP. 151-Volkmar Wentzel, NGS.

ASIA
152-Barry C. Bishop, NGS. 153-Howard S. Friedmar. 158, 159-Dean Conger, NGS. (bottom left) Thomas J. Abercrombie, NGS. 160,161-Lev Nosov, Novosti Press Agency. 161-(top) Dean Conger, NGS. (bottom) Howard Sochurek. 164-(top & bottom) Thomas J. Abercrombie, NGS. (right) Burt Glinn, Magnum. 165-Thomas J. Abercrombie, NGS. (bottom) James L. Stanfield, NGP. 166-Howard Sochurek. 167-H. Edward Kim, NGS. 170-Brian Brake. 171-(top & bottom) Audrey Topping. (top right) Jørgen Bisch. 172,173-Helen and Frank Schreider. 173-Dean Conger, NGS. 177-(top & bottom) Dean Conger, NGS. (right) David Alan Harvey, NGP. 178-William F. Kuykendall. (right) Malcolm Kirk. 179-Ted Speigel, Black Star. (bottom) Bruce Dale, NGP. 182,183-W. E. Garrett, NGS. 184-Peter Robinson. (right) W. E. Garrett, NGS. 185-Dean Conger, NGS. (bottom) Michael Kuh. 188-John Scofield. (bottom) Raghubir Singh. 188,189-Harry Miller. (bottom) Raghubir Singh. 190, 191-John Scofield. 191-(top) Raghubir Singh. (bottom) Schuyler Jones. 194-Sabrina and Roland Michaud. (bottom) Helen and Frank Schreider. 194,195-Albert Moldvay. (bottom left) Igne Morath, Magnum. (right) James P. Blair, NGP. 198,199-Mehmet Biber. 200-Emory Kristof, NGP. (right) David F. Cupp. 201-Thomas J. Abercrombie, NGS. (bottom) Robert Azzi. 204,205-Thomas Nebbia. 205-B. Anthony Stewart. (bottom) Winfield Parks. 206-Gordon W. Gahan, NGP. (right) James L. Stanfield, NGP. (bottom) Nik Wheeler, Black Star. 207-Winfield Parks.

AFRICA
208-Sara Conn Thompson. 209-Howard S. Friedman. 214,215, 216-Thomas J. Abercrombie, NGS. 217-Thomas J. Abercrombie, NGS. (bottom) Winfield Parks. 218-Pamela Johnson Meyer. (top right) Victor Englebert. (bottom) Georg Gerster. 219-Victor Englebert. (bottom) Jonathan Blair. 222-John G. Ross. (bottom) Winfield Parks. 222,223-Thomas J. Abercrombie, NGS. 224-Brian Brake, Photo Researchers. (right) James Holland. (bottom) Horst Luz. 225-Brewster Morris. (bottom) John Scofield. 228,229-Bellorget Ghislain, Black Star. 228-(bottom) James P. Blair, NGP. 229-(bottom) Bruce Dale, NGP. 230-John Scofield. (bottom) James P. Blair, NGP. 230,231-James P. Blair, NGP. (bottom) W. D. Vaughn. 234,235-Bruno Barbey. (bottom) Georg Gerster. 236-John Scofield. 237-Albert Moldvay. (right) James Wells. (bottom) Bruce Dale, NGP. 240,241-Volkmar Wentzel, NGS. (right) Paul A. Zahl. 242-Eliot Elisofon. (bottom left) Alyette DeMunck. 243-Eliot Elisofon. 247-Victor Englebert. (bottom) Georg Gerster. 248-M. Philip Kahl, Jr. (right) Bruce Dale, NGP. (bottom) Robert M. Campbell. 249-George F. Mobley, NGP. 250-Joseph J. Scherschel, NGS. 251-Emory Kristof, NGP. (bottom) Robert M. Campbell. 254-Volkmar Wentzel, NGS. 255-Helen and Frank Schreider. 256,257-Albert Moldvay. 261-W. D. Vaughn. (right) Roger Tory Peterson. 262-Walter Meayers Edwards. (center) James L. Stanfield, NGP. (right) Dick Durrance II. (bottom) James L. Stanfield, NGP. 263-James P. Blair, NGP. 264-Fred Ward, Black Star. (top & bottom) Thomas Nebbia. 265-Volkmar Wentzel, NGS. (bottom) Walter Meayers Edwards. (right) Thomas Nebbia.

AUSTRALIA and NEW ZEALAND
266-Gordon De'Lisle. 267-Howard S. Friedman. 270-Winfield Parks. (right) Joseph J. Scherschel, NGS. (bottom) David Moore, Black Star. 270,271-Robert W. Madden, NGP. 271-Valerie Taylor. (right) Winfield Parks. 272-Jeff Carter. (bottom) William Albert Allard. 272,273-Robert E. Gilka, NGS. 273-Bates Littlehales, NGP. (right) M. F. Soper, Bruce Coleman Inc.

ANTARCTICA and the ARCTIC REGIONS
276-Robert W. Madden, NGP. (bottom) William R. Curtsinger. 276,277-William R. Curtsinger.

ATLANTIC OCEAN ISLANDS
280,281-Walter Meayers Edwards. 282-Emory Kristof, NGP. 283-(top & bottom right) O. Louis Mazzatenta, NGS. (left) Jonathan Blair.

PACIFIC OCEAN ISLANDS
289-Nicholas DeVore III. (bottom) Mike Holmes. (right) Jack Fields. 290-Edwin Stewart Grosvenor. (bottom) David S. Boyer, NGS. 290,291-Nicholas DeVore III. (bottom) Thomas J. Abercrombie, NGS.

INDIAN OCEAN ISLANDS
294-Quentin Keynes. (right) Robert F. Sisson, NGP. 295-Robert F. Sisson, NGP. (bottom) Alan Villiers.

We'd like to thank ...

We are grateful to many people and organizations for help in preparing this book. Special thanks go to Peter Stifel of the Department of Geology at the University of Maryland, and to Whitney Smith of the Flag Research Center, Winchester, Massachusetts. We are indebted to the following teachers, and their students, for advice: Charlotte Kovach in Washington, D. C., and Ann McKay in Falls Church, Va.

We thank the State Department, the Central Intelligence Agency, the Department of Agriculture, the Bureau of the Census, the Population Reference Bureau, the United Nations, and the embassies of many countries.

We are also grateful to the staffs of many public and private libraries. Books and pamphlets of broad scope we found most useful include publications of the United States government, particularly the *National Basic Intelligence Factbook* and the State Department Background Notes; the Peoples of the Earth Series published by The Danbury Press; the Area Handbooks prepared by Foreign Area Studies of The American University; Fodor's travel guides; the Life World Library; the Visual Geography Series published by Sterling Publishing Co., Inc.; *The Europa Year Book;* the *Statesman's Year-Book;* the *Commercial Atlas and Marketing Guide* published by Rand McNally & Company; the *Guinness Book of World Records;* the Portraits of the Nations Series published by J. B. Lippincott Company; *Atlas of World Population History* by Colin McEvedy and Richard Jones; *Frontiers of Life* by Joseph Lucas, Susan Hayes, and Bernard Stonehouse; the *Encyclopedia of the Third World* by George Thomas Kurian, Facts on File, Inc.; the *New Encyclopedia of World Geography,* Octopus Books Ltd.

The National Geographic Magazine abounds with stories and pictures of all parts of the world, as do many National Geographic Society books. For detailed country maps, see the *National Geographic Atlas of the World.*

Facts at Your Fingertips

Geographic Extremes

RAINIEST SPOT
Mount Waialeale, Hawaii; annual average rainfall 460 inches (1,168 cm). Heaviest rainfall ever recorded: Cilaos, Reunion Island, Indian Ocean; 73.6 inches (186.9 cm) in less than 24 hours.

DRIEST SPOT
Atacama Desert, Chile; rainfall barely measurable.

COLDEST RECORDED TEMPERATURE
Vostok, Antarctica; –127° F (–88° C), in 1960.

HOTTEST RECORDED TEMPERATURE
Al Aziziyah, Libya, south of Tripoli; 136° F (58° C), in 1922.

STRONGEST RECORDED WIND
Mount Washington, New Hampshire, 231 mph (372 kmph), on April 12, 1934.

FOGGIEST PLACE (Sea Level)
Grand Banks, off Newfoundland, Canada; more than 120 days a year of fog, often for weeks at a time.

HIGHEST POINT
Mount Everest, Nepal-Tibet; 29,028 feet (8,848 m).

LOWEST POINT
Dead Sea, Israel-Jordan; surface of water 1,302 feet (397 m) below sea level.

LONGEST RIVER
Nile, Africa; 4,145 miles (6,671 km).

HIGHEST WATERFALL
Angel Falls, Venezuela; 3,212 feet (979 m).

LARGEST GORGE
Grand Canyon, Colorado River, Arizona; 277 miles (446 km) long, 1 to 18 miles (1.6 to 29 km) wide, 1 mile (1.6 km) deep.

DEEPEST GORGE
Hells Canyon, Snake River, Idaho; 7,900 feet (2,408 m).

BIGGEST CAVE
Mammoth-Flint Ridge cave system, Kentucky; more than 180 miles (290 km) of passageways.

LARGEST DESERT
Sahara Desert, North Africa; 3,320,000 sq mi (8,598,761 sq km).

DEEPEST OCEAN TRENCH
Mariana Trench, Pacific Ocean; 36,198 feet (11,033 m).

HIGHEST TIDES
Bay of Fundy, Nova Scotia; 53 feet (16.2 m).

DEEPEST OCEAN
Pacific; average depth 14,000 feet (4,267 m).

LARGEST LAKE
Caspian Sea, Europe-Asia; 143,550 sq mi (371,793 sq km), 3,360 feet (1,024 m) deep.

DEEPEST LAKE
Lake Baykal, in U.S.S.R.; 5,315 feet (1,620 m) deep.

HIGHEST LAKE
Unnamed glacial lake, 19,300 feet (5,883 m) high, near Mount Everest, Nepal-Tibet.

LOWEST LAKE
Dead Sea, Israel-Jordan; surface of water 1,302 feet (397 m) below sea level.

LARGEST ICEBERG
Seen 150 miles (241 km) west of Scott Island, in the South Pacific, in 1956; at least 12,000 sq mi (31,000 sq km), bigger than Belgium.

LARGEST ISLAND
Greenland; 840,000 sq mi (2,176,000 sq km).

HIGHEST TOWN
Wenquan, China; 16,732 feet (5,100 m) above sea level.

LOWEST TOWN
Towns on the shore of the Dead Sea, almost 1,300 feet (396 m) below sea level.

NORTHERNMOST CAPITAL
Reykjavik, Iceland.

SOUTHERNMOST CAPITAL
Wellington, New Zealand.

LARGEST COUNTRY BY AREA
U.S.S.R.; 8,594,500 sq mi (22,259,700 sq km).

LARGEST COUNTRY BY POPULATION
People's Republic of China; 1,003,855,000.

SMALLEST COUNTRY BY AREA
Vatican City; .2 sq mi (.5 sq km).

SMALLEST COUNTRY BY POPULATION
Vatican City; 1,000.

MOST CROWDED COUNTRY
Monaco; 41,667 people per sq mi.

LEAST CROWDED COUNTRY
Mongolia, 2.6 people per square mile.

Engineering Marvels

LONGEST RAIL TUNNEL
Dai-Shimizu, north of Tokyo, Japan; 13.8 miles (22.2 km). Seikan Undersea Tunnel, from Honshu to Hokkaido, Japan; 22.6 miles (36.4 km), scheduled completion in 1980's.

LONGEST ROAD TUNNEL
Mont Blanc, Alps, France-Italy; 7.2 miles (11.6 km). St. Gotthard, Alps, Switzerland; 10.1 miles (16.3 km), to open in 1980's.

TALLEST DAM
Grand Dixence, Switzerland; 932 feet (284 m).

BIGGEST DAM (Earthfill)
New Cornelia Tailings, Ajo, Arizona; 274,026,000 cubic yards (209,508,000 cu m).

BIGGEST DAM (Concrete)
Grand Coulee, Columbia River, Washington; 10,585,000 cubic yards (8,093,000 cu m).

TALLEST TOWER (Free-standing)
Canadian National Railroad tower, Toronto, Canada; 1,822 feet (555 m).

TALLEST OFFICE BUILDING
Sears Tower, Chicago, Illinois; 1,454 feet (443 m); 110 stories.

LONGEST BRIDGE SPAN
Humber Estuary, Hull, England; 4,626 feet (1,410 m).

HIGHEST BRIDGE
Royal Gorge, Arkansas River, Colorado; 1,053 feet (321 m) above water.

DEEPEST MINE
Western Deep Levels gold mine near Johannesburg, South Africa; 12,600 feet (3,840 m).

DEEPEST WELL
Natural gas well, Washita County, Oklahoma; 31,441 feet (9,583 m).

GREAT PYRAMID OF CHEOPS
450 feet (137 m) high; base covers 13.1 acres (5.3 ha).

GREAT WALL OF CHINA
1,500 miles (2,414 km) long; averages 25 feet (7.6 m) high; 15 feet (4.6 m) wide at top; 25 feet (7.6 m) wide at base.

LONGEST RAILROAD
Trans-Siberian, Moscow to Nakhodka, near Vladivostok, U.S.S.R.; 5,777 miles (9,297 km).

Index

Map pages are in **boldface type (126)**. Letters and numbers following in lightface (M8) will locate the place named. See page 35 for help in using them.

Illustrations are in *italic (250)*. Text references are in lightface type (181).

Abbreviations Used In This Book

° C — *degrees Celsius or Centigrade*
cm — *centimeter*
° F — *degrees Fahrenheit*
gm — *gram*
ha — *hectare*
kg — *kilogram*
km — *kilometer*
kmph — *kilometers per hour*
kw — *kilowatt*
l — *liter*
m — *meter*
mi — *mile*
mm — *millimeter*
mph — *miles per hour*
sq km — *square kilometer*
sq m — *square meter*
sq mi — *square mile*
t — *metric ton*

Mali **212**; 26, 213, *218*, 229
Malili, Indonesia **174** N16
Mallawi, Egypt **220** E14
Malmo, Sweden **108** S9
Malta **138** T4; 139
Mamberamo River, Indonesia **175** N24
Man, Isle of, England **114** L11
Man, Ivory Coast **226** O13
Manado, Indonesia **174** L17
Managua, Lake, Nicaragua **58** L12
Managua, Nicaragua **58** M11; 60
Manama, Bahrain **196** C12
Manaus, Brazil **82** F7
Manchester, England **114** N14; 116
Manchuria (region), China **168** C17; 169
Mandalay, Burma **180** G5
Mangalore, India **186** P6
Manila, Philippines **174** D15; 176
Manisa, Turkey **202** D3
Manitoba (province), Canada **48** N9; 49
Manizales, Colombia **76** H5
Mannar, Gulf of, India-Sri Lanka **186** S7
Mannheim, West Germany **120** O9
Mano River, Liberia **226** O9
Manresa, Spain **148** D16
Manta, Ecuador **88** D7
Manufacturing 43, 67, 107, 139, 163, 169; heavy industry 83, 115-116, 121, *125*, 127, 143, *161*, 233; light industry *116*, 127, 143, 144, 163, *164*, 182, 203, 233; *see also* Steel industry
Manzanillo, Cuba **64** J9
Maoke Mountains, Indonesia **175** O24
Maps and mapmaking *29-35*, 152; photomapping *30;* projections 34, *34;* sound-wave mapping *30*
Maputo, Mozambique **252** T10; *254*
Mar del Plata, Argentina **98** L9
Maracaibo, Lake, Venezuela **76** D9; 77, *81*
Maracaibo, Venezuela **76** C9
Maracay, Venezuela **76** C12
Marajo (island), Brazil **82** F11
Marakei (island), Kiribati **284** Q10
Maramba, Zambia **252** L5
Maranon River, Peru **88** G12
Maras, Turkey **202** F10
Marathon, Greece 135
Marble Canyon, Ariz. *15*
Marchena Island, Galapagos Islands **88** R5
Mardan, Pakistan **192** D17
Mare (island), Loyalty Islands **285** O35
Margarita Island, Venezuela **76** C16
Margherita Peak, Zaire **238** H18

Mariana Islands **284** C4
Maribor, Yugoslavia **130** D9
Marie Byrd Land (region), Antarctica **274** K6
Maritsa River, Europe **134** J8
Marmara, Sea of, Turkey **202** B3; 204
Marne River, France **142** E13
Marquesas Islands, French Polynesia **284** J19
Marrakech, Morocco **212** E7
Marseille, France **142** N14; 143
Marshall Islands, Trust Territory of the Pacific Islands **284** E9; 288
Martaban, Gulf of, Burma **180** M5
Martinique (island), Caribbean Sea **65** P25; 68, *69*
Masampo, South Korea *see* Masan
Masan, South Korea **162** L5
Maseru, Lesotho **258** N15
Mashhad, Iran **192** C10
Masuria (region), Poland 127
Matadi, Zaire **238** M8
Matagalpa River, Nicaragua **58** L15
Matamoros, Mexico **54** H18
Matanzas, Cuba **64** F5
Mataro, Spain **148** E17
Mato Grosso Plateau, Brazil **82** M8
Matrah, Oman **196** E18; 197
Matsuyama, Japan **162** N9
Matterhorn (mountain), Italy-Switzerland **142** J16; *145*
Maturin, Venezuela **76** D17
Maui (island), Hawaii **43** E10
Mauna Loa (volcano), Hawaii **43** G10
Mauritania **212**; 213, *219*
Mauritius, Indian Ocean **292** G10; 293, *294*
Mayaguana Island, Bahamas **64** G13
Mayotte, Indian Ocean **292** U6; 293
Mazatlan, Mexico **54** K10
Mbabane, Swaziland **258** L17; *265*
M'Bakaou Reservoir, Cameroon **232** H16
Mbandaka, Zaire **238** J11
Mbuji Mayi, Zaire **238** N14
Mecca, Saudi Arabia **196** G5; 197, *198-199*
Medan, Indonesia **174** K4
Medellin, Colombia **76** G5; 77
Medina, Saudi Arabia **196** E5
Mediterranean Sea **134, 202, 212;** 107, 139, 152, 211, 221, 222; coast 143, *150-151*
Mekong River, Southeast Asia **168, 180;** 155, 181, 182
Mekong River Delta, Vietnam **168, 180** R12
Mekrou River, Benin **232** D8
Melanesia, Pacific Ocean **284;** 287
Melbourne, Australia **268** N15
Melos (island), Greece **134** Q7

Memphis (site), Egypt **220** D15
Mendoza, Argentina **98** J4
Meneng Point, Nauru **285** Q29
Mergui Archipelago, Burma **180** Q6
Merida, Mexico **55** M25
Merida, Venezuela **76** E9
Meridians 32, *32*
Mersin, Turkey **202** F8
Messalo River, Mozambique **252** F16
Messina, Italy **138** R15
Meta River, Colombia **76** H10
Metz, France **142** D14
Meuse River, Europe **120, 142**
Mexicali, Mexico **54** A3
Mexico **54-55;** 55, *56-57*
Mexico, Gulf of **42** K14
Mexico City, Mexico **54** O17; 55, 56
Michigan, Lake, U. S. **42** C14, 48 R12
Micronesia, Pacific Ocean **284** E6; 288
Middle America *see* Central America; Mexico
The Midlands (region), England **114** O15
Midway Islands, Pacific Ocean **284** A11; 288
Mikonos (island), Greece **134** P8; *136-137*
Miladummadulu Atoll, Maldives **292** B3
Milan, Italy **138** D6; 139
Milford Sound, New Zealand *272-273*
Millet *218*, 225
Milo River, Guinea **226** K11
Mindanao (island), Philippines **174** G18; 176, *179*
Mindoro (island), Philippines **174** E15
Minerals and metals 26, 41, 49, 60, 83, 158, 169, 227, 233, 234, 240, 245, 259, 260, *270*, 275, 287; bauxite 66, 67, 84, *230;* copper 176, 253; iron *165*, 213, 228; salt 68, 129, 131, 245, *247;* tin 95, *96; see also* Gems; Gold; Silver
Mines and mining 41, 77, 84, 95, *96, 103*, 182, 234, 259, *262, 265*, 270; coal *119*, 121, 129; iron 131, 228; open pit 49, 103, 131, 287
Mino River, Spain **148** D4
Minorca (island), Spain **148** G20
Minsk, U.S.S.R. **156** E4
Miquelon Island, Atlantic Ocean 48 O19
Miri, Malaysia **174** J11
Misery, Mount, St. Christopher-Nevis 67
Miskolc, Hungary **130** A16
Mississippi River, U. S. **42** C12, H13; 41
Missouri River, U. S. **42** D10
Mitumba Mountains, Zaire **238** P16
Mmabatho, Bophuthatswana **258** K13

Moa River, Guinea **226** M11
Mogadishu, Somalia **244** L15
Moheli (island), Comoro Islands **292** T3; 293
Mohotani (island), Marquesas Islands **285** Q39
Mokpo, South Korea **162** L3
Moldavian S.S.R., U.S.S.R. **156** F1
Molokai (island), Hawaii **43** C9
Mombasa, Kenya **244** P12; *248*
Monaco **142**; 143
Monaco-Ville, Monaco 143
Monclova, Mexico **54** G15
Mongolia **168;** 155, 169, *173*
Mongolia, Inner (region), China **168** F15
Mono River, Togo-Benin **232** F7
Monrovia, Liberia **226** P9; 228
Monte Carlo, Monaco 143
Monte Lindo River, Paraguay **94** Q13
Montego Bay, Jamaica **64** L8
Montenegro (region), Yugoslavia **130** M14
Monterey Peninsula, Calif. **42** F2; *47*
Monteria, Colombia **76** E5
Monterrey, Mexico **54** H16
Montevideo, Uruguay **98** J10; 99
Montpellier, France **142** N12
Montreal, Canada **48** Q15; 49
Montserrat, Caribbean Sea **65** M23; 67, 68
Moorea (island), French Polynesia **285** S28
Morava River, Czechoslovakia **126** P10
Morava River, Yugoslavia **130** J17
Moravia (region), Czechoslovakia **126** P9; 127
Morelia, Mexico **54** O15
Morioka, Japan **162** F16
Morocco **212;** 213-214, *216, 217*
Moroni, Comoro Islands **292** R2
Moscow, U.S.S.R **156** F5; 157, *160-161*
Mosel River, Europe **120** N7
Mosquito Coast, Nicaragua **58** G16, H17; 60
Mosquito Gulf, Panama **58** R20
Most, Czechoslovakia **126** L4
Mosul, Iraq **202** G15
Motagua River, Guatemala **58** F7
Moulmein, Burma **180** L6
Mount Hagen, Papua New Guinea **175** O26
Mountains 8, 12, 15, 41, 89, 144; highest 12, *12-13, 152*, 188, *190-191;* longest chain 75; undersea *30-31*, 275, *282*, 288; *see also* Volcanoes *and mountains by name*
Mountains of the Moon *see* Ruwenzori
Mozambique **252;** 208, 253, *254-255*
Mozambique, Mozambique **252** H19

Mozambique Channel, Africa **252** N14; 253
Mueru, Lake, Zambia **252** B8
Mukden, China *see* Shenyang
Mulaku Atoll, Maldive Islands **292** E3
Mulhacen (peak), Spain **148** N10
Mulhouse, France **142** F15
Multan, Pakistan **192** H16
Munich, West Germany **120** R14
Munster, West Germany **120** H8
Murat River, Turkey **202** D13
Murcia, Spain **148** L13
Mures River, Romania **134** C4
Muritz, Lake, East Germany **120** E15
Murmansk, U.S.S.R. **156** C9
Murray River, Australia **268** L14
Muscat, Oman **196** E18
Muslim *see* Islam
Musi River, Indonesia **174** N7
Mweru, Lake, Zaire **238** O17
My Tho, Vietnam **180** Q13
Myingyan, Burma **180** G3
Mysore, India **186** P7

Nagano, Japan **162** J13
Nagasaki, Japan **162** O6
Nagoya, Japan **162** L12
Nagpur, India **186** K8
Naha, Japan **162** P16
Nahuel Huapi, Lake, Argentina **98** N4
Nairobi, Kenya **244** N10; *248*
Nakhon Ratchasima, Thailand **180** N9
Nakhon Sawan, Thailand **180** M7
Nakhon Si Thammarat, Thailand **180** S8
Naktong River, South Korea **162** K5
Nam Dinh, Vietnam **180** H13
Namib Desert, Namibia **258** G4; 259, *264*
Namibia **258;** 259, *264*
Nampo, North Korea **162** G3
Nampula, Mozambique **252** H17
Namsen River, Norway **108** H9
Namur, Belgium **120** L5
Nan River, Thailand **180** K8
Nanchang, China **168** M16
Nancy, France **142** D14
Nandi Devi (peak), India **186** D8
Nanjing, China **168** K17
Nanking, China *see* Nanjing
Nanning, China **168** O13
Nantes, France **142** G6
Naples, Italy **138** M13
Napo River, Ecuador-Peru **88** C13
Narew River, Poland **126** F16
Narmada River, India **186** J7
Nassau, Bahamas **64** D9
Nasser, Lake, Egypt **220** H16
Nata River, Zimbabwe Rhodesia-Botswana **258** E14
Natal *see* South Africa

Natural resources 26 *see also* Minerals; Oil
Nauru, Pacific Ocean **284, 285;** 287, *289*
Naxos (island), Greece **134** Q8
Nazare, Portugal **148** H2; *151*
N'djamena, Chad **220** O5
Ndola, Zambia **252** F7
Neagh, Lake, Northern Ireland **114** K9
Neblina (peak), Brazil **82** E4
Neckar River, West Germany **120** Q10
Negev Desert, Israel **202** N8; 203
Negro River, Argentina **98** M5
Negro River, Guatemala **58** F4
Negro River, South America **58, 82**
Negros (island), Philippines **174** G16
Neisse River, Europe **120** J18, **126** K6
Nellore, India **186** O9
Nelson's Dockyard, Antigua 65
Nepal **186;** *152,* 188, *190-191*
Ness, Loch, Scotland **114** E11; 116
Netherlands **120;** 122, *122-123*
Netherlands Antilles, Caribbean Sea **64** R17; 68, *70*
Neuchatel, Lake, Switzerland **142** G15
Nevis *see* St. Christopher-Nevis
New Britain (island), Papua New Guinea **175** O30
New Brunswick (province), Canada **48** O16
New Caledonia, Pacific Ocean **284, 285;** 287
New Delhi, India **186** E7
New Georgia (island), Solomon Islands **285** G31
New Guinea, Pacific Ocean **175** O25; 175, 176, *178*
New Hebrides, Pacific Ocean **284, 285;** 287
New Ireland (island), Papua New Guinea **175** N32
New Siberian Islands, U.S.S.R. **156** E19, **275** D5
New South Wales (state), Australia **268** K15
New York, N.Y. **42** D19; 7, 43, *44*
New Zealand **269;** 266, 269, *272-273,* 286
Newcastle, Australia **268** L17
Newcastle upon Tyne, England **114** K15
Newfoundland (province), Canada **48** L17
Newfoundland, Island of, Canada **48** N18; 38, 41, 49
Ngau (island), Fiji **284** S4
Ngoko River, Cameroon **232** L18
Ngorongoro Crater, Tanzania **244** P9; 246
Nha Trang, Vietnam **180** P15
Niamey, Niger **212** Q12
Nicaragua **58;** 60
Nicaragua, Lake, Nicaragua **58** N13; 60

Nice, France **142** N16
Nicholson River, Australia **268** C13
Nicobar Islands, Indian Ocean **292** D15
Nicosia, Cyprus **202** H7; 203
Nicoya, Gulf of, Costa Rica **58** Q14
Niger **212;** 214, *218, 219*
Niger Delta, Nigeria **232** J11
Niger River, Africa **212** Q7, **226** J10, **232** F10; 213, 214, 227, *235*
Nigeria **232;** 211, 233, *234-235*
Niigata, Japan **162** H14
Nile River, Africa **220** E15; 72, 211, 221, 222, *223 see also* Blue Nile; Victoria Nile; White Nile
Nimba Mountains, Guinea **226** N12
Nimes, France **142** M12
Nis, Yugoslavia **130** L18
Nitra, Czechoslovakia **126** R11
Nizhniy Tagil, U.S.S.R. **156** J9
Nkongsamba, Cameroon **232** J14
Nogales, Mexico **54** B7
Nonouti (island), Kiribati **284** S11
Norfolk Island, Pacific Ocean **284** N8
Norilsk, U.S.S.R. **156** G14
Norrkoping, Sweden **108** P11
Norrland (region), Sweden **108** J10; 110
North America **40;** *38-71,* 104, 107, 152 *see also* Canada; Greenland; Mexico; United States
North Atlantic Ocean **278** D13
North Cape, Norway **108** A15
North Island, New Zealand **269** A5; *273*
North Keeling Island, Cocos Islands **292** L2
North Korea *see* Korea, North
North Land, U.S.S.R. **275** C7
North Magnetic Pole **48** F8
North Pole **275** E7; 16, 275
North Sea **114, 120;** 110, 116, 121
North-West Frontier, Pakistan **192** D16
North Yemen *see* Yemen, North
Northern Ireland **114** K9; 115, 116, *118*
Northern Karroo (region), South Africa **258** P11
Northern Mariana Islands, Trust Territory of the Pacific Islands **284** C4
Northern Territory, Australia **268** D10; *266*
Northwest Territories, Canada **48** K7
Norway **108;** 110, *110, 111*
Norwegian Sea **108** F8
Norwich, England **114** O18
Notec River, Poland **126** E9
Nottingham, England **114** O15; 116
Nouakchott, Mauritania **212** N2; *219*

Noumea, New Caledonia **285** P33; 287
Nova Scotia (province), Canada **48** O17; 49
Novaya Zemlya (islands), U.S.S.R. **156** D12, **275** B8
Novi Sad, Yugoslavia **130** G15
Novokuznetsk, U.S.S.R. **156** N13
Novosibirsk, U.S.S.R. **156** M12; *161*
Nuba Mountains, Sudan **220** P14; *224-225*
Nubian Desert, Sudan **220** J16
Nuevo Laredo, Mexico **54** F16
Nukualofa, Tonga **284** T18; 287
Nuremberg, West Germany **120** O13
Nuuk, Greenland **48** G16; 49
Nyala, Sudan **220** P11
Nyasa, Lake, Malawi *see* Malawi, Lake
Nyasaland *see* Malawi
Nyiregyhaza, Hungary **130** B17
Nyong River, Cameroon **232** K15

Oahu (island), Hawaii **43** B6
Oaxaca, Mexico **54** Q19
Ob River, U.S.S.R. **156** H11
Oberndorf, Austria **130** B5; 131
Ocean Island *see* Banaba
Oceans 8, 15, *18-19,* 23, 275, **278, 284-285, 292;** currents 107, 110, 111, 275; floor **30-31,** 75; spreading and shrinking 8
Odense, Denmark **108** S7
Oder River, Europe **120** F17, **126** E6, J8; 127
Odessa, U.S.S.R. **156** G2
Ogbomosho, Nigeria **232** F9
Ogooue River, Gabon **238** J6
Ohio River, U.S. **42** F15
Ohre River, Czechoslovakia-West Germany **126** L4; 127
Ohrid, Lake, Albania-Yugoslavia **130, 134**
Oil 23, 26, 41, 55, *56,* 77, *81, 136, 166,* 175, *200, 214,* 224, 235
Ojos del Salado (mountain), Argentina **98** F3
Okara, Pakistan **192** G17
Okayama, Japan **162** M10
Okhotsk, Sea of, U.S.S.R. **157** K24
Oki Islands, Japan **162** K9
Okinawa (island), Japan **162** O17
Oland (island), Sweden **108** R11
Oldenburg, West Germany **120** F9
Olduvai Gorge, Tanzania **244** O9; 246
Olifants River, South Africa **258** J16
Olomouc, Czechoslovakia **126** O9
Olsztyn, Poland **126** D14
Olt River, Romania **134** D7
Olympia, Greece 135

Olympus, Mount, Greece **134** M5; 135
Oman **196** D18; 197, *201*
Omdurman, Sudan **220** M15
Omo River, Ethiopia **244** H10
Omsk, U.S.S.R. **156** L10
One and Half Degree Channel, Maldives **292** G2
Onega, Lake, U.S.S.R. **156** E7
Onitsha, Nigeria **232** H11
Ontario (province), Canada **48** P12; *50-51*
Ontario, Lake, Canada-U.S. **42** C17, **48** Q15
Opole, Poland **126** L11; *129*
Oporto, Portugal **148** E3; 149
Oradea, Romania **134** B5
Oran, Algeria **212** C11
Orange Free State *see* South Africa
Orebro, Sweden **108** O10
Orense, Spain **148** D4
Orhon River, Mongolia **168** D11
Orinoco River, Venezuela **76** E17, K14; 75, 77, 83
Orizaba, Mexico **54** O19
Orkney Islands, Scotland **114** B13
Orleans, France **142** F10
Orohena Mountains, Tahiti **285** T31
Orontes River, Asia **202** J10
Oruro, Bolivia **94** K5
Osa Peninsula, Costa Rica **58** S15
Osaka, Japan **162** M11; *164, 165*
Oshogbo, Nigeria **232** G10
Osijek, Yugoslavia **130** G13
Oslo, Norway **108** N8; *110*
Osnabruck, West Germany **120** H9
Ostend, Belgium **120** K2
Ostrava, Czechoslovakia **126** N11; *128*
Osumi Islands, Japan **162** Q6
Oti River, Ghana **232** E6
Ottawa, Canada **48** Q15; *50-51*
Ouagadougou, Upper Volta **232** C4; *234, 237*
Oueme River, Benin **232** F8
Ouham River, Central African Empire **238** D10
Oujda, Morocco **212** D10
Oulu, Finland **108** G15
Oulu River, Finland **108** G16
Outer Banks, N.C. **42** F19
Outer Hebrides (islands), Scotland **114** C9
Oviedo, Spain **148** B7
Oxford, England **114** Q16
Oymyakon, U.S.S.R. **157** H22; 158
Oyo, Nigeria **232** F9

Pacific Ocean 8, *47,* 75
Pacific Ocean Islands **284-285;** *286-291*
Padang, Indonesia **174** M4
Padova, Italy **138** D10

Paektu, Mount, North Korea **162** D5; 163
Pag (island), Yugoslavia **130** H8
Pagan, Burma **180** H3
Pago Pago, American Samoa **285** Q23
Pakanbaru, Indonesia **174** L4
Pakistan **192;** 155, 187, 193, *194-195*
Pakistan, East *see* Bangladesh
Pakxe, Laos **180** M12
Palawan (island), Philippines **174** G13
Palembang, Indonesia **174** N7
Palencia, Spain **148** D8
Palermo, Italy **138** R12
Palestine *see* Israel; Jordan
Palma, Spain **148** H18
Palmas, Cape, Liberia **226** S13
Palmyra Island, Line Islands **284** F14; 288
The Pampas (region), Argentina **98**
Pamplona, Spain **148** C12
Pan American Highway **58, 88, 98**
Panama **58-59;** 60, *62, 63*
Panama, Gulf of, Panama **59** T23
Panama Canal, Panama **59** R22; 38, 60, *63*
Panama City, Panama **59** R23; 60
Panay (island), Philippines **174** F15
Pangani River, Tanzania **244** P10
Panuco River, Mexico **54** L18
Paotuo, China *see* Baotou
Papeete, Tahiti **285** S30; 286
Papua New Guinea **175;** 176, *178*
Paraguana Peninsula, Venezuela **76** B10
Paraguari, Paraguay **94** S15
Paraguay **94;** 95, *97*
Paraguay River, South America **94, 98;** 95, *97*
Paramaribo, Suriname **82** B9; 84
Parana River, South America **82, 94, 98**
Paris, France **142** D10; 143, *147*
Parma, Italy **138** E8
Parry Islands, Canada **48** E7
Pasadena, Calif. **42** G3; *46*
Pasion River, Guatemala **58** D6
Pasto, Colombia **76** M3
Patagonia (region), Argentina **98** Q4; 99, *101*
Patna, India **186** G11
Patos Lagoon, Brazil **82** T10
Patrae, Greece **134** O4
Patuca River, Honduras **58** G14
Pau, France **142** N7
Paysandu, Uruguay **98** H9
Peanuts 227, 228, *230, 231*
Pearl Harbor, Hawaii **43** C5
Peat 115, *118*
Pecs, Hungary **130** E13
Pegu, Burma **180** L5

309

Ujung Pandang, Indonesia **174** O15

Ukrainian S.S.R., U.S.S.R. **156** F3; 157, *158-159*

Ulaanbaatar, Mongolia **168** D12; 169

Ulan Bator *see* Ulaanbaatar

Ulsan, South Korea **162** L6; *166*

Ulster *see* Northern Ireland

Umea, Sweden **108** J13

Umtata, Transkei **258** P15

Union of Soviet Socialist Republics **156-157**; 155, 157-158, *158-161*

United Arab Emirates **196**; 198

United Arab Republic *see* Egypt

United Kingdom **114**; 115, *116-119*

United States **42, 43**; 24, 26, 43, *44-47*, 55, 110, 211

U.S. Territories in the Pacific **284**; 288, *290, 291*

United States Trust Territory of the Pacific Islands, Pacific Ocean **284** D6

U.S. Virgin Islands **65** L21; 69

Upolu (island), Western Samoa **285** T25

Upper Volta **232**; 229, 234, *237*

Uppsala, Sweden **108** N12

Ural Mountains, Asia-Europe **156** J8; 104, 152, 157

Ural River, U.S.S.R. **156** K5

Urfa, Turkey, **202** F12

Urmia, Lake, Iran **192** A2

Uruapan, Mexico **54** O14

Urubamba River, Peru **88** N15; 89

Uruguay **98**; 99, *102*

Urumchi, China *see* Urumqi

Urumqi, China **168** F6

Urundi *see* Burundi

Ushuaia, Argentina **98** U5

Usti, Czechoslovakia **126** L5

Utrecht, Netherlands **120** H5

Utsunomiya, Japan **162** J15

Uvea (island), Loyalty Islands **285** M33; 288

Uvea (island), Wallis and Futuna Islands **285** C29

Uxmal, Mexico **55** N24

Uzbek S.S.R., U.S.S.R. **156** O6; *158*

Vaal River, South Africa **258** M13

Vaasa, Finland **108** K14

Vadodara, India **186** J5

Vaduz, Liechtenstein **142** G18

Valdes Peninsula, Argentina **98** N7

Valdivia, Chile **98** M2

Valencia, Spain **148** J14

Valencia (region), Spain 149

Valencia, Venezuela **76** D12

Valera, Venezuela **76** D10

Valladolid, Spain **148** E8

Valletta, Malta **138** S6

Valparaiso, Chile **98** J2; 99

Van, Turkey **202** D15

Vancouver, Canada **48** P3; 49

Vanern, Lake, Sweden **108** O9

Vanilla beans 253, *257*

Varanasi, India **186** G10

Varna, Bulgaria **134** G11; 135

Vasteras, Sweden **108** N11

Vatican City **138** K10; 139, *141*

Vattern, Lake, Sweden **108** P10

Vaupes River, South America **76**

Vella Lavella (island), Solomon Islands **285** F29

Venezuela **76**; 77, *80-81*

Venice, Italy **138** D10; 139, *140-141*

Veracruz, Mexico **54** O20

Verde, Cape, Senegal **226** C1

Vereeniging, South Africa **258** L15

Verkhoyansk, U.S.S.R. **156** H20; 158

Verona, Italy **138** D9

Vesuvius (volcano), Italy **138** M13

Veszprem, Hungary **130** C12

Victoria (state), Australia **268** N14

Victoria, Canada **48** P3

Victoria, Lake, Africa **244** N7; 245, 246

Victoria, Seychelles **292** T11

Victoria Falls (waterfall), Zambia-Zimbabwe Rhodesia **252, 258**; 253, 260, *261*

Victoria Island, Canada **48** H7

Victoria Nile River, Africa **244** M8; 246

Vienna, Austria **130** A10; 131

Vientiane, Laos **180** K10

Vietnam **180**; 181, 182, *184*

Vigo, Spain **148** D3

Vijayawada, India **186** M9

Vila do Porto, Azores **278** E7

Vila Junqueiro, Mozambique **252** J15; *254-255*

Villach, Austria **130** D6

Villahermosa, Mexico **55** P22; 55

Villavicencio, Colombia **76** J7

Vilnius, U.S.S.R. **156** D4

Vina del Mar, Chile **98** H2

Vindhya Range, India **186** H7

Vinh Loi, Vietnam **180** R12

Virgin Islands *see* British Virgin Islands; U.S. Virgin Islands

Virunga Mountains, Africa 246

Virunga National Park, Zaire **238** J17; *242-243*

Vishakhapatnam, India **186** M10

Vistula River, Poland **126**; 127

Vitoria, Brazil **82** O15

Vitoria, Spain **148** C11

Vladivostok, U.S.S.R. **157** P23

Vlore, Albania **134** L2

Volcanoes 7, 7, 8, 12, 41, 43, 55, *57*, 59, 60, 66, 67, 68, 75, 89, *91, 93*, 109, 139, 176, *177, 206*, 246, 279, 280, *282*, 286, 288, 289, 293; largest active 163

Volga River, U.S.S.R. **156** J5; 157, 161

Volgograd, U.S.S.R. **156** J4; *161*

Volos, Greece **134** N6

Volta Lake, Ghana **232** G5; 233

Volta River, Ghana-Upper Volta **226, 232**; 233

Volta River, Black, Ghana-Upper Volta **226, 232**

Volta River, Red, Ghana-Upper Volta-Ivory Coast **232** D5

Volta River, White, Ghana-Upper Volta **232** D4

Volturno River, Italy **138** L13

Voodoo 66, 233

Vorkuta, U.S.S.R. **156** G11

Vostok Station (Soviet Union), Antarctica **274** J14

Wad Medani, Sudan **220** N16

Waingapu, Indonesia **174** R15

Wakamaya, Japan **162** M11

Wakasa Bay, Japan **162** K11

Wake Island, Pacific Ocean **284** C8; 288

Walbrzych, Poland **126** L8

Wales **114** P12; 115, 116, *119*

Wallis and Futuna Islands, Pacific Ocean **284, 285**; 288

Wankie National Park, Zimbabwe Rhodesia 260

Warangal, India **186** M8

Warri, Nigeria **232** J10; *235*

Warsaw, Poland **126** G15; 127

Washington, D. C. **42** E18

Waterfalls *15*, 67, *79*, 83, 131, *240-241*, 253, 260, *261*, 286; highest 77, *80*

Waterways: canals 38, 157, 181, 182, *184*, 221; lakes 41, 49, 60, 109, 110, *110-111*; rivers 41, 49, 95, 107, 121, 127, 131, 152, 157, *179*, 181, 187, 227, 233, 239

Wau, Sudan **220** S13

Weather *see* Climate, weather, seasons

Welkom, South Africa **258** M14

Wellington, New Zealand **269** D5

Weser River, West Germany **120** G10

West Africa 219

West Bengal (state), India **186** H12

West End, Bahamas **64** B7

West Germany *see* Germany, West

West Indies **64-65**; 8, 38, 41, *65-71*

Western Australia (state), Australia **268** G5

Western Desert, Egypt **220** F13

Western Ghats (mountains), India *see* Ghats

Western Samoa, Pacific Ocean **284, 285**; 288

Wheat 41, *43, 44, 45*, 127, 131, 157, *158-159*, 169, 187, *194*, 204, *217*

Whiskey, Colombia **76** M4

White Nile River, Sudan **220** P16, S15; 222

White Volta River, Upper Volta-Ghana **232** D4

Wieliczka, Poland **126** N14; 129

Wiesbaden, West Germany **120** M9

Wight, Isle of, England **114** S16

Wild game *18-19*, 72, 89, 95, 99, 176, 269; caribou 43; crocodiles 221, 239; elephants *188-189*, 211, 227, 229, *242*, 246, 260; giraffes 211, *248*; gorillas *251*; hippos 221, 239, *242-243*, 246; jaguar *86*; lions *208*, 211, 239, 245, 246; wild game reserves *86*, 208, 211, *242-243*, 246, *248*, 259, 260, *264, 270*; wildebeests 208, 211, 246, *250*

Wilhelmshaven, West Germany **120** E9

Willemstad, Curacao **64** S18; *70*

Windhoek, Namibia **258** H6

Windsor, Canada **48** S13

Winnipeg, Canada **48** P9

Winnipeg, Lake, Canada **48** O9

Wismar, East Germany **120** D14; *124*

Wloclawek, Poland **126** G12

Wolfsburg, West Germany **120** G13; *125*

Wollongong, Australia **268** M17

Wonsan, North Korea **162** G4

World maps 24-25, 36-37

Wrangel Island, U.S.S.R. **157** B23; **275** D3

Wroclaw, Poland **126** K9

Wuhan, China **168** L15

Wuhsi, China *see* Wuxi

Wuppertal, West Germany **120** K8

Wurzburg, West Germany **120** N12

Wuxi, China **168** K18

Xai-Xai, Mozambique **252** S11

Xau, Lake, Botswana **258** F12

Xiamen, China **168** N17

Xian, China **168** K13; *171*

Xingu River, Brazil **82** K10

Yakutsk, U.S.S.R. **156** K20

Yalu River, China-Korea **162** E3; 163

Yamuna River, India **186** E7

Yangku, China *see* Taiyuan

Yangtze River, China **168** K9, L14; 155, 169

Yaounde, Cameroon **232** K15; 233

Yazd, Iran **192** F6

Yellow River, China **168** K10, J16; 155, 169

Yellow Sea, China-Korea **162, 168**

Yellowstone National Park, Wyo. 18, *38*

Yemen, North **196**; 198, *201*

Yemen, South **196**; 198

Yerevan, U.S.S.R. **156** L2

Yinchuan, China **168** H12

Yogyakarta, Indonesia **174** Q9

Yokohama, Japan **162** L15

York, England **114** M15

Yosu, South Korea **162** L4

Yucatan Peninsula, Mexico **55** N25; 55

Yugoslavia **130**; 131, *132-133*

Yukon River, Canada-U. S. **42, 48**

Yukon Territory, Canada **48** H3; 49

Yumen, China **168** G9

Zacatecas, Mexico **54** L14

Zagreb, Yugoslavia **130** F9

Zahedan, Iran **192** H10

Zaire **238**; 211, 240, *242-243*

Zaire (Congo) River, Africa **238** H12, K9; *243*

Zambezi River, Africa **252, 258**; 253, 260, *261*

Zambia **252**; 253

Zamboanga, Philippines **174** H15

Zamora, Mexico **54** N14

Zamora, Spain **148** E7

Zanjan, Iran **192** B3

Zante (island), Greece **134** P3

Zanzibar, Tanzania **244** R12; 246

Zanzibar Island, Tanzania **244** Q11

Zaragoza, Spain **148** E13

Zaria, Nigeria **232** D12

Zealand (island), Denmark **108** S8; 109

Zenica, Yugoslavia **130** J12

Zhengzhou, China **168** J15

Zhob River, Pakistan **192** G15

Zielona Gora, Poland **126** H7

Ziguinchor, Senegal **226** G2

Zilina, Czechoslovakia **126** O12

Zimbabwe Rhodesia **258**; 260, *261*

Zonguldak, Turkey **202** B6

Zrenjanin, Yugoslavia **130** G16

Zurich, Switzerland **142** F17

Zwickau, East Germany **120** L15

Type composition by National Geographic's Photographic Services. Color separations by Colorgraphics, Inc., Forestville, Md.; Graphic Color Plate, Inc., Stamford, Conn.; Chanticleer Company, Inc., New York, N.Y.; Beck Engraving Co., Inc., Philadelphia, Pa. Printed and bound by Holladay-Tyler Printing Corp., Rockville, Md. Paper by Westvaco Corp., New York, N.Y., and Mead Corp., Publishing Paper Division, New York, N.Y.

Library of Congress CIP Data

National Geographic Society, Washington, D.C.   Book Service

National Geographic picture atlas of our world.

1. Atlases. I. Title. II. Title: Picture atlas of our world.
G1021.N36 1979 912 79-17204
ISBN 0-87044-311-9 regular bind.
ISBN 0-87044-312-7 library bind.